Communities and Crime Reduction

Edited by Tim Hope and Margaret Shaw

London: Her Majesty's

© Crown copyright 1988
First published 1988

ISBN 0 11 340892 7

Contents

Implementation

International Perspectives on Policy

Endpiece

Foreword

We need to change the way in which we think about crime. Understandably, people look to the formal criminal justice agencies—the police, the courts and prisons—as their shield against crime. But we must not overlook the enormous, largely untapped, potential for preventing crime which exists amongst ordinary citizens. Crime is not just wished upon us from outside; it has its roots in the values and standards—or the lack of them—in neighbourhoods throughout the land.

Preventing crime is a matter for all of us. It has a moral and social dimension in addition to the practical business of fitting proper locks and bolts—and remembering to use them. We need to look to individuals—to parents, teachers and broadcasters—and to institutions—the family, schools, the churches, the media—to help us re-build those values and a sense of individual responsibility which prevents crime from taking a hold. It is only when these values fail that we come to rely upon the police and the courts.

Rebuilding values will, in many cases, also involve re-building communities. Crime flourishes in neighbourhoods with shallow roots, where there is little sense of pride or loyalty and where the disapproval of neighbours does not matter. Crime is often at its most acute in inner urban areas and on some estates located in bleak isolation on the edge of some cities. In these places litter, for example, is not just a sign of local authority inefficiency but a potent symbol of the "couldn't care less, let someone else clear it up" attitude to life. In many of these places the sense of community has been lost through a combination of discouragement, powerlessness, fear and apathy. The drive to revitalise our urban communities and to return hope and opportunity to them is of crucial importance if we are to stop crime.

I am pleased to see lively debate and enquiry within the pages of this volume about how the potential and energy of individual citizens, working together, can be mobilised against crime—even if I do not agree with every point of view or conclusion. I am greatly encouraged that many distinguished international scholars have addressed the theme of rebuilding communities in their research, and that their creative thinking will stimulate those within society who have the means to take action. The problem of crime confronts all the countries of Western Europe; we have a common problem and we have much to learn from each other.

The restoration of the values and standards of behaviour which should form the foundation for any 'community' is a moral imperative which we must pursue in the coming years. But this cannot be achieved by relying on the exhortation of politicians; nor just by legislation. It requires resolution from people in all walks of life to play their part in restoring a collective sense of responsibility and, therefore, safety to our streets. At the very centre of our ideas on how to control crime should be the energy and initiative of the active citizen. His or her contribution must be mobilised and should be the core of the radical rethinking we need on prevention and control of crime.

JOHN PATTEN MP
Minister of State
Home Office

February 1988

Contributing Authors

SUSAN F. BENNETT is co-principal investigator of the Eisenhower Foundation's Neighbourhood Program Evaluation at the Centre for Urban Affairs and Policy Research, Northwestern University, Evanston, Illinois.

HARRY BLAGG is Lecturer in Social Policy in the Department of Social Administration, University of Lancaster.

ANTHONY E. BOTTOMS is Wolfson Professor, and Director of the Institute of Criminology in the University of Cambridge.

ELLIOT T. CURRIE is a Visiting Scholar at the Center for the Study of Law and Society, University of California, Berkeley.

LYNN A. CURTIS is President of the Milton S. Eisenhower Foundation, Washington, DC.

JAN J. M. van DIJK is Director of the Research and Documentation Centre, Ministry of Justice, The Netherlands.

ERIC DUNNING is Senior Lecturer in Sociology and Co-Director of the Sir Norman Chester Centre for Football Research, University of Leicester.

STEPHEN D. GOTTFREDSON is Chair of the Department of Criminal Justice, Temple University.

KEVIN HEAL is Head of the Home Office Crime Prevention Unit.

TIM HOPE is a Principal Research Officer in the Home Office Research and Planning Unit.

MIKE HOUGH is a Principal Research Officer in the Home Office Research and Planning Unit.

JOSINE JUNGER-TAS is Deputy Director of the Research and Documentation Centre, Ministry of Justice, The Netherlands.

PAUL J. LAVRAKAS is Associate Professor at the Centre for Urban Affairs and Policy Research, Northwestern University, Evanston, Illinois.

GLORIA LAYCOCK is a Principal Research Officer, Home Office Crime Prevention Unit.

MARIE-PIERRE de LIEGE is at the Bureau de lat Protection des Victimes et de la Prévention, Ministère de la Justice, France.

PATRICK MURPHY is Lecturer in Sociology, University of Leicester, and a director of the Sir Norman Chester Centre for Football Research.

CHRISTOPHER P. NUTTALL is Assistant Deputy Solicitor General, Canada.

GEOFFREY PEARSON is Professor of Social Work at Middlesex Polytechnic.

PAUL ROCK is Professor of Sociology at the London School of Economics.

DENNIS P. ROSENBAUM is Associate Professor of Criminal Justice at the University of Illinois at Chicago.

ALICE SAMPSON was formerly a Research Fellow, Middlesex Polytechnic and is now a Research Officer at the Home Office Crime Prevention Unit.

JOANNA SHAPLAND is a Research Fellow of the Centre for Criminological Research, Oxford University and of Wolfson College, Oxford.

MARGARET SHAW was formerly a Principal Research Officer in the Home Office Research and Planning Unit and is now a research consultant based in Montreal, Canada.

WESLEY G. SKOGAN is Professor of Political Science at Northwestern University, Evanston, Illinois.

DAVID SMITH is Lecturer in Social Work in the Department of Social Administration, University of Lancaster.

PAUL STUBBS was formerly a Research Fellow, Middlesex Polytechnic.

RALPH TAYLOR is Associate Professor, Department of Criminal Justice, Temple University.

PAUL WILES is Director of the Centre for Criminological and Socio-Legal Studies, University of Sheffield.

JOHN WILLIAMS is Co-Director of the Sir Norman Chester Centre for Football Research at the University of Leicester.

1. Community approaches to reducing crime

Tim Hope and Margaret Shaw

It often seems as though no two people understand the same thing by the use of the word 'community', and the term 'crime reduction' is broad enough to encompass a wide range of measures. Their use—together—in this book is purposeful. It is intended to demonstrate the range of possibilities which exist in our society for preventing crime, as well as the varied, localised and very different nature of individual communities or neighbourhoods, and their experience of and capacities to deal with crime.

The purpose of the book, which represents the outcome of a conference convened by the Home Office Research and Planning Unit in 1986, is to bring together some current ideas, experience, practice and policy, from those who have been working on the problems of how to prevent crime. In doing so, it is hoped to clarify directions for future policy and practice. The authors, coming as they do from a number of different countries and backgrounds, illustrate the current collective concern with crime prevention. Each country has its own characteristic set of crime problems, cultural and population mix, housing, policing and administrative structures. Nevertheless, it is fruitful to examine the range of approaches being explored in parts of Europe and North America, often with considerable vigour. No simple or consistent approach is advocated here. Contradictions and confusions are evident, either in the nature of the problems, their definition, or in the different ways people have tackled them, and these need to be aired. Yet it is these very contradictions which are probably the most useful spur to developing more appropriate policy and research. And it was as a stimulus to practitioners and policy-makers that this book was conceived. The very vagueness of most people's understanding of community crime prevention, the tentative nature of the links with crime of some current activity and the lack of articulation of theories underlying the genesis of crime in the community, all acted as signals that it was time to think more coherently about these issues.

While the chapters in the book vary in their style and emphasis—some are concerned with theoretical problems or seek explanations, some with broad policy initiatives, some with the evaluation of specific programmes—the focus of the book is upon the elusive concept of community, 'a word rich in symbolic power' (Cohen, 1985). It is concerned with small areas, recognisable to their inhabitants and often to outsiders, and set apart in some way. There is a focus upon living space, upon the areas in which groups of people live, move around and perhaps work. They are often small neighbourhoods in which the inhabitants seem to have particular cultural and social characteristics, although not necessarily uniform; they may be identified by reputation, physical cues, architectural styles, environmental features, and by the way they experience crime. Rather than concentrating on individuals, as has so often been the case when considering crime, whether by offenders or involving victims, the focus is upon small areas as collectivities. The importance of this focus lies not just in its apparent neglect in recent years, but primarily in the fact that, as Reiss argues, the structure and organisation of a community affects the crime it experiences over and above the individual characteristics of its residents (Reiss, 1986).

This introductory chapter first of all reviews the background to current interest in community crime prevention and then goes on to outline some of the themes raised by the various contributors. There is one common theme which runs throughout the book: the possibility of developing and strengthening community *institutions* as a means of reducing crime. By 'institution' is meant a whole range of groupings and organisations—families, friendship networks, associations of various kinds, means of employment, markets, public and private services, administrative structures—which bring individuals together and which serve to transmit norms and values to guide and shape behaviour. The underlying principle of this book is that social institutions necessarily complement and mutually reinforce the operation of the formal institutions of the state—police, courts, prison—in the regulation and prevention of behaviour which comes to be defined as criminal.

Trends in community crime prevention

The idea that the residential community should be the focus of measures to reduce crime has been a recurring theme in policy and research. Yet there have been differences over the years in the definition of the nature of the crime 'problem' in communities, and thus in the means to tackle it. Different national experiences have also tended to influence the way crime prevention in the community has been treated. These constitute a legacy of inheritance for what might be done now to reduce crime in residential communities. By way of introducing the specific themes which emerge in this book, it is worth describing some of this legacy of community crime prevention.

The disorganised community

Permeating much discussion about crime in the community is the idea that crime results from a *failure* of community life—in particular, a failure of those positive mechanisms of socialisation and informal control which work against the development of offending. The idea took criminological form primarily in the work of Shaw and McKay (1942) and other sociologists associated with the University of Chicago. They identified areas within American cities which had persistently high rates of resident delinquents, and of other social problems, despite changing populations and ethnic identities. These were the low rent areas, where newly arriving groups to the city first settled—the 'zones of transition'. No recently arrived immigrant group was able to maintain its community bonds in the dislocation of urban life, thus social disorganisation—the absence of shared norms of behaviour and of effective ways of rearing the young into a law-abiding way of life—came to characterise the life of these areas.

The theories of the Chicago sociologists were based upon a relatively free urban market during a period of rapid economic and population growth.

Thus neighbourhoods with the lowest property values were always inhabited by the poorest, most recently arrived immigrant groups. Given expanding urban economic opportunities, each group which bettered itself and moved to a more desirable neighbourhood was replaced by the latest arrivals to the city. With successive waves of new arrivals, community life in the zone of transition would always be inherently unstable, disorganised and criminogenic. In contrast, crime-free neighbourhoods were those where upwardly mobile groups had established themselves socially and politically and had thus acquired a stable culture and set of institutions. 'Successful' urban communities, therefore, were essentially self-selecting and self-organising—the urban market determining their extent and location. For those communities lacking in interal organisation it followed that

> '... if the causes of delinquency were to be found in the attenuation of social controls born of "social disorganisation", then the most effective responses should be the fostering of such potential for social organisation as did exist in the areas most affected. Since the approach stressed the inherent capacity of communities to mobilise their own social control resources, the main burden ...... should be to enhance the capacity of local residents to take the initiative in promoting links with "disaffiliated" youth and in seeking indigenous sources for the promotion of their welfare.' (Downes and Rock, 1982; p. 229.)

The legacy of the Chicago school for crime prevention is therefore threefold: first, it suggests that the distribution of both crime and social disorganisation between communities can be affected by the broader policies and trends which shape the urban scene; second, that measures against offending should somehow seek to socialise and integrate residents, especially youth, into a shared set of norms and standards of behaviour, and third, that the most effective resource for this is to be found amongst ordinary members of the community, though they may need considerable assistance in the trying and difficult circumstances which exist in their neighbourhoods.

The disadvantaged community

A later perception, dominating American attempts at delinquency prevention in the 1960s, expressed another persistent idea about the communal nature of crime. This was the notion that crime would develop as a way of life amongst youth in neighbourhoods where opportunities for personal economic advancement were blocked. In this view, crime was seen as reaction by embittered slum youth to a failure to attain qualifications, a good job, a decent income, which are widely valued and seem to be available to people who live elsewhere (Cloward and Ohlin, 1960). It followed from this analysis that programmes designed to increase the ability of slum youth to participate in the employment market, and to become full members of society, would diminish their participation in illicit activities. This strategy could also be seen as providing a 'stake in conformity' for disadvantaged youth.

In the Britain of the 1950s and 1960s, these two American themes—the failure of community controls and the lack of access to economic opportunity—did not seem to characterise the experience of young people in poor areas. Although studies of youth in the traditional slum areas of London's East End (Willmott, 1966; Downes, 1966) and the Liverpool docklands (Mays, 1954) found widespread offending, this seemed of a predominantly petty nature. There was little evidence of frustration regarding economic failure, or of oppositional values. Rather, the outlook of the youth studied was more one of fatalistic resignation about their future prospects, cushioned by a strong working-class culture, a plentiful, if unrewarding, supply of jobs, and access to lively teenage leisure opportunities (see also Parker, 1974). Generally, the poorer communities of most British cities during the middle of this century seemed together more communal and safer than either their American equivalents or their nineteenth-century counterparts. There is emerging a view that the period roughly between the 1880s and 1950s in Britain can be seen, with some justification, as the steady development of a consensus around the rule of law, even in the poorer areas (see Clarke, 1987). Though episodes of political or industrial unrest periodically brought citizens into conflict with the police, there had emerged by the 1950s a broad, if conditional, measure of support for the *institutions* of the police and the law (Reiner, 1985). What is also striking to the modern observer is that in the early post-war period there seemed little publicly expressed 'fear' of crime. Obviously private citizens became victims of crime but neither the fact, nor the prospect, of victimisation seemed to occasion undue personal worry or demands for action. The policy 'problem' of crime was more one of deciding what to do with the individual miscreant than of protecting society from the predatory actions of criminals.

Many reasons can be advanced for this state of affairs (and important exceptions could also be found) but recent analyses suggest two broad contributory developments. In the first place, there had been the evolution of a particularly British philosophy of policing, resting upon the idea of a non-partisan, professional constable as a 'citizen in uniform', tightly circumscribed by the rule of law and using minimal force in the execution of his duties, whose primary purpose was to prevent crime by visible uniformed patrol and who, as a consequence, was available to deal with a whole range of emergencies and difficulties at the behest of the ordinary citizen (Reiner, 1985). Second, there had been the eventual 'settling' of urban areas by the first part of the twentieth century following the dislocations of rapid population expansion and industrialisation during the nineteenth century. This encouraged within working-class districts both the development of informal networks of family and kin and the emergence of indigenous institutions—for instance, pubs, recreational clubs, co-operative and friendly societies, churches, local trade unions, etc. —alongside the increasing political enfranchisement and partici-pation of the new urban population in local and central government (Clarke, 1987).

These two developments may have worked together to create conditions which, for a time, successfully preserved order in urban communities and, at least, ensured general support for the police. Such areas had developed, through their range of institutions and networks of kin and friendship, formal and informal means for maintaining order and dealing with offending within their midst. In addition, the police had become an effective institution by virtue of having the tacit support of the community. Each aspect reinforced the other (Clarke, 1987): the community gave the police the kind of information which would allow them to deter or apprehend offenders reasonably effectively; the police exercised sensitive discretion in enforcing (or not) aspects of the law in ways which did not alienate the community, often maintaining a very minimal presence. Informal measures were probably important too: members of the community may have been able to deploy sanctions of various kinds—e.g. gossip, exclusion, physical force—to deter or punish 'predatory' crimes, such as burglary or robbery, against fellow residents (especially the elderly); the police may have dealt informally with many acts of petty crime (particularly by youth) by relying upon their own, and the community's, close surveillance as a sufficient deterrent against future misconduct.

Of course, such a picture is a somewhat crude caricature of what must have been a more complex and varied reality. It would certainly have had its limitations and much wrong-doing would have gone unreported and unpunished. Petty theft, receiving stolen goods, illegal gambling, brawling and, most importantly, domestic violence and child abuse were probably all common and, to a large extent, condoned. Neither would the process of law enforcement have been uniformly fair or just in terms of individual rights and liberties. Urban poverty too, may have been continually undermining fragile community institutions and networks—and there would always have been 'rough' areas where the rule of law would have been minimal indeed. But for a time in many communities there may have been brought together the necessary ingredients of formal and informal social regulation in a way which kept crime rates down to tolerable levels, which did not induce fear or damage communities, and which ensured a reasonable measure of support for the rule of law, despite severe poverty and lack of opportunity.

The publication of this book comes at a time when a wide spectrum of public opinion in Britain believes that this situation no longer obtains. Regardless of the actual risk (which is usually less), crime is felt to be a pressing everyday problem by many urban residents—over half of those who live in areas with the highest risk of crime (see Chapter 2) believe they are likely to be burgled within the next twelve months (Hough and Mayhew, 1985). These areas contain only 12 per cent of the households but suffer over a third of the total burglaries in England and Wales (Chapter 2). Neither are the offenders seen as some remote group—at least half the residents of the poorest council estates think most burglaries are committed by people who live in their area (Chapter 2).

Crime in the large American cities is still much greater than in Britain but the difference is now seen as merely quantitive rather than qualitative; and American theories linking crime in urban areas with social disorganisation and economic marginality have more relevance than before. Arguably, the compact between informal and formal regulation no longer functions to any great degree in many British urban communities. Many of the informal institutions and networks necessary to discourage offending have gone; while surveys of inner urban residents suggest that, although there still remains support for the police as an institution necessary to control crime, there is also a worrying degree of disaffection with the everyday practice of policing, especially amongst the young and ethnic minorities (Kinsey *et al.,* 1986; Jones *et al.,* 1986; Smith and Gray 1985).

It is this transformation which forms the backdrop to this volume. In a variety of ways, and by international comparison, it seeks to address some of the causes and possible remedies for the apparent failure of urban communities to regulate crime. The emphasis, in part reflecting the current state of research and policy analysis, tends to be on informal institutions but the role of the formal system is no less important. Discussion returns at the end of this chapter to consider the compact between community and the formal regulation of crime.

Neighbourhood crime in modern cities

The early post-war period in Britain did not produce the kind of criminal areas described by the Chicago sociologists. Morris (1957) found that although there were areas with high rates of resident offenders, they did not appear to have high rates of offences committed within them, nor were they necessarily the inner zones of transition. In fact, since the Second World War, the development of both American and British cities has diverged from the Chicago model, most notably, due to greatly increased government intervention in the urban market. As contemporary American writers such as Jacobs (1962) and Suttles (1972) noted, the culture and organisation of residential communities over this period have also become increasingly affected by urban planning and redevelopment.

The urban communities which established themselves during the expansion of cities in America and Europe seemed to have a life of their own—their identity, institutions and political representation tending to emerge from within the community itself. The relative stability in the ranking of neighbourhoods within the city was buttressed by a combination of market forces, which distributed income groups around a city's housing stock, local employment opportunity (which was determined by the location of industry) and the growth of local government representation based upon neighbourhood political identities. With the development of the modern city, large-scale urban redevelopment began to replace established communities with new neighbourhoods, where the type and mix of population and housing were decided in advance of settlement, as were the amount and type of available community facilities, and where employment was often separated from the area of residence. As such, the identity of communities was rapidly becoming defined by their 'external relations' (Suttles, 1972), particularly by planning and policy decisions taken by local or central government operating from outside the local community. Modern city neighbourhoods are now shaped by a 'mixed economy' of public planning and individual or corporate actions within urban economic and housing markets. Amongst other things, this has produced a shifting pattern of neighbourhood crime rates as community life changes in response to complex interactions between market forces and government interventions. For instance, the relative ordering of neighbourhood crime rates in American cities now appears to change quite markedly over time (Schuerman and Kobrin, 1986; Bursik, 1986) while studies both in Chicago

(Taub, Taylor and Dunham, 1984) and in Sheffield (Bottoms and Wiles, 1986) have demonstrated the need to look at the complex interplay of a range of social, economic and demographic factors over some years in order to understand a particular neighbourhood's current experience of crime. Such shifting patterns now call for explanations of community crime rates which take account of the processes creating urban *change* rather than those which once produced stability (Reiss, 1986).

Housing tenure and the British city

Despite some undoubted similarities, British cities nevertheless differ quite markedly from those in North America, primarily in their structure of housing tenure. The post-war task of reconstruction in many European countries was to facilitate the rapid provision of housing needed as a result of war damage and slum clearance programmes. British cities underwent considerable renewal, characterised in particular by the increased role of the public sector in the provision of housing, and by the decline of private renting. In 1945, 62 per cent of households in Great Britain were privately rented, 26 per cent of households were in owner-occupation, and 12 per cent were rented from public local authorities; by 1979, the private rental sector had shrunk to 13 per cent, owner-occupation had grown to be the majority tenure (55%) and a third of households, predominantly the lower income groups, rented dwellings provided by local government (Bottoms and Wiles, 1986).

Comtemporary British concern with community aspects of crime has been greatly influenced by the transformation of cities brought about by these changes in housing tenure. Of particular significance has been the disappearance of the classic English slum and the emerging problems of the mass council estate. Initially, public concern focused on the growth of vandalism in these new residential environments (Ward, 1973) and on the consequences for family life of high rise dwelling (Jephcott and Robinson, 1971). Oscar Newman's *Defensible Space* (1973) offered a timely and intuitively plausible account to a British audience of the problems engendered by the newly constructed environment of the inner city. During the 1970s, vandalism on the mass estate came to be seen as the consequence of environments lacking defensible space, built on an inhuman scale, and with too many families with children, living at too high a residential density (Clarke, 1978). Since the late 1970s, however, perceptions have gradually changed towards an awareness of the interlocking problems of the 'difficult-to-let estate'—often large, poorly managed and run-down council estates with high levels of crime and deprivation, unpopular with current and prospective tenants alike. The specific focus on vandalism has given way to a wider concern with the quality of life in these areas, and with the emergence of serious crime and drug problems. Of particular significance has been the growing awareness that some estates contained both high rates of offenders and of residents likely to be victimised from crime. With only a little exaggeration, the problem estate has now come to represent, rightly or not, the modern British image of the high crime community.

7

Explanations of community crime rates couched in terms of social disorganisation or economic disadvantage are explanations of how the residents of
particular communities come to engage in criminal activity. They are thus
oriented towards offenders or potential offenders and offer 'social' measures
of prevention inasmuch as they direct attention towards the deployment of
social policies in housing, employment, job creation, recreation, etc. in the
interests of crime prevention. Yet during the 1970s, research and policy shifted
away from a concern with offenders within the community towards a focus on
preventing offences and reducing victimisation from crime suffered by
ordinary community members. In Britain, partly as a result of disillusionment
with the efficacy of measures of penal treatment and social reform (Clarke and
Cornish, 1983), criminologists and policy-makers turned their attention
towards specific situational measures designed to reduce the opportunities
which are available for offending, and thus to reduce the risk of victimisation
to individual citizens and corporate bodies (Clarke and Mayhew, 1980; Heal
and Laycock, 1986).

There has been a tendency during this period to make a distinction between
social and situational measures of crime prevention. Clarke (1981), for
instance, saw 'social' measures as dealing with the 'fundamental causes' of
crime, whether broad social policies designed to integrate the young or
promote respect for moral values, or localised measures designed to increase
community solidarity, improve facilities or strengthen relationships with the
police. These were to be distinguished from situational measures, particularly
involving the manipulation of aspects of the physical environment to reduce
opportunities, which aimed to deter would-be criminals from the commission
of specific offences. Whereas social crime prevention came to be seen as an
effort to inculcate a permanent disposition against offending in general,
situational prevention has concentrated on developing shorter-term measures
to prevent specific offence behaviour, either by 'designing out' the possibility
of crime altogether or by increasing the risk of detection, and thus logically
resting upon the deterrence of crime by legal sanction. Although there is
nothing intrinsically communal about situational crime prevention—measures
can take many forms as long as they reduce opportunities as perceived by
potential offenders—its implementation often demands a focus on residential
communities. In as much as the situational approach calls for targeted action
based on an assessment of risk, communities which suffer high rates of
offences then become likely locations for implementing situational measures
(Clarke and Hope, 1984). Involving communities also seems a promising way
of reaching ordinary people and encouraging them to adopt protective
measures (Heal and Laycock, 1986). Neighbourhood Watch, for instance, has
come to be seen as a popular medium for implementing opportunity reduction
in local communities especially since it relies upon co-operative effort to
reinforce preventive actions taken by individuals—that is, keeping watch on
neighbours' dwellings, installing security devices, taking precautions against
burglary and marking property.

While situational prevention has evolved a community approach to foster
the implementation of measures, most discussion of social crime prevention in
recent years has largely ignored the community dimension, focusing on

measures to offset the development of individual criminality and criminal behaviour or to strengthen the socialising potential of, in particular, the family or the school. For example, the Parliamentary All-Party Penal Affairs Group report on the prevention of crime among young people (1983) presented some suggestions for social crime prevention which included general measures to strengthen family support, to improve the education system's response to truancy and disruptive behaviour in school, to improve recreational and leisure facilities and access to employment opportunities, and to discourage the abuse of alcohol and drugs by teenagers. There was little emphasis in the report, however, on a localised or community dimension, nor on focusing social measures in high crime areas. Reiss (1986) too points to the current emphasis within American criminology on individual-level explanations of offender or victim behaviour and to the dominant concern to explain individual 'criminal careers'.

Nevertheless, there are also signs of a recent renewal of interest in the socialising structures of society found in the basic institutions of the family and social network—the building blocks of community. Recent research on the family, for example, (see e.g. Riley and Shaw, 1984) points to the need for support and encouragement to parents in bringing up their children in a society which has changed rapidly over the past few years. At the most crime-prone periods of their life, young people perhaps lack the support and supervision—much of it informal—which may have existed in previous generations. In The Netherlands, France and Canada, as Chapters 15–17 indicate, there is a similar concern with the lack of socialising structures, most dramatically illustrated in the case of the Netherlands by the analysis of the increase in crime among young people following the collapse of the 'columns', organisations which integrated religious, political and cultural activities and effectively helped in socialising young people.

Additionally, a general move towards the concept of community care, initiated within the field of health and social services, has in turn prompted a revival of interest in exploring informal resources of care and concern amongst neighbours (Bulmer, 1986; Willmott, 1984). Bulmer (1985), in tracing the decline of community studies since the 1960s, shows too how changes in the definition of the field, developments in method and theory, and interest in local politics, have all contributed to a revival of interest in community action, neighbourhood mobilisation and participation, and the role they play in linking 'the personal sphere to the broader political and bureaucratic structures of society'.

Notwithstanding developments in other spheres of social policy, much crime prevention analysis over the past decade and a half—whether 'social' or 'situational'—has ignored the community dimension, seeing crime as it occurs in specific communities (whether from a victim-or offender-perspective) as little more than an aggregation of individual behaviour. But there have also been specific objections raised against community-level social measures. For instance, Wilson (1975) points to the seeming intractability of those conditions within the family, local economy or peer group which criminology has suggested are correlated with offending, compared with the possibilities of deploying legal sanctions; while Clarke and Cornish (1983) baldy state that.... 'there is little evidence to date that youth work, voluntary welfare, school liaison work by the police, community self-help groups and tenant associations have any effect on levels of crime' (p.46).

Nevertheless, while there is substance to these arguments, it is also reasonable to point out that, on the whole, there have been relatively few reliable evaluation studies of social policy measures taken against crime, especially in contemporary circumstances. And there may also be an element of selective perception in overlooking the contemporary evidence which is available (for which see, *inter alia* Curtis, 1985; Currie, 1985; McGahey, 1986). Even so, some have sought to impute guilt by association by brigading community interventions under the broad rubric of a 'medico-psychological' or 'treatment' model and then citing evidence of this model's ineffectiveness in reducing recidivism amongst convicted offenders as evidence also against preventive work in the community (Clarke and Cornish, 1983). But, in any case, critics have perhaps been to ready to pose a dichotomy between community measures and those resting on increasing the risks of offending via the criminal justice system. In doing so, they tend to underestimate the contribution of families, peers and neighbours in reinforcing standards of conduct. As Gottfredson (1982) remarks:

> 'Adolescents who do not commit delinquent acts may be unaware of the average time in prison and the probability of conviction given an offence, but they do have a fair idea of (and care about) what their mothers would think if they were caught breaking the law.'

Neither are measures to improve the employability of young people, or to divert them into constructive leisure activities, incompatible with perspectives which see potential offenders as rational calculators of risk and reward, given that these measures can be construed as benefits increasing the incentives to abstain from offending (Wilson and Herrnstein, 1985). Thus although some critics may be keen to use an absence of contemporary evidence on the efficacy of social measures in the promotion of their own favoured approach to crime control, the case against social crime prevention in the community remains unsubstantiated. However, the difficulty of finding the right way of intervening in the community should not be underestimated.

'Social engineering' in the community

To some quite considerable degree, the relative absence of a focus on social prevention in the community within contemporary thinking about crime prevention reflects a reaction to the perceived follies of past interventions in communities (cf.Wilson, 1975). On both sides of the Atlantic, the 1950s saw the initiation of community development programmes designed to redress the problems of deprivation within specific urban neighbourhoods. In the United States, delinquency in slum neighbourhoods was diagnosed as arising from poverty, stemming from a lack of employment opportunities and the inability of local people to compete on equal terms in the job market. Cloward and Ohlin's (1960) theory of delinquency, described above, linked these concerns with crime prevention and became the justification for mounting intensive job creation and community programmes in slum neighbourhoods. The Mobilisation for Youth (MFY) programme in New York, formed on the basis of this analysis, in turn became a model for the 'War on Poverty' of the Kennedy and Johnson administrations (Marris and Rein, 1974).

In Britain, influential reviews of the provision of education (the 'Plowden Committee', 1967) and social services (the 'Seebohm Committee', 1968) focused on the pocketing of poverty and social pathology (including delinquency) in identifiable areas and argued for a targeting of resources, and co-ordination of service delivery, to tackle the problems on the ground. As a consequence, special programmes within education (the Educational Priority Area (E.P.A) projects) and community development (the Community Development Projects—CDP) were established. It is, in fact, almost twenty years since CDP was launched as 'a neighbourhood-based experiment aimed at finding new ways of meeting the needs of people living in areas of high social deprivation'. A similar mood of optimism pervaded both the American and British schemes: that the problems of urban neighbourhoods could be resolved by local action projects, conducted in the form of social 'experiments'— guided by the spirit of 'experimental social administration' (Halsey, 1978).

The subsequent history of these programmes has become part of the folklore of social policy in both countries. Though to this day, partisan positions are taken as to 'what happened' or 'what went wrong', there seems general agreement that the specific and focused objectives of the projects became subordinated in a drift towards political activism as programme workers engaged in conflict with local authorities and other interests, and as the researchers moved from evaluation to social critique. In particular, the specific aim of reducing delinquency tended to disappear in the pursuit of wider goals of social change. The political conflict involved in these projects, their consumption of resources, their perceived lack of tangible effect, their grandiose designs and aims, and their raising of expectations within the community which could not be met, all fuelled a reaction in the 1970s against 'social engineering' for crime prevention purposes. In contrast, more low-key methods of intervention have begun to emerge.

Citizen involvement and multi-agency co-ordination

Over the past decade, there seems to have been a movement in many countries towards widening the sense of responsibility for crime prevention beyond the criminal justice system. Two broad developments have encouraged this: in the first place, there has been an increasing sensitisation to the social problem of the 'fear of crime' and, in particular, to the harmful effects which such fear was thought to be having on community life. With this has come the realisation that many people—as victims or friends of victims—are touched by crime, and that crime is nowadays a common public concern, no longer the sole province of the specialist, whether policeman, psychiatrist or social worker (Lavrakas, 1985).

There has also been a growing awareness, evident in the contributions in this volume from other countries, of the limitations of what the criminal justice system can do: that the burden of crime prevention cannot be carried solely by the police, the courts and the penal system. As well as citizens themselves, those responsible for housing, for schools, for employment and leisure provision also have a more crucial role in crime prevention than has been acknowledged previously. These shifts in thinking have lead to two approaches

11

to organising preventive effort in the community: citizen involvement; and multi-agency co-ordination.

A community hypothesis has emerged in a number of countries (but particularly in North America) which serves as a rationale for citizen involvement. As DuBow and Emmons (1981, p.171) describe it:

'i. Neighbourhood residents can be mobilised by community organisations to participate in collective crime prevention projects.

ii. Involvement in these activities creates a stronger community because people will take greater responsibility for their own protection and local problems, and interactions among neighbours will be increased, both formally, through the activities of crime prevention projects, and informally, as a byproduct of these activities.

iii. A stronger sense of community and increased social interaction leads to more effective informal social control.

iv. Aside from the direct effects of community crime prevention activity in reducing crime and fear of crime, these activities may also reduce crime or the fear of crime by rebuilding local social control in the neighbourhood.'

Nevertheless, what seems to distinguish this approach to community crime prevention from that, say, of the Chicagoans has been called the 'victimisation perspective' (Lewis and Salem, 1986; Podolefsky and DuBow, 1981). For Shaw and McKay, crime was a problem which originated *within* particular kinds of community. The task was to promote community control to monitor and shape the behaviour of residents, particularly youngsters, and to inculcate a disposition against offending, including offending within the neighbourhood. In contrast, the victimisation perspective, though also relying on the mobilisation of informal community controls, directs these in the *defence* of communities against a perceived predatory threat from outside.

Attention is focused on ameliorating the impact of crime on the individual and on community institutions. In the short-run, measures predicated on this perspective are aimed principally at providing mutual self-protection; in the longer term, it is hoped that these will enhance the greater integration of community members, itself seen as a defence against invasion from crime. Though there may be some disagreement as to whether it is victimisation itself which destroys communities, or whether crime merely acts as a potent symbol of neighbourhood decline which is occurring for other, primarily economic, reasons (Lewis and Salem, 1981), there nevertheless seems to be a common theme of the 'invasion' of crime into the community from persons or agencies who come from a largely unspecified elsewhere.

Recently, though, there has been an increasing awareness that while the introduction of Neighbourhood Watch into Britain has been very popular overall, it has been less easy to initiate or sustain in poor, inner-city neighbourhoods—an experience also found in the United States (Titus, 1984). Various chapters in this volume address this issue, but the experience perhaps highlights the difficulty of applying a purely 'defensive' model in communities where the source of crime comes from within. Interestingly, comparison of crime prevention schemes in the United States revealed different approaches and emphases according to the nature of the host community (Podolefsky, 1983; Podolefsky and DuBow, 1981). In particular, schemes which emerged within poorer, high crime communities, tended to take a 'social problem', approach, seeing crime as a problem involving local people, which needed to be addressed in ways which would tackle these endemic causes. Similarly, in a recent review of American research on community organisations in crime prevention, Skogan (in press) contrasts 'preservationist' with 'insurgent' organisations: the former tend to see crime as undermining the character of their neighbourhood which they wish to preserve; the latter are concerned to change the conditions in their neighbourhood which they perceive as causing crime. An emerging issue, then, within citizen crime prevention is the extent to which local definitions of the crime problem come to shape the solutions which may emerge to tackle it.

In contrast, the move towards a co-ordinated, multi-agency approach in tackling crime within local communities has emerged, in Britain at least, primarily as a response by those agencies charged with dealing with crime. The basic premise underlying the approach has been that, inasmuch as crime within local communities is likely to be sustained by a broad range of factors—in housing, education, recreation, etc.—the agencies and organisations who are in some way responsible for, or capable of, affecting those factors, ought to join in common cause so that they are not working at cross-purposes or sustaining crime inadvertently.

The multi-agency approach in Britain has developed from three sources. In the first place, various police forces, from about the mid-1970s, began to initiate links with other agencies as part of a move towards 'community policing' so as to renew the partnership between the police and the community they serve (Moore and Brown, 1981; Weatheritt, 1986). Second, there have been moves, usually at local level, towards developing co-ordinated approaches to juvenile justice, involving increased collaboration between police, social work agencies and schools, and taking a variety of forms including juvenile liaison schemes, police juvenile bureaux, cautioning panels, as well as more thoroughgoing attempts to co-ordinate local juvenile justice 'systems'. Thirdly, an impetus has come from central government in the form of joint, inter-departmental circulars offering advice and guidance. In 1978 a circular urged greater co-ordination amongst agencies dealing with juveniles; and another in 1984 commended systematic co-ordination in all aspects of crime prevention. The Home Office in particular has taken a lead in encouraging other central government departments to be mindful of the implications of their work for crime prevention, and in encouraging co-ordination at the local level (for which see Chapter 14).

The trend in community intervention in recent years has thus been towards building and organising from the local level—whether through the involvement of citizens at the grass-roots or by co-ordinating the efforts of local agencies—rather than seeking to engineer change, or to impose solutions, according to diagnoses of community problems formulated by external agencies.

The inner city

In parallel with these specific developments within crime prevention, central and local government in many of the industrialised countries has struggled with the problems of urban economic decline, especially the problems generated by the shrinkage of manufacturing and population from the inner urban core of the older industrial cities. Surprisingly though, thinking about crime prevention has tended until recently to develop in isolation from the debates and programmes surrounding the issues of urban renewal. Yet as Lord Scarman's enquiry into the Brixton disorders of 1981 noted, the roots of local youth's involvement in crime may well be found amongst the difficulties of community life in these deteriorating inner city areas, in much the same way as Cloward and Ohlin (1960) identified for slum youth in the American cities of the 1950s and 1960s:

> '. . .they share the desires and expectations which our materialistic society encourages. At the same time, many of them fail to achieve educational success and on leaving school face the stark prospect of unemployment . . . Without close parental support, with no job to go to and with few recreational facilities available, the young black person makes his life on the streets and in the seedy commercially run clubs of Brixton. There he meets criminals, who appear to have no difficulty in obtaining the benefits of a materialist society . . . Many young black people do not of course resort to crime . . . But it would be surprising if they did not feel a sense of frustration and deprivation' (Scarman, para. 2.23)

To the extent that life for young people in inner-city communities resembles this picture, or that conditions on the large, decaying, council estates place obstacles in the way of maintaining community cohesion and control over conduct, there is scope for looking towards policies of urban economic regeneration to bring about reductions in crime within the community. Currently, the British Government is engaged in wide-ranging effort to increase employment, employability and enterprise in blighted inner-city neighbourhoods—to develop skills, focus training and employment opportunities on the needs of local firms, and encourage new businesses to start up and grow. The emphasis is on building a capacity amongst local people to take positive action themselves—to improve their chances of employment, to upgrade their skills and education and to participate in economic recovery. Nevertheless, the task of connecting these aims with the goal of preventing crime, and of integrating crime control initiatives within the broader programmes of urban regeneration, remains to be carried through. Modestly, the contributions to this volume represent a move in this direction.

Summary

This outline of trends in the perception of how crime might be tackled at the community level does not suggest that a simple solution or definition of approach is likely to emerge from this volume. Indeed, the pursuit of single-focus, universal solutions may be illusory, given the complexity and variety of ways of thinking about crime in communities. Likewise, the motivation for a renewal of interest in tackling the causes of crime at the community level comes from a number of directions. Yet this does not reflect merely a return to old ideas for the sake of change. Given the gains that have been made in recent years in our understanding of the environmental patterning of crime and the application of careful targeting of offender behaviour with the development of the situational approach, it is rather a question of looking afresh at community problems with new insights. Indeed it is in part in recognition of the rapid and often successful development and adoption of the situational approach in Britain (although as Chapter 14 suggests there is still a long way to go) that it was felt to be time to take stock of alternative approaches, and to explore compatibilities and differences around the problem of crime in the community.

Themes rather than conclusions

The community context of crime

The book is organised around a number of themes and the first, that of the location of crime in particular areas, provides the 'evidence' as it were for a community focus. As Reiss has recently pointed out, there is nothing new about the territorial distribution of crime, whether in terms of offenders or victims (Reiss, 1986). However, as he demonstrates, almost all data collected about crime patterns (whether official statistics, victimisation surveys or self-report studies) is based upon individual behaviour rather than collective behaviour at the community level. Thus Chapter 2, which looks at the area context of crime using the British Crime Survey, bases its conclusions on a national sample of individuals taken to be representative of particular types of residential neighbourhood. Nevertheless, there is powerful evidence of the pocketing of crime—a factor also obscured by an historic concentration on trends in national criminal statistics. Most notably, it is the poorer council estates where burglary in particular is heavily concentrated, and this serves also to illustrate the link between crime, area and tenure. The geographical concentration of crime is further underlined in Chapter 4 which shows the very limited range of types of neighbourhood to which adult offenders are released.

Neighbourhood deterioration

A second, and related theme, is the role of crime in the process of neighbourhood deterioration. One noteworthy consequence of bringing together contributors from North America and Britain is to illustrate how writers from different urban contexts make use of an essentially similar theoretical model to describe the way in which crime may be linked to neighbourhood decline (Chapter 3 and Chapters 5 and 6; see also Hope, 1986). This model also represents an attempt to organise thinking about the process by which crime comes to be localised in particular communities. The model postulates a series of stages leading to the social breakdown of neighbourhoods. It suggests that certain visible neighbourhood conditions such as delapidated buildings, litter and vandalism, and such things as noisy neighbours, unruly youths hanging about, and drunks in the street (collectively termed 'incivilities') can come to signal to outsiders and residents alike that the neighbourhood is in decline. This perception has further psychological effects on residents, increasing their worries about crime and diminishing their satisfaction with the neighbourhood. If residents continue to observe increasing signs of neighbourhood disorder they may then begin to withdraw from community life. Such withdrawal can take a variety of forms: for instance, residents may lose interest in participating in local voluntary activities; they may also be afraid to venture out at night to attend them; they may retreat behind closed doors and develop strategies to minimise their contact with neighbours; and, at the extreme, they may move away from the neighbourhood altogether if they can.

The consequence of such withdrawal is to greatly reduce the reservoir of informal control which community members exercise amongst themselves. Additionally, flight from the neighbourhood and reduced social activity starts to cut into the neighbourhood's economic base, particularly in retailing and small business enterprise. The neighbourhood (or council estate) begins to acquire an adverse reputation, the area becomes unattractive to prospective residents and only those in greatest housing need—who have least personal resources to participate in communal life or to stem the increase in neighbourhood problems—start to move in. Offenders from outside now begin to perceive this absence of community control and commit crimes within the neighbourhood, knowing that residents are unlikely to intervene. Local youth increasingly offends within the residential environment in the absence of persons to monitor their leisure-time behaviour or who offer non-criminal alternatives.

As a result of this vacuum in community life, incivilities now begin to escalate into increasing rates of serious crime. Additionally, as conventional retailing and business activity withdraws from the shopping centres of the neighbourhood, they are replaced with 'twilight enterprises' such as massage parlours, pornographic retailers, etc. which in themselves attract further criminal activity. The process is circular and, if unarrested, may continue with accelerating force, such that the greater accumulation of signs of neighbourhood disorder comes to signify the further deterioration of the neighbourhood, and so on.

It is, of course, possible to refine further the model as described here. Gottfredson and Taylor (Chapter 4), for example, distinguish between active and passive responses to disorder, and the relative ability of neighbourhoods to resist or accommodate signs of deterioration. Neither is the process inevitable. Taub, Taylor and Dunham (1984), for instance, present evidence to suggest that neighbourhoods can withstand quite high levels of crime and incivility if there are other amenities—parks, schools, housing—which residents value. But there may also be a point at which resistance to disorder gives way as crime rises and interest in the other benefits of the neighbourhood are outweighed by the deterioration and level of incivility (Chapter 9).

Notwithstanding the need for further theoretical refinement (and it is not the purpose of this book to provide a final analysis of its utility), the current significance of the model is that it seems to provide the rationale for a number of different options for intervention to arrest the process of deterioration. They differ, however, in their identification of the appropriate point to intervene in the spiral of decline, and the appropriate means to do so. One popular version, the 'Broken Windows' model (Wilson and Kelling, 1982), suggests that it is important to intervene early in the cycle to clean up the environment and reduce incivilities—the metaphor being that unrepaired damage encourages further broken windows. Wilson and Kelling advocate the deployment of police to fill the vacuum of informal social control and to act in support of community norms against those creating a nuisance within the neighbourhood. But the metaphor can also be applied literally, as encouragement for local authorities to maintain their estates to a high standard and act quickly to repair outbreaks of vandalism (Clarke, 1978).

An alternative model suggests that residents in private sector neighbourhoods that look as if they are in danger of 'tipping' into a spiral of deterioration can be encouraged to stay and act to stem the tide if they are given some incentive to do so. In particular, this points to the need for broader economic investment in an area to increase its desirability, especially in keeping house prices buoyant, and neighbourhood facilities—schools, parks, shops—clean, safe and attractive. Taub, Taylor and Dunham (1984) point, in particular, to the beneficial consequences for some Chicago neighbourhoods of investment by institutions and 'corporate actors'—banks, universities, insurance companies, manufacturing firms, etc. The benefit for the institution (and not without profit) is to buttress the neighbourhood in which they already have a financial stake; and residents' confidence is boosted by the confidence of the institution in their neighbourhood.

Another mode of intervention involves the more concerted attempt to improve both environmental factors as well as community cohesion and confidence. Two strong examples of such intervention in problem housing estates which are well on the road of decline, and which attempt to reverse it, are the current programmes being conducted by the Priority Estates Project sponsored by the Department of the Environment, and a number of projects including the work of the Safe Neighbourhoods Unit being run by the National Association for the Care and Resettlement of Offenders (NACRO) (see Chapter 6). Here, in areas where crime and fear of crime are a normal feature of daily life, and the cycle of decline is well established, intervention comes late. While the two programmes are based upon rather different premises, that by PEP emphasising the importance of management and maintenance, that by NACRO stressing participation and involvement by tenants in decision-making, both are characterised by the focus on specific, small-area neighbourhoods, and working on issues which go much beyond crime and its companions, fear, vandalism, violence, damage and disorder.

Another model of neighbourhood change is one which is possibly more specific to Britain than other countries without a major public housing sector. The work of Bottoms and Wiles (Chapter 5) has enabled them to develop the concept of the community crime career. Based on their longitudinal study of housing areas in Sheffield, they have been able to identify estates with similar environmental and architectural characteristics but very varied crime and offender rates. Thus the determinists, who have argued for the overriding importance of design and environment on behaviour, find no room in Sheffield. The alternative explanation favoured by Bottoms and Wiles is of the power of tenure allocation patterns which have helped to channel particular groups of people into particular estates, with consequent wide variations in the kinds of social relationships and cohesion found to exist. Nor is high crime, in terms of the presence of offenders resident in an estate, necessarily associated with social breakdown and depressed communities. As with Taub, Taylor and Dunham's model, Bottoms and Wiles see housing policy at both national and local level as having a significant influence on the pocketing and maintenance

17

of criminal areas, a trend they see as particularly important in a period which is witnessing a change of tenure patterns towards owner-occupation.

Finally, in an attempt to examine the interaction of offenders and environments, Gottfredson and Taylor consider how far the presence of offenders in a neighbourhood influences the perceptions of residents about the kind of place they live in, and how far the behaviour of offenders is in turn influenced by the nature of that community. Offenders, they argue, are themselves part of the community and of the process of neighbourhood change, and crime prevention policies need to take account of their presence in designing community activities. Though their work is exploratory, it does suggest that there may be some mileage in looking at the extent to which current policies of resettling and housing offenders or, indeed, of other vulnerable or minorities groups, might affect the communities to which they are allocated and, of course, the effect of those communities upon their own future well-being.

Informal social control

A third major theme of the book is *informal social control* currently exemplified by neighbourhood watch. This form of police-led community crime prevention provides a useful case study of some of the problems and possibilities inherent in crime prevention based on a situational approach. It is a form of practice which has considerable appeal both for the police and local communities as well as policy-makers. It is readily understandable, not costly, and designed to capitalise on the natural inclination of most individuals to protect their property. It is apparently simple to set up and operate and it demonstrates one of the essential elements of current crime prevention, that it helps to shift the burden of responsibility for prevention on to the community.

As a form of opportunity reduction, neighbourhood watch raises a number of questions about the extent to which it is applicable in different communities. The authors concerned here raise a range of questions about the potential for setting up schemes (Chapter 9), their implementation and maintenance (Chapter 13), and their effectiveness (Chapter 8). All of them helpful considerations for the development of future schemes. Thus Chapter 9 considers the scope for the development of neighbourhood watch schemes in different types of community setting in Britain, based on an analysis of the British Crime Survey. Here, again, the elements of neighbourhood change are traceable: where satisfaction with one's neighbourhood is high in spite of a high crime rate, there seems a willingness to participate in a neighbourhood watch scheme, but a critical point is reached where increasing crime erodes satisfaction.

In America this form of crime prevention has a much longer pedigree, and Dennis Rosenbaum's chapter examines the assumptions underlying the establishment of neighbourhood watch—that it helps to reduce fear of crime and restores a sense of community. While public awareness and attitudes about such schemes are high, participation, even in America, is still felt to be low and difficult to sustain. He challenges the assumptions that it is easy to implement on a large scale; that given the opportunity to do so most citizens will participate; and that fear of crime and criminal activity will decrease as participation in crime prevention activity increases; and indeed that such schemes are easily sustained. Based on an evaluation of a neighbourhood watch programme in Chicago, Rosenbaum's research suggests that fear of crime may actually be increased by such schemes if not properly handled, but more importantly, that it is inherently a defensive approach which sees offenders as outsiders and works to deflect them, and does not rely on the more constructive reformative instincts of a community's resources. While Rosenbaum claims that much research on the effectiveness of neighbourhood watch has failed to meet the standards of rigorous evaluation, his findings are themselves challenged by Curtis (Chapter 11), on the rather separate grounds that it is unrealistic to expect a programme based on opportunity reduction, even with the involvement of the community, to reduce crime over a short period, and without tackling the more fundamental causes of crime.

What these chapters bring out most clearly is the conundrum that it is precisely those areas and neighbourhoods which are most affected by crime and fear of crime, and most in need of such schemes, which are least able to sustain them. Such areas do not exhibit the ability to act collectively, do not have strong social networks, and are least able to see their neighbours as a force for crime prevention.

The importance of informal social controls based on 'watching' and 'noticing' are raised in another chapter by Joanna Shapland (Chapter 7) which documents the essential supportive role of the police in any rural or urban community, and beyond the more 'formalised' organisation implied by neighbourhood watch schemes. In her view it is essential 'that methods of policing and official programmes for crime prevention and crime reduction should build on the existing work being done by the public, rather than ignoring or even countering it'. One significance of the research on which the chapter is based is that it looks not just at the urban setting and its problems, but at those areas such as small villages and suburban neighbourhoods, where it is possible to see communities working as we would like them to, an approach to the understanding of crime and its patterning which looks for positive influences, after decades in which the focal point has been the offender or the areas of greatest criminal activity (cf.the interest in protective factors in delinquency causation discussed by Rutter and Giller, 1983).

Community interventions and young people

A rather different focus is taken by two chapters which consider prevention policies aimed more specifically at young people. Chapters 10 and 11 provide detailed accounts of approaches concerned to prevent the development of offending behaviour among the poorest and, in the case of America, minority communities. Thus John Williams and his co-authors give an account of some of the history of attempts in Britain to prevent football violence. Again the interplay between preventive techniques based on deterrence or on opportunity reduction, and that grounded in a concept of the need for a longer-term community reform solution is evident, with the development of football clubs as a resource within a community, in partnership with other local agencies. Both past policies, and research and theory, are felt to have been inadequate based as they often have been on a notion that it represents a social problem which is 'inexplicable'. Yet football hooliganism is a predominantly male preserve, and community initiatives which stress equalising and integrating both men and women within those localised communities from which most hooliganism stems, seem the most productive. Chapter 11 provides some challenging material on the successful implementation of policies to reduce crime among young people in America, and which are concerned with dealing with causes rather than opportunity. Three well-established neighbourhood-based self-help projects known as Argus, El Centro and The House of Umoja are examined. All are directed primarily at young people at risk or in trouble with the criminal justice system. Curtis repudiates the notion that 'nothing works' and sees the need for a concerted return to crime prevention based on the notion that it possible to effect changes by early intervention in the cycle, and the provision of such supportive institutions as employment creation and training, the development of self-esteem and social skills, and good support which recreates that with which a strong family provides its members. This is not to reject the accumulation of experience and gains made by opportunity-based crime prevention, which he sees as an important aspect of an overall crime prevention policy, but only if it is pursued in conjunction with prevention 'which addresses causes'.

Implementation issues

Good theory and careful research are not the only prerequisites for the development of successful policies. It would be foolish to promise too much, or to assume that recent wisdom will necessarily lead to workable solutions. In the literature on situational prevention, the problems of actually implementing schemes has been apparent from the start (e.g. Hope and Murphy, 1983). Several chapters of the book touch on the problems to be faced. Thus Chapter 14 points out that popular support for crime prevention has not yet been won:
> 'the . . . majority of individuals and organisations persist in the view that responsibility for crime control rests with the police alone'. It is evident that interest in prevention will depend upon the costs of crime, the capacity of organisations to do something about it, and their willingness to take responsibility for its prevention. This, Heal and Laycock argue, calls for a programme of public re-education on the lines of a public health campaign.

Chapter 13, based on an analysis of community schemes, considers in some detail the prerequisites of establishing and maintaining successful community schemes. The authors outline the community characteristics which are necessary for successful community involvement in crime prevention activities. These include a shared understanding or knowledge of the underlying causes of crime, an articulate and persuasive leader, public-spirited volunteers who are not motivated primarily by fear of crime, adequate resources within the community including both a self-confidence to carry group activity forward, and perhaps both financial and administrative support. This point is made by Curtis (Chapter 11) too who places good managerial capacities and financial self-sufficiency high on the agenda for community-based schemes to enable them to become not only well established and effective, but continuing. He warns also against the notion that voluntary-based initiatives can be expected to maintain a programme without financial and managerial assistance. Another implementation issue underlying much crime reduction is the notion that horizontal links between agencies working in the community are easily made. *Inter-agency co-operation* is the subject of current research discussed in Chapter 12 and specifically established to explore some of the problems which arise and to counter, in their terms, the rhetoric and well-meaning sentiments which surround policy statements about the value of inter-agency co-operation in crime prevention. (Not everyone agrees it is a good thing. For example, it may be widen the net of those dealt with punitively, or the exchange of information may infringe civil liberties.) Yet, they argue, different agencies do not start on equal terms and this inequality of power which helps the shape outcome of collaboration should not be neglected. Liaison problems may be greatest where the goals of a particular programme are least clearly defined.

The implications of power differentials between agencies and formal differences in their roles and objectives is illustrated by the consequences this may have for the definition of crime problems in a local area. Because of their close and traditional relationship to the formal system of criminal justice, the police, for example, or the probation service may define the problems to be tackled differently. Thus local residents may feel the real problems to be vandalism, petty theft or rowdiness, problems which are not in the eyes of the police 'real' crimes. Nor are they characteristic of the kinds of offending behaviour or clientele which the probation officer may deal with in a routine way. Thus the authors question the 'key role' which is assumed to belong to those agencies in many crime prevention initiatives, and where crime prevention technology can become a 'definer of status in an inter-agency forum'.

There is the problem also that inter-agency groups may develop into 'talking shops', reaching only surface agreement, rather than identifying areas of conflict and attempting to remedy them. They discuss too what they refer to as the 'silences' in crime prevention, with the failure of much current preventive activity to confront crimes such as violence against women, or racial attacks. Finally, they point to the informal neighbourhood care networks which form a base upon which local projects in crime prevention could be built, but which have tended to be neglected in the emphasis upon the linking of statutory organisations.

Bubbling-up

It is possible to discern among these chapters a clear distinction between the methodology thought appropriate for different types of crime preventive activity. What is apparent, is that for a community initiative to begin to be successful, it must involve the members of the community, and not just the organisations or agencies working in the community. Lynn Curtis distinguishes between 'bubble up' and 'top down' approaches. In the latter, a crime prevention package, often based on very careful assessment of the crime problem of an area may be designated; in the former, the emphasis is upon allowing ideas about the definition of the problems facing the community, and the ways in which the residents feel they might be tackled, to come from the community itself. This process, in the form of tenant participation, is very much the starting point for the NACRO initiatives, as well as the current programme being funded by the Eisenhower Foundation (see Chapter 11), and community football initiatives outlined in Chapter 10. In his discussion of 'what it is' that makes 'something' happen in such projects, Paul Rock hints at, among other factors, the central importance of community leaders—often women—and informal networks.

Evaluation

Discernable too, in these chapters, is a tension between those who regard evaluation as an essential part of good crime prevention policy and those who have little time for it. Paul Rock (Chapter 6) gently reproves the activists who have been so involved in the problems of the inner city housing estate for being too busy to write down what has been happening. Yet, he argues, if we are not to waste energy and resources, it is necessary to be able to understand what has been happening on those estates to help build up a sense of community and to reduce fear and crime. Curtis too (Chapter 11) notes that those responsible for successful community crime initiatives do not have time to worry about the minutiae of formal academic evaluation (or indeed for the requirements of bureaucratic grant application). Yet clearly there is a high emphasis placed by funding agencies and the academic community in America on the careful evaluation of projects, and certainly, sensible policy development requires some attempt to assess efficacy and impact.

For the present, there seems a clear difference in this approach and that being taken in France (Chapter 16) where national policy is emphasising the importance of energising local co-operation and practical initiative, and does not place a particularly high value on demonstrating effectiveness. And among those who stress the need for evaluation, there are disputes about whether the emphasis should be upon fear of crime or upon crime itself. In Curtis's view, fear of crime has been developed too much as a bureaucratic convenience, since it is often easier to show changes in fear levels than in crime itself.

Across national boundaries

The final section of the book provides a glimpse at current policy developments at government level in France, The Netherlands, Canada and Britain. In The Netherlands, a broad and well-balanced programme of measures ranging from situational to social crime prevention, and backed by evaluative research, is now well established. In France, there is a determined effort to foster crime prevention initiatives of a wide-ranging kind at local level, bringing together representatives of local organisations and criminal justice agencies to assess the problems experienced in their communities and develop policies to tackle them locally. Recent Council of Europe efforts to establish a European alliance of local municipalities, and a data bank to support their work, is indicative of a movement spreading beyond France's national borders. In Canada, while there seems to some extent less urgency or need to confront crime as a national problem—although as Chapter 15 shows, fear levels in Canada reflect those of its American neighbour—it is instructive to note the uniqueness of Canadian society. While having a North American lifestyle, a far higher emphasis is placed upon community health and well-being. This has meant that it has been comparatively easy to set up a wide range of preventive schemes.

Defining boundaries and future trends

The attraction of situational and opportunity models of crime prevention lies primarily in their ability to provide rational, often simple and cheap solutions to particular crime problems, infinitely adaptable to a variety of locations, and based on what Clarke and Cornish have termed 'good enough' explanations of criminal behaviour (Cornish and Clarke, 1985). Running through this book is the tension between what has been achieved so far by this approach, and what, inevitably, are the problems which have been thrown up—inevitably, because all social change programmes have to be constantly adapted to shifting circumstances and ideas, and measured against their initial aims. Elliott Currie's postscript, which formed a commentary on the discussions generated at the conference on which the book is based, provides an account of where in his view we should be going now.

He does this by polarising, deliberately for the sake of emphasis, what he calls Phase I and Phase II crime prevention. Essentially he classifies what he sees to be the differences between a defensive and a reformist approach. Defensive crime prevention is characterised by opportunity reduction models based on a victim perspective and emphasising the need to protect the community against offenders who are seen as outsiders. It thus makes use of notions of fear of crime, and does not tap or build on more altruistic feelings or try to develop social awareness of members of the community. It is restrictive in the crimes it targets, focusing particularly on property theft or damage or neighbourhood incivilities, but tends to ignore more 'hidden' crimes such as violence against women or child abuse, racial harassment and drug misuse, which may well be taking place within the community. It tends to work best in areas with fewest social problems and those which already have established neighbourhood networks of participation. Phase II for Currie represents a reformist model of community crime prevention, and is characterised by strategies to change the conditions which enable crime to develop. It accepts that offenders and potential offenders may be part of the community and that the aim is to tackle the processes which create and sustain criminal motivation and involvement. Thus the emphasis is upon the basic institutions which help to sustain a community, on providing support where these are weak and upon targeting areas most at risk. But in addition to these factors, the Phase II approach to community crime prevention places more emphasis upon issues such as maintenance and the management of programmes, and on good evaluation at a variety of levels.

It is clear from these chapters that some of the activity which has characterised situational crime prevention has swelled over into approaches which are more akin to a reformist approach, and that some of those working at the neighbourhood level from a reformist stance, are also making use of situational approaches to crime prevention. What is important is less the rejection of one model in favour of another, as of being more aware of the limitations in terms of coverage, energy, costs and long-term effects of both approaches. In Currie's analysis we are moving from Phase I to Phase II crime prevention, to a period which takes account of all we have learnt and is not afraid to tackle the causes of community decline.

Reviving the compact?

The emphasis in this volume is on the problems and possibilities for community control over crime. As such it concentrates on the development of institutions and organisations comprising ordinary citizens. But what about the role of the criminal justice system itself in crime control and, importantly, the compact between community control and the rule of law enacted by the police? Perhaps as a reaction to many difficulties faced by the police in tackling crime effectively, much recent discussion of crime prevention (reflected in this volume) has developed in isolation from a consideration of police as an institution whose purpose is to prevent crime. Yet, though unacknowledged, the police presence does, in fact, underlie much current activity, not just as a participating actor in crime prevention 'projects' but, more fundamentally, as an everyday presence in all communities. No matter how imperfect, the police presence and the 'rule of law' still persist even in the highest crime areas.

By overplaying the role of informal institutions we may be 'relying too much on the sociability of man' (Dahrendorf, 1985, p. 139). There are obvious dangers:

'. . . . strengthening local communities must not mean that the state, and the norms upheld by general and formal sanctions, are abandoned in favour of an unworkable Rousseauean mutuality or, more likely, an intolerable Hobbesian system of vigilantes exercising private power' (ibid, p.74).

As Currie (Chapter 18) and others remind us, we must not 'let the police off the hook'. This is not, of course, meant to imply that there is any wish on behalf of the police to be let off the hook. The caution is merely against placing the burden of crime control solely on social institutions. Currie reflects a common feeling ' . . . people who live in badly crime-ridden communities desperately want a more effective and visible police presence—especially to cope with some of their toughest and most frightening problems'. The police wish, and try, to provide this presence. Nevertheless, the problem remains of how to integrate formal justice with a community approach to crime without either inadvertently co-opting community institutions into an extended system of repressive control (Cohen, 1985) or of underestimating the importance of law in underwriting the ability of such institutions to tackle crime. The general task must be to seek the right balance between the control of crime through social institutions and through the institutions of law. It is unlikely that either mechanism can prevent crime without the support of the other. The problem for policy is to decide on the appropriate weight to be placed on each and how to ensure that each acts effectively in harmony, without incurring unacceptable costs to civil society.

In recent years, the police have begun to involve themselves actively in social institutions with the express purpose of preventing crime. Two examples from this book—neighbourhood watch (Chapter 8) and multi-agency collaboration (Chapter 12)—illustrate how this process is happening at both informal and organisational levels within local communities. They also illustrate just how crucial is the institutional structure of communities to the success of this enterprise. In the case of neighbourhood watch, the ability of police or government to implant informal control depends, paradoxically, on the resources for control already existing within the community. Likewise, the collaboration of the police with other agencies—seemingly commonsensical—actually raises profound issues about boundaries, powers and responsibilities between the agencies of civil society, which in turn have practical consequences (Chapter 12).

The movement of the police towards greater involvement with social institutions is one example of how the balance between the formal and informal control of crime is being negotiated but perhaps a more profound question is whether and how the enforcement of law underwrites the ability of social institutions to affect crime. Shapland (Chapter 7) alerts us to the separation that exists between policing by the police and policing by the public. Yet it is clearly impossible for social institutions to work without a certain level of order—in high crime communities neighbours neither have the incentive nor the opportunity to witness, admonish or report offenders if they are living in fear behind their doors; nor can vital public and private services be made available if their operatives refuse to enter for fear of victimisation. To the extent that crime *in itself* (or more accurately the way crime is interpreted by communities) can undermine the ability of social institutions to tackle crime, their benign effects may never materialise unless another agency—most often the police—underwrites at least a minimal level of order. The fact that some minimal order can be taken for granted even in many high crime communities should not obscure the necessary role that law enforcement plays.

In the evolution of community crime prevention, a future task may be to determine the level of 'law and order' which is necessary to allow social institutions to work against crime. Both components are necessary—it makes little sense to divide 'order maintenance' from 'law enforcement' when the visible un-enforcement of the law against crimes which harm their victims and occasion fear in others itself becomes a threat to those institutions which are necessary for the preservation of order in the community (Kinsey *et al.*, 1986). A consequence of this objective is, of course, to improve the ability of the criminal justice system as a whole (with a major role accorded the police) to guarantee the required level of order. Far from being alternative means of preventing crime, formal justice and social institutions are mutually dependent.

Intervention at the community level

For some people the pressure to broaden the base of crime prevention will be reminiscent of earlier eras, of the Community Development Project (CDP) in Britain, or of the Office of Economic Opportunity in the United States; of large amounts of money or effort being directed in a general way at areas with multiple problems. What this book tries to argue is that our understanding of the processes and possibilities of social change have shifted considerably since that time. We have learnt a great deal about the dangers of raising expectations too high, or promising too much. We have learnt a considerable amount about action research and evaluation—much of it initially from programmes such CDP and more recently from victim surveys and situational crime prevention—and about the need to target areas and problems more closely. There is less money available and that too must be targeted more carefully. And there is evidence of a concerted attempt to provide a theoretic base to guide intervention. Finally, we are wary of nostalgia and a search for some arcadian vision of neighbourhood, or of attempts to recreate some earlier kind of 'Bethnal Green' closeness—much of which, as Abrams pointed out, was really based on unacceptable material circumstances: 'Those [old] networks are dying and should be allowed to die' (Abrams, 1980, in Bulmer, 1986).

Yet as Currie stresses, and others have pointed out (e.g. Reiss, 1986), there remain assumptions that it is less costly to intervene at the individual level, and that we are unlikely to be able to create social change at the neighbourhood level by altering local structures, or that community dynamics cannot be controlled, or take too long to influence. Currie goes further in suggesting that there has been a loss of faith in the ability of the police and other public agencies to do much about crime. It is perhaps worth recalling too the disenchantment which became associated with the concept of community during the 1960s: 'it is doubtful whether the concept "community" refers to a useful abstraction' (Stacey, 1969).

Nevertheless, what these chapters demonstrate is the fundamental importance for crime prevention of an awareness of the location of people—offenders, victims, community leaders—within specific social and physical environments, and the need to approach them on their own terms. If there is in the 1990s a recognisable shift on the part of organisations responsible for housing, environment, education, employment, as well as the citizens themselves towards accepting that something can be done about crime as part of everyone's responsibility, then the current energy in exploring crime reduction will have been worthwhile. The warning signs against over-enthusiasm are there, and one way of ensuring that it does not take over is to maintain a balance between practice, evaluation and theory.

We need to know what has happened, and how best to adapt an approach from one place and time to another. There are also clear signs of a determination which crosses national boundaries to find workable ways of cementing societies most in need, or creating networks of neighbours, to provide support against 'the ... inability of the local urban community to regulate itself' (Janowitz, 1978).

References

ABRAMS, P. (1980). 'Social change, social networks and neighbourhood care'. *Social Work Service*, 22, February, pp. 12–23.

BOTTOMS, A. E. and WILES, P. (1986). 'Housing tenure and residential community crime careers in Britain'. In Reiss, A.J. Jr., and Tonry, M. (Eds.), *Communities and Crime*. Chicago: University of Chicago Press.

BULMER, M. (1985). 'The rejuvenation of community studies: Neighbours, networks and policy'. *The Sociological Review*, 33, pp. 430–448.

BULMER, M. (1986). *Neighbours: The Work of Philip Abrams*. Cambridge: Cambridge University Press.

BURSIK, R. J., Jr. (1986). 'Ecological stability and the dynamics of delinquency'. In Reiss, A. J. Jr., and Tonry, M. (Eds.), *Communities and Crime*. Chicago: University of Chicago Press.

CLARKE, M. J. (1987). 'Citizenship, community, and the management of crime'. *British Journal of Criminology*, 27, pp. 384–400.

CLARKE, R. V. G. (1978). (Ed.), *Tackling Vandalism*. Home Office Research Study No.47. London: HMSO.

CLARKE, R. V. G. (1981). 'The prospects for controlling crime'. *Research Bulletin* No. 12 London: Home Office Research and Planning Unit.

CLARKE, R. V. G. and CORNISH, D. B. (1983). *Crime control in Britain: A Review of Policy Research*. Albany: State University of New York Press.

CLARKE, R. V. G. and CORNISH, D. B. (1985). 'Modelling offenders' decisions: framework for research and policy'. In *Crime and Justice: An Annual Review of Research*. Tonry, M. and Morris, N. (Eds), Chicago: University of Chicago Press.

CLARKE, R. V. G. and HOPE, T. (Eds.), (1984). *Coping with Burglary*. Boston: Kluwer-Nijhoff.

CLARKE, R. V. G. and MAYHEW, P. (Eds.) (1980). *Designing Out Crime*. London: HMSO.

CLOWARD, R. A. and OHLIN, L. (1960). *Delinquency and Opportunity: a Theory of Delinquent Gangs*. Glencoe; III: Free Press.

COHEN, S. (1985). *Visions of Social Control*. Cambridge: Polity Press.

CURRIE, E. (1985). *Confronting Crime*. New York: Pantheon Books.

CURTIS, L.A. (Ed.), (1985). *American Violence and Public Policy*. New Haven: Yale University Press.

DAHRENDORF, R. (1985). *Law and Order. The Hamlyn Lectures*. London: Stevens and Sons.

DOWNES, D. (1966). *The Delinquent Solution: A Study of Subcultural Theory*. London: Routledge and Kegan Paul.

DOWNES, D. and ROCK, P. (1982). *Understanding Deviance*. Oxford: Oxford University Press.

DUBOW, F. and EMMONS, D. (1981) 'The community hypothesis'. In Lewis, D. A. (Ed.), *Reactions to Crime*. Newbury Park, CA: Sage Publications.

GOTTFREDSON, M. R. (1982). 'The social scientist and rehabilitative crime policy'. *Criminology*. 20, pp.29–42.

HALSEY, A. H. (1978) 'Government against poverty in school and community'. In Bulmer, M. (Ed.). *Social Policy Research*. London: Macmillan.

HEAL, K. and LAYCOCK, G. (Eds.), (1986). *Situational Crime Prevention: from theory into practice*. London HMSO.

HOPE, T. (1986). 'Crime, community and environment'. *Journal of Environmental Psychology*, 6, pp. 65–78.

HOPE, T. and MURPHY, D. J. I. (1983). 'Problems of implementing crime prevention: the experience of a demonstration project'. *The Howard Journal*, 22, pp. 38–50.

HOUGH, M. and MAYHEW, P. (1985). *Taking Account of Crime*. Home Office Research Study No.85. London: HMSO.

JACOBS, J. (1961). *Death and Life of Great American Cities*. New York: Random House.

JANOWITZ, M. (1978).*The Last Half-Century: Societal Change and Politics in America*. Chicago: University of Chicago Press.

JEPHCOTT, P. and ROBINSON, H. (1971). *Homes in High Flats*. Edinburgh: Oliver and Boyd.

JONES, T., MacLEAN, B., YOUNG, J. (1986). *The Islington Crime Survey*. London: Gower.

KINSEY, R., LEA, J. and YOUNG, J. (1986). *Losing the Fight Against Crime*. Oxford: Basil Blackwell.

LAVRAKAS, P. J. (1985). 'Citizen self-help and neighbourhood crime prevention policy'. In Curtis, L. (Ed.). (1985). *American Violence and Public Policy.* New Haven and London: Yale University Press.

LEWIS, D. A. and SALEM, G. (1981). 'Community crime prevention: an analysis of a developing strategy.' *Crime and Delinquency,* 27, pp. 405–421.

LEWIS, D. A. and SALEM. G. (1986). *Fear of Crime.* New Brunswick, NJ: Transaction Books.

MARRIS, P. and REIN, M. (1974) *Dilemmas of Social Reform.* Harmondsworth: Penguin Books. Originally published in 1967 by Routledge and Kegan Paul.

MAYS, J. B. (1954). *Growing Up in the City.* Liverpool: University Press.

McGAHEY, R.M. (1986). 'Economic conditions, neighbourhood organization, and urban crime'. In Reiss, A. J. Jr., and Tonry, M. (Eds.), *Communities and Crime,* Chicago: The University of Chicago Press.

MOORE, C. and BROWN, J. (1981). *Community versus Crime.* London: Bedford Square Press/NCVO.

MORRIS, T. (1957). *The Criminal Area.* London: Routledge and Kegan Paul.

NEWMAN, O. (1973). *Defensible Space: crime prevention through urban design,.* New York: Macmillan. (Published by Architectural Press, London, in 1973).

PARKER, H. (1974). *View from the Boys.* Newton Abbot: David and Charles.

PARLIAMENTARY ALL-PARTY PENAL AFFAIRS GROUP (1983). *The Prevention of Crime among Young People.* Chichester: Barry Rose.

PLOWDEN REPORT (1967). *Children and their Primary Schools.* Central Advisory Council for Education (England). London: HMSO.

PODOLEFSKY, A. (1983). *Case Studies in Community Crime Prevention.* Springfield, Ill.: Charles C. Thomas Publishing Co.

PODOLEFSKY, A. and DUBOW, F. (1981). *Strategies for Community Crime Prevention: Collective Responses to Crime in Urban America.* Springfield, Ill.: Charles C. Thomas.

REINER, R. (1985). *The Politics of the Police.* Brighton: Wheatsheaf.

REISS, A. J. Jr. (1986). 'Why are communities important in understanding crime?' In Reiss, A. J. Jr., and Tonry, M. (Eds.), *Communities and Crime.* Chicago: University of Chicago Press.

RILEY, D. and SHAW, M. (1985). *Parental Supervision and Juvenile Delinquency.* Home Office Research Study No. 83. London: HMSO.

RUTTER, M. and GILLER, H. (1983). *Juvenile Delinquency: Trends and Perspectives.* Harmondsworth: Penguin Books.

SCARMAN REPORT (1981). *The Brixton disorders, 10–12 April 1981.* Report of an Inquiry by the Rt. Hon. Lord Scarman, OBE. CMND 8427.

SCHUERMAN, L. A. and KOBRIN, S. (1986). 'Community careers in crime.' In Reiss, A. J. Jr. and Tonry, M. (Eds.), *Communities and Crime.* Chicago: University of Chicago Press.

SEEBOHM REPORT (1986). *Report of the Committee on Local Authority and Allied Personal Social Services.* CMND 3703. London: HMSO.

SHAW, C. R. and McKAY, H. D. (1942). *Juvenile Delinquency and Urban Areas.* Chicago: University of Chicago Press.

SKOGAN, W. G. (in press). 'Community Organizations and Crime.' In Tonry, M. and Morris, N. *Crime and Justice.* Volume 9. Chicago: University of Chicago Press.

SMITH, D. J. and GRAY, J. (1985). *Police and People in London.* Aldershot: Gower.

STACEY, M. (1969). 'The myth of community studies.' *British Journal of Sociology,* 20, pp. 134–147.

SUTTLES, G. D. (1972). *The Social Construction of Communities.* Chicago: University of Chicago Press.

TAUB, R. P., TAYLOR, D. G. and DUNHAM, J. D. (1984). *Paths to Neighborhood Change.* Chicago: University of Chicago Press.

TITUS, R. M. (1984). 'Residential burglary and the community response.' In *Coping with Burglary.* Clarke, R. V. G. and Hope, T. (Eds.), Boston: Kluwer-Nijhoff.

WARD, C. (1973) (Ed.). *Vandalism.* London: Architectural Press.

WEATHERITT, M. (1986). *Innovations in Policing.* London: Croom Helm.

WILLMOTT, P. (1966). *Adolescent Boys in East London.* London: Routledge and Kegan Paul.

WILLMOTT, P. (1984). *Community in Social Policy* Discussion Paper No. 9. London: Policy Studies Institute.

WILSON, J. Q. (1975). *Thinking About Crime.* New York: Basic Books.

WILSON, J. Q. and HERRNSTEIN, R. J. (1985). *Crime and Human Nature.* New York: Simon and Schuster.

WILSON, J. Q. and KELLING, G. L. (1982). 'Broken windows: the police and neighbourhood safety.' *The Atlantic Monthly,* March, pp. 29–38.

The Community Context

The three chapters in this section examine a range of evidence about the location of crime, disorder, and fear in urban communities. Chapter 2, based upon an analysis of the 1984 British Crime Survey provides a detailed picture of the patterns of crime and incivilities in different types of residential areas in Britain, using the ACORN classification of neighbourhood type. It attempts too to test the 'Broken Windows' hypothesis, and examines the pocketing of crime. Council house tenants in particular are shown to be most at risk from the major domestic crime of burglary. Chapter 3 reviews recent North American research on the impact of crime and disorder on the social and economic processes which influence the stability of neighbourhoods. Residential commitment to an area, the capacity of communities to exercise informal social control, and their capacity to organize themselves are all eroded by the growth of crime and disorder.

Chapter 4 examines the case for bringing together two mainstream traditions in criminology—the risk-assessment tradition and the environmental tradition. It examines the impacts of community environments on criminal offenders, and the impacts of offender concentrations on communities. Results from a preliminary study provided support for their person-environment integrity model. While this was not replicated by a subsequent study, there was substantial evidence that offender concentrations have an impact on neighbourhoods even when the social and economic characteristics of those areas are controlled.

2. Area, crime and incivilities: a profile from the British Crime Survey

Tim Hope and Mike Hough

This chapter presents a selection of findings from the British Crime Survey (BCS) on crime, area and 'incivilities'. Its aim is partly and unashamedly descriptive—to document some of the variation across area in crime and related phenomena. But it is also intended to shed light on recent theories about incivilities and crime; and a little space should first be given to the development of these.

The tradition of ecological or areal research into crime is a long and respectable one, from Shaw and McKay (1942) onward. The main responses to the research by policy-makers have been attempts to resuscitate 'natural communities', to arrest community decline and to avoid the 'tipping' of neighbourhoods into a spiral of deterioration (see Chapter 1). The crime-preventive emphasis of these community programmes has generally been in the integration of potential offenders *within* communities. In Britain, the heyday of community development programmes was in the late 60s and early 70s.

The first sign of a break with this tradition came not from a criminologist but an architectural journalist—Jane Jacobs. In *The Death and Life of Great American Cities* (1961) Jacobs took a sceptical attitude towards the urban pastoral which underpinned many community projects, arguing that the attempt to generate or regenerate close-knit urban communities was fundamentally misconceived and that the anonymity of city life was part of its richness. She emphasised the informal social control which a (well-planned) city could yield, in contrast to the potential for integration of deviants which an active community promised; and she identified diversity of land-use as the lever for maximising informal social control. Though the book did not achieve an immediate impact, it has subsequently infused thinking about neighbourhood to a considerable degree.

As its title suggests, Oscar Newman's *Defensible Space* (1972) developed Jacobs's theme of defensive urban design (in contrast to the engineering of communities). Newman's contribution was in importing the concept of territoriality from ethology; the essence of Defensible Space was that housing design could and should engender both a sense of territoriality amongst residents and the opportunity for surveillance. In contrast to Jacobs, Newman achieved an immediate and highly visible impact, and architectural design now routinely incoporates at least a token piece of territory for urban residents.

The role of informal social control became increasingly prominent as a means of prevention in the late 1970s. Informal surveillance—by householders, shopkeepers, bus-drivers, etc.—was an important plank in the 'situational approach' to crime prevention developed by the Home Office (e.g. Clarke and Mayhew, 1980) and was also stressed in American CPTED (Crime Prevention Through Environmental Design) programmes (Wallis and Ford, 1980).

A more recent strand of thought about 'informal social control' is to be found in the 'Broken Windows' theory of J. Q. Wilson and George Kelling (1982; see also Chapter 1). Like Jacobs and Newman, they emphasised the centrality of informal social control, but the distinctive feature about the Wilson/Kelling hypothesis is the idea that the level of 'incivilities'—something they believe to be within police control—is one of the factors which shape the nature and strength of informal control. They suggest that certain levels of disorderly behaviour (on the part of drunks, tramps, rowdy youths, prostitutes and other disreputables) can trigger a spiral of neighbourhood decline, with increased fear of crime, migration of the law-abiding from the area, weakening of informal social control and, ultimately, increases in serious crime. According to this view, beat policemen should be assigned long term to areas at risk to break the spiral, clamping down on the 'incivilities' which lead to decline.

Testing theories of informal social control

Theories about how informal social control within neighbourhoods is related to changes in neighbourhood conditions, population, policing and community life (see Chapter 1) have been fairly resistant to evaluative research and it is worth briefly mentioning some of the reasons for this:

i. the theories are usually dynamic (with models which specify feedback loops)—which cross-sectional studies cannot fully assess;

ii. the theories often posit only a long-term effect, which outstretches the timescales of almost all social research;

iii. the theories are usually highly complex and multi-factorial—and studies tend to 'run out of numbers' before the required multivariate analysis can be carried off;

iv. measurement of the 'dependent' variable, crime, is problematic: only crime surveys offer an adequate index of crime—and these are beyond the pocket of most evaluations;

v. measuring the factors which are meant to affect crime is also hard: few studies actually quantify whether people intervene when they see anti-social behaviour (but see Chapter 7); and the variables which in turn are thought to shape preparedness to intervene are notoriously 'soft' to measure—such as 'sense of territory' or 'commitment to neighbourhood'; and

vi. neighbourhood itself is a slippery concept: do we mean simply, the area within a given radius or individuals' homes? Or an area which corresponds to individuals' cognitive maps of their neighbourhoods? Or an area whose identity has a social reality—whose boundaries are agreed and recognised by a proportion at least of the residents?

In large measure, theories of neighbourhood decline such as 'broken windows' have been deduced either from associations found in surveys of neighbourhoods taken at one moment in time (e.g. Taub et al., 1984; Skogan, 1987), from retrospective statistical analyses of census tracts (e.g. Schuerman and Kobrin, 1986) or from the unanticipated consequences of community crime control interventions (e.g. Wilson and Kelling, 1982). In all these studies, including that presented in this chapter, it has been necessary to estimate the appropriate sequence of events within the process of neighbour-hood change. Without controlled prospective studies of change in actual neighbourhoods, such theories must remain essentially as working hypotheses. Nevertheless, despite these methodological limitations, patterns of findings from survey data like the British Crime Survey are suggestive, at least, of links between incivilities, crime and community life in different types of community.

BCS findings on area, crime and incivilities

The findings presented in this chapter are drawn from the British Crime Survey (BCS). This is a sample survey designed primarily to estimate the extent of crime, including incidents which are neither reported to, nor recorded by, the police. But the survey also collects a great deal of additional information, and the 1984 sweep asked amongst other things about attitudes to neighbour-hood, levels of perceived 'incivilities', neighbourhood 'cohesiveness' and preparedness to participate in neighbourhood watch (see also Chapter 9). In other words, it is a fairly large data set measuring (with variable success) many of the ingredient variables of theories of informal control—and in particular that of 'Broken Windows'.

The BCS also made use of the ACORN classification of area, developed from Census data by CACI (see Annex). ACORN was derived from cluster analysis of some 40 Census variables including age, class, tenure, dwelling type and car-ownership: and on the basis of this, each Enumeration District in the country (comprising 150 households on average) has been assigned an ACORN code. It is important to remember, however, that ACORN categories used in the following analyses are not actual areas. As used here, ACORN refers to the type of area in which groups of individual BCS respondents live.

Neighbourhoods and crime: an ACORN profile

It is one of the criminological truisms that crime belongs in the cities. The British Crime Survey has shown very clearly that rates for burglary, autocrime, bike theft and vandalism all increase with population density (Hough and Mayhew, 1983, 1985; Gottfredson, 1984). Crimes of violence—in many of which victim and offender are known to each other—show a similar, but less marked, relationship. The ACORN classification offers an accessible way of displaying area patterns (see Table 1).

Table 1 picks out very clearly three categories of area where risks of crime are high:

     *ACORN I—high status non-family areas—one archetype of the inner city—split between the homes of the rich and the more 'twilight' areas of the urban transients—privately owned buildings in multiple occupation.

     *ACORN H—multi-racial areas—poor, private rentals mixed with owner occupation—again in inner cities.

     *ACORN G—the poorest council (or local authority) estates, located either in inner cities, or in the outer ring of conurbations.

Table 1 *Crime rates, by ACORN neighbourhood group, 1983*

	Crime rates		
	Burglary including attempts	Robbery and theft from person	Theft of and from vehicles outside home
	% of HHs victim	% persons victim	% owners victim
Low Risk Areas			
A. Agricultural areas (n = 476)	1	1.3	5
C. Older housing of intermediate status (n = 2001)	2	0.8	10
K. Better-off retirement areas (n = 463)	3	1.1	6
J. Affluent suburban housing (n = 1659)	3	1.1	7
B. Modern family housing high incomes (n = 1537)	3	0.9	8
Medium Risk Areas			
E. Better-off council estates (n = 1018)	4	1.4	14
D. Poor quality older terraced housing (n = 759)	4	1.4	18
F. Less well-off council estates (n = 1175)	4	1.4	15
High Risk Areas			
I. High status non-family areas (n = 609)	10	3.9	15
H. Multi-racial areas (n = 400)	10	4.3	26
G. Poorest council estates (n = 543)	12	3.3	21
National Average	4	1.4	11

Weighted data
Source: 1984 BCS.

Table 2 gives information by ACORN type on residents' attitudes to their area, showing levels of satisfaction, perceived anonymity and fear of crime. In general and as one would expect, fear of crime increases with crime, and satisfaction with the area falls; and areas where strangers are conspicuous generally have little crime. But the table also exemplifies exceptions to these rules: area satisfaction is only slightly below average for ACORN group I, for example, and residents of ACORN group G do not rate their area as anonymous.

Table 2 *Perceptions of area, by ACORN type*

	% 'very satisfied' with area	% rating area as anonymous	% feeling 'very unsafe' in area
	%	%	%
Low Risk Areas			
A. Agricultural areas (n = 460)	65	8	3
C. Older housing of intermediate status (n = 1936)	50	17	10
K. Better-off retirement area (n = 443)	60	20	11
J. Affluent suburban housing (n = 1589)	56	22	8
B. Modern family housing higher incomes (n = 1475)	47	22	9
Medium Risk Areas			
E. Better-off council estates (n = 975)	40	20	12
D. Poor quality older terraced housing (n = 735)	34	18	12
F. Less well-off council estates (n = 1129)	34	23	18
High Risk Areas			
I. High status non-family areas (n = 573)	42	39	18
H. Multi-racial areas (n = 379)	24	28	23
G. Poorest council estates (n = 523)	24	23	27
National Average	46	21	12

Weighted data
Source: 1984 BCS.

Table 3 shows perceptions of the prevalence of three sorts of incivility, by ACORN group. This shows clearly that there is a broad correlation between crime and incivilities: residents are most likely to perceive incivilities as common in the three ACORN groups which have been labelled 'high risk' on the basis of their crime rates; and areas with low risks of crime seem comparatively free of incivilities. But again, the exceptions to this rule should be emphasised: there is not a linear relationship between crime rates and perceptions of incivilities. Indeed one high-crime group, ACORN I, seemed less beset by 'teenagers hanging around' than average. More important, the existence of a correlation between incivilities and crime must not be taken as evidence of cause and effect.

Table 3   *Perception of incivilities, by ACORN neighbourhood group*

	Perceived Incivilities		
	drunks, tramps on streets	litter lying around	teenagers hanging around
	% saying 'common'	% saying 'v. common'	% saying 'v. common'
Low Risk Areas			
A. Agricultural areas (n = 476)	1	4	3
C. Older housing of intermediate status (n = 2001)	9	14	12
K. Better-off retirement areas (n = 463)	11	13	8
J. Affluent suburban housing (n = 1659)	4	8	7
B. Modern family housing high incomes (n = 1537)	5	11	11
Medium Risk Areas			
E. Better-off council estates (n = 1018)	9	17	18
D. Poor quality older terraced housing (n = 759)	16	32	20
F. Less well-off council estates (n = 1175)	14	25	23
High Risk Areas			
I. High status non-family areas (n = 609)	25	21	12
H. Multi-racial areas (n = 400)	19	34	17
G. Poorest council estates (n = 543)	19	40	31
National Average	10	17	14

Weighted data
Source: 1984 BCS.

Crime and incivilities

Wilson and Kelling's theory specifies a process involving the following elements:

i. incivilities are perceived as signs of crime and disorder;

ii. this reduces the sense of community and communal control exercised by residents in a neighbourhood;

iii. the diminution of informal community control leads to increased criminal activity;

iv. this in turn leads to increasing fear of crime;

v. which reduces the commitment of residents to the neighbourhood; and so on.

An important feature of the theory is that it is dynamic, predicting an increasing spiral of decline, once the process has taken root in an area. The proper test of this general theory would also be dynamic—charting the sequence over time of incivility, crime, diminished control and deterioration in particular neighbourhoods. Little if any reliable research of this kind has been carried out, especially in Britain.

The BCS can take us a little further forward. It allows comparison of levels of crime, incivility, fear and social cohesion of people living in the different ACORN neighbourhoods of England and Wales. Though this data is cross-sectional, it nevertheless affords us an opportunity to see if the expected relationships between incivility and crime emerge in different areas at one point in time.

The analyses in this part of the chapter were carried out on BCS data aggregated to the level of the ACORN neighbourhood, of which there were 36 different types within the sample drawn from England and Wales (see Annex). Variables were constructed to express the average characteristics of people living in each type of neighbourhood (see note to Table 4). Table 4 suggests that levels of perceived incivilities are linked strongly to worries about crime, satisfaction with the neighbourhood and perceptions of its social cohesiveness, and with crime levels themselves. All these co-vary to a substantial degree—areas where people perceive a high degree of incivility also have high levels of crime and fear, and low levels of neighbourhood cohesion and satisfaction.

Table 4 *Incivility, crime, fear of crime, social cohesion and satisfaction with neighbourhoods.* ACORN areas (n = 36)

| | Correlation coefficients | | | |
	incivility	*victim rate*	*fear of crime*	*social cohesion*
victim rate	.81			
fear of crime	.90	.79		
social cohesion	—.62	—.50	—.56	
satisfaction	—.90	—.73	—.85	.59

Notes:
1. Source: 1984 British Crime Survey
2. Variable are rates per 100 residents of each type of ACORN neighbourhood within the BCS sample (n = 36) and are constructed from responses to BCS survey questions. The incivility rate is constructed by aggregating each individual's responses to questionnaire items about incivilities. The victim incidence rate is the number of offences per 100 residents reported in the BCS. Fear of crime is a rate combining scores from items about feelings of safety and worries about specific crimes. Social cohesion is a rate of persons who think that 'people in their area help each other'. Neighbourhood satisfaction is the rate of people who are 'very satisfied' with their area.
3. All the correlation coefficients are statistically significant at p< .01.

Rates of perceived incivilities are more strongly related to levels of fear of crime (p.< .05) and neighbourhood satisfaction (p.< .01) than the level of victimisation itself. Indeed, the correlations are so strong that, at the neighbourhood level, the perception of incivilities, and self-reported fear of crime and neighbourhood satisfaction might be thought of as equivalent indicators. This finding could be useful because information on disorderliness in a neighbourhood could be used as an index of residents' well-being, though it remains to be established how closely people's perceptions of incivility are related to actual levels in neighbourhoods (it seems likely that the equivalence will be greater when aggregated across the neighbourhood population than for any particular individual).

We do not know whether there is any threshold of tolerance—for example, whether people who are dissatisfied with their neighbourhood are more likely to notice or report greater incivility than others. Neither can we say that incivilities are necessarily a 'cause' of neighbourhood dissatisfaction, both may be a reflection of other conditions in the neighbourhood. We can be confident, however, that the perception of incivilities is a sensitive indicator of a related set of worries about the neighbourhood, including worries about its level of crime. Interestingly, the measure of social cohesion employed here is significantly less strongly correlated with each of the other variables than they are with each other. Admittedly, it is not possible to say whether this measure fully captures people's sense of community or whether the latter is not as dependent upon perceptions of incivility and crime as we might suppose.

The 'broken windows' hypothesis does not simply assert a relationship between incivility and crime but also assumes it has a certain form, corresponding to a 'development sequence' of events (Chapter 3). This could be expressed as some form of exponential relationship: at first crime rates rise gently with increasing incivility but after a certain level is reached, a vicious spiral of decline sets in, and crime rates increase at a much greater rate with increasing increments of incivility.

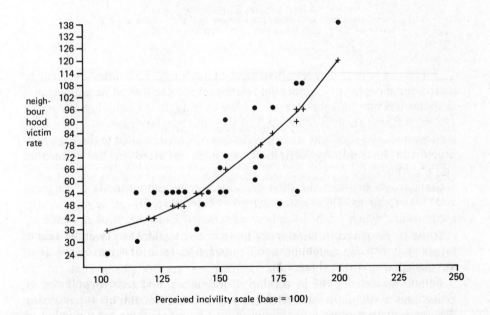

FIGURE 1A. __ACORN victimisation rates by perceived incivilities__

(per 100 persons, aged 16 yrs and over)

Perceived incivility scale (base = 100)

Note

The data were analysed using the GLIM statistical package. For a linear fitted model with an identity link function, R^2 = .65. For a non-linear fitted model (illustrated) with a logarithmic link R^2 = .68.

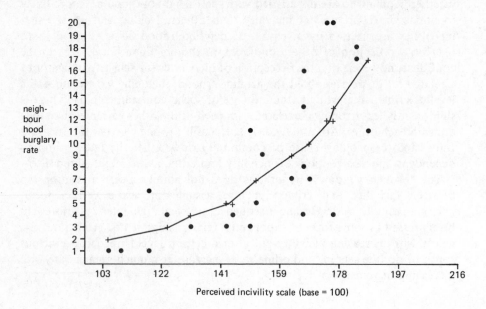

FIGURE 1b. **Acorn burglary rates by perceived incivilities (n=35)**

(per 100 persons, aged 16 yrs and over)

neigh-
bour
hood
burglary
rate

Perceived incivility scale (base = 100)

Note

1. The graph excludes ACORN type 28 — see annex — which had much higher rates of perceived incivility and burglary than the other high rate areas.

2. The data were analysed using the GLIM statistical package. For a linear fitted model with an identity link function, R^2 = .53. For a non-linear fitted model (illustrated) with a logarithmic link function, R^2 = .58.

Figures 1a and 1b suggest that rates of perceived incivilities do seem to exhibit some degree of exponential relationship to the overall neighbourhood victimisation rate and the rate of residential burglaries (including attempts). The exponential form is more marked with the burglary rate, which perhaps underscores the hypothesis since it is the one offence recorded in the 1984 BCS which can be said, by definition, to have occurred in the residential neighbourhood.

Comparison between the different ACORN neighbourhoods of England and Wales, using BCS data, affords some support, at least, for the relationships which might have been anticipated from the 'broken windows' hypothesis. As perceptions of incivility increase, so does worry about crime; satisfaction with the neighbourhood diminishes and crime begins to grow at an increasingly rapid rate (Figure 2).

These findings do not in themselves validate the specific hypotheses of Wilson and Kelling nor, importantly, their policy prescriptions for reversing the spiral of deterioration. As discussed in Chapter 1, there are a number of variants on the general model linking incivilities to crime and neighbourhood deterioration, of which Wilson and Kelling's is merely one. It is, of course, a big step to move from the form of relationship identified here between the

FIGURE 2. **Incivility, burglary rates, fear of crime and satisfaction with neighbourhood**

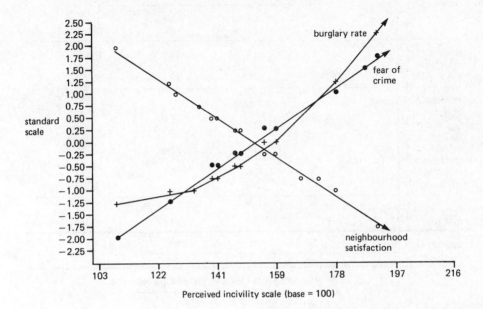

ACORN AREAS (n=35). Fitted values.

Note

For definitions of rates see Table 4 and Figure 1b. The figure shows
the fitted values obtained by regressing the perceived incivility rate
against: i. the burglary rate (R^2 = .58, see Figure 1b); ii. the
fear of crime rate (R^2 = .81); iii. the rate of neighbourhood
satisfaction (R^2 = .78). The values of the y-axis have been
standardised to create a common scale.

individuals elements of the general model, to causal assertions about changes
over time in real neighbourhoods. Nevertheless, this BCS snapshot adds
weight to the need to take such a step if we are to understand and prevent
processes of neighbourhood deterioration in which incivility may play an
important part.

The pocketing of crime

There is a growing realisation within policy debate that crime and problems of
law and order are, in very large measure, local and 'pocketed' problems
(Home Office, 1986). The historic focus on trends over time of national or
regional criminal statistics, classified by crime type, has obscured a truth
apparent when small-area variations in crime rates are examined (cf. Baldwin
and Bottoms, 1976). The pocketing of crime is evident when one looks at the
relationship between 'incidence' (the number of victims) and 'prevalence' (the
probability of becoming a victim) for people who live in the different ACORN
neighbourhoods. Table 5 shows the number of victims of crimes in England
and Wales (estimated from the BCS) 'produced' by ACORN areas with
different prevalence rates of becoming the victim of crime (see Table 1).

Table 5 *Offences by ACORN/risk areas in England and Wales, 1983*

A. HOUSEHOLD OFFENCES (row percentages)

| | ACORN | | | |
	low risk	medium risk	high risk	n (thousands)
households	61	27	12	18,489
vehicle-owning households	69	21	10	11,278
household offences				
burglary (incl. attempts)	37	27	37	904
theft of motor vehicle	40	38	23	283
theft from motor vehicle	56	24	20	1,364
vandalism	56	31	13	2,953
total household offences	51	29	20	7,588

Source: 1984 British Crime Survey

A. HOUSEHOLD OFFENCES (row percentages)

| | ACORN | | | |
	low risk	medium risk	high risk	n (thousands)
persons over 16 years	61	27	12	39,149
personal offences				
theft from person/robbery	38	28	33	650
assault	54	28	18	1,852
other personal theft	58	25	18	1,770
total personal offences	53	26	20	4,343

Notes:
1. The numbers of offences in thousands for England and Wales are 'best estimates' derived from the 1984 British Crime Survey (see Hough and Mayhew, 1985, Table 1).
2. Assault includes the sub-categories of common assault and wounding. These sub-categories have been combined because of problems in developing consistent and objective criteria for distinguishing between the two. For the same reason, theft from the person and robbery have been combined.

On the one hand, the contribution of the high-risk ('inner city') areas is greatest with regard to the victims of more serious crimes: burglary, theft and robbery from the person. On the other hand, the disparity is less for other kinds of crime. Fighting and thieving are probably practised quite widely. The relatively low incidence of households reporting vandalism (including damage to vehicles) in otherwise high-risk areas presumably reflects the relative lack of private property belonging to residents, especially that kept outside the dwelling. Probably the incidence of vandalism to publicly-owned property would show the opposite distribution (Clarke, 1978).

The distribution of victims of motor vehicle crime falls somewhere in between. Differences in the proportion of victims living in each type of risk area in part reflect the distribution of vehicle-owning households (Table 5), but they also reflect the fact that, in general, households with motor vehicles are more likely to be at risk when they are resident in areas of low vehicle ownership—that is, the poorer neighbourhoods (Table 1, and Hope, 1987). That the risk of becoming the victim of motor vehicle crime may be influenced by the type of area in which the owner lives is reinforced by the BCS findings that 61 per cent of all autocrime occurs while cars are parked at home, and a further 12 per cent within about a mile of home (Hope, 1987).

These findings seem to suggest that the somewhat broader distribution of victims of the less serious offences across the different types of neighbourhood reflect widely available opportunities and lifestyles, such as car usage and going shopping, or to pubs and clubs—where many assaults recorded in the BCS seem to occur (Hough and Sheehy, 1986). In contrast, the likelihood of becoming a victim of the more serious 'predatory crimes' (and contributing disproportionately to the overall number of victims) seems to be more a reflection of where people live. The 'community dimension' of criminal victimisation thus appears particularly marked for burglary and theft and/or robbery from the person. As such, residents of the high-risk areas are disproportionately victimised from the kinds of crimes which the country as a whole finds the most worrying (Hough and Mayhew, 1985).

Crime, area and tenure

A number of chapters in this volume discuss the links between housing tenure, community life and crime. One of the difficulties here is whether it is tenure itself which is associated with crime, or the ecological distribution of tenure types between different neighbourhoods. Table 6 suggests that it is the latter. The table shows that it is the interaction between individual tenure and the predominant tenure of the neighbourhood which is important, especially so with the concentration of council tenure in small residential areas, that is, on 'estates'. Council tenants in council areas face a risk of burglary considerably higher than the national average, while owner-occupiers in non-council areas face a risk much closer to the average. Similarly, both owner-occupiers in predominantly council areas (who might either live adjacently to council estates or actually within them), and council tenants in non-council areas, have a risk of burglary around the national average. It is thus council tenants on estates who seem particularly vulnerable to burglary.

Examination of differences in burglary risk between the different kinds of council area identified by ACORN (Table 7) shows that burglary is even more concentrated within the council housing sector. Council tenants in the poorest council areas have a rate of burglary five times that of tenants on the better-off estates and those in predominantly non-council areas. Crime is a considerable problem for tenants on the poorer estates, with 42 per cent of residents 'very worried' about being the victim of burglary. Almost half of these tenants personally knew someone locally who had had their home burgled in the year

Table 6 *Burglary and the Ecology of Tenure burglaries per 1,000 households. (% of total households)*

	Tenure		
	owner occupiers	council tenants	total
non-council areas	33 (56%)	39 (11%)	34 (67%)
council areas	38 (8%)	66 (14%)	56 (22%)
total	34 (64%)	55 (25%)	40 (89%)

Notes:
1. Weighted data. Unweighted N = 10,631.
2. 'Council' areas are ACORN Groups E, F and G where the majority of households in the ED rent their dwellings from the local authority. BCS respondents in private rental or other tenures have been excluded from the analysis.

prior to the survey (compared to 29 per cent of residents on the better-off estates) and more residents thought that most burglaries were committed by people who lived locally.

Table 7 *Burglary and council tenants: area, risk, worry and beliefs about burglars.*

	better-off council estates	average council estates	poor council estates	all council tenants
Burglaries, incl. attempts (per 1000 households)	38	66	190	64
'very worried about burglary' (%)	27	34	42	29
'most burglaries committed by people who live in area' (% agree)	38	50	51	38
unweighted n	519	771	374	2867

Weighted data.   Source 1984: British Crime Survey.

There are, of course, other ways in which we might look at the pocketing of crime between neighbourhoods—for example, by different offence types, or between recognisable communities within cities (Baldwin and Bottoms, 1976; Reiss and Tonry, 1986)—but it is an inescapable conclusion of this analysis that the planned distribution of public housing in England and Wales matches the distribution of at least the major domestic crime of burglary. Furthermore, the variation in burglary rates between areas *within* the public housing sector is sharper than the overall areal variation between council tenure and owner occupation. Here, it is the poorer, run-down or 'problem' estates which differ dramatically from the others. Subsequent chapters in this book (in particular, Chapters 5 and 6) address the implications of this finding for crime prevention.

Summary

This chapter has sought to shed some light from the British Crime Survey on two themes also raised elsewhere in this volume: (i) the relationship between incivility and crime in neighbourhoods; and (ii) the distribution (or 'pocketing') of crime across different kinds of residential neighbourhood. Some support is given to the general relationship between incivility, crime and neighbourhood deterioration described in a number of theoretical models (see Chapter 1), of which Wilson and Kelling's (1982) 'broken windows' hypothesis is one version (see also Chapters 3 and 6). The chapter has also shed light upon the marked concentration of victimisation from crime (particularly, burglary) in certain communities—especially the poorer council housing estates. These findings reinforce the importance of studying the spatial ecology of housing tenure, and the market mechanisms which affect it, as factors related to the variation in crime rates between different communities, as Bottoms and Wiles argue (Chapter 5).

The analyses presented here have the limitation that they are based upon information collected from a national sample of individuals who are taken to be representative of those who live in different kinds of neighbourhood (as defined by ACORN)—they do not refer to actual neighbourhoods in England and Wales. There are certainly major difficulties in seeking to identify the correct sequence of events in the history of individual neighbourhoods which lead to deterioration, and even greater problems in trying to predict whether and when neighbourhoods are likely to tip into the spiral of decline. Moreover, though increasing incivilities may be a powerful motor in accelerating this spiral, reducing them by some means may not necessarily lead to positive improvements. Much remains to be seen from studies of planned and unplanned change in actual neighbourhoods. But for the meantime, we can be cautiously confident that neighbourhood incivilities play an important part in the dynamics of crime and community.

References

BALDWIN, J. and BOTTOMS, A. E. (1976). *The Urban Criminal*. London: Tavistock.

CLARKE, R. V. G. (Ed.) (1978). *Tackling Vandalism*. Home Office Research Study No. 47. London: HMSO.

CLARKE, R. V. G. and MAYHEW, P. (Eds.). (1980). *Designing out Crime*. London: HMSO.

GOTTFREDSON, M. R. (1984). *Victims of Crime: the dimensions of risk*. Home Office Research Study No. 81. London: HMSO.

HOME OFFICE, (1986). *Criminal Justice: a working paper* (revised edition). London: Home Office.

HOPE, T. (1987). 'Residential aspects of autocrime'. *Research Bulletin* No. 23. London: Home Office Research and Planning Unit.

HOUGH, M. and MAYHEW, P. (1983). *The British Crime Survey: first report*. Home Office Research Study No. 76. London: HMSO.

HOUGH, M. and MAYHEW, P. (1985). *Taking Account of Crime: key findings from the 1984 British Crime Survey*. Home Office Research Study No. 85. London: HMSO.

HOUGH, M. and SHEEHY, K. (1986). 'Incidents of violence: findings from the British Crime Survey'. *Research Bulletin* No. 20. London: Home Office Research and Planning Unit.

JACOBS, J. (1961). *The Death and Life of Great American Cities*. New York: Random House. (Published by Penguin Books Ltd., Harmondsworth, in 1965.)

NEWMAN, O. (1972). *Defensible Space: crime prevention through urban design*. New York: Macmillan. (Published by Architectural Press, London, in 1973.)

REISS, A. J. and TONRY, M. (Eds.) (1986). *Communities and Crime*. Chicago: University of Chicago Press.

SCHUERMAN, L. and KOBRIN, S. (1986). 'Community careers in crime'. In Reiss, A. J. and Tonry, M. (Eds.) (1986). *Communities and Crime*. Chicago: University of Chicago Press.

SHAW, C. R. and McKAY, H. D. (1942). *Juvenile Delinquency and Urban Areas*. Chicago: University of Chicago Press.

SKOGAN, W. G. (1987). *Disorder and Community Decline:* final report to the National Institute of Justice. Evanston, Ill: Center for Urban Affairs and Policy Research, Northwestern University.

TAUB, R. P., TAYLOR, D. G., and DUNHAM, J. D. (1984). *Paths to Neighborhood Change: race and crime in urban America*. Chicago: University of Chicago Press.

WALLIS, A. and FORD, D. (1980). *Crime Prevention through Environmental Design: an operational handbook*. National Institute of Justice. Washington, DC: Government Printing Office.

WILSON, J. Q. and KELLING, G. L. (1982). 'Broken windows': the police and neighbourhood safety'. *The Atlantic Monthly*, March, 29–38.

Annex
The Acorn system of area classification

ACORN stands for 'A Classification of Residential Neighbourhoods'. It is a system of classifying households according to the demographic, employment and housing characteristics of their immediate area. It was produced by CACI, a market analysis consultancy, by applying the statistical technique of cluster analysis to variables from the 1981 Census. ACORN is now used for planning and marketing by a wide range of commercial organisations, and is beginning to be employed by social research.

There are 38 ACORN area types, these aggregating up to 11 neighbourhood groups. Each of the 130,500 enumerations districts (EDs) in Great Britain (an average ED comprises about 150 households) has been assigned to an ACORN area type on the basis of its scores on 40 selected Census variables. As CACI have 'mapped' postcodes into enumeration districts, any household in the country can be given an ACORN score provided its full postcode is known.

The principle of ACORN is that people who live in the same neighbourhood share characteristics of class, income and lifestyle. Naturally, there will be differences between individual EDs with the same ACORN classification, and between households within the same ED—particularly in heterogeneous areas such as those in inner cities. Nevertheless, ACORN is a useful way of determining the immediate social environment of different households, and can be more illuminating for some purposes than individual characteristics such as income or class. In this case for instance, ACORN will show what types of target for crime different areas might offer and what risks their residents might face from those living nearby.

Each respondent in the 1984 BCS was allocated to an ACORN area type on the basis of the postcode for their address. The 11 ACORN groups are shown in Figure A, with the percentage of the 1981 population in each group.

A **AGRICULTURAL AREAS**
1 Agricultural villages
2 Areas of farms and smallholdings
Represents 3.3% of total households in G.B.

B **MODERN FAMILY HOUSING, HIGHER INCOMES**
3 Cheap modern private housing
4 Recent private housing, young families
5 Modern private housing, older children
6 New detached houses, young families
7 Military bases
Represents 14.8% of total households in G.B.

E **BETTER-OFF COUNCIL ESTATES**
15 Council estates, well-off older workers
16 Recent council estates
17 Council estates, well-off young workers
18 Small council houses, often Scottish
Represents 12.2% of total households in G.B.

F **LESS WELL-OFF COUNCIL ESTATES**
19 Low rise estates in industrial towns
20 Inter-war council estates, older people
21 Council housing for the elderly
Represents 10.4% of total households in G.B.

I **HIGH STATUS NON-FAMILY AREAS**
30 High status areas, few children
31 Multi-let big old houses and flats
32 Furnished flats, mostly single people
Represents 4.9% of total households in G.B.

J **AFFLUENT SUBURBAN HOUSING**
33 Inter-war semis, white collar workers
34 Spacious inter-war semis, big gardens
35 Villages with wealthy older commuters
36 Detached houses, exclusive suburbs
Represents 15.9% of total households in G.B.

C OLDER HOUSING OF INTERMEDIATE STATUS
8 Mixed owner-occupied and council estates
9 Small town centres and flats above shops
10 Villages with non-farm employment
11 Older private housing, skilled workers
Represents 18.7% of total households in G.B.

D POOR QUALITY OLDER TERRACED HOUSING
12 Unimproved terraces with old people
13 Pre-1914 terraces, low income families
14 Tenement flats lacking amenities
Represents 4.6% of total households in G.B.

G POOREST COUNCIL ESTATES
22 New council estates in inner cities
23 Overspill estates, high unemployment
24 Council estates with overcrowding
25 Council estates with worst poverty
Represents 6.8% of total households in G.B.

H MULTI-RACIAL AREAS
26 Multi-occupied terraces, poor Asians
27 Owner-occupied terraces with Asians
28 Multi-let housing with Afro-Caribbeans
29 Better-off multi-ethnic areas
Represents 3.5% of total households in G.B.

K BETTER-OFF RETIREMENT AREAS
37 Private houses, well-off elderly
38 Private flats with single pensioners
Represents 4.8% of total households in G.B.

47

3. Disorder, crime and community decline

Wesley G Skogan[1]

Introduction

This chapter reviews recent North American research on the relationship between crime and disorder and the social and economic forces which underlie stability or change in private-market residential communities. Its focus on crime is familiar; perhaps more unusual is the attention given to the role of *disorder* in stimulating neighbourhood decline. Communities are troubled when they cannot realise their values with regard to public behaviour. Some of those values clearly are protected by the criminal law and fall within the purview of routine police operations. Other widely approved standards of conduct are not so clearly supported by statute, and many more seem to present intractable enforcement problems despite their unlawful status. But those legal and operational distinctions have little to do with the impact of these problems upon community life, which appears to be considerable.

'Disorders' are conditions and events widely interpreted as signalling a breakdown in the realisation of conventional norms about public behaviour. Their presence appears to provide observable evidence of neighbourhood decline. Disorders include both visual signs of physical deterioration and behavioural evidence of social disorganisation. Deterioration is apparent in the widespread appearance of junk and trash in vacant lots, poor maintenance of homes, boarded-up buildings, vandalism of public and private property, graffiti, and the presence of stripped and abandoned cars in the streets and alleys. Disorganisation is signalled by bands of teenagers congregating on street corners, public solicitation for prostitution, begging, public drinking, verbal harassment of women on the street, and open gambling and drug use. Some of these conditions and events are not clearly unlawful, and the police find it hard to do much about any of them; their significance is to be found in their impact on urban communities.

Almost 20 years ago, Biderman *et al.*, (1967) argued that people's major impressions about area crime are derived from such '. . . highly visible signs of what they regard as disorderly and disreputable behaviour in their community'. Surveys and observational studies suggest that disorder may have numerous ill consequences for urban neighbourhoods. Disorder sparks concern and fear of crime among neighbourhood residents, and may actually increase the level of serious crime. It apparently undermines the processes by which stable neighbourhoods exercise informal control over local events and conditions, and drives out residents for whom stable community life is

1. Preparation of this report was supported in part by Grant 85-IJ-CX-0074 from the National Institute of Justice, US Department of Justice, awarded under the Omnibus Crime Control and Safe Streets Act, as amended. Points of view or opinions in this report are those of the author and do not necessarily represent the official position or policies of the US Department of Justice.

important. In this view, disorder is a source of neighbourhood destabilisation and decline.

Disorder and fear of crime

Surveys enquiring about the extent of disorder problems find responses are closely related to fear of crime and perceptions that serious crimes are neighbourhood problems. Some research suggests visible disorderly activity by people has a greater impact than physical deterioration, but that both independently are important determinants of fear and some fear-related behaviours (McPherson et al., 1983). This parallels Hunter's (1978) conceptual distinction between 'social' and 'physical' signs of what he dubbed 'incivility'.

Deterioration and disorder can be discomforting, and run counter to many adults' expectations about proper public conditions, although, of course, they will vary in their tolerance of such situations. Taylor, Schumaker and Gottfredson (1985) found that observational measures of physical deterioration had the greatest effect in blue collar, rather than in poor or more well-to-do areas of Baltimore. In wealthy areas, instances of these problems may be ignored as atypical and non-threatening, and residents of poor areas have many things to worry about. However, in moderate income areas of cities, where market conditions for housing are insecure, residents may be more sensitive to such barometers of decline. This may account as well for the high negative correlation they found between indicators of decay and neighbourhood confidence. People may take disorder as a sign of the disintegration of the standards which guide local public life. Local residents may be distressed about continuous confrontations with obstreperous and unpredictable people, many of whom seem hostile and potentially dangerous. Americans generally associate visible deterioration, gang graffiti, loitering teens and public drinkers, and other disorderly activities with a heightened risk of being victimised; they serve as what Stinchcombe et al., (1980) called 'the signs of crime'. These conditions generate fear because they signal that the community is out of control. Lewis and Salem (1986) find that disorder popularly signals a diminished capacity for local problem solving, gives residents a feeling of personal isolation, and spreads the sense that no one will come to the rescue when they find themselves in trouble (see also Greenberg, 1984).

Disorder and conventional crime

Wilson and Kelling (1982) have suggested that disorder actually spawns more serious crime. They allude to a 'developmental sequence' by which unchecked rule-breaking fosters petty plundering and even more serious street crime and theft. The nature of the relationship between crime and disorder is still unclear, and Maxfield (1984) illustrates how perceptions of crime and disorder are differentially related to fear, depending upon their absolute level. However, several studies report high correlations (+.45 to +.60) between area-level measures of crime and perceived disorder. There apparently are few high-disorder low-crime neighbourhoods, which suggests the effect of one condition upon the other is either quite powerful or due to their strong joint association with some other factor (Skogan 1983).

Wilson and Kelling argued that disorder undermines the processes by which communities ordinarily maintain order. In stable neighbourhoods families care for their homes, and residents supervise the activities of youths, watch over one another's property, and challenge those who seem to be up to no good. Wilson has elsewhere referred to the 'moral tutelage, reciprocal obligations, and public humiliations' which maintain order in such places. Where public drinking, street gambling, begging, teenage loitering, and the like, go on, those arrangements do not work very effectively. Respectable people then use the streets less often; when they do, they avoid contact with strangers and potentially threatening situations, and believe it is safer to 'not get involved'. They think of the area as a 'place to live', but have little commitment to it. In such areas, no one takes responsibility for rowdy behaviour in public places, the residents' sense of 'territoriality' shrinks to include only their own households, and untended property is fair game for plunder or destruction. Where communal barriers against crime are low, local youths ramble freely.

Wilson and Kelling (1982) argued further that a neighbourhood's reputation for being tolerant of social disorder serves as an invitation to outside troublemakers. Criminals are attracted into such areas because of the opportunities for crime they offer. Areas which tolerate (or cannot counter) rowdy taverns, sex-oriented paraphernalia shops, public drinking, prostitution, and other disorders, quickly will attract street robbers to prey upon the trade. Thieves will sense the limited surveillance capacity of the area, and that it presents easy pickings for burglars. Where disorder is common they feel their chances of being identified are low, and are more confident no one will intervene. Many disorderly activities create their own criminal sub-industries. Drinking and gambling lead to assaults and fights; prostitution and drug sales attract those who prey upon the consumers of vice. Wilson and Kelling suspect that the concentration of supposedly 'victimless' activities can in short order inundate an area with serious and victimising crime.

One important feature of this interest in disorder is its policy implications. Speculation about the ill consequences of disorderly acts and conditions, and of the presence of deviant persons on city streets, has led to calls for action to suppress them. Early analysts merely found it interesting that factors other than 'real crime' were related to community decline; more recently some have taken that finding as licence to recommend direct intervention by the police to break up disorderly activity and presumably intervene in the spiral of disorder, fear, crime and neighbourhood decline.

This is controversial because it seems to call for the reversal of trends in American social policy, including the decriminalisation of status and victimless offences, community-based treatment of drug addicts, and the deinstitutionalisation of sentenced offenders and the mentally ill. These policies presumably account for some of the disorder plaguing urban neighbourhoods. Wilson and Kelling also advocate that the police take the initiative in discovering and acting on disorder, on the basis of what they dubbed 'communal needs'. Many of these needs would not be found in the criminal code. Aggressive order maintenance activity by the police raises the spectre of racial and class discrimination in 'norm enforcement', problems which are difficult enough to control in 'law enforcement'. It also raises significant civil liberties issues.

The consequences of crime and disorder for communities

Most neighbourhoods form stable social systems, and this is one reason why their names often are useful labels. Their future generally resembles their past. Through individual initiatives and collective action, residents find ways to retard unwanted change and preserve their community's character.

However, when things happen which disrupt the processes by which neighbourhoods renew themselves, dramatic changes can ensue. Forces can be set loose which stimulate further changes rather than dampen them. In such areas, one problem leads to another. Systems characterised by such 'positive feedback' change rapidly. These changes do not necessarily make crime or the quality of life in those areas worse (see McDonald, 1986), but when they do neighbourhoods can quickly decline.

Once areas slip into the cycle of decline, feedback processes rapidly take control of neighbourhood conditions. The problems which emerge include crime, physical deterioration and social disorder. These in turn undermine the capacity of the community to deal with its problems. Crime and disorder stimulate physical and psychological withdrawal from the community, a weakening of informal social control mechanisms, a decline in the organisational and political capacity of the neighbourhood, and deterioration of local business conditions. These problems feed upon themselves, spiralling neighbourhoods deeper into decline. As Schuerman and Kobrin (1986) report, area crime shifts from being just a 'dependent' variable to being an 'independent' variable as well, in areas characterised by long periods of decline.

Thus, crime and disorder play an important role in stimulating urban decline. A major consequence of post-war mobility in American society is that all but the black and poor can flee urban problems. When disorder makes people uncomfortable and encounters with strangers leave them uneasy, communities grow unpleasant and they feel unsafe, many can leave. Measures of crime and disorder problems are strongly related to residential dissatisfaction and the desire to move (Kasl and Harburg, 1972; Droettboom *et al.*, 1971). Moving is selective, and families and the middle class leave first, often to be replaced by unattached and transient individuals (Frey, 1980; Duncan and Newman, 1976). Those who cannot leave may psychologically withdraw, finding friends elsewhere or simply isolating themselves (Kidd and Chayet, 1984). This further limits participation in neighbourhood organisations, reduces supervision of youths, and undermines any general sense of mutual responsibility which may have been felt by area residents.

Crime and disorder erode residential commitment

One critical role of crime and disorder appears to be their impact upon the number and mix of people moving into and out of a neighbourhood. Selective out-migration is the most fundamental source of neighbourhood change (Frey,

1980). Neighbourhoods never remain the same; even in places which appear tranquil, families are moving in and out, the building stock is ageing, and macro-economic forces are continually changing the price and demand for housing there. However, if about the same number of people move into a neighbourhood as move out, and if they resemble those who left, it can be counted as 'stable'. Areas are stable when the housing stock is continually renewed, and if people can sell and buy homes there at prices appropriate for the structures and their social class; stability means that the neighbourhood as a social system reproduces itself.

However, many will not want to remain in an area characterised by crime and disorder, and fewer still will want to move in. Measures of both are strongly related to residential dissatisfaction and the desire to move to a safer place (Kasl and Harburg, 1972; Droettboom et al., 1971). However, studies of actual moving—as opposed to residential dissatisfaction—document the realities of economics and race (Duncan and Newman, 1976). In the US, middle-class and white residents actually move on, and their replacements are different. A comparison of 'movers' and 'stayers' in the Chicago metropolitan area indicated that households which left the central city were more affluent, more educated, and more often formed intact families. This was despite the fact that blacks, unmarried adults and the poor were far more likely to be unhappy about their neighbourhood. Those who moved out were 'pulled' by the attractiveness of safe suburban locations as well as 'pushed' by fear and other concerns (Skogan and Maxfield, 1981).

As this implies, flight from neighbourhoods may carry away somewhat less fearful residents, leaving behind those who were more fearful to deal with the area's problems. A few elderly and long-time residents may remain behind after this transition because they are unwilling to move or cannot sell their homes for enough to buy another in a nicer neighbourhood. They find themselves surrounded by unfamiliar people whom they did not choose to live with. Loneliness and lack of community attachment are significant sources of fear among the urban elderly (Yin, 1980; Jaycox, 1978), especially among women (Silverman and Kennedy, 1985). It also appears that perceived social diversity (measured by questions about whether neighbours are 'the same' or 'different' from the respondent) has a strong effect on fear only among the elderly (Kennedy and Silverman, 1985).

Demographic changes are very significant for the local housing market. If fewer or poorer people want to move in, real estate values shift. A soft demand for housing due to the undesirability of the area can be stimulated by reducing its price and changing standards for tenant selection, but this further effects the mix of in-movers. Kobrin and Schuerman (1983; 1981), using census figures and recorded crime, place demographic change near the beginning of the decay process. Land use, housing, and population changes at first lead to shifts in crime rates. Changes in the socio-economic status of residents of destabilising areas follow population turnover. The consequences which follow can stimulate even further change, including mounting levels of crime and disorder.

If residential buildings are unprofitable, owners have few incentives to maintain them adequately or even to pay the real estate and utility bills. If there is no demand for them they may sit boarded up. The arson rate reflects the same calculations (Sternlieb and Burchell, 1983). Future investments in a neighbourhood appear to be affected by a relatively low level of building abandonment, perhaps 3 to 6 per cent (Department of Housing and Urban Development, 1973). Abandonment has increased as migration into many American industrial cities has slowed to a trickle; the 'waystation' role historically played by the worst housing in inner-city, mixed land-use areas, which gave it continued economic value, has vanished with the disappearance of new migrants.

Mounting levels of crime and disorder may further reduce real estate values (Frisbie *et al.*, 1977). Multiple regression models of the crime-property value nexus find area-level crime rates are so highly correlated with other physical and social determinants of property values that the independent effect of crime cannot be estimated. However, Taub, Taylor and Dunham's (1984) survey data indicates that individual's market evaluations and investment plans are affected by dissatisfaction with safety, perceived risk of victimisation in the area, and actual victimisation. Crime affects the upkeep of the neighbourhood, and together the two affect perceptions that the neighbourhood is changing for the worse and desire by residents to move away.

Crime and disorder undermine informal social control

There are other psychological and behavioural consequences of crime and disorder. People can feel powerless, impotent and vulnerable in the face of crime. High area levels of perceived crime and disorder appear to undermine residents' beliefs that problems can be solved locally, it increases their sense of personal isolation, and spreads the perception that no one will come to their rescue when they find themselves in trouble (Lewis and Salem, 1986). Not surprisingly, concern about crime and fear of crime do not stimulate constructive, preventive responses to crime (Tyler, 1984; Lavrakas, 1981). Surveys and experiments indicate that fear reduces people's willingness to take positive actions when they see crimes—including simply calling the police. The reduction in the number of legitimate users of the streets caused by fear, coupled with the unwillingness of bystanders to intervene because they are afraid, can create easy opportunities for predators.

Fear of crime also decreases the radius which individuals feel responsible for defending. When that boundary is expansive, individuals monitor more strangers, youths and suspicious sounds and activities. Where territories encompass only people's homes and families, untended persons and property are fair game for plunder. Territoriality is an important component of the larger process of surveillance, which may be an important mechanism for controlling crime. Surveillance entails both 'watching' and 'acting'. Acting is facilitated by personal recognition, shared standards about appropriate public behaviour, a sense of responsibility for events in the area, and identification with potential victims. There is some evidence (summarised in Shotland and Goodstein, 1984; Goodstein, 1980) that crime is encouraged by low levels of surveillance of public places, and reduced by people willing to act to challenge strangers, supervise youths, and step forward as witnesses.

One of the most significant consequences of crime and disorder may be withdrawal from community life. Fearful people report they stay at home more, especially after dark. When they do go out, they carefully avoid coming into contact with strangers or potentially threatening situations, and they confine their path to the safest times and routes possible. They avoid people they do not know, and 'not getting involved' in events seems the wisest course. Among women in particular, adoption of such defensive tactics is related to levels of neighbourhood disorder as well as to perceived risk of victimisation (Riger et al., 1982). At best this can result in a form of 'ordered segmentation' of the community which enables diverse and potentially conflictful people to share the same turf without coming into contact; they divide the area among themselves by time and space, thus avoiding potentially unsettling encounters (Suttles, 1968).

There has been a great deal of research on the effect of the strength of 'local social ties' on interventions (or intentions to intervene) of a variety of kinds, especially to control juveniles. The effect of social ties is strong, but they are affected by fear. In stable neighbourhoods residents supervise the activities of youths, watch over one another's property, and challenge those who seem to be up to no good. Neighbourhood change brings newcomers, changes in patterns of street life, and unpredictable people to the neighbourhood. This further rebounds to the disadvantage of such areas through the impact of dense social relationships on fear. Surveys often find that the strengths of local social ties are a strong and independent correlate of feelings of safety. They also increase the scope of individual territoriality, cement identification to one's area, and encourage participation in organised community activity (Taylor et al., 1984; DuBow and Emmons, 1981; Hunter, 1974). Thus, another consequence of individual passivity, weak informal social control, and collective incapacity, is that neighbourhoods caught in decline lose the ability to control problems caused by youths living in the area.

Crime and disorder erode organisational capacity

Both concern about crime and disorder and simple demographics work against organised community life in neighbourhoods caught in the cycle of decline. Research indicates that fear of crime does not stimulate participation in collective efforts to act against crime; rather, it often has the effect of undermining commitment to an area and interest in participation (Lavrakas et al., 1981). Where fear promotes suspicion in place of neighbourliness it can be difficult to forge formal linkages between residents to attack neighbourhood problems.

When neighbourhoods spiral into decline, demographic factors related to participation in community organisations can shift unfavourably. Those who move in tend to be harder to organise; they are renters, single-parent families, the poor and less educated, younger and unmarried persons and nonfamily households. They report having little economic or emotional commitment to the community, and usually expect to move again.

As a result of these demographic changes, the political capacity of the area is diminished. This affects the ability of residents to effectively demand that landlords and governments act on their behalf. Where they are strong, organisations can provide a mechanism for combating crime and disorder. One important function of community organisations is to convey the image—to residents and outsiders alike—of a mobilised community which will resist unwelcome change (Unger and Wandersman, 1983). Organisations can restore or reinforce a local value consensus and emphasise the shared interests of people living together (DuBow and Emmons, 1981). Where informal organisation is limited, there may be few other mechanisms for generating community cohesion around the issues of crime, disorder, and decline. For example, Cohen (1980) finds that street prostitution flourishes only where community consensus is weak and there is no organised resistance to deviant public behaviour.

Another role of neighbourhood groups is to extend face-to-face contacts between residents and generate optimism about the future of the area, both important factors facilitating crime-prevention efforts (DuBow and Emmons, 1981). Perceptions registered in surveys that 'neighbours help each other' are an important source of morale in urban communities and seem to stimulate a variety of positive actions against crime (Lavrakas, 1981). Participation in neighbourhood organisations seems to stimulate homeowner investments as well (Taub, Taylor and Dunham, 1984). However, in neighbourhoods in decline, mutual distrust and hostility are rampant and antipathy between newcomers and long-term residents prevails. Residents of poor, heterogeneous areas tend to be more suspicious and feel less communality with one another (Taub, Taylor and Dunham, 1984; Greenberg *et al.*, 1982; Taylor *et al.*, 1981). Greenberg (1983) concludes that crime prevention programmes requiring social contact and neighbourhood co-operation are less often found in heterogeneous areas and those with high levels of fear. Surveys indicate that respondents who think that local crime is carried out by 'people in the neighbourhood' are more fearful than those who think it is the responsibility of 'outsiders'. This perception is a corrosive one, for it undermines trust among neighbours. It certainly violates one of the assumptions behind Neighbourhood Watch and other programmes which attempt to promote mutual co-operation to prevent crime—it may not seem wise to inform the neighbours that you will be out of town when it is their children whom you fear (Greenberg, 1983).

Intervening in the cycle of decline

Despite the trends reviewed above, urban neighbourhoods do not inevitably shift into a cycle of decline, even where crime and disorder are common. There is some evidence of a modest reversal of these processes, with a 'return to the cities' affecting areas in the United States with locational advantages and housing suited to affluent, childless households (Laska and Spain, 1980). Neighbourhoods can improve their standing through both gentrification and 'incumbent upgrading' (cf. McDonald, 1983). This can force up rents, increase the value of land, and upgrade the housing stock in small areas through economic pressures acting in reverse of the trends described above.

Concern about crime and disorder are only two features of urban life, and are not necessarily the most important determinants of decisions to move or to invest in an area. Taub, Taylor and Dunham's (1984; 1981) study of fear of crime and real estate prices in Chicago neighbourhoods suggests that fear has substantial negative effects on moving and investment decisions only if *other* neighbourhood factors are pushing in the same direction. If they are, people who live there view crime as a leading indicator of community decline. Among white Chicagoans, for example, fear of local crime was related to the perception that investment in the neighbourhood was unwise only among those who thought their area was racially unstable. In areas which were deteriorating crime was seen as a sign of neighbourhood decay, and people who lived in deteriorating areas reported feeling helpless in the face of large-scale social forces which seemed to be working against them.

However, factors other than concern about crime are important in determining the demand for property or rental housing which pushes real estates values up or down. These include closeness to the downtown, the quality and style of the housing stock, access to amenities and transportation, and the availability of loans. When other factors are positive and (especially) when property values are appreciating, residents find ample reason to be satisfied with the area, and they tolerate surprisingly high levels of crime. The same seems to be true for small retail businesses in urban residential areas. McPherson *et al.*, (1983) found that even in disorderly, problem-ridden, high-crime areas, owners were more likely to plan to remain in business and make future investments where they believed the future of their market area looked bright, and if they were optimistic about local development efforts. Concern about crime does not *in itself* determine levels of investment, the confidence of residents in the future, or property values. Rather, it is one strand in a bundle of features which make up a community's character. Where people are optimistic about the bundle as a whole, crime counts for less.

This does not mean that residents of higher-crime but appreciating areas are not personally fearful. McDonald (1986) summarises several studies indicating residents of inner-city gentrifying neighbourhoods are concerned about crime; the difference is, they are willing to tolerate that condition despite their ability to move elsewhere. One reason they can do so is that residents of gentrifying areas often are childless, and thus able to ignore a number of local problems, including school safety. A survey in poor neighbourhoods of Philadelphia found that the safety of their children in and on the way to school was the number one crime-related concern among parents. Interviews with their children revealed that they also saw schools as dangerous places (Savitz *et al.*, 1977). Another reason why they tolerate untoward neighbourhood conditions is they may have well-founded optimism for the immediate future. Economically advantaged areas often succeed in steering more city resources into building the stock of local amenities which underlie appreciating property values. 'Rehabbers' often prove to be effective petitioners for better services, including police protection, and understand the change in neighbourhood dynamics associated with stimulating negative rather than positive feedback processes.

This means dealing with population turnover. Schuerman and Kobrin (1986) have some hope for what they dub 'emerging crime areas'. These are 'middle-aged' rather than old residential areas, with changing populations but substantial pockets of middle-class residents. Here they recommend (without elaborating upon the mechanisms) 'declaration of demographic and socio-economic change'. Wilson and Kelling (1982) focus upon 'the ratio of respectable to disreputable people' in an area to foresee its fate. Neighbourhoods not too far past their 'tipping point' are those with substantial levels of legitimate street use and a critical mass of residents interested in keeping the area in good repair. Taub, Taylor and Dunham (1984) found that defensively 'stabilising the real estate market' was the first concern of community organisations in the Chicago neighbourhoods they studied, and that '... [m]ost of the strong community organisations considered in this book arose in response to impending or actual racial change' (p 184). At best, they found that this was accomplished by self-consciously promoting the virtues of racial integration and appealing to class interests instead. They also found that neighbourhood efforts to reverse tendencies toward decline primarily were successful when supported by large but immobile corporate institutions (hospitals, banks, universities) with an investment to protect.

Recent US experiments in community policing also speak to the problem of controlling crime and – especially – disorder. One programme in Newark, New Jersey, was specifically designed to test Wilson and Kelling's 1982 recommendations. In one target area, a special task force cracked down on disorderly public conduct, aggressively driving groups of younger males off the streets. This was combined with extensive foot patrol in residential parts of the area, and blockades and radar checks to enforce drinking and speeding laws. Also, there was an effort to intensify city services in the area, clean up unsightly lots, and control minor delinquency. This effort was dubbed 'Reducing the "Signs of Crime"', reflecting its intellectual origins.

This and other programmes in both Newark and Houston, Texas, were rigorously monitored and evaluated. Measures of perceived problems with crime and disorder and residential commitment were included in pre-intervention and post-intervention surveys conducted in both target and control areas of both cities. The evaluation indicated that Newark's special disorder control programme had no discernible positive effects. (For a further discussion see: Pate *et al.*, 1986; Skogan *et al.*, 1986).

However, several other programme packages in the two cities met with some apparent success in reducing levels of perceived disorder and increasing levels of residential commitment. Perhaps the most successful was a form of directed foot patrol. In target areas in both Houston and Newark, teams of patrol officers went 'door-to-door' interviewing residents to gather information on neighbourhood problems of all kinds. In Newark this programme was linked to a store-front police office offering a range of services. In both cities (but in most organised fashion in Newark) the teams acted to solve the problems they identified, either on their own or by mobilising other city agencies. The evaluation indicated that these activities were widely known in the target areas, and they appear to have reduced levels of perceived disorder and increased satisfaction with the neighbourhood. These patrols also tested certain aspects of Wilson and Kelling's original argument. They thought it was critical that the police devise mechanisms for identifying neighbourhood problems and understanding the sometimes varying standards of public conduct which communities wish maintained. Directed foot patrol is one such mechanism, a systematic way of gaining contact with ordinary area residents and assessing local order problems. Much earlier, Bittner (1967) found that policing public drinking on Skid Row was more effective when the officers involved had a detailed knowledge of those who frequented the area and their different yet still understandable patterns of behaviour. The Houston and Newark efforts appear to have combined at least a bit of this with the general benefits of foot patrol identified in previous experiments, which include reduced fear and lower levels of perceived crime (Police Foundation, 1981). The resulting package may provide a vehicle for facilitating police intervention in the disorder-decline nexus.

Summary

This chapter reviewed recent North American research on the impact of disorder and crime upon neighbourhood social and economic processes. Disorder undermines the private residential housing market through its impact upon neighbourhood commitment and satisfaction, the desire of residents to move away from troubled areas, and the market value of the housing stock. Both disorder and crime erode the capacity of communities to exercise informal social control, through their impact upon territoriality, intervention efforts, and even the extent of self-help. Instead, people in troubled areas physically and psychologically withdraw from community life. Disorder and crime also handicap communities politically, through their corrosive impact upon neighbourhood organisational capacity. Research suggests that under some circumstances the operation of private-market economic forces can reverse cycles of neighbourhood decline. Efforts to do this by community organisations in the US typically focus upon controlling land-use and population turnover. Finally, recent experiments with community policing hint that decentralisation, directed foot patrol, and other efforts to increase co-operation between the police and neighbourhood residents may have an impact upon both disorder and fear of crime.

References

BIDERMAN, A. D., JOHNSON, L. A., McINTYRE, J. and WEIR, A. W. (1967). *Report on a Pilot Study in the District of Columbia on Victimization and Attitudes Toward Law Enforcement*. Washington, DC: US Government Printing Office.

BITTNER, E. (1967). 'The police on skid row: a study of peace keeping'. *American Sociological Review*, 32, pp. 699–715.

COHEN, B. (1980). *Deviant Street Networks: Prostitution in New York City*. Lexington, MA: Lexington Books.

DEPARTMENT OF HOUSING AND URBAN DEVELOPMENT. (1973). *Abandoned Housing Research: A Compendium*. Washington, DC: Department of Housing and Urban Development.

DROETTBOOM, T., McALLISTER, R. J., KAISER, E. J. and BUTLER, E. W. (1971). 'Urban violence and residential mobility'. *Journal of the American Institute of Planners*, 37, pp. 319–325.

DuBOW, F. and EMMONS, D. (1981). 'The community hypothesis'. In Lewis, D. A. (Ed.), *Reactions to Crime*. Newbury Park, CA: Sage Publications, pp. 167–182.

DUNCAN, G. and NEWMAN, S. (1976). 'Expected and actual residential moves'. *Journal of the American Institute of Planners*, 42, pp. 174–186.

FREY, W. H. (1980). 'Black in-migration, white flight, and the changing economic base of the central city'. *American Journal of Sociology*, 85, pp. 1396–1417.

FREY, W. H. (1984). 'Lifecourse migration of metropolitan whites and blacks and the structure of demographic change in large central cities'. *American Sociological Review*, 49, pp. 803–827.

FRISBIE, D., FISHBEIN, G., HINZ, R., JOELSON, M. and NUTTER, J. B. (1977). *Crime in Minneapolis*. St. Paul, MN: Community Crime Prevention Project, Governor's Commission on Crime Prevention and Control.

GOODSTEIN, L. I. (1980). 'The crime causes crime model: a critical review of the relationships between fear of crime, bystander surveillance, and changes in the crime rate'. *Victimology*, 5, pp. 133–151.

GREENBERG, S. W. (1983). 'External solutions to neighbourhood-based problems: the case of community crime prevention'. Unpublished paper presented at the Annual Meeting of the Law and Society Association (June).

GREENBERG, S. W., ROHE, W. M. and WILLIAMS J. R. (1982). *Safe and Secure Neighbourhoods: Physical Characteristics and Informal Territorial Control in High and Low Crime Neighbourhoods*. Washington, DC: National Institute of Justice, US Department of Justice.

GREENBERG, S. W., ROHE, W. M. and WILLIAMS, J. R. (1984). *Informal Citizen Action and Crime Prevention at the Neighbourhood Level: Synthesis and Assessment of the Research*. Unpublished grant report to the National Institute of Justice, US Department of Justice, from the Research Triangle Institute.

HUNTER, A. (1974). *Symbolic Communities*. Chicago: University of Chicago Press.

HUNTER, A. (1978). 'Symbols of Incivility: Social Disorder and Fear of Crime in Urban Neighbourhoods'. Unpublished paper presented at the Annual Meeting of the American Society of Criminology.

JAYCOX V. H. (1978). 'The elderly's fear of crime: rational or irrational'. *Victimology*, 3, pp. 329–333.

KASL, S. V. and HARBURG, E. W. (1972). 'Perceptions of the neighbourhood and the desire to move out'. *Journal of the American Institute of Planners*, 38, pp.318–324.

KENNEDY, L. W. and SILVERMAN, R. A. (1985). 'Perception of social diversity and fear of crime'. *Environment and Behaviour*, 17, pp. 275–295;

KIDD, R. F. and CHAYET, A. F. (1984). 'Why do victims fail to report: the psychology of criminal victimization'. *Journal of Social Issues*, 40, pp. 39–50.

KOBRIN, S. and SCHUERMAN, L. A. (1981). *Interaction Between Neighbourhood Change and Criminal Activity*. Los Angeles: Social Science Research Institute, University of Southern California.

KOBRIN, S. and SCHUERMAN, L. A. (1983). 'Crime and urban ecological processes: implications for public policy'. Unpublished paper presented at the Annual Meeting of the American Sociological Association.

LASKA, S. and SPAIN, D. (Eds.) (1980). *Back to the City: Issues in Neighbourhood Renovation*. New York: Pergamon Press.

LAVRAKAS, P. J., HERZ, E. J. and SALEM, G. (1981). 'Community organization, citizen participation, and neighbourhood crime prevention'. Unpublished paper presented at the Annual Meeting of the American Psychological Association.

LAVRAKAS, P. J. (1981). 'On households'. In Lewis, D. A. (Ed.), *Reactions to Crime*. Newbury Park, CA: Sage Publications, pp. 67–86.

LEWIS, D. A. and SALEM, G. (1986). *Fear of Crime: Incivility and the Production of a Social Problem*. New Brunswick, NJ: Transaction Books.

MAXFIELD, M. G. (1984b). 'The limits of vulnerability in explaining fear of crime: a comparative neighbourhood analysis'. *Journal of Research in Crime and Delinquency*, 21, pp.233–250.

McDONALD, S. C. (1983). *Human and Market Dynamics in the Gentrification of a Boston Neighbourhood*. PhD. dissertation, Department of Sociology, Harvard University.

McDONALD, S. C. (1986). 'Does gentrification affect crime rates?'. In Reiss, A. and Tonry, M. (Eds.), *Communities and Crime*. Chicago: University of Chicago Press, pp. 163–202.

McPHERSON, M. (1978). 'Realities and perceptions of crime at the neighbourhood level'. *Victimology*, 3, pp. 319–328.

McPHERSON, M., SILLOWAY, G. and FREY, D. (1983). *Crime, Fear, and Control in Neighbourhood Commercial Centres*. Unpublished grant report to the National Institute of Justice, US Department of Justice, from the Minnesota Crime Prevention Center, Inc.

PATE, A., WYCOFF, M. A., SKOGAN, W. G. and SHERMAN, L. (1986). *Reducing Fear of Crime in Houston and Newark: A Summary Report*. Washington, DC: The Police Foundation and the National Institute of Justice.

POLICE FOUNDATION. (1981). *The Newark Foot Patrol Experiment*. Washington, DC: The Police Foundation.

RIGER, S., GORDON, M. T. and LEBAILLY, R. (1982). 'Coping with urban crime'. *American Journal of Community Psychology,* 10, pp. 369–386.

SAVITZ, L. D., LALLI, M. D. and ROSEN, L. (1977). *City Life and Delinquency: Victimization, Fear of Crime, and Gang Membership*. Washington, DC: National Institute for Juvenile Justice and Delinquency Prevention, US Department of Justice.

SCHUERMAN, L. A. and KOBRIN, S. (1986). 'Community careers in crime'. In Reiss, A. and Tonry, M. (Eds.), *Communities and Crime,* Chicago: University of Chicago Press, pp. 67–100.

SHOTLAND, R. L. and GOODSTEIN, L. I. (1984). 'The role of bystanders in crime control'. *Journal of Social Issues*, 40, pp. 9–26.

SILLOWAY, G. and McPHERSON, M. (1985). 'The limits to citizen participation in a government-sponsored community crime prevention program'. Unpublished paper presented at the annual meeting of the American Society of Criminology, San Diego.

SILVERMAN, R. A. and KENNEDY, L. W. (1985). 'Loneliness, satisfaction and fear of crime'. *Canadian Journal of Criminology*, 27, pp. 1–13.

SKOGAN, W. G. (1983). 'Disorder, crime and community deterioration: a test of the Wilson-Kelling hypothesis'. Unpublished paper presented at the 9th International Congress on Criminology (September).

SKOGAN, W. G. and MAXFIELD, M. G. (1981). *Coping with Crime: Individual and Neighbourhood Reactions*. Newbury Park, CA: Sage Publications.

SKOGAN, W. G., PATE, A., WYCOFF, M. A. and SHERMAN, L. (1986). 'Reducing public disorder: an experiment in formal social control'. Unpublished manuscript, Center for Urban Affairs and Policy Research, Northwestern University.

STERNLIEB, G. and BURCHELL, R. W. (1983). 'Fires in abandoned buildings'. In Rapkin, C. (Ed.), *The Social and Economic Consequences of Residential Fires*. Lexington, MA: Lexington Books, pp. 261–270.

STINCHCOMBE, A., ADAMS, R., HEIMER, C., SCHEPPELE, K., SMITH, T. and TAYLOR, D. G. (1980). *Crime and Punishment in Public Opinion*. San Francisco: Jossey-Bass.

SUTTLES, G. D. (1968). *The Social Order of the Slum*. Chicago: University of Chicago Press.

TAUB, R. P., TAYLOR, D. G. and DUNHAM, J. (1984). *Paths of Neighbourhood Change: Race and Crime in Urban America*. Chicago: University of Chicago Press.

TAUB, R. P., TAYLOR, D. G. and DUNHAM, J. (1981). 'Neighbourhoods and safety'. In Lewis, D. A. (Ed.), *Reactions to Crime,* Newbury Park, CA: Sage Publications, pp. 103–122.

TAYLOR, R. B., GOTTFREDSON, S. D. and BROWER, S. (1981). *Informal Control in the Urban Residential Environment*. Report to the National Institute of Justice, US Department of Justice, from the Center for Metropolitan Planning and Research, Johns Hopkins University.

TAYLOR, R. B., GOTTFREDSON, S. D. and BROWER, S. (1984). 'Block crime and fear: defensible space, local social ties, and territorial functioning'. *Journal of Research in Crime and Delinquency*, 21, pp. 303–331.

TAYLOR, R. B., SCHUMAKER, S. A. and GOTTFREDSON, S. D. (1985). 'Neighbourhood-level linkages between physical features and local sentiments: deterioration, fear of crime, and confidence'. *Journal of Architectural Planning and Research*, 1985, pp. 261–275.

TITUS, R. (1984). 'Residential burglary and the community response'. In Clarke, R. and Hope, T. (Eds.), *Coping with Burglary*. Boston: Kluwer-Nijhoff, pp. 97–130.

TYLER, T. R. (1984). 'Assessing the risk of crime victimization'. *Journal of Socal Issues*, 40, pp. 27–38.

UNGER, D. and WANDERSMAN, A. (1983). 'Neighbouring and its role in block organizations'. *American Journal of Community Psychology,* 11. pp. 291–300.

WILSON, J. Q. and KELLING, G. (1982). 'Broken windows'. *The Atlantic Monthly,* March, pp. 29–38.

YIN, P. (1980). 'Fear of crime among the elderly'. *Social Problems,* 27, pp. 492–504.

4. Community contexts and criminal offenders

Stephen D Gottfredson and Ralph B Taylor[1]

Considerable criminological research has focused on the individual, while largely ignoring physical and social environmental influences on behaviour. Conversely, most research focusing on environmental factors has ignored the individual. The research reported in this paper has sought to incorporate both approaches by examining the interactions between offenders and their communities. The questions addressed may be stated quite simply. First, by considering the socio-environmental context into which an offender is released after incarceration, can we improve recidivism predictions based solely on personal characteristics of the offender? Second, what are the effects of offender populations on communities?

This chapter describes our recent efforts to examine the effects of community contexts on criminal offenders, and the effects of criminal offenders on their communities. Section I discusses two salient bodies of criminological research, risk assessment and ecological work, and summarises their core findings. Section II outlines a theoretical framework for thinking about interactions between community characteristics and criminal offenders and explains why it is believed that community differences are likely to affect criminal behaviour. Section III summarises the methods, data sources, analyses, and findings of preliminary and follow-up studies of community and offender interactions in several neighbourhoods in Baltimore. Finally, Section IV presents conclusions and discusses their implications.

I. Theoretical background

Two extensive research traditions have been important to much of modern criminology. One, the risk-assessment tradition, dates at least from Goring (1913), and has provided much of what we now know concerning individual-level correlates of criminality. Research in this tradition generally has been predictive in nature and directly policy-relevant in intent. The second research tradition, ecological studies, essentially ignores the individual—even though it is clear that many sociological theories of crime causation deal largely with the social environment and its interaction with individuals or groups (see, as examples, Merton, 1957; Sutherland and Cressey, 1974; Hirschi, 1969; Cloward and Ohlin, 1960; Matza, 1969; Reckless, 1973; Gibbons and Jones, 1975). Ecological and areal research findings have been important to much of this theory construction (e.g., Willie, 1967; Hirschi and Selvin, 1967; Maccoby, Johnson and Church, 1958). The two traditions developed virtually

1. Funding for this research was provided by the National Institute of Justice. Points of view or opinions expressed are those of the authors and do not necessarily reflect the positions or policies of the United States Department of Justice.

independently, although some persons have been influential to both (e.g. Burgess, 1925; 1928). In particular, ecological research findings have been little used to inform the risk-assessment tradition.

The risk-assessment tradition

The prediction literature relating to criminal justice, and particularly recidivism, is enormous (see Gottfredson and Gottfredson, 1986, for a review). Research findings on behavioural and demographic correlates that have predictive utility across a range of samples and studies provide a reasonably clear picture of the factors most closely associated with recidivism. Thus past criminal behaviour is found to be one of the best predictors of future criminal conduct. This generalisation tends to hold regardless of the measure to prior criminal conduct used or of the specific operational definitions of that conduct. Age, usually measured at time of release, appears to be positively associated with criminal outcomes, but the relation is slight, particularly when considered in multivariate contexts. When examined in relation to age of onset of notified (or official) criminal behaviour, the evidence is compelling, however; the earlier the onset, the poorer the prognosis. Other factors such as marital status, education, employment history, offence, alcohol and drugs are all found to have some predictive power in relation to recidivism, although their contribution tends to be less powerful than others and weak or non-existent when multivariate analyses are used. Factors such as gender, race and ethnicity have been little studied, and few significant effects are reported. Dozens of other variables have also been examined for association with recidivism, but fail to have a systematic effect.

There is some evidence of the predictive power of 'community correlates', variously defined and measured, from early risk-assessment studies. The evidence is discouraging, however, because it is routinely found that demographic and, more strikingly, behavioural correlates of delinquency or recidivism overwhelm 'community' correlates. Other evidence is available from studies conducted in response to the bail reform movement. Since (until recently) assurance of appearance at trial was the overwhelming consideration in bail and pre-trial decisions, a variety of studies examined the relation between community and contextual factors—principally social and familial-environmental influences and offender behaviour. Although the evidence is mixed, behavioural correlates generally overwhelm the environmental, although in relation to failure to appear for trial, community ties can prove predictive.

The ecological and areal research tradition

Investigations in this area have differed substantially with respect to their conceptual bases. A brief summary of three relatively distinct perspectives is given below.

(i) Human ecology
The human ecological perspective (Park, 1916) developed from the ecological framework used in biology. According to this view, locales were seen to be

differentially influenced by large scale economic and social forces, resulting in social disorganisation in some. Thus, Shaw and McKay (1942) observed that delinquency rates were high in areas where physical deterioration was also high, and that delinquency varied inversely with distance from the city centre. Later work replicated these findings, associating delinquency and/or crime rates with socio-economic status. Factors relating to housing, employment and family characteristics were found to co-vary with delinquency rates.

Many sociological theories of crime causation deal largely with the social environment and its interaction with individuals or groups. Not surprisingly ecological research has been important to much of this theory construction. However, the association between crime or delinquency rates and social characteristics, although strong and consistent, is not perfect, and likely operates through several (often unspecified) mediating factors which, if specified, are difficult to measure adequately (Greenberg, Rohe and Williams, 1984).

(ii) Positive local forces

A different body of work focuses on neighbourhood and community qualities. Burgess (1925) suggested that there were three types of social forces operating at the neighbourhood level: ecological, cultural and political. Warren's work on riots (Warren, 1969, 1977, 1978) is a compelling demonstration of this framework's utility. She suggested that neighbourhoods vary on three dimensions: (i) the extent of attachment to local community, (ii) the degree of informal social exchange among neighbours, and (iii) 'vertical' ties to the larger community. Warren observed that riotous behaviour was more extensive in neighbourhoods lower in social exchange and attachment and that 'counter-riot' activity was greater in neighbourhoods in which neighbouring linkages were extensive.

(iii) Situational factors

A third ecological approach has investigated physical environment factors that may create 'opportunities' for crime (see Taylor, Gottfredson and Brower, 1980; Taylor, 1982, 1985 for reviews) and social, environmental and family-related stressors. This situational approach, as articulated by Monahan and Klassen (1982) includes family-related stress (Strauss, 1980), peer-related stress (Davies, 1969) and job-related stress (Cook, 1975).

II. A theoretical perspective

Person-environment interactions

The research traditions briefly described above can be characterised as analogous to the *trait* and *situational* perspectives on personality. The former suggests that most of personality may be explained by some set enduring dispositions (traits), while the latter suggests that personality is relatively more situation-specific. The influence of environments on behaviour has been well documented in psychology (Barker, 1968), and in addition to the ecological studies reviewed later in this paper, has received some attention in recidivism studies (Reitzes, 1955; Glaser, 1964).

64

The third approach, the interactionist, may hold promise as a perspective from which to articulate theories concerning the causes of criminal recidivism. On one level, the interactionist perspective is very simple and has considerable common sense or 'face' validity; it simply is a statement that behaviour is a function both of the person and the environment. Olweus (1977) has proposed a number of different interactionist perspectives, one of which, the *person-environment integrity* model, suggests that the person, the environment, and the person's behaviour in that environment, are interwoven or integrated in a system-like fashion; that these three classes of variables have a functional integrity; and this is reflected in processes of reciprocal influence.

It is felt that the person-environment integrity model will prove most useful for providing advances to the risk assessment problem. First, an offender's adjustment represents not only the influence of the environment on the person, but the person's influence on that environment. The environment may influence the offender's behaviour in many ways. By itself, it may serve as a discriminating stimulus to elicit some behaviours which are reinforcing, such as drug abuse. The environment produces social agents who may encourage behaviours leading to recidivism, or behaviours leading to successful adjustment. Social agents may indirectly influence the course of events by encouraging police or other crime control agents to keep track of the offender. Physical and land use factors may provide (or limit) targets or opportunities for crime.

Likewise, there are many ways in which offenders and their behaviour may influence the environment. The mere presence of a known offender may be a cause of increased vigilance, watchfulness, concern, or perhaps fear. Of course, the offender's behaviour contributes to the environment by making it more or less orderly. If the offender's behaviour becomes extremely antisocial, leading to the commission of crimes, this also influences environmental quality. Both the offender's presence and behaviour may contribute to or detract from the quality of community life, and may stimulate local formal or informal control mechanisms.

It consistently has been observed that, at the aggregate-level, socio-demographic variables are related to delinquency and crime rates. Further, social cohesion or community integration factors appear to augment or mediate these effects (Maccoby *et al.*, 1958; Warren, 1969; Schmid, 1960). The inference might be drawn that social network correlates of delinquency or crime may also be good correlates of post-release adjustment.

Some direct evidence to support this inference is available (Glaser, 1964; Reitzes, 1955). For example, Reitzes found that compared with non-recidivists, recidivists (a) have less stable employment upon release, work more frequently in unskilled professions, and are more 'occupationally mobile'; (b) have less stable marital and parental relationships; and (c) report themselves as 'friendless', but associate more with other offenders, and work more often in occupations likely to involve them in contact with other offenders. Finally, recidivists were much less likely to join organisations than were non-recidivists. Reitzes concluded that 'the adjustment of ex-convicts to law-abiding society depends on the social conditions under which this adjustment takes place'. Clearly, several of these factors identified by Reitzes primarily involve socio-environmental factors. Other, less comprehensive studies, also have found these variables predictive of recidivism (Davies, 1969; Cook, 1975).

The neighbourhood perspective

Areal socio-demographic factors are correlated with crime-related outcomes, and these relations obtain even when individual-level characteristics are statistically controlled (Sampson, 1982a,b). If the *nature* of these relations is to be understood, we need conceptual tools to help in deciding the appropriate areal unit(s) to study, which ecological variables theoretically are important, and how best to measure them. Thus, we have a geographical problem, a conceptual problem, and a measurement problem. The concept of *neighbourhood* may help provide a resolution.

There would appear to be three advantages to using a neighbourhood perspective. First, the neighbourhood may be a clearly bounded spatial unit. Second, neighbourhoods have substantial ecological integrity, and the areas are recognised by insiders and outsiders alike (Taylor, Brower, and Drain, 1979; Goodman and Taylor, 1983). Finally, their social and psychological functions have been extensively studied (Popenoe, 1973; Warren, 1977).

Thus, the neighbourhood concept can help solve the geographic and conceptual problems concerning socio-environmental characteristics. Three classes of neighbourhood-related variables should be associated with crime-related outcomes. The first is the nature and extent of *local social ties* (Fischer *et al.*, 1977; Mitchell, 1969; Granovetter, 1973). Informal sanctions or controls are asserted through local ties (Warren, 1963). Thus, pressure to conform with local norms may be mediated by local social networks. Local ties are important for such practical things as finding a job (Granovetter, 1974) or a place to live, or using local services (Froland and Pancoast, 1979).

The second class of neighbourhood variables concern *attachment to locale* (Schumaker and Taylor, 1983; Gerson, Stueve and Fischer, 1977; Warren, 1978), that is, the extent to which residents are involved in local events and feel positively about and responsible for what goes on in the neighbourhood.

The third relevant class of neighbourhood variables concerns the extent, location, and distribution of *local services*. Conceptions of 'community' (Froland and Pancoast, 1979; Gerson *et al.*, 1977; Warren, 1963) rely heavily on the location and type of local service institutions. A reasonable hypothesis is that some local services and community elements may prove supportive to offenders (e.g., presence of local churches, places of employment, social services agencies, job location agencies, etc.), while others may pose a risk (bars, liquor stores, concentrations of other offenders, etc.).

III. The Baltimore studies

Since it makes both theoretical and common sense to hypothesise that people and environments affect one another and that they both, independently and in various interactions, affect crime, a series of studies of interactions between released offenders and neighbourhoods in Baltimore was undertaken.

The preliminary study

The preliminary investigation of the impacts of community environments on released offenders (Gottfredson and Taylor, 1986) provided results which although limited in scope, were very encouraging, and a brief summary is given below.

The study involved the collation of detailed social and criminal history information on all men released from state institutions to any of 90 randomly sampled neighbourhoods in Baltimore over a period of two years from 1978 to 1980. Follow-up information was obtained in 1982 including, as far as possible, data on details of any re-arrest, its seriousness, and subsequent sentence, using FBI rap sheets. Secondly, assessments were made of the physical environments to which the men were released. Of the 90 neighbourhoods selected, a 20 per cent sub-sample was chosen for on-site assessment by teams of trained raters, in terms of types of street use, appearance, land use, and social climate. All items which prior theoretical or empirical work have suggested are related to crime, crime-related outcomes or social disorder were included. These environmental variables were correlated with average neighbourhood crime levels for the 1978–81 period, and a series of sub-scales was developed which reflected particular environmental influences on social control, including incivilities.

Detailed analysis of the data confirmed the expected strong effects of prior criminal history and offender characteristics on recidivism, as well as time available in which to offend. On their own, however, the environmental scales proved not to be significantly related to outcome. As this paper has discussed, there are three general approaches that can be taken to predicting recidivism: focusing solely on the characteristics of the offender (the trait approach), upon the characteristics of the situation to which the offender is released (the situational approach), or upon the interaction between offender and environmental characteristics (the interactionist approach). This latter basic hypothesis was confirmed, in that while there was no main effect for environment, interaction terms did add to the predictive power of the model. However, it also was found that different types of offenders performed differently in different types of environments. For example, those offenders with an extensive history of criminal involvement failed more seriously when released to 'bad' environments than to 'good' ones. However, good-risk offenders did better in poorer environments and worse in better ones.

It is possible that the observed interactions were related to some of the measures used, both predictor and criterion (e.g., prior criminal conduct and arrest). Both of these measures are likely related to police or neighbourhood surveillance. Surveillance is likely to be targeted on offenders with extensive criminal records, enabling good-risk offenders to fare better in poor environments than poor-risk offenders, for example. In other words, a differential arrest/charging phenomenon could be invoked to explain the observed interaction.

The results of this preliminary investigation were encouraging both statistically and theoretically, and the person-environment interactions appeared most successful when more complex criteria than simple success/failure dichotomies were used. Nevertheless, this preliminary research was subject to severe limitations since it was not possible to assess the effect of socio-economic and demographic variables adequately. Since these are likely to have a substantial effect on and co-vary with environmental characteristics, it is important to examine the latter net of socio-demographic characteristics. The problem may be stated quite simply: socio-economic and demographic characteristics co-vary with crime-related behaviours. Concepts such as social networks, cohesion and incivilities are hypothesised to co-vary with crime-related behaviours and appear to. Finally, social and demographic variables also are known to co-vary with these concepts of social cohesion and incivility. The research question is whether the concepts of cohesion, networks and incivilities are related to crime-related behaviours beyond their relation to socio-economic and demographic characteristics.

Additionally, the environmental characteristics measured were limited to observable physical characteristics, and provided only crude proxies for such variables as social networks, social cohesion and attachment.

A more complete study

A follow-up study was designed to overcome these limitations, and this section of the paper outlines the ways in which neighbourhoods were characterised on the basis of resident surveys and demographic data, sources of data on offender outcomes, and the findings of the analysis. This covers assessment of the interactions between neighbourhood, individual and aggregate offender outcomes. Finally, some observations on the effects of offenders on their communities are described.

Of the original sample of 90 Baltimore neighbourhoods selected for assessment in the preliminary study, only 66 were finally included after elimination of those which were too small, or because of non-cooperation by local leaders. The final pool of neighbourhoods varied widely with respect to race, income and crime rates. Within these areas the final sample of residential surveys was based on 1,406 telephone interviews and 216 face-to-face interviews, with a response rate of 73 per cent.

Survey scale development

The survey of neighbourhood residents asked a broad range of questions about local social dynamics, aspects of residents' attachment to the locale, place dependence, territorial attitudes, comparisons of the neighbourhood vis-à-vis others, confidence in and expectations for the neighbourhood, knowledge of the neighbourhood, its features and organisations, responses to crime and other forms of social threat, perceptions and fear of crime and neighbourhood disorder, and restriction of activities. Scales were developed to assess each of these constructs.

The following section provides a few examples of these scales, and the manner in which they were developed (for detailed information see Taylor, Schumaker, and Gottfredson, 1985).

Local social involvement

Social network items such as presence of local friends, acquaintances and relatives; awareness of and membership in various types of local organisations; and instances of assistance and friction between neighbours, were submitted to principal components analysis, and four components were extracted (accounting for more than 60 per cent of the variance available in this set of questionnaire items).

The first component appeared to reflect *trust* among residents. Neighbourhoods with a high score on this component were those in which residents have done things for one another which imply confidence and trust, such as giving a neighbour a key, asking them to take in mail, or to watch the house during an absence. Neighbourhoods where trust is higher are also those in which a greater proportion of respondents belong to the local neighbourhood or improvement organisation. This bond of shared membership implies further shared understandings, allegiances, and concerns among residents. This also is implied by more respondents reporting having friends in the neighbourhood.

The second component seemed to reflect *social ties*. Neighbourhoods with high scores on this component were those where respondents were aware of many different types of local organisations (e.g., PTA, church, and youth-oriented groups), where large numbers of local friends are reported, and where many respondents have relatives living nearby. These patterns of ties and awareness do not necessarily imply intimacy or shared confidence among neighbours.

Component III reflects *local instrumental helping*. Neighbourhoods with a high score on this component contained residents who reported that they have helped or worked with other residents on the block. Although these items reflect a willingness to assist and co-operate, they do not imply shared trust.

Component IV appeared to reflect *on-block friction*. Neighbourhoods where residents had 'tangled' with other neighbours on the block, or been bothered by the opinions or activities of them would score high on this component.

Attachment and territorial functioning

Survey respondents were asked about several aspects of their attachment to the locale, including standard items (e.g., 'feel neighbourhood is home vs. just a place to live'), items relevant to place dependence, and those reflective of territorial attitudes.

Three components were extracted. The first appeared to reflect *territorial responsibility* and how the current neighbourhood compares with prior neighbourhoods in which respondents have lived. Neighbourhoods with a high score on this component are those whose residents felt a strong sense of territorial responsibility for what happened on the block and elsewhere, were satisfied with their neighbourhood, felt it compared favourably to their last place of residence, and that they exercised choice in moving to their current location.

Component II was the dimension most clearly reflecting *attachment to place*. The item with the highest loading on this component was that which has most widely been used as a measure of attachment; feeling that the neighbourhood is 'home' v. 'just a place to live'. Neighbourhoods with high scores on this component had stable residents, who have moved little in the past and expected to be where they were now five years in the future.

69

Respondents with a high score on this dimension also reported a strong sense of community, and of being attached to both the block and the neighbourhood.

The third component reflected *current comparisons* of the neighbourhood *vis-à-vis* others. Neighbourhoods with a high score on this component contained residents who thought their neighbourhood was more attractive and safer than others, and who were not seriously contemplating moving from it.

Neighbourhood confidence and expectations

A five-item scale concerned with ratings of and perceived changes in neighbourhood appearance and overall quality was developed. With respect to the former, respondents estimated the overall condition of homes in the neighbourhood, and also indicated whether the appearance of the neighbourhood has got better, stayed the same, or got worse during the time he or she has lived there. Respondents also rated overall neighbourhood quality as it is currently, as it was two to three years ago, and as it will be two to three years in the future.

Neighbourhood knowledge

Two ordinal items reflecting an awareness of neighbourhood features were combined to form one general scale reflecting knowledge of the neighbourhood.

Response to crime and threat scales

Scales from survey items that appeared to reflect various types of potential community responses to crime and threat were constructed. The *informal social control* scale measured the predisposition to intervene in relatively non-serious but annoying incidents such as late night noise and vandalism. The *post-hoc informal response* scale is concerned with informal, resident-initiated responses to a (hypothetical) rash of burglaries on the home block. A scale reflecting the *level of organised community crime prevention activities* in each community also was developed. A *responding to break-in* scale assesses predisposition to intervene and solicit help from neighbours in the event a break-in appears to be in progress. A *fear* scale uses the standard National Crime Survey items, repeating them for block as well as neighbourhood; it also includes a 'fear of retaliation' item, and an 'awareness of dangerous places' item. A *restricted activity* scale measures the extent to which people stay in more, or go out less frequently, due to a perception of vulnerability. Finally, *awareness of active organisations* is the proportion of respondents in a neighbourhood who are aware of an active, problem-oriented neighbourhood organisation involved in activities like crime prevention, neighbourhood clean-up, etc.

It is suggested that several of these items are related to a larger concept of *resistance to disorder*, and that several are related to a more passive *accommodation to disorder*. Examination of the zero-order neighbourhood-level correlations among these items provides suggestive evidence concerning these more general response strategies. Fear and behavioural restriction are significantly related, in support of the notion of an accommodation dimension. Informal social control correlates with post-hoc responses to crime, awareness of active organisations, and awareness of active community crime prevention initiatives, providing support for the notion of a resistance dimension.

Scale and variables based on census data

Three types of scale which reflected different characteristics of neighbour-hoods were constructed using data from the US Census of Population and Housing. The allocation of census data into neighbourhoods required approximation in some cases. A great deal of important information is only available at the level of the block-group (a cluster of up to nine blocks in a census tract), and in many cases, neighbourhood and block-group boundaries do not coincide.

Economic status

Neighbourhoods vary with respect to the amount and type of economic resources available. Typically, those with more economic resources will have higher housing values, higher household income, and residents with higher educational levels. The following variables were used to attempt to define this factor:

House value percentile score. This variable transforms raw housing prices into a percentile score ranging from 0 to 100.

Household income percentile score. This allows for the assessment of each neighbourhood relative to all others in the city.

Status employment. This variable represents the sum, in percentage terms, of a neighbourhood's labour force that is in either white collar or managerial/professional occupations.

Education. This is represented as the percent of a neighbourhood's adult population that has at least completed high school and obtained a degree.

Lifestyle or 'families'

A second way that neighbourhoods may differ is in terms of a lifestyle or 'familism' dimension. Such a dimension contrasts areas where homeow-nership, married couples, and children are predominant with those where renters, working women, and single or non-married households are predomi-nant. The following variables were selected as representatives of this dimension:

Percent of population from zero to five years of age;

Percent of population from six to thirteen years of age;

Percent of households which are 'married couple' households; and

Percent of housing units which are single-unit structures (as opposed to multi-unit, and therefore probably rental).

71

Race and ethnicity represent the third dimension on which neighbourhoods have been held to differ. Two variables were used to attempt to identify this factor, based on the 1970 and 1980 censuses:

Percent of the total population who are black; and

Percent of the total population who are 'other' (e.g., neither black nor white). In Baltimore, these people predominately are Korean, Hispanic, or Amerindians.

In an effort to provide empirical validation for the three theoretical constructs identified above, a series of principal components analyses were conducted. The *status* dimension appeared precisely as predicted, and included house value, income, type of employment, and educational level. The second component, however, did not completely conform to expectation. Rather than reflecting a lifestyle or 'familism' dimension, the scale appeared to reflect *stability*. It did include married couples, one-unit structures and homeownership, but not the two 'children' variables. The latter loaded on a third component including the proportion of black population (but not the 'other' races). Thus, this dimension appeared to reflect race and youth, rather than ethnicity alone.

Because of the statistical approach taken, these three factors or dimensions are independent of one another; thus, a neighbourhood may be high (or low) on any given dimension, and have virtually any score on either of the other dimensions.

Outcome data: sample attrition

Because the State Police failed to provide FBI rap sheets for several hundred subjects, follow-up information was recoded for all offenders using 'rap sheets' made available by the State Division of Parole and Probation. Thus, the outcome information data source for the analyses to be reported here, and that reported in that preliminary study, differs and excludes information on seriousness of offences.

In this study, sample attrition occurred in three ways. First, some of the 1,033 offenders originally identified as having returned to one of the 90 Baltimore City neighbourhoods sampled later were found *not* to have returned to the designated neighbourhood (that is, the Parole and Probation headquarters office records were incorrect). This was the case for 235 (23%) of the original sample. Second, follow-up information for 179 offenders originally sampled (17.3%) could not be obtained due to errors. Third, sample attrition occurred based on differences in the neighbourhoods studied in the two projects (132 offenders—12.8 %—were so affected). As described above only 66 of the original 90 neighbourhoods could be studied given the requisite sampling procedures. Finally, it was found that no offenders were released to 23 of the neighbourhoods originally sampled. Thus, analyses based on survey information were limited (in this study) to 57 neighbourhoods and 487 offenders. Analyses based on the physical assessments were based on 619 offenders and 67 neighbourhoods.

For all practical purposes, this attrition appears to have been random; that is, no differences in offender characteristics were discovered between offenders removed from and remaining in the sample. Differences in neighbourhood characteristics were encountered, however; the 23 neighbourhoods to which no offenders were released during the project period generally were more socially cohesive, of higher socio-economic status, and were lower on the incivilities measure developed.

Findings

Analyses reported here are based on three outcome criteria; a simple success/failure measure (arrest/no arrest during follow-up period), the proportion of the follow-up period arrest-free, and the number of arrests experienced during the follow-up period. In an effort to examine the stability of any effects observed over the follow-up period, both six- and twelve-month periods were investigated. Table 1 provides a summary of individual-level outcomes for three follow-up periods. By the end of the first twelve months following release from incarceration, over one-half of this sample of offenders had experienced at least one re-arrest; the average offender had experienced 2.16 arrests, and had remained arrest-free about eight and one-quarter months.

Table 1 *Individual-level outcomes at six, nine and twelve months*

Outcome measure	Six months	Nine months	Twelve months
Arrest/No Arrest	.36	.46	.53
Number of Arrests	1.55	1.95	2.16
Months Arrest-Free	4.88	6.70	8.23

Contributions of offender characteristics

Risk models developed using only information concerning offenders' characteristics provided results very typical of those commonly found and the power of the models was in the mid- to upper-ranges typically observed. In short, variables commonly found predictive, as described earlier in this paper, were predictive in this sample as well.

Contributions of environmental characteristics

What of efforts to identify environmental effects and person-environment interaction effects? Unfortunately a brief and disappointing answer must be given: virtually no such effects were observed. Neither any of the census scales, nor any of the carefully constructed survey scales yielded either main effects or interaction effects when entered (after personal characteristics) in the models. The encouraging findings reported in the preliminary study completely failed to replicate here.

One possible explanation has to do with data quality. Although the data bases used in the two studies contained considerable overlap in terms of offenders studied and variables investigated, they also were different. Some offenders studied in the preliminary research could not be studied in the more complete investigation, and vice versa. Measurement was, with one important exception, careful in both studies. The exception, unfortunately, has to do with the outcome criterion measure: recidivism. It was a clear impression that the follow-up information available from the Division of Parole and Probation, and used in the more complete study, was substantially less valid than that available from the FBI (and used in the preliminary investigation). This was not only the impression gained from coding the data, but it was evident that although risk-assessment models developed in both studies were similar, those developed in the preliminary study had considerably more power.

If this impression is correct, the modest effects observed in the preliminary study may in fact be reliable; given the poorer quality of the outcome measures used in this study, it proved not possible to replicate them.

Effects of offenders on community environments

Findings concerning the second of the 'general research questions', relative to the impacts of offenders on community, were less discouraging. For purposes of these analyses, the neighbourhood survey scales were treated as indices of 'community outcomes' (whereas, of course, they were treated as independent, rather than dependent variables, in the individual-level analyses). This seems quite reasonable, and in keeping with the 'person-environment integrity' approach to interactionism outlined earlier. Of interest at the neighbourhood level, then, is the extent to which the presence of offenders influences factors such as the community perception of its social climate, residents' fear of crime, and accommodation to social threat (e.g., through restriction of activities). In particular, the extent to which these influences are manifest over and above other socio-demographic characteristics of the neighbourhoods is of interest (e.g., as assessed by the census-based scales.)

Both the ecological and risk-assessment literatures provide ample evidence that offenders tend to come from similar kinds of environments, and that they return to environments which, if not the same, are similar to those from which they came. This clearly is true of the offenders in this study (about which more will be said shortly). Figure 1 gives the observed distribution of number of offenders per neighbourhood. No offenders were returned to 23 neighbourhoods, and the distribution drops off very sharply, but exhibits a very long tail (the final figure for number of offenders actually represents 30+). Two neighbourhoods, for example, each contained over *one-tenth* of the total of offenders available for study.

Using census information, two rate measures were developed (offenders per 10,000 residential population, and per 10,000 households). The former ranged from 1.29 to 212.7; the latter from 3.10 to 588.24. Table 2 summarises bivariate correlations of the three census-based scales, the two rate measures, and the raw number of offenders per neighbourhood with the community outcome measures described earlier. (Interestingly, none of the census measures correlates better than .3 with any of the offender-based measures.)

The first three columns of the table confirm 'typical' ecological research findings. Indices of socio-economic status, stability, ethnicity and age composition are rather powerfully correlated with indices of community

Table 2 *Comparison of zero-order correlations between census factors and offender rates—various community outcomes*

	Census or offender-based predictor					
Community Outcome	Status	Stability	Race/ Youth	Number of Offenders	Offenders/ Nbhd. Pop.	Offenders/ Nbhd. Hshlds.
Community Perception of Social Climate (57)	.616	.204	−.161	−.420	−.472	−.486
Residents' Attachment to Community (54)	−.219	.367	.560	.150	.118	.187
Residents' Expectations for Community (57)	.609	.207	−.179	−.381	−.538	−.559
Physical Signs of Incivility (64)	−.490	−.391	.083	.617	.738	.732
Community Perception of Physical Problems (57)	−.672	−.278	.252	.423	.587	.591
Community Perception of Social Problems (57)	−.628	−.227	.009	.302	.387	.375
Residents' Fear of Crime (57)	−.295	−.409	.262	.373	.488	.492
Community Perception of Crime Problem (54)	−.347	−.521	.176	.490	.641	.633
'Actual' Community Crime Problem (57)	−.295	−.511	.243	.512	.694	.683
Reported Restriction of Activities (57)	−.181	−.036	.426	.377	.440	.476

Notes:
a) Number of neighbourhoods/outcome measure is given in parentheses.
b) Status dimension reflects mean housing value, income, type of employment, education.
c) Stability dimension reflects married couple households, one-unit housing structures, and owner-occupancy.
d) Race/Youth dimension reflects per cent black, young (0–5) children, and children (6–13).

decline, anomie, incivility, and crime rates. The last three columns are suggestive that offender concentration also is powerfully correlated with community decline, anomie, incivility, and crime. To observe otherwise, of course, would be surprising at best, and would require the validity of the community outcome measures to be questioned.

The remaining question is whether *knowledge* of offender concentration provides information about community outcomes over that which is provided by socio-economic status, stability, and ethnicity and age composition. The answer seems to be yes (Table 3). Offender/population rate (for example) adds significantly to the prediction of all but two of the community outcomes examined (these are Attachment to the Neighbourhood and Community Perceptions of Social Problems). In some cases, the increments in explanatory power are quite substantial (e.g., the offender rate adds 11 per cent explained variance to Residents' Expectations for the Neighbourhood, 10 per cent to Community Perceptions of Physical Problems, 15 per cent to Residents' Perception of Crime as a Neighbourhood Problem, 13 per cent to self-reported Restriction of Activities (but only 6 per cent to Fear of Crime), and 20 per cent to the explanation of the actual neighbourhood crime rate).

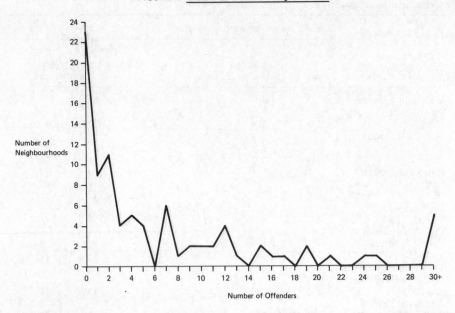

FIGURE 1. **Number of Offenders/Neighbourhood**

Table 3 *Regression of various community outcomes on census factors and offender rates*

Community outcome (Criterion)	Beta	Increment in R-sq.	F–Test
Community Perception of Social Climate			
Predictor cluster			
Census based			
Status	.572		
Stability	.182	.456	$F(2,54) = 22.61$ $p < .001$
Offender/population			
rates	− .288	.070	$F(1,53) = 7.81$ $p < .01$
Total R-sq. = .526; $F(3,53) = 19.57$; $p < .001$			
Residents' Attachment to Community			
Predictor cluster			
Census based			
Race/youth	.544		
Stability	.342	.430	$F(2,51) = 19.22$ $p < .001$
Offender/population			
rates	—	—	(Insufficient association to enter model)
Total R-sq. = .430; $F(2,51) = 19.22$; $p < .001$			
Residents' Expectations for Neighbourhood			
Predictor cluster			
Census based			
Status	.545		
Stability	.158	.449	$F(2,54) = 21.98$ $p < .001$
Offender/population rate	− .368	.114	$F(1,53) = 13.78$ $p < .001$
Total R-sq. = .563; $F(3,53) = 22.71$; $p < .001$			

76

Community Perceptions of Physical Problems
  Predictor cluster
    Census based
      Status   − .610
      Stability   − .248
      Race/youth   .124   .618 $F(3,53) = 28.62$
                                                              $p < .001$
      Offender/population rate   .347   .096 $F(1,52) = 17.43$
                                                              $p < .001$

Total R-sq. = .714; $F(4,52) = 32.48$; $p < .001$

Community Perceptions of Social Problems
  Predictor cluster
    Census based
      Status   − .617
      Stability   − .245   .485 $F(2,54) = 25.43$
                                                              $p < .001$
      Offender/population rate   .175   .026 $F(1,53) = 2.786$
                                                              $p < .10$

Total R-sq. = .511; $F(3,53) = 18.44$; $p < .001$

Residents' Fear of Crime
  Predictor cluster
    Census based
      Stability   − .363
      Status   − .255
      Race/youth   .191   .348 $F(3,53) = 9.43$
                                                              $p < .001$
      Offender/population rate   .278   .062 $F(1,52) = 5.42$
                                                              $p < .05$

Total R-sq. = .410; $F(4,52) = 9.01$; $p < .001$

Community perception of crime problem
  Predictor cluster
    Census based
      Stability   − .428
      Status   − .292
      Race/youth   .069   .465 $F(3,50) = 14.49$
                                                              $p < .001$
      Offender/population rate   .431   .147 $F(1,49) = 18.64$
                                                              $p < .001$

Total R-sq. = .612; $F(4,49) = 19.36$; $p < .001$

'Actual' community crime problem
  Predictor cluster
    Census based
      Stability   − .391
      Status   − .215
      Race/youth   .127   .442 $F(3,53) = 14.01$
                                                              $p < .001$
      Offender/population rate   .499   .198 $F(1,52) = 28.56$
                                                              $p < .001$

Total R-sq. = .640; $F(4,52) = 23.12$; $p < .001$

Reported restriction of activities
  Predictor cluster
    Census based
      Race/youth   .344   .181 $F(1,53) = 12.17$
                                                              $p < .001$
                                                              $F(1,53) = 7.81$
      Offender/population rate   .363   .125 $F(1,54) = 9.72$
                                                              $p < .01$

Total R-sq. = .306; $F(2,54) = 11.91$; $p < .001$

These findings are important theoretically, since they indicate how, if the neighbourhood is the level of analysis, offenders may shape the communities to which they are released—resulting in differences in how residents of those neighbourhoods view one another and their community. The presence of offenders has an impact on the community climate: as offenders per capita increase, positive bonds among residents, and between co-residents, decrease.

Offender outcomes in the aggregate

The analyses thus far have left unanswered the question of whether, at the neighbourhood level, the community fabric influences offender outcomes. This question is different from those already explored. So far, when considering offender outcomes, the individual offender has been the unit of analysis. Here, offenders released to a neighbourhood are treated as a sample.

The approach is justified for several reasons. First, each offender in the sample is influenced by the same community environment. Second, offenders within neighbourhoods are more like one another than are offenders across neighbourhoods; there is a homogeneity suggestive of some natural grouping process. Finally, since the neighbourhoods investigated are relatively small, especially when compared to neighbourhoods in Chicago, Philadelphia, or Los Angeles (sites of other neighbourhood-based research), there is a small probability that different members of a sample of offenders in a neighbourhood may have communicated with one another.

Also, should these analyses indicate that neighbourhood climate influences offender behavioural outcomes, this will provide, at the neighbourhood level, support for the transactional interactionist perspective. Although aggregate offender characteristics were found to explain by far the bulk of the aggregate outcome variance, socio-demographic and community factors did add significant increments in some of the models.

At the neighbourhood level, between half and one-third of the variation in offender recidivism rates may be explained (depending upon the length of the follow-up period and the recidivism measure used) by offender and environment characteristics. Offender characteristics are the most powerful class of predictors, followed by socio-demographic, census-based measures of neighbourhood, and by survey-based measures of community climate. Indices of community, particularly those based on census variables, contribute significantly to the prediction of recidisivm rates even when offender characteristics and 'offender density' are controlled.

Considered in conjunction with findings of the previous section, the pattern of results at this level of aggregation suggests confirmation of the transactionalist perspective. The per capita density of offenders released to a neighbourhood influences residents' perceptions of community and one another. Also, the behaviour of offenders in communities is influenced by the nature of those communities. This relation holds even when offender density and characteristics are held constant. In short, this suggests evidence of a process of mutual, system-like influence between communities and offender groupings.

IV. Summary and conclusions

This paper began with a consideration of two research traditions that have, rather independently, been important to much of current criminology—the risk assessment and the ecological traditions. A reading of these literatures strongly suggested that the risk assessment tradition could be greatly informed and strengthened by the ecological, and it was posited that people's behaviour—including offender criminal behaviour—is a function both of the person and the setting in which that behaviour takes place. Borrowing from Lewin (1936) and the interactionist perspective, a complex but none the less compelling theoretical foundation for the study of situational influences was developed.

A preliminary study was conducted with very encouraging results; person × environment interaction terms of modest power were observed, and the results appeared consistent with criminological theory concerning the etiology of crime. A more extensive study then was conducted, which disappointingly failed to replicate the preliminary study; no effect of environment (or of environmental/individual interactions) could be demonstrated at the individual level.

At the neighbourhood level, effects of environment on aggregate offender outcomes were demonstrated, but these need to be considered in the context of the more substantial effects of aggregate offender characteristics on recidivism rates. Still, even controlling for offender characteristics, the relation between neighbourhood composition and attitudes and offender behavioural outcomes is clear. Further, it is clear that offender concentrations have an impact on neighbourhood environments, and that this obtains even after socio-demographic factors are controlled.

These studies are subject to several limitations. First, it was not possible to 'track' offenders. It is not known how long they remained in study neighbourhoods, but there is evidence that this is a very mobile group. Second, outcome measures used in both studies must be considered as crude proxies for recidivism. Indeed, some have considered arrests to be a better measure of police performance than of offender behaviour. Third, for community factors to be influential, the offender must to some extent be integrated into the social fabric of the community. No measure of this was available. Finally, in the individual level, the research suffered a peculiar sort of range-restriction problem. There is very little variability in the kinds of places in which these offenders resided. In one series of analyses designed to 'type' neighbourhoods with respect of socio-demographic factors, it was observed that the vast majority of offenders resided in one or two neighbourhood classifications. Accordingly, it may well be that many more offenders than were available for study are needed to examine fully the kinds of effects sought here (for perforce, if no offenders returned to one of our study neighbourhoods, the effect of environment could not be investigated; and if only one or two offenders were available for study, the contribution made by that neighbourhood/offender combination must be considered of suspect reliability). Several series of analyses designed to deal with this problem were performed (e.g., through weighting of the samples, through proportionate sampling), but there is no confidence that it was dealt with adequately. It also must be noted that the 'problem' is a natural ecological fact (recall Figure 1).

The authors remain committed to the person-environment integrity model, despite the mixed results of the present investigations: it simply makes too much theoretical sense to dismiss. What is needed now are careful and detailed micro-level studies. These studies probably should be 'crime-specific' in nature. Further, careful attention must be paid to the issue of offender decision-making. Since it is through the offender that all environmental influences are presumed to be mediated, much attention must be paid to this 'black box'.

Finally, it is clear that community-based crime prevention efforts must attend well to the fact that offenders themselves are very much a part of the community fabric. From our studies, it appears that concentrations of offenders in our midst affect not only the nature and quality of neighbourhood life, but are very likely to affect also the very kinds of community activities designed to meliorate the impact of crime.

References

BARKER, R. (1968). *Ecological Psychology*. Stanford, Ca: Stanford University Press.

BURGESS, E. W. (1925). 'Can neighbourhood work have a scientific basis?' In Park, R. E., Burgess, E. W., and McKenzie, R. *The City*. Chicago: University of Chicago Press.

BURGESS, E. W. (1928). 'Factors determining success or failure on parole'. In Bruce, A. A., Burgess, E. W., and Harno, A. J. (Eds.), *The Workings of the Indeterminate Sentence Law and the Parole System in Illinois*. Springfield, Ill.: Illinois State Board of Parole.

CLOWARD, R. A. and OHLIN, L. E. (1960). *Delinquency and Opportunity*. New York: Free Press.

COOK, P. (1975). 'The correctional carrot: better jobs for parolees'. *Policy Analysis* 1, pp. 11–54.

DAVIES, M. (1969). *Probationers in their Social Environment*. Home Office Research Study No. 2. London: HMSO.

FISCHER, C., JACKSON, R. M., STEUVE, C. A., GERSON, K., AND JONES, L. M. (1977). *Networks and Places: Social Relations in the Urban Setting*. New York: Free Press.

FROLAND, C. and PANCOAST, D. S. (Eds.) (1979). *Networks for Helping: Illustrations from Research and Practice*. Portland, Oregon: Regional Research Institute, Portland State University.

GERSON, K., STEUVE, C. A, and FISCHER, C. (1977). 'Attachment to place'. In Fischer, C. *et al.*, (Eds.), *Networks and Places: Social Relations in the Urban Setting*. New York: Free Press.

GIBBONS, D. C. and JONES, J. F. (1975). *The Study of Deviance*. Englewood Cliffs, NJ: Prentice-Hall.

GLASER, D. (1964). *The Effectiveness of a Prison and Parole System*. New York: Bobbs-Merrill.

GOODMAN, A. C. and TAYLOR, R. B. (1983). *The Baltimore Neighbourhood Fact Book: 1970 and 1980*. Baltimore, Md.: Center for Metropolitan Planning and Research, The Johns Hopkins University.

GORING, C. (1913). *The English Convict: A Statistical Study*. London: HMSO.

GOTTFREDSON, S. D., and GOTTFREDSON, D. M. (1986). 'Accuracy of prediction models'. In Blumstein, A. *et al.*, (Eds.), *Criminal Careers and 'Career Criminals'*. Washington, DC: National Academy Press.

GOTTFREDSON, S. D., and TAYLOR, R. B. (1982). *The Impact of Community Environments on Supervised Offenders*. Final Report to the National Institute of Justice. Baltimore, Maryland: The Johns Hopkins University.

GOTTFREDSON, S. D., and TAYLOR, R. B. (1986). 'Person-environment interactions in the prediction of recidivism'. In Sampson, R. and Byrne, J. (Eds.), *Environmental Criminology*. New York: Springer/Verlag.

GRANOVETTER, M. S. (1973). 'The strength of weak ties'. *American Journal of Sociology*, 78, pp. 1360–1380.

GRANOVETTER, M. S. (1974). *Getting a Job*. Cambridge, Mass.: Harvard University Press.

GREENBERG, S. W., ROHE, W. M. and WILLIAMS, J. R. (1984). *Informal Citizen Action and Crime Prevention at the Neighbourhood Level: Synthesis and Assessment of the Research*. Research Triangle Park, NC: Research Triangle Institute.

HIRSCHI, T. (1969). *Causes of Delinquency*. Berkeley, Ca.: University of California Press.

HIRSCHI, T., and SELVIN, H. (1967). *Delinquency Research*. New York: Free Press.

LEWIN, K. (1936). *Principles of Topological Psychology*. New York: McGraw-Hill.

MACCOBY, E., JOHNSON, J. and CHURCH, R. (1958). 'Community integration and the social control of juvenile delinquency'. *Journal of Social Issues*, 14, pp. 30–51.

MATZA, D. (1969). *Becoming Deviant*. Englewood Cliffs, NJ: Prentice-Hall.

MERTON, R. K. (1957). *Social Theory and Social Structure*. New York: Free Press.

MITCHELL, J. C. (1969). 'Social networks'. *Annual Review of Anthropology*, 3, pp. 279–299.

MONAHAN, J., and KLASSEN, D. (1982). 'Situational approaches to understanding and predicting individual violent behaviour'. In Wolfgang, M. E. and Weiner, N. A. (Eds.), *Criminal Violence*. Beverly Hills, Ca.: Sage.

OLWEUS, D. (1977). 'A critical analysis of the "modern" interactionist position'. In Magnusson, D. and Endler, N. S. (Eds.), *Personality at the Crossroads: Current Issues in Psychology*. Hillsdale, NJ: Erlbaum.

PARK, R. E. (1916). 'The city'. *American Journal of Sociology*, 20, pp. 577–612.

81

POPENOE, D. (1973). 'Urban residential differentiation: an overview of patterns, trends, and problems'. *Sociological Inquiry*, 3, 00. 35–56.

RECKLESS, W. C. (1973). *The Crime Problem*. New York: Appleton—Century Croft.

REITZES, D. C. (1955). 'The effect of social environment upon former felons'. *Journal of Criminal Law, Criminology, and Police Science*. 46, pp. 226–231.

SAMPSON, R. (1982a). The Neighbourhood Context of Criminal Victimization: Quarterly Progress Report (81-IJ-CX-0042) (February). Washington DC: National Institute of Justice.

SAMPSON, R. (1982b). The Neighbourhood Context of Criminal Victimization: Quarterly Progress Report (81-IJ-CX-0042) (March). Washington DC: National Institute of Justice.

SCHMID, C. F. (1960). 'Urban crime areas'. *American Sociological Review*, 25, pp. 537–542 (Part I); pp. 655–678 (Part II).

SCHUMAKER, S. A. and TAYLOR, R. B. (1983). 'Toward a clarification of people-place relationships: a model of attachment to place'. In Feimer, N. R. and Geller, E. S. (Eds.), *Environmental Psychology: Directions and Perspectives*. New York: Praeger.

SHAW, C. R. and McKAY, H. D. (1942). *Juvenile Delinquency and Urban Areas*. Chicago: University of Chicago Press.

STRAUSS, M. A. (1980). *Behind Closed Doors*. Garden City, New York: Anchor.

SUTHERLAND, E. and CRESSEY, D. R. (1974). *Principles of Criminology*. Philadephia: Lippincott.

TAYLOR, R. B. (1985). 'Toward an environmental psychology of disorder'. In Altman, I. and Stokols, D. (Eds.), *Neighbourhood Environmental Psychology*, New York: Wiley.

TAYLOR, R. B. (1982). 'Neighbourhood physical environment and stress'. In Evans, G. W. (Ed.), *Environmental Stress*. New York: Cambridge University Press.

TAYLOR, R. B., BROWER, S., and DRAIN, W. (1979). *Toward a neighbourhood-based data file*. Baltimore, Md.: Center for Metropolitan Planning and Research, The Johns Hopkins University.

TAYLOR, R. B., GOTTFREDSON, S. D., and BROWER, S. (1980). 'The defensibility of defensible space'. In Hirschi, T., and Gottfredson, M. (Eds.), *Understanding Crime*. Beverly Hills, Ca.: Sage.

TAYLOR, R. B., SCHUMAKER, S. A. and GOTTFREDSON, S. D. (1985). 'Neighbourhood-level links between physical features and local sentiments'. *Journal of Architectural Research and Planning*, 2, pp. 261–275.

WARREN, R. L. (1963). *The Community in America*. Chicago: Rand McNally.

WARREN, D. I. (1969). 'Neighbourhood structure and riot behaviour in Detroit'. *Social Problems*, 16, pp. 464–484.

WARREN, D. I. (1977). 'The functional diversity of urban neighbourhoods'. *Urban Affairs Quarterly*, 13, pp. 151–180.

WARREN, D. I. (1978). 'Explorations in neighbourhood differentiation'. *Sociological Quarterly*, 19, pp. 310–331.

WILLIE, C. V. (1967). 'The relative contribution of family status and economic status to juvenile delinquency'. *Social Problems*, 14, pp. 326–335.

Housing policy

The chapters in this section provide complementary material on the stark neglect of housing policies in the exploration of the genesis of crime over the past decades, and particularly the inner city public housing estate. Chapter 5 which is based upon a ten year study of housing tenure and crime patterns in different types of residential area in Sheffield, considers the implications which housing tenure patterns have for crime prevention policies. Central to the argument is the notion of the 'residential community crime career', the changing patterns of crime in a community over time, which it is essential to understand if sensible policies to alter that profile are to be planned. It stresses that it is important to develop a theory of crime reduction and practice which encompasses a broader notion of the purpose of government than e.g. a narrow and mechanistic one based on technical issues such as physical repair and the reduction of incivilities.

Chapter 6 traces the work of three recent initiatives in problem housing estates which are directed, among other things, at the reduction of crime and the improvement of conditions on those estates. It traces the genesis of the problem estate with the failure of architectural design, public housing allocation, and poor management policies, all combining to create vulnerable areas of stigmatised and demoralized populations suffering high crime and victimization. The implicit processes which guide the three approaches are examined. The initiatives promise a remarkable ability to reduce crime, but as yet it is unclear why or how they bring about the effects they claim, and the chapter argues for a more careful exploration of the diffuse and interacting processes at work, and which with their strong emphasis on action, at least two of the projects have had little time to consider.

5. Crime and housing policy: a framework for crime prevention analysis

Anthony E Bottoms and Paul Wiles

In a recent paper, we sought to show in some detail that an understanding of housing policy (and especially policies affecting housing tenure and the housing market) is necessary if one is to explain crime patterns in differing residential areas in Britain (Bottoms and Wiles, 1986). That paper in turn drew heavily upon the lessons learned from earlier research into contrasting small residential areas in Sheffield (see, e.g. Baldwin, 1974; Baldwin and Bottoms, 1976; Mawby, 1979; Bottoms and Xanthos, 1981; Mawby, 1984; Bottoms, Mawby and Walker, 1987).

This chapter aims to build upon the 1986 paper, and to consider the implications for crime prevention policies that can be derived from the general approach we have developed. But this task is not wholly straightforward, because the Sheffield research has been primarily *explanatory*, that is, concerned to explain why different kinds of housing areas have very different crime rates; it has not, in the main, been specifically policy-oriented, and has so far contained no evaluations of particular crime prevention policies adopted in the studies areas. Hence, no precise crime prevention programmes can be advocated here. Rather, it is intended here to lay out a *framework of analysis* for the consideration of housing-based crime prevention programmes in residential areas in Britain, based on an understanding of the housing market.

Before proceeding to the substances of the analysis, three key concepts central to the 1986 paper need to be explained. The first, which has already been used above, is that of the 'housing market'; this refers to all processes which enable people to move into residential properties (by buying or renting), or which inhibit them from doing so; and also to all processes enabling or inhibiting the termination of residence in a property when desired. Such a broad definition of course covers a much wider ambit than simply the private housing market, and includes *inter alia* the bureaucratically-determined rules of public housing authorities.

The second key concept, or pair of concepts, refers to a distinction known to criminology for at least thirty years (see Morris, 1957 pp. 20–1, 119–30), yet still insufficiently appreciated by many. This is the contrast between *area offender rates* (based on where offenders live) and *area offence rates* (based on where crimes are committed) (for an elaboration of the distinction, see Bottoms and Wiles, 1986, pp. 158–60). Although in residential areas these two indices are usually positively correlated (*ibid.*, pp. 106–7), in particular areas this may not be so, and it is always important to bear in mind the potential contrast between the two rates.

The third key concept is that of the 'residential community crime career', which refers to the changing crime patterns (offender-based or offence-based) in a residential community over time. This term is an elaboration of an idea originally suggested by Albert Reiss; in a recent paper, Reiss (1986) spells out the gains to be made by studying communities over time, and emphasises both the need to bring together criminological research work on communities and on individuals, and the failure of most existing governmental data-sets and social science research to collect information that can be used to explain community variation in crime rates. Yet 'communities like individuals can have careers in crime, [and] today's safe environment can become tomorrow's dangerous one' (p.2). This chapter will argue that an understanding of a community's 'crime career' is crucial to sensible community-based crime prevention, and indeed area-based crime prevention programmes can be regarded as a way of trying to intervene in the life of a community so as to alter its community crime career.

Housing and crime: general approaches

Traditionally, criminologists have shown relatively little interest in housing policy, the housing market, or housing-based crime prevention programmes. An important exception to this generalisation, in recent years, has been the work influenced directly or indirectly by Oscar Newman's (1972) ideas of 'defensible space'. The two major British writers in this *genre* in the 1980s have been Barry Poyner (Poyner, 1983; Poyner *et al.*, 1985) and Alice Coleman (1985), though the emphases of these two writers have been interestingly different.

Poyner's main thrust has been that the design of housing (and other aspects of urban areas) can influence crime rates by denying or offering opportunties for offending; his work is, therefore, within the tradition of 'situational crime prevention' (see Clarke and Mayhew, 1980; Heal and Laycock, 1986). Situational crime prevention is primarily oriented to the prevention of high area *offence rates*. It can lead to straightforward design-focused policies for crime prevention, and for this reason has an immediate attractiveness; moreover, there is some empirical evidence in support of it, for example in Allatt's (1984) study of target-hardening on a difficult-to-let council estate in Newcastle. However, the opportunity-based nature of this approach naturally raises the problem of displacement (which was apparent to some extent in Allatt's study), though the importance of displacement within situational crime prevention is a matter of some dispute (see Heal and Laycock, 1986, especially the chapters by Cornish and Clarke, Trasler, Bennet, and Heal and Laycock). Furthermore, since crime reduction is not the only goal of social policy, the broader social impact of opportunity-based policy suggestions needs to be considered; for example, Poyner's suggestion that, in the interests of burglary prevention,

'areas of wealthy or middle-class/middle-income housing should be separated as far as possible from poorer housing' (Poyner, 1983, p. 36)

—is clearly unlikely to appeal to those wishing to create a more egalitarian society, or to those concerned to foster a sense of common interest between people of different social classes and income levels.

Coleman's work, in some contrast to Poyner's, argues that the design of certain apartment blocks may encourage various forms of uncivilised behaviour among those who live in them, and, by extension, may also influence crime. These blocks, therefore, tend to 'breed anti-social people' (p. 133). Living in a high-rise block—

'does not force all its inhabitants to become criminals, but by creating anonymity, lack of surveillance, and escape routes, it puts temptation in their way and makes it probable that some of the weaker brethren will succumb' (p. 22.)

In short, in criminological terms Coleman's work emphasises primarily the influence of design on the production of *offender rates*. If her propositions were substantiated, they could perhaps be regarded as even more interesting than Poyner's work, since they would not be subject to possible displacement limitations. From our perspective, however, there are a number of problems with Coleman's research. There are some methodological queries about her interpretation of her own data; despite the rhetoric about 'crime' at various points in the book (see the quotation above), there are no data about crimes other than vandalism except in one short section (pp. 178–9); and most importantly of all, there is no satisfactory research consideration of relevant social variables (see Hope, 1986), so that Coleman is certainly not justified, on her data, in claiming that 'design appears to be *the chief factor* affecting the six types of social malaise' (p. 149, emphasis added).

None of this is intended to deny the potential importance of design in crime prevention in residential areas; the evidence does indeed suggest that design solutions can sometimes lead to crime reduction. But it is noteworthy that a recent North American review of empirical work in the 'defensible space' tradition has concluded that:

'simple effects of physical environment on crime range from small to moderate ... It appears that alteration of physical environment features cannot have stand-alone crime prevention effectiveness. Resident dynamics are the key mediators of the environment-crime linkage' (Taylor and Gottfredson, 1986).

If this view is correct (and we believe that it is), then the case for examining non-design-related crime prevention possibilities, linked to 'resident dynamics', looks strong. This is so despite the historic neglect of housing policy by criminologists.

Before looking in detail at crime prevention possibilities of this sort, it is important to consider, in a general and preliminary way, how non-design-related housing policies and offending behaviour might in principle be related. The key to this is the housing market (as defined above) and its allocative mechanisms, for it is these allocative mechanisms which bring together people and houses to create residential communities, and it is within such communities that much social behaviour, including crime, takes place. But the link between housing market allocation mechanisms and offending is not, as some have supposed, a simple once-for-all effect; rather it is an ongoing social process with three main aspects:

i. the immediate effects of allocating different groups in the population within the framework of a given housing market;

ii. the secondary or long-term effects of such allocations; and

iii. the consequences of changes in the market and/or its mechanisms of allocation.

These three aspects must be considered separately.

At any one point in time the housing market's allocative mechanisms will distribute groups of the population in specific ways. One key to this in Britain has been the policies pursued by each local authority, and how these policies have affected both the size of the public housing sector in a given city, and the criteria for access to the sector. These policies can affect the age, social class, ethnic, occupational, or family-type mix of those living in particular areas of public housing. Furthermore since such policies are largely determined at local level and in response to local conditions, there have been both local and regional variations in the results. In a similar way, access to the other housing sectors in Britain is partly determined by the policies of building societies in granting mortgages, and government policies with regard to private rentals. The effect on community offender rates of patterns of allocation *per se* will depend on the relative criminogenic potential of different groups, and how they are distributed within the housing market at one point in time. For example, if vandalism occurs disproportionately in housing areas of high child density (see Wilson, 1980), then an allocation process which concentrates families with young children in certain areas will tend to produce high vandalism offender and offence rates in those areas. It this were all that was involved, then we could influence the geographical distribution of offender rates by housing allocation, but not the overall crime rate. However, such a model takes no account of the dynamics of social process.

Allocation mechanism can influence not only the differential distribution of social groups within the housing market, but also the mix of groups within an area, and the social life they create. The interactive effects within and between groups, and/or the development of particular cultural patterns may be more criminogenically important than any initial propensity to offend. Furthermore, once the population of an area is allocated, and its community crime profile established, this will be further influenced by the wider social response to that community. In any case, some of the factors which may influence a community crime pattern as a result of allocation, such as age distribution, are not static. Allocation policies at one point in time, therefore, may have many indirect and longer-term effects. Even though many housing areas in post-war Britain have had relatively stable populations, this does not mean that they will necessarily have had stable residential community crime careers.

Equally important, allocation mechanisms and housing policies can, and have, changed over time. Sometimes the effects of such changes are intended: for example, a local authority making its housing more available to disadvantaged groups, or the building societies encouraging owner-occupation by lower-paid workers. However, the effects may also be unintended: for example, either of the above changes could alter the relative population stability of a local authority housing estate. The interplay of intended and unintended effects, both within a housing sector and between sectors, can produce complex long-term consequences for residential community crime careers in particular local areas.

If we are interested in influencing crime rates by housing-related policies, we must pay careful attention to these various effects. A residential community's crime career may be influenced by physical design or location; initial allocation; the interactive effects within and between groups in the community; the social reputation of the area and residents' response to that reputation; changes in allocation mechanisms; changes in general policies about forms of tenure; and so on. Hence, if we are to use interventionist housing policies to try to change a residential community crime career, we need to know something about the past history of the area—including the unintended past history—and what has given it its high criminality (offence- or offender-based). Only with such an understanding of a community's previous crime career can we begin to devise housing-related crime prevention programmes whose possible influence on crime has a degree of predictability.

Crime reduction strategies and housing areas

With the above framework as a background, how can one begin to move towards housing-related crime prevention strategies in residential areas in Britain?

The British housing stock has historically had three main tenure types, each of which has its own different market for property allocation. These three tenure types are owner-occupied housing (including mortgaged properties); privately rented housing; and housing rented from the local authority. In most British cities, the majority of houses in small local areas have tended to be of a single tenure type, so that the market has developed, in effect, 'tenure areas'. However, the relative size of the three main tenure types has varied a good deal historically. Since the Second World War there has been a huge growth in the owner-occupied sector, and a more modest growth in the local authority ('council') sector, with a concomitant decline in private rentals. Since 1980, however, the growth in the local authority sector has ceased, in response to central government policy. These are the overall national trends, but the relative sizes and rates of change of the three tenure types has varied considerably both regionally and locally. (For a much fuller discussion, see Bottoms and Wiles, 1986). As for crime, it has been shown that offence and offender rates vary both between and within tenures (see below), so, given this and the very different market mechanisms, it is important to discuss the three tenure types separately in considering crime prevention strategies. Since the largest series of relevant research studies has been conducted in Sheffield, the discussion will be based especially upon that work.

Owner-occupied housing areas

The majority of housing areas in Britain are owner-occupied. The Sheffield study showed that owner-occupied areas had uniformly low offender rates with little variation between areas (Baldwin and Bottoms, 1976), and such evidence as is available for other parts of the country confirms that owner-occupied areas have generally had low offender rates (Herbert, 1982). We will return later to whether this situation may change. In so far as the pattern remains unaltered, then strategies designed to reduce offender rates are obviously not very relevant in this tenure sector.

Owner-occupied areas, however, may have relatively high *offence* rates especially for burglary, household theft, and auto-theft. Such a situation is especially likely where owner-occupied areas are located near to high offender rate areas, or on main roads which are well known to potential offenders (see Brantingham and Brantingham, 1981). Also, the Sheffield study showed that offence rates of recorded burglary per 1000 dwellings were positively related to the rateable value, with a particularly high rate among the most affluent houses (Baldwin and Bottoms, 1976, p. 63). For such crimes, offence-reduction strategies have some obvious potential effectiveness. On the one hand 'target hardening' techniques can be used to make entry to the area more difficult ('sleeping policemen', etc.), houses harder to burgle (alarms, locks, etc.), or property more difficult to dispose of after theft (property and vehicle marking). On the other hand such communities can adopt a variety of tactics for communal defence from offenders from other areas, including 'neighbour-hood watch' schemes, encouragement of community policing or even the private employment of security firms.

Such policies may or may not, in practice, reduce offence rates in any given area: that is a matter for empirical testing. But given the 'communal defence' nature of the strategies (which will not of themselves necessarily reduce overall offending levels), displacement of offences to other areas must be a possibility (see e.g. Lowman, 1983). Additionally, one necessarily has to consider—as noted earlier—the potentially divisive social consequence of adopting some forms of 'communal defence'; the development of fortress-like housing complexes in some parts of the USA may not be an attractive example.

Private rental housing areas

The proportion of the housing stock in Britain which is privately rented has declined dramatically in the post-war period—from 62 per cent of all households in 1945 to 11 per cent in 1983. London still contains significant-sized private rental areas, but elsewhere rented houses are often scattered among owner-occupied or sometimes council properties, and private rental *areas* are small and rare. Where such areas do exist they are increasingly seen as temporary dwellings for tenants seeking either a mortgage or council accommodation, or those who are only resident in the city for a short period.

Historically the offender rates of privately rented areas varied greatly, but with the decline of the tenure, and its increasing marginalisation, it is probably the case—there is no adequate research—that most privately rented areas outside London now have high offender rates. Also, some private rental areas, because of their marginal status and the availability of short tenancies, are a prime location for the supply of illegal goods and services such as drugs and prostitution.

What crime prevention initiatives can be attempted in private rental areas as at present constituted? If these areas are now mainly of the kind we have postulated, they will probably have high offender rates (see above, and note also the likely over-representation of young single males among a transient population), and also high offence rates fostered by such features as multi-occupation of large houses (rendering burglaries relatively easy) and considerable garaging of cars on the street. That being the case, such areas differ importantly from the owner-occupied areas previously discussed, and the crime-reductive strategies mentioned for owner-occuped areas may have only limited applicability. Moreover, one obvious possible reduction strategy for an area of high population turnover—namely stabilisation of residence, a strategy sometimes used within the local authority sector—is scarcely available in this context since the economic role of the area is precisely to provide short-term accommodation.

In practice, few major recent area-based crime prevention initiatives in Britain seem to have focused on privately rented areas, and these areas are now so few that no general strategy likely to prove successful can be readily suggested. Rather, any local strategy would have to depend upon a close examination of the features of the particular area within the context of its particular local town and its housing market.

In Sheffield, the main crime prevention strategies developed in one high offender and offence rate, privately rented area have been complicated by the area's role as the principal red-light district for the city, and its (non-crime-related) designation as a Housing Action Area under the Housing Act 1974. Crime prevention techniques used in this area have included policing initiatives, and the creation of access difficulties for motorists (road schemes, one-way streets, and 'sleeping policemen') designed *inter alia* to inhibit 'kerb-crawling'. None of these techniques seems to have had clear success, though the initiatives have not been fully researched (for a much fuller account, see Bottoms and Wiles, 1986). An issue raised in relation to this area, which may be of more general applicability for some other privately rented districts, is how far the supply of illegal services (prostitution and drugs) can be successfully suppressed, rather than displaced; or whether, if displacement occurs, displacement to a non-residential form (rather than to another residential area) is feasible or desirable (see also Lowman, 1986).

Local authority housing areas

Given the previous anlaysis, it will be clear that high *offender* rate areas in Britain are now generally speaking concentrated in the local authority sector. And, as with private rental tenures, research in Sheffield has shown that there is in general a correlation between offender and offence rates in residential areas, so that high offender rate council estates also have high crime.

It might be tempting to conclude that local authority tenure is *per se* criminogenic, but this is in fact totally false. There is huge variation in the offender and offence rates of different council estates, ranging from very high to very low. This variation is in part class-related (i.e., comparing the estates in their proportions of skilled working class to unskilled working class), but more detailed research in Sheffield has shown conclusively that two estates of almost identical social class composition can have very different offender and offence rates (Bottoms *et al.*, 1987). Design variables, too, though not definitively studied, certainly do not show straightforward associations with offender and offence rates.

The most interesting areas for analysis are of course the local authority estates with high offender and offence rates: these seem, at least at first sight, to be the most obvious target within the British housing market for intervention with crime reduction techniques which are not just defensive in nature. It is worth noting that such estates probably constitute no more than 5–10 per cent of residential areas in the country, and therefore strategies can be targeted in a highly specific way. However, it is also important to realise that such estates are by no means all the same, whether in terms of social composition, or architecture and design variables, or their history.

From the Sheffield research it has been possible to identify at least three different kinds of local authority high offender and offence rate estates; further research in Sheffield or elsewhere might well identify additional types. It is worth discussing the three Sheffield estates in a little detail, as a basis for subsequent discussion of housing-related crime prevention strategies.

The Blackacre estate. This (housing) estate was built in the 1930s as a specifically slum-clearance estate. A group of residents was transferred into it *en bloc* from an inner-city area with a highly criminal reputation; the area then developed, and retained, a high offender rate and an active criminal sub-culture. The estate had considerable residential stability: at the time of a 1972 survey, more than half the families had lived there for more than thirty years (see Baldwin, 1974).

The Gardenia estate. This (housing) estate was built under earlier legislation than Blackacre, but also in the inter-war period. It began life as a select estate for the artisan section of the working class, and was a model 'garden-city' estate of the period. Sometime in the 1940s, for now unknown reasons, it 'tipped' and became a highly criminal estate, again with an active, if mild, criminal sub-culture. Like Blackacre, it has considerable residential stability: at the time of a 1975 survey, half the residents had lived there for more than fifteeen years (see Bottoms and Xanthos, 1981).

The Skyhigh estate. This estate of high-rise flats was opened in the 1960s. It has one central multi-storey block, surrounded by some lower-rise blocks. It did not easily achieve residential stability; at the time of a 1975 survey a quarter of its residents had lived there less than two years, and three-quarters expressed a wish to leave. It had many complaints from its residents about litter, vandalism, etc., and was the most unpopular estate in Sheffield. Its official crime data were also high, although not as high as Blackacre or Gardenia; and the ratio of survey crime to official crime was particularly high (Bottoms *et al.*, 1987). In the late 1970s it was the subject of a stabilisation programme by the Sheffield Housing Department because of its 'difficult-to-let' status (see Bottoms and Xanthos, 1981).

What policy implications flow from these three types of high crime areas? Blackacre shows the danger of transplanting an existing criminal culture *en bloc*. When the populations of such areas are being rehoused, a policy of dispersal may be appropriate where family ties, etc. permit. Gardenia well illustrates the problem of 'tipping' in the crime career of a residential community. The task here is a dual one: first of identification that tipping is occurring, and secondly implementing policies to prevent it. Early identification requires careful and sensitive monitoring, perhaps of crime data, if available, but certainly of applications to leave the estate and potential tenants' refusals of offers of accommodation on the estate. Once identified, then remedial measures against tipping could include careful selection of new residents for a period, encouragement of positive features of community life on the estate, and publicity for desirable developments on the estate to offset any adverse reputation. If identified early enough, such measures may halt the 'tipping' process.

However, Blackacre and Gardenia have now developed settled criminal sub-cultures. Policies to reduce crime in such cases are extremely difficult. An attempt has been made in Gardenia to tackle the problem by a social work programme with children on the estate, but there is no published evaluation of this. More generally the projects run by NACRO and PEP on difficult estates may seem to offer some possibilities, though it is doubtful whether the mechanisms they use are really appropriate for the tackling of crime issues on a stable criminally sub-cultural estate. The social stability of these estates, together with the link between criminal activity and the black economy, makes social change particularly difficult.

In the case of Skyhigh, a socially highly unstable area with a high crime profile, stabilisation would appear to be the obvious solution, and might be successful, but runs the risk of creating a stable criminal sub-culture like Gardenia. One could try to guard against it by attempts to attract stable, non-criminal groups into the area. This would be allied to a general programme to increase the satisfaction of existing tenants by a mixture of physical management and social interventions. This would, of course, be not dissimilar to the strategies adopted by PEP and NACRO on difficult council estates.

The PEP and NACRO policies certainly represent the most important crime reduction strategies which have been attempted within the local authority sector (see Chapter 6 in this volume by Rock). On the basis of existing research work, these strategies appear to contain considerable promise for crime reduction (see Hedges et al., 1980; Burbidge, 1984), though this promise has not been definitely confirmed in research terms. From our point of view, however, the fact that apparently some crime reduction has been achieved in some estates is interesting but ultimately unsatisfying. What we really need to know, and usually do not, is precisely what kind of local authority areas (in terms of the sort of typologies discussed above) were involved in the action programmes, and how success or otherwise in crime reduction was related to this typology.

Ideally, in the future, one would like to see research developments whereby the kind of estate is identified with some precision (on variables such as offender rate, offence rate, vandalism in public spaces, tenant turnover, letting difficulty, rent level, design features, and history of the estate), and this is then related to particular kinds of intervention, to test for crime reduction effects. Even then one would also have to monitor the development for unintended consequences as well as for expected outcomes.

It could be argued that this ideal strategy is too expensive and difficult. If so, a less ambitious alternative which could be attempted straightaway would be first, to reconsider the existing NACRO and PEP experience in the light of a more sophisticated typology of types of estate; and secondly to identify theoretically some key types of local authority estate, decide on what is the most appropriate likely intervention for each type, and then run some model crime prevention projects with full evaluation.

Speculation about the future

The discussion so far has focused upon residential community crime careers within the three major tenure types in Britain, and the possible crime reduction strategies they suggest, based on research carried out in the 1970's. Although process and change within tenure types have been discussed, macro-level changes in the housing market as a whole, and their effects on tenure type, allocation and crime have not been mentioned. At the broadest level, however, housing policy influences the overall structure of the relevant markets and can therefore affect the crime career of residential areas—consider, for example, the indirect effects of the policies which led to the shrinkage of the private rental sector, as discussed above. These broad housing policy considerations are especially important at present, since recent government policy has in part been designed to change tenure distribution away from the local authority sector and towards owner-occupation.

There is at present no research evidence concerning the consequences of these recent changes for residential community crime careers. However, it is worthwhile offering some speculative comments about this matter, especially since this will highlight research which now needs to be undertaken.

The post-war period has seen a continual growth of the *owner-occupied sector* aided by gentrification of previously privately rented property, and more recently by the privatisation of public housing. One interesting speculation is whether the expansion of owner-occupation is itself offender-reductive. Such an effect might be thought to occur *either* because owning increases occupiers' freedom and control over their housing (a parallel notion to that which underlies NACRO crime reduction strategies in council estates), *or* because owner-occupation helps to develop a set of social values which is inimical to crime commission. There is some tentative correlational support for an effect of this kind (Herbert, 1982, pp. 87–8), but nobody would claim this to be decisive. If owner-occupation in and of itself does not reduce potential offender rates, then the further expansion of this sector will undoubtedly produce differential offender rates *within* the sector. Should this happen, then the price mechanism will probably produce in some areas the kind of criminal tipping consequences we have already observed in the public sector. In such a case the policy interventions to prevent tipping by controlling population movements (as in the public sector) would, because of the different allocation mechanisms, not be available. Nevertheless, other strategies which use public funds might be possible: these include improvements grants, housing action area status, and the fostering of housing associations.

Housing associations are, in legal tenure form, private rentals, but their allocation mechanisms can be administrative, and they therefore offer the kinds of population controls previously discussed for the local authority areas (see Donnison and Ungerson, 1982). Though relatively few properties in Britain are let by housing associations, this proportion has increased in recent years, and housing associations now take a significant proportion of the central government expenditure on housing. The combination of central government intervention in local housing stock, plus private management at a local level, together with the fact that housing associations tend to be encouraged to operate especially in a rehabilitative role in relatively run-down housing environments, suggests that they may potentially have a considerable part to play in future housing-related crime prevention policies in Britain.

Although there have been recent suggestions to revitalise the *private rental sector* (National Federation of Housing Associations, 1985) all the signs are that this is unlikely to happen. If private rental areas continue to disappear, then the marginal social groups they currently cater for will either have to be absorbed into the public sector, or be dispersed to individual private rental properties within owner-occupied areas. In the first case local authority regulation would make it difficult for illicit goods and services to be provided in such a setting, and in the latter case resident pressures might also prevent such provision, though both of these constraints could be weakened if an area became residual within its tenure market. The most likely result is perhaps that such crimes will move to non-residential locations or develop new forms (see Bottoms and Wiles, 1986).

The shifts in tenure patterns which have been discussed may have particularly interesting effects on crime patterns on *local authority estates*. In regions where owner-occupation expands dramatically, public housing could become a residual tenure and would carry with it the danger of re-creating the Victorian criminal ghettoes. The potential implications of this for urban disorder are obvious. A more likely immediate possibility is that privatisation of local authority housing stock will be uneven. In many areas, of course, the better estates with low offender rates are the most likely to become owner-occupied. However, it is possible that some estates will only partly change tenure. We know that even on estates which generally have either high or low offender rates, there can be small areas which differ from the general pattern. Such differences could now be reinforced by differential legal status, and this could produce quite new social conflicts within such estates. On the one hand, a growth of owner-occupation on an estate might produce improvements in an area which local authority management could reinforce, as part of a crime-reduction strategy, provided the position in the local authority as a whole allowed them to provide allocative support against tipping. On the other hand, a growth of owner-occupation in only one part of an estate might produce a separate owner-occupier culture which would not co-operate with such local authority policies. The effect of this might be to split the estate into two distinct areas with different offender rates, and possibly different community crime careers.

These recent developments in housing policy, because they vary regionally, open up very interesting research possibilities. The research community should, if possible, begin to compare residential community crime patterns in regions in which the owner-occupied sector has grown to a wholly dominant position, with those in regions where this has not occurred. We are, in effect, being presented with a naturally occurring experimental situation in different parts of Britain, which should allow us to understand much more fully the interaction between the housing market and residential community crime careers, and hence also the differing crime prevention possibilities in different kinds of housing area.

Conclusion

The previous section has dealt with the macro-economic and national political dimensions of housing policy, and shown their possible links to residential community crime careers. It should be obvious from this discussion that residential community crime careers, at least in part, are a product of both national and local housing policies. Nevertheless, housing policies have been the result of many considerations other than community crime levels. A history of post-war British housing policy would not highlight crime reduction as having been, in any serious sense, a specific goal helping to drive policy (for example, Donnison and Ungerson's (1982) authoritative book on housing policy does not cite 'crime' in its index at all). The consequences of this has been that the effects of changing housing policies on residential community crime careers have been largely unintended.

However, this situation has begun to change, not least as a result of a housing-crime link having been identified by some policy-makers as associated with the disorders in areas such as Brixton (1981 and 1985) and Broadwater Farm (1985). Hence, crime reduction is now on the agenda of housing policy, though not necessarily in a dominant position on that agenda.

Criminologists are, in some respects, bound to welcome this shift; for criminological research could inform housing policy-makers of the likely criminogenic consequences of their policy options. At another level, however, there is a danger that thinking about crime and housing may become far too narrowly focused, and this may in the end inhibit true crime reduction. The reason crime reduction as such featured so little in post-war housing policy was because the main goal of that policy was to improve the quality of social life and this would, so it was believed, *inter alia* reduce crime. The fact is, however, that this broad attempt to improve social life did not reduce crime. That may have been because the policies to improve the quality of life were misconceived, and/or because the link to crime was more complex than had been assumed: there is some evidence to support both of these views. One result of these failures is that broad, large-scale planning no longer commands the widespread support that it did in the immediate post-war period. We are learning a proper respect for keeping our plans to a scale which can maintain contact with what citizens actually prefer, and over which they can exercise some control. But smallness of scale and modesty of objectives are not the same as lack of vision, and we believe that an overall social vision remains essential as one considers the links between crime and housing. By contrast, some crime reduction ideas have conceived of crime in a very particularistic way, ignoring its relationship to the broader fabric of people's lives. Some proponents of crime reduction in residential areas have focused on one causal variable, or even worse one correlational variable, to the exclusion of all else. It is possible to reduce some offence rates, or even some offender rates, by specifically targeted crime reduction strategies, but, as previously indicated, we must also evaluate the broader social implications of these strategies, for in the end short-term crime prevention may not be worth a massive increase in, for example, residential social divisiveness.

It is worth developing this point a little more generally. In the early 1970s Albert Reiss (1971) introduced the concept of 'civility' into the criminological literature; he took the concept from the work of Edward Shils (1962), who had argued that the development of a truly civilised society necessitates civility in mundane, day-to-day human interaction. Reiss used this idea in a study of policing by proposing that a good police force was one whose contact with citizens developed civility, and argued that this was most likely to occur when policing was a reactive response to citizens demand. Shils's concept, and Reiss's use of it, was an attempt to produce policy proposals which operationalised an answer to the question posed by political philosophy; 'What is the good society?' Reiss was thereby insisting that any answer to specific questions about policing policy, or crime reduction, must be set within a philosophy of the overall purpose of government. Crime reduction, therefore, should not be conceived simply in negative terms as a lower incidence of some offences, but also positively as part of the attempt to create a more civilised and ordered society.

A complaint made by a number of writers (see e.g. Habermas, 1976) is that modern advanced industrialised societies have turned basic philosophical or moral questions about human association into purely technical questions of instrumental rationality. The fate of the concept of 'civility' in criminology is in danger of following this pattern. Some recent American criminological writers have suggested that residential areas with high crime rates are distinguished by lack of civility because this lack creates fear which weakens informal social control, and so allows crime to develop unchecked (see Wilson and Kelling, 1982). This thesis has been operationalised by some researchers using incivility indices which are partly social (public drinking, drug use, and unruly children) and partly physical (litter, graffiti, broken windows, etc.). The claim is then made that if these particular indices are corrected, then crime will be reduced, or prevented from developing (for a summary, see Taylor and Gottfredson, 1986). The danger with this approach is that a theory of crime reduction which was capable of locating its policies within a broader notion of the purpose of government has been transformed into a simple mechanistic theory of physical repairs and potentially petty social control. By contrast, this paper has sought to argue for an approach to housing-based crime-reduction strategies in residential ares which sets such strategies in the wider context of housing policy and its broader social goals and purposes.

[The authors wish to express their gratitude to Susan J. Smith for her helpful comments on an earlier draft of this paper.]

References

ALLATT, P. (1984). 'Residential security: containment and displacement of burglary'. *Howard Journal of Criminal Justice*, 23, pp. 99–116.

BALDWIN, J. (1974). 'Problem housing estates: perceptions of tenants, city officials and criminologists'. *Social and Economic Administration*, 8, pp. 116–135.

BALDWIN, J. and BOTTOMS, A. E. (1976). *The Urban Criminal*. London: Tavistock.

BOTTOMS, A. E., MAWBY, R. I. and WALKER, M. A. (1987). 'A localised crime survey in contrasting areas of a city'. *British Journal of Criminology*, 27, pp. 125–154.

BOTTOMS, A. E. and WILES, P. (1986). 'Housing tenure and residential community crime careers in Britain'. In Reiss, A.J., Jr., and Tonry, M. (Eds.), *Communities and Crime*. Chicago: University of Chicago Press.

BOTTOMS, A. E. and XANTHOS, P. (1981). 'Housing policy and crime in the British public sector'. In Brantingham, P. J. and Brantingham, P. L. (Eds.), *Environmental Criminology*. Beverly Hills: Sage Publications.

BRANTINGHAM, P. L. and BRANTINGHAM, P. J. (1981). 'Notes on the geometry of crime'. In Brantingham, P.J. and Brantingham, P.L. (Eds.), *Environmental Criminology*. Beverly Hills: Sage Publications.

BURBIDGE, M. (1984). 'British public housing and crime: a review'. In Clarke, R. and Hope, T. (Eds.), *Coping with Burglary*. Boston: Kluwer-Nijhoff.

CLARKE, R. V. G. and MAYHEW, P. (Eds.), (1980). *Designing Out Crime*. London: HMSO.

COLEMAN, A. (1985). *Utopia on Trial*. London: Hilary Shipman.

DONNISON, D. and UNGERSON, C. (1982). *Housing Policy*. London: Penguin.

HABERMAS, J. (1976). *Legitimation Crisis*. London: Heinemann.

HEAL, K. and LAYCOCK, G. (Eds.), (1986). *Situational Crime Prevention: from theory into practice*. London: HMSO.

HEDGES, A., BLABER, A. and MOSTYN, B. (1980). *Community Planning Project: Cunningham Road Improvement Scheme*. London: Social and Community Planning Research.

HERBERT, D. T. (1982). *The Geography of Urban Crime*. London: Longman.

HOPE, T. (1986). 'Crime, community and environment'. *Journal of Environmental Psychology*, 6, pp. 65–78.

LOWMAN, J. (1983). 'Target hardening, burglary prevention and the problem of displacement phenomena'. In Fleming, T. and Visano, L. A. (Eds.), *Deviant Designations: Crime, Law and Deviance in Canada*. Toronto: Butterworths.

LOWMAN, J. (1986). 'Prostitution in Vancouver: some notes on the genesis of a social problem'. *Canadian Journal of Criminology*, 28, pp. 1–16.

MAWBY, R. I. (1979). *Policing the City*. Westmead: Saxon House.

MAWBY, R. I. (1984). 'Vandalism and public perceptions of vandalism in contrasting residential areas'. In Levy-Leboyer, C. (Ed.), *Vandalism*. Amsterdam: North-Holland.

MORRIS, T. (1957). *The Criminal Area*. London: Routledge and Kegan Paul.

NATIONAL FEDERATION OF HOUSING ASSOCIATIONS (1985). *Enquiry into British Housing*. London: NFHA.

NEWMAN, O. (1972). *Defensible Space: crime prevention through urban design*. New York: Macmillan.

POYNER, B. (1983). *Design against Crime*. London: Butterworth.

POYNER, B., HELSON, P. and WEBB, B. (1985). *Layout of Residential Areas and its Influence on Crime*. London: Tavistock Institute of Human Relations.

REISS, A. J., Jr. (1971). *The Police and the Public*. New Haven: Yale University Press.

REISS, A. J., Jr. (1986). 'Why are communities important in understanding crime?'. In Reiss, A.J., Jr., and Tonry, M. (Eds.), *Communities and Crime*. Chicago: University of Chicago Press.

SHILS, E. A. (1962). 'The Theory of mass society'. *Diogenes*, 39, pp. 45–66.

TAYLOR, R. B. and GOTTFREDSON, S. (1986). 'Environmental design, crime and prevention: an examination of community dynamics'. In Reiss, A. J., Jr., and Tonry, M. (Eds.)., *Communities and Crime*. Chicago: University of Chicago Press.

WILSON, J. Q. and KELLING, G. L. (1982). 'Broken windows: the police and neighbourhood safety'. *Atlantic Monthly*, 249, pp. 29–38.

WILSON, S. (1980). 'Vandalism and defensible space on London housing estates'. In Clarke, R. V. G. and Mayhew, P. (Eds.), *Designing Out Crime*. London: HMSO.

6. Crime reduction initiatives on problem estates

Paul Rock

Recent British initiatives to reduce crime on problem housing estates have taken three principal forms: work conducted by the National Association for the Care and Resettlement of Offenders has focused on the creation and maintenance of 'neighbourliness' in weak, demoralised communities: the Department of the Environment has concentrated on the reform and decentralisation of housing management and repairs: and the Land Use Research Unit has attended to the physical remodelling of poor architecture. Their work is of major interest because it promise to diminish rates of crime and make unpleasant conditions more tolerable. It has been discussed in a number of reports but many of its aims, assumptions and practices remain quite obscure. It seemed important to discover more about the initiatives.

The problem

This chapter explores some facets of the new wave of initiatives on council housing estates in England and Wales, giving special attention to their explicit and implicit ideas of social relations. In a policy environment permeated by the belief that little or nothing works, the initiatives promise a remarkable ability to reduce crime. Intervention is taking place on an ambitious scale although it is not always clear what processes are actually at work.

Alice Coleman has argued that 'the twentieth century in Britain has been split in two by a great revolution in housing' (Colemen, 1985) and, indeed, the substantial provision of local authority housing is really quite new. Councils began building in the 1880s and were to own some 20,000 dwellings in 1914 (Power, 1985). By 1977, 30 per cent of the seventeen million dwellings in England were publicly owned (Mayhew and Clarke, 1982). Recent movements to build were driven first by the slum clearance programmes of the 1930s; then by the rehabilitation of derelict, bombed areas after the Second World War; and finally by massive, utopian social engineering in the 1960s and early 1970s. The proportion of single schemes swelled over time as building techniques became industrialised; arguments were advanced about potential economies of scale; confidence and experience were acquired in huge planning; architects were given a chance to create 'design fantasies' (Power, 1985) and make their 'mark as impressively as possible' (Coleman, 1985); financial rewards were offered by the government for building high and large; and a few contractors acquired an oligopolistic position in the housing market.

Styles of management echoed the pattern of growth: political re-organisation, mass building projects and a commitment to substantial administrative structures enlarged the average number of properties controlled by each authority from 1400 after the Second World War to 14,000 in 1975. The larger authorities became the owners of between 20,000 and 30,000 units

(Power, 1981). As ever-growing organisations were instructed to search for more economic management strategies from 1963 onwards, so they began to concentrate power and activity at the centre (Power, 1985). Staff were taken away from the estates: 'over the last 15 years, many local authorities, mainly in urban areas, have withdrawn rent collectors, resident caretakers, repairs men and managers to central offices or town halls' (Department of the Environment, 1984).

The problem of the local authority estate took time to emerge. Slums were so patently offensive that their destruction and replacement could not be anything but intrinsically right. For a long while, too, it seems to have been assumed that many social problems, and the problems of the slums in particular, were largely material in origin and that an improvement of a physical environment must bring about eventual social regeneration. Difficulties on new estates were ascribed to the transitional troubles of 'settling' (Reynolds, 1986). There was obvious merit in that assumption, but it was not subjected to much scrutiny and the consequences of rehousing in this fashion and to this extent were neither controlled nor assessed until very late. Like many other sizeable pieces of social change in Britain, the 'great revolution in housing' was allowed to occur without visible management or monitoring. Poor designs were 'used repeatedly before their unsuitability became apparent' (Department of the Environment, 1981). Most councils did not establish specialised housing departments for some fifty years (Power, 1986) and professional housing management was in abeyance. Power observed, 'local authorities were undertaking a task they had never set out to accomplish. Building decent homes and clearing slums had been an objective. Running them as good landlords had not' (Power, 1985).

To be sure, a few estates did acquire an early local notoriety. Some were initially occupied by outsiders who never seemed to become absorbed because of their strangeness and the physical isolation and marginality of their housing (Herbert, 1979; Reynolds, 1986). Miscalculations and congestion in the planning process made it difficult to let large portions of other new estates and, being unlet, they began to appear unkempt and devalued, plunged into a 'self-fuelling decline' (Priorities Estates Project, 1985). A number were stigmatised from the first because they housed marked people from slum clearance schemes (Gill, 1977; Armstrong and Wilson, 1973).

But the more general and disembodied issue of 'problem', 'difficult', or 'run-down' local authority estates was a little slow in becoming translated into a political problem. In part, there was most probably a presumption that building design and community organisation must be innocent of blame. Indeed, the architecture and planning of the new estates had been lauded as adventurous exercises in communal engineering. If things went awry it could be argued that 'problem' estates merely imported the older difficulties of people who had been associated with social problems even before they had been moved. Many estates were sited at a distance from centres of population or were constructed as enclosed, separate and distinct areas of what was virtually private space (Power, 1985). Damer actually called his 'Wine Alley' a 'dreadful enclosure' (Damer, 1974) Estates attained a kind of ecological isolation, apart from other neighbourhoods, their doings invisible to all but those who had good reasons to intrude. They shielded problems from outsiders, and outsiders often shunned them (Power, 1986). And even those whose business it was to be instrusive sometimes refrained from entering the larger estates. Although one useful definition of the problem estate is that it 'causes problems for the authorities' (Reynolds, 1986), the problem estate may receive inattention as well. From time to time, the police appeared reluctant to move into areas which were neither public nor private but marked by an anomalous 'semi-privacy' (Wilson, 1982; NACRO 1983). Residents talked about a lack of effective policing and, indeed, the police themselves regarded the problem estates as communities of discredited and possibly dangerous people. Further, the centralisation and consolidation of housing services estranged landlord from tenant, encouraging residents to think that they were 'neglected and ignored by an inaccessible bureaucracy' (Bright and Petterson, undated). Slum clearance may have transformed private tenants into public problems (Wilson, 1963) but it could lead to a decline in routine surveillance.

What seems finally to have galvanised a political response was an analytic shift that was made compelling by a succession of provocative incidents. The shift was prompted by Oscar Newman's work on 'defensible space' (Newman, 1972), a book which began to be read widely in America and the United Kingdom. Newman promoted a new sensitivity to the part played by design in shaping behaviour. He gave intellectual organisation to the relations between rising crime, an apparent decline of neighbourhood life and the emergence of high-rise buildings (Hope, 1986). He brought about the rediscovery and subsequent importance of Jane Jacobs's writing on space and control (Jacobs, 1961). There was an elective affinity between his ideas and those stirring in the Home Office Research Unit (Clarke, 1982; Poyner, 1983). Poyner, Wilson (Wilson, 1978), Coleman (Coleman, 1985) and NACRO (Osborn, 1986) were all influential in lending structure to the spate of British initiatives and they all acknowledge their borrowings from Newman's work. Several spectacular incidents, and the collapse of Ronan Point, in particular, dramatised the problem of the difficult estate. They seemed to signal and feed a growing consumer revolt. There were reports in the early 1970s that councils were being forced to advertise vacant accommodation in unpopular estates (Power, 1985). On some estates, too, it become apparent that there would never be an unaided transition to the once anticipated phase of 'settling' (Reynolds, 1986). Surveys of hard-to-let and troublesome estates were commissioned by the Department of the Environment in 1974, 1976 and 1978. Partly in response to the disclosures made by those surveys (Power, 1985) initiatives were started. NACRO began the pioneering Cunningham Road Improvement Scheme in 1976 (Hedges, Blaber and Mostyn, undated). The Priority Estates Project was founded in 1979. The Greater London Council funded the Safe Neighbourhoods Unit in 1980. Alice Coleman's Land Use Research Unit embarked on its own mammoth survey of problem estates.

In a dialectical process characteristic of the natural history of many social problems, the political designations of an issue as troubling led to a phase of investigation that gave new urgency and clarity to a once vague phenomenon. The process moved on to be amplified by other incidents including riots, and the riot on the Broadwater Farm Estate especially. Difficult estates inevitably loomed large once the gaze was no longer averted. Some 300,000 dwellings or 5 per cent of the local authority stock were to be classified by the Department of the Environment as 'difficult-to-let' (although 'difficult-to-let' and 'problem' estates were not necessarily taken to be interchangeable) (Burbidge, 1984). The estates came to be seen as distinct entities beset by a mass of conspicuous troubles. In some measure, they became the new rookeries of criminal areas marked off by 'unhelpful myths' (NACRO, 1983). The Brantinghams captured the matter nicely, English 'criminal areas near the city center prior to World War II have leapfrogged in a way not predicted at all ... The answer ... is now seen in the fact of government entry into the housing market' (Brantingham and Brantingham, 1981).

The description

Surveys and initiatives furnished a cluster of linked portraits of the problem estate and the portraits were themselves something of an encoded explanation of what had gone wrong and what needed to be done. Running through them is the theme of 'anomie' although the actual word seems never to have been used. An instance is Burbidge's description, 'poor and slow repairs, unlet and boarded-up dwellings, unswept litter and refuse, not only make for resident dissatisfaction, but also provide an invitation to crime and vandalism. Residents see an uncontrolled environment outside their front doors and fear crime' (Burbidge, 1984). The Priority Estates Project wrote of the Norley Hall Estate in Wigan: 'the now familiar picture has emerged of a concentration of disadvantaged people, outward signs of decay, decreasing confidence in the council, and more residents placing their long-term hopes in a move away rather than any improvement in the estate' (Priority Estates Project, 1985).

Description emanating from those initiatives turns repeatedly around the same features. Physically, the problem estate is large, consisting of some 200 or more dwellings (Power, 1986) clearly insulated from their environment by material and symbolic boundaries. Outside London, that isolation may be reinforced by the geographical distance that separates many of the satellite estates from older centres of population. Internally, the estates are composed of substantial tracts of what has become known as 'confused space', areas whose ownership, custody and character are uncertain, readily accessible to outsiders and difficult to superintend. The huge open areas around some large blocks may be confused. So may the numerous walkways, communal areas, staircases, garages and gardens of flatted estates. Confused space is impersonal, belonging to no one, and the clear responsibility of no one. The result can be an unpatrolled 'no man's land' in which dogs, children and anonymous groups of adolescents congregate and roam (NACRO, 1983).

There are other ways in which design exacerbates problems of control. Flimsy locks, doors and windows make people 'feel insecure within their flats' (Bright and Petterson, undated). The maintenance of 'defensible space' requires a continuous stream of decisions about the significance of movement and position, but there can be no effective supervision when entrances give promiscuous access to large numbers of dwellings (Coleman, 1985). Long interlocking corridors and balconies do little to regulate the flow of people. Concealed turnings and recesses, and rooms, lifts and garages hidden from public view, resist monitoring, appear menacing, and invite damage and clandestine activity. They attract drug users, drunks and young people who may behave in a manner that others find disturbing.

Problem estates are typically presented as dilapidated, unkempt and badly maintained. Thus a Priority Estates Project survey report of twenty estate management projects stated baldly, 'all the estates had a neglected and rubbish-strewn environment ...' (Department of the Environment, 1984). Many estates had a large number of empty, often vandalised properties. There was an extensive problem of deliberate damage and graffiti (Coleman, 1985). Repairs were usually dilatory, inefficient and haphazard, administered by a staff and management working from a distant office. The Safe Neighbourhoods Unit observed, 'tenants on many estates feel that much of the problem of poor housing services lies in the simple fact that there is often no person(s) responsible for, or resident in, each block, whose job it is to care for it, clean it, patrol it and report repairs. Some councils ... employ no resident staff at all' (Safe Neighbourhoods Unit, 1985).

The description has a demographic emphasis: local populations, patterns of demand, allocation policies and transfers will combine to give a particular character to problem estates. The residents will often be very young (Power, 1986; Bright and Petterson, undated) and youth is associated with high levels of petty crime and vandalism (Wilson, 1980). There will be an unusual concentration of one-parent families who find it difficult to superintend their young, being obliged to delegate informal control during the children's adolescence to groups of peers (Coleman, 1985). The residents will often include a collection of somewhat disparate marginalised groups, composed in various proportions of ethnic minorities, squatters, the unemployed, the very poor, the elderly, the youthful, the transient, ex-prisoners, former mental patients, gypsies and travellers (Zipfel, 1985; Department of the Environment, 1984).

Disparate populations plagued by diverse problems do not necessarily share an identity (Newman, 1981; Power, 1985). On the contrary, neighbours can be a source of disunity. The styles of different generations and groups often jar. People may be anxious about one another, regarding one another as a source of trouble. Fear of crime, irritation and mistrust can then breed when residents, often in personal hardship, become estranged. Reynolds devoted an entire chapter of her study of a problem housing estate to 'neighbour trouble': relations with neighbours were a major determinant of satisfaction with the estate and there was a discernible group who 'specifically caused annoyance, property damage, even fear and suffering, to those living around them' (Reynolds, 1986). Remedies are not always readily available. The poor, vulnerable and troubled are not the best candidates for major voluntary initiatives or self-help. Divided neighbours may not imagine that they have the authority, mandate or competence to interfere in each others' lives. Moreover there can only be the most modest development of co-operation in such a divided world: 'it was hard to collaborate with neighbours who were often seen as part of the problem' (Power, 1985).

Finally, the problem estates suffer from acute criminal victimisation. Crime is preponderantly urban, and it swells exceptionally in certain estates in the inner city (Herbert, 1979) and the demoralised satellite estates. Fifty-five per cent of the residents of Reynolds's 'Omega Estate' had been victims of some crime in the two years before her study (Reynolds, 1986). The Stamford Hill Estate was described by the Safe Neighbourhoods Unit as having 'extensive vandalism, abandoned cars, burglaries ...' (Safe Neighbourhoods Unit, 1985b). More generally, the British Crime Survey of 1981 made it clear that local authority dwellings are much more vulnerable than other kinds of housing to residential burglary, 'theft in dwelling', 'other household thefts' and theft of bicycles. Significant victimisation is married to significant offending: the council sector in Sheffield also had the highest offender rate (Bottoms and Xanthos, 1981). Much naïve crime is committed within a very short radius of the offender's home (Baldwin and Bottoms, 1976) and the residents of estates are not infrequently the prey of their neighbours. Indeed, high levels of victimisation tend generally to be accompanied by high levels of offending. Fellow residents were sometimes a problem but police were believed to be reluctant to accept anonymous calls (Power, 1986b) and reporting might lead to retribution (Reynolds, 1986). The outcome is a marked fearfulness allied to a distrust of neighbours. A further outcome could be a sense of powerlessness coupled with a loss of will: ' "defensible space" does not automatically operate in a very poor, demoralised community, residents can simply give up all attempts at guarding or caring for their own property' (Power, 1985). So constituted, problem estates acquire a symbolic identity that can be amplified by experience, in gossip and in press reports. They can appear awesome even to their own residents.

The initiatives

The initiatives mustered to deal with the problem estates reflected their distinctive mandates. The National Association for the Care and Resettlement of Offenders is concerned with crime and the criminal justice system. Its work on problem estates flowed out of a meeting on crime and architecture that was one of a series of conferences on crime and the professions. Its first project began in 1976 on a 'heavily vandalised and unpopular estate in Widnes' (Osborn, 1982). The Crime Prevention Unit was established in 1979 and the Safe Neighbourhoods Unit in 1980. By 1985, that latter unit had worked on nineteen estates in five inner London boroughs. Its aims were to confront vandalism and more minor crime by 'involving the residents on demoralised estates in planning improvements in such a way that they will feel inclined to maintain and protect them' (NACRO, 1982). The victimisation and decay of problem estates were explained by a lack of pride, co-operation, power and cohesion and the remedy was held to lie in a restoration of structure and purpose. 'Estate improvement programmes' were to be co-ordinated in liaison with different agencies and with 'tenant participation'; tenants organisations were to be established and strengthened; consultations were to be held with tenants, tenants' associations and local authorities; councils and tenants' were to be assisted 'in planning and implementing the localisation of housing services to an estate or neighbourhood level'; attempts were to be made to improve and develop policing; and facilities provided for the young (Safe Neighbourhoods Unit, 1985b).

The other major initiative, the Department of the Environment's Priority Estates Project, also incorporated the diagnosis of demoralisation and the recommendation of social reconstruction. Those ideas had been developed independently by its chief consultant, Anne Power, who had been active in community development in the United States and Islington. They were imported with the migration of another consultant, Ann Blaber, from the

NACRO Crime Prevention Unit.

The Department of the Environment is not concerned expressly with crime and the criminal justice system; crime and vandalism arise as indirect policy issues because of their 'effect on the environment' (Burbidge, 1982). The direct impetus for the Priority Estates Project was the 'alarm' felt by councils and government about 'the declining popularity of many housing estates' (Department of the Environment, 1984). The initiative was launched in 1979 to improve housing management and decrease the number of vacant properties on difficult-to-let estates. Octavia Hill's methods of 'intensive, locally-based and locally-controlled management' (Department of the Environment, 1984) were revived and reapplied. 'The aim is to move management and maintenance staff from the Town Hall and put them on the housing estate where they can work closely with residents. Experience shows that a tightly-controlled, autonomous, resident-supported approach to housing management can bring about great improvements on the most run-down of estates' (Priority Estates Project, undated).

Thus a Priority Estates Project which began work on the Penrhys Estate in the Rhondda in July 1984 is involving tenants in consultations and programmes, working with the local authority and different agencies, initiating major repairs, improving lighting, treating walls with anti-graffiti paint, reducing the number of dwellings per block, localising lettings and repairs, intensifying beat policing and instituting night police patrols. The larger objective throughout is to 'deal with the problem of social disarray and give people the feeling that there is some hope' (Power, 1986b).

The Land Use Research Unit at King's College borrowed from Jacobs and Newman to centre its own work on the spatial control of movement and behaviour. It undertook a massive empirical analysis of 4,099 blocks of flats in two inner London boroughs to establish the design features that correlated with such observable signs of decay and abuse as litter, graffiti, vandalism and the number of children in care, (although see Hope, 1986, for criticism of statistical methods used and architectural determinism). The conjecture was that poor design encourages social breakdown by estranging members of a community from one another, obscuring visibility, inhibiting surveillance and providing escape routes that give confidence to potential predators. Some fifteen design variables were thought to be linked with most of the mischief on estates. By altering such design characteristics of the built environment it is argued that confused space is reduced; private and defensible space is enlarged; surveillance is increased; the circulation of criminals and outsiders is controlled; and people are allowed to make their own mark on their environment, reducing anonymity. By early 1986, the Unit had been consulted on some ten projects, the most notable being the Mozart Estate in Westminster (Land Use Research Unit, undated). While the Unit feels that estate reform is best undertaken with the consent and support of tenants, such consultation has low priority and design is seen as paramount in bringing about change. Its director, Alice Coleman, asserts that the scientific evaluation of design gives the Unit its special identity and she holds it against the Department of the Environment that research on design has been neglected (Coleman, 1985), a charge that the Department resists with some vigour.

The effects of these three initiatives are not uniform but they are none the less impressive at a time when most major indicators map a steady growth of

105

crime. NACRO's early Cunningham Road Project in Widnes was reported to have brought about an appreciable decline in crime: 'the consensus of opinion is that crime and vandalism on the estate has abated, although by no means disappeared. There is less sign of graffiti and malicious damage around the estate, and on the whole less evidence of nuisance to residents' (Hedges, Blaber and Mostyn, undated). Eighteen per cent of a sample of households on the estate claimed to have had a break-in in 1976. By 1979, the comparable figure was eleven per cent. There was also a major decrease in the volume of damage noticed by residents. NACRO's Safe Neighbourhoods Unit reported similar improvements on a number of its estates; thus, the Pepys Estate had had 'a considerable reduction in crime', and, on the Haggerston Estate, 'the level of street crime around the estate is reported to have fallen and the police have also reported a drop in the number of burglaries' (Safe Neighbourhoods Unit, 1985b). The results elsewhere were sometimes less certain. In the Titford Link Project, for instance, there was a decline in perceived levels of violence but no reported lessening of burglary, criminal damage and crime associated with motorcars (NACRO, 1985).

The Priority Estates Project was not directed explicitly at crime, but it none the less seems to have had very real consequences. Tricia Zipfel, one of its consultants, asserted that there is evidence of burglary rates decreasing on all but one of the Project's estates. The most conspicuous change was observed on the Broadwater Farm Estate in Haringey; between 1982 and 1984, the burglary rate had dropped by 62 per cent (Zipfel, 1986). On what Tricia Zipfel described as a 'nightmare estate', 'burglaries have virtually been eliminated ... and the crime rate generally has plummeted' (Zipfel, 1985).

The Land Use Research Unit recommends the physical alteration of estates, manipulating spatial control, and it too claims a major decline in the victimisation of residents. For instance, the removal of walkways on the Lisson Grove Estate was held to have halved the crime rate. It was maintained that graffiti, litter and the fear of crime virtually vanished when walls were installed around blocks of flats on the Brandon Estate in Southwark. Not a single burglary was reported for two years after the bottom floors of blocks on the Less View Estate in Hackney were turned into houses with backs and fronts, becoming 'a normal sort of street' (Coleman, 1986).

The explanation

A miscellany of reasons have been advanced in public for what appear to be quite dramatic changes, but the reasons tend not to be lengthy or detailed.

It is the main contention of the National Association for the Care and Resettlement of Offenders that crime reduction flows from the structure and communality that are injected into run-down housing estates; 'on a well-managed estate with a stable population, there is likely to be a degree of neighbourliness conducive to good neighbour relations. It is argued by many that the gradual development of 'neighbourly behaviour' and informal networks of support among tenants is the most effective deterrent of anti-social behaviour' (Bright and Petterson, undated). NACRO character-istically enters into elaborate liaison with institutions delivering services to estates, and that coupling is also part of the work of crime reduction. It leads to an 'improvement in relations between residents and service providers' (NACRO, 1982). More extensive and sympathetic policing, in particular, is likely to enhance feelings of security and erode the fear of crime (NACRO, 1983b).

The Priority Estates Project's account reflects its special preoccupation with the decentralisation of housing services and management. Explanation turns chiefly to the benign consequences of delegating services, management and lettings. Thus, a devolved system of lettings will reduce the numbers of vacant and squatted properties that damage 'local morale' and are 'a public announcement of trouble'. It will help to construct and restore community, being a 'guarantee that people who apply locally actually want to live there, and a chance to strengthen local ties' (Department of the Environment, 1984). It will install tenants who are prepared to act as the willing, unpaid and unofficial custodians of space that was formerly unprotected. It will increase the homogeneity and like-mindedness of a community. And it will remove squatters and others who can be a source of mischief. Similarly, the decentralisation of maintenance work will improve the quality and rate of repairs, transforming the physical appearance and symbolic presence of an estate. Such a decrease in visible public damage can eventually become self-propelling, reducing the number of cues that invite vandalism. Resident caretakers can act as peripatetic guardians and channels of information, playing 'a key role in helping to reduce vandalism, patrolling public areas and supervising the cleaning of them, and dealing at first hand with tenants' problems' (Department of the Environment, 1981). Again, the devolution of practical control may provide the justification for a remodelling of the physical environment. When boundaries are instated, there may be a decline in the amount of confused, impersonal public space and an increase in the area of private, defended space. (Department of the Environment, 1981). Consultation with the police and other agencies can demystify relations; enabling groups to reassess one another, respond more sympathetically, and then collaborate; a 'commonly reported situation is one where, as a result of beat policing allied to better management of the estate, the tenants are more willing to report damage or challenge hooliganism' (Burbidge, 1984). Above all, the very process of implicating tenants in plans and programmes can soften relations between suspicious neighbours and imbue them with a novel sense of organisation, purpose and effectiveness. It gives an opportunity to reassert control.

Alice Coleman's is an empirically-grounded strategy that centres on the observable controls exerted by design. When the physical structures of estates are remapped, there can be control over the entrances that give predators access to property; a reduction in the spatial anonymity that subverts a sense of territoriality; a decrease in the numbers of escape routes that lend criminals confidence; and an enhancement of the opportunities for surveillance that will lead to the identification of criminals. In small, private and enclosed areas of residence outsiders will become more circumspect, and insiders will feel more proprietorial. Social change thereby flows out of material change; 'the residents do it themselves' (Coleman, 1986).

The problem of the explanation

Those explanations are the accounts given in public by men and women who have spent a number of years in the field, they stem from impressive experience, and they possess considerable authority. None the less, they are markedly incomplete and tentative, tending to reiterate very broad assumptions about the likely movements of events rather than representing minute analysis. Before understanding can advance, it would be well to review some of the reasons why such an analysis has not yet emerged. People involved at the core of the initiatives are quite candid about the relative opacity of the processes they are attempting to control. There is a confidence that material changes are occurring but less certainty about their precise mechanics and composition. Thus, Michael Burbidge of the Department of the Environment asked 'how far is crime related . . . to the way council housing is managed? We do not have a fully researched answer to that question' (Burbidge, 1984). Steven Osborn of NACRO voiced a similar response (Osborn, 1986). So did Alice Coleman when she said 'there's something out there in the housing market having an effect. We may not know what it is but it's affecting things' (Coleman, 1986b).

Part of their perplexity may be attributed to the scale of the work, the methodology employed and the process by which it was reported. Housing estates are a little-explored morass of social worlds and processes that lend themselves to a great array of contrasting descriptions. For example, Parker's closely observed study of a difficult estate (Parker, 1983) revealed how 'multivocal' such a community could be. 'Providence' was very many different things. From time to time, indeed, its residents did not seem to dwell in the same place at all. To some, it was a warm, comfortable and neighbourly estate. To others, it was alienating and frightening.

Interestingly, different researchers may go to the 'same' area and return with quite different accounts of what they saw. What is true on one side of the street may not be true on the other. What is true at one point in time may not hold indefinitely. Thus, those whom Gill depicted as the dedicated deviant inhabitants of a distinct criminal area were later described by Davies as people who 'can be hard on crime . . . have a soft spot for policemen, and think the courts too soft' (Davies, 1978). It is not surprising that it has been difficult to supply simple interpretations of the impact of initiatives.

There are, however, added problems which flow particularly from the special objectives and style of the initiative. Difficult estates are afflicted by so many problems that modest reforms tend to be regarded as inappropriate. There are, indeed, principled objections to the 'experimental' introduction of single alterations. Instead, most initiatives have consisted of sizeable 'packages' of many different measures administered in varying proportions. Consider NACRO's Titford Link Project: the project was intended to 'improve living conditions and reduce crime problems' and it proceeded by devising an 'action plan' composed of 'internal decorations, installation of 'phone entry systems in tower blocks, fencing schemes, alterations to refuse chutes, improvements to bathrooms, upgrading of fire safety features, installation of gas fires, introduction of mobile repair team systems, creation of a social centre, creation of an activities centre, development of a residents' association, development of youth activities, new policy arrangements'

(NACRO, 1985). At any distance, it is impossible to conceive how those individual measures worked. And problems of understanding are compounded because measures, and their effects, and the effects of their effects, release a great spate of complicated interchanges (Hope, 1986). For instance, the Cunningham Road Improvement Scheme was initiated by a local authority working in tandem with a group from NACRO. In time, consultations with the estate's tenants were to introduce changes in the authority's own procedures and work practices which would in turn affect tenants on the estate (Hedges, Blaber and Mostyn, 1980). Similarly, work on the Titford Link Project was reported to have affected the local police, councillors, housing department, technical services department and recreation and amenities department (NACRO, 1985).

The authors of the different initiatives themselves acquired evolving stocks of knowledge, experience and motivation. Their interpretation, interests and ambitions shifted over time. Their work was set in an environment of political and organisational change. Unemployment and other urban problems multiplied during the lifetime of the initiatives. When it is recalled that an arithmetical increase in the number of figures involved in a scene will be accompanied by an exponential increase in the numbers of their relations (Simmel, 1908), it becomes evident that the interactions stirred up by an initiative defy even the most efficient and comprehensive analysis. Poyner reflected on the problem of assessment at large, 'undoubtedly, many of these tactics can contribute to a reduction in crime in the appropriate setting, but when they are all bundled together in the same demonstration project it is almost impossible to decide those tactics which are the most effective ...' (Poyner, 1983).

To make analysis even more intricate, the initiatives were manned by a few people who were engaged in daily negotiations with diverse and difficult groups who had strong moral commitments and who were too busy to continuously record and assess what was happening about them. No systematic monitoring and observation were conducted in most instances (Safe Neighbourhoods Unit, 1985; Burbidge, 1984; Department of the Environment, 1984). As one of the principal figures reflected, 'it's very difficult to know what's going on. You have to be on the spot to know and then one gets caught up in the operation of the initiative. Community development is very stressful. You can't sit back. In the end, you give (analysis) up because there isn't time to do it.'

The result has been a succession of reports which offer simple, condensed glosses on what must have occurred, each gloss passing as an explanation for practical purposes. Such a championing of one uncomplicated standpoint may entail what Douglas has chosen to call 'simplificationism' (Douglas, 1977): the reduction of complexitiy to a comparatively simple theorem in which the author assumes a proprietorial stake. It is apparent that the movers of the different initiatives have given their own special inflections to what they observe. Alice Coleman has laid claim to design as the pre-eminent variable. The Priority Estates Project has been mobilised around the reform of housing mangement and, within the sphere of criminal justice policy at least, that inflection has made the business of analysis particularly fraught because the Project was not intended originally to make an impact on crime (Burbidge, 1984). Such emphases are not only ways of seeing the effects of an initiative, but they are also ways of not seeing those effects.

Much that could have been said about the unwinding of initiatives has not been said because it was regarded as unduly subjective. There has been little detailed observational and ethnographic work on the social processes of housing estates. Nothing of any great substance has been written about the extent, interplay and variability of changes in different parts of the project estates. What is of great moment to some groups of residents may have no effect on others. What achieves one result in certain quarters may have contrary results elsewhere (Bottoms and Xanthos claim that some problem estates have no lack of social organisation but support coherent criminal sub-cultures). There has been no reporting of the fashion in which offenders and potential offenders made sense of the changes introduced by the initiatives; the surveillance and custodial practices of those assumed to be concerned about their defensible space; the everyday movements, practices and behaviour of tenants; confrontations between tenants and predators; the manner in which adolescents deploy their time; the social formation and evolution of communities; the workings of informal social control in the private and public spaces that compose an estate; methods of dispute settlement; the activities of outsiders on estates; policing behaviour. There has instead been reliance on conjectures about what reasonable men and women would do in specified circumstances. 'So far research has proceeded mainly by inference from the ''revealed traces'' of behaviour' (Hope, 1986). Ideal types replace identifiable figures. So it is that Alice Coleman argues that spatial organisation 'has the strongest effect on crime. If there's only one access point, you can't take a short cut. Criminals feel they can be identified.' (Coleman, 1986b). Yet the criminals who feel in this manner are no more than working conjectures. So, too, Burbidge writes how 'criminals, in all probability, see a place where they will face little hindrance' (Burbidge, 1984) on problem estates, but the assessments made by the criminal mind are really provided by the Department of the Environment. Such a loose use of common-sense typification is prevalent and adequate enough. It is undoubtedly frequent in economics and politics. When analysis is novel and uncertain, however, it is useful to gain reassurance that common-sense typification is actually well-founded. It would be prudent to establish that criminals and tenants make use of logic and behave in the way that they are supposed to.

A hidden explanation

It seems that a number of half-formed ideas have not been published because they do not conform to the canons of scientific reporting. A whole area of knowledge is systematically suppressed by the limitations of prevailing research methods (Clarke, 1975). While there is much to commend an approach which focuses on the 'factual' and the 'objective' it leads to a form of self-censorship of 'soft' data. Thus, those who work in the initiatives operate with an impressive practical knowledge of the social life of the estates, but it is a knowledge that has been exposed to censorship. Informally, in seminars and conversation, they make use of an interesting working analysis that is rarely permitted to enter whole into their writing. It would be unwise to exaggerate the extent of that censorship, but public knowledge of the initiatives has been impoverished in consequence. What has been 'banned' consists in the main of evidence that is thought to be too personal, subjective and qualitative. It includes the methods and topics of reasoning that are actually employed by experts when they speak and work. In particular, it includes a number of little illustrative histories or stories about the effects of initiatives. One such 'story' told by consultants on the Priority Estates Project, for example, contains the germ of an explanation of the impact that intervention can make.

It is now a virtual axiom that initiatives in crime-ridden neighbourhoods and estates must proceed by constructing communities that are capable of policing themselves. Thus Curtis and Kohn remark of American initiatives 'one emphasis of the Anti-Crime Programme is enabling the poor to take charge of their own lives ...' (Curtis and Kohn, 1982). What is publicly inaccessible in Britain is a series of detailed natural histories of how the poor do begin to take charge of their own lives. A process observed on a number of the Department of the Environment's priority estates has the makings of just such a detailed natural history.

In the poorer urban areas, and especially those populated by large numbers of young people, absent fathers and single-parent families, it is inevitable that one of the significant figures exercising local authority is the mother (Liebow, 1967). From time to time, her authority can become the basis of a more diffuse influence, generalised beyond the family to embrace a wider grouping. A common source and model of such extended power flows from participation in a trade union. On a number of the Department of the Environment's priority estates, processes of consultation and collaboration between influential outsiders and tenants have succeeded in amplifying local power. Particular people will come to the fore or attain greater prominence as the projects progress. In turn, the status conferred on tenants by project staff makes it imperative that they receive recognition from the housing authorities, and their standing with fellow residents will grow in proportion. In effect, efforts to implicate tenants in decision-making, planning and action prepare the social structures which bestow eminence on tenants. Initiatives manufacture and confirm the role of powerful local intermediaries who can 'fix' things. Going to people who have been so elevated reinforces their standing in what can become a self-fuelling cycle (at least during the life of an initiative). Processes culminating in the emergence of influential indigenous leaders have been discerned on estates in Hornsey, the Rhondda, Finsbury Park and elsewhere.

What marks a critical phase in the natural history of a reform is the decision taken by a strong matriarch or leader to embrace all or some large part of the estate as her own, assume a proprietorial stance and impose a disciplining organisation. If, for instance, she is black, she will move beyond the narrow interests of blacks to encompass other races. She may assist in injecting organisation herself or call upon the police and, perhaps for the first time, give names and identify incidents.

Much of the disarray on problem estates has been attributed to 'the mayhem' introduced by a few people who are so frightening that others will not act. It is when a community turns on what Wilson called 'the difficults' (Wilson, 1963) that social order may be conferred and a transition will occur. On one estate, for example, a benchmark was passed when a matriarch 'came out against the winos and prostitutes (who had squatted there) and called in the police'. Perhaps the archetypal matriarch is Dolly Kiffin of Broadwater Farm, described by a PEP consultant as 'very stong and charismatic'. It was she who animated the moves behind the formation of the Broadwater Farm Youth Association, an association predominantly of young blacks whose work with the elderly began to dispel some of the 'shrill polarisation' that had hitherto divided older whites and younger blacks. She secured substantial funding and a physical base for the Association, exercising internal discipline within it:

'... the Youth Association had become a force on the estate. Although "youth" had been the initial focus, the Association increasingly saw itself as fighting to improve conditions for the whole community ... New Urban Aid money enabled the Association to take a large corner unit in [a] shopping precinct ... providing recreational space, kitchens, work-shops and office space for the rapidly expanding work of the Youth Association. The meal programme was extended to cater for many of the pensioners and the Youth Association won a contract with Social Services to provide meals on wheels locally. This service, plus the regular outings and parties organised by the Youth Association for the pensioners, has brought the two groups together and done more to show the potential for good community relations than almost anything else on the estate. Although many tenants still do not feel safe, burglaries have virtually been eliminated ... and the crime rate generally has plummeted. The youths instead of being labelled the cause of all the problems are now viewed by many as allies ...' (Zipfel, 1985).

Of course, there is no certainty about how many projects on the transformed estates did generate matriarchs, leaders and youth associations. These are contingent processes. Yet the projects' 'Hawthorne Effect' must wield a pervasive influence, creating organisation and identities where none existed before and giving structure, urgency and interest to relations that were formerly obscure or weak.

Conclusion

Quite quietly and very recently there has emerged a spate of major social engineering projects in areas which have great need of change. 'Hard-to-let' and problem estates are very close to becoming the new rookeries. They combine stigmatisation, demoralisation and anomie with unusually high rates of offending and victimisation. NACRO, Department of the Environment and other initiatives appear to reverse those processes and restore some measure of informal social control. Yet their workings are complex, indefinite and diffuse, a compound of many different and interacting activities. They are not fully understood by their authors, busy people who feel obliged to describe their accomplishments in the special opaque language of funded projects. It is apparent that something stirs when an initiative starts, but what it is and how it moves are not yet evident. What must now be attempted is the patient observation and analysis of the impact of those initiatives on the everyday life of the estates.

The author wishes to express his thanks to Alice Coleman, Tim Hope, Anne Power and Steven Osborn for their help and advice.

References

ARMSTRONG, G and WILSON, M. (1973). In Taylor, I. and Taylor, L. (Eds.), *Politics and Deviance*. Harmondsworth: Penguin.

BALDWIN, J. and BOTTOMS, A (1976). *The Urban Criminal: a Study in Sheffield*. London: Tavistock.

BOTTOMS, A. and XANTHOS, P. (1981). 'Housing Policy and Crime in the British Public Sector'. In Brantingham, P. and Brantingham P. (Eds.), *Environmental Criminology*. Beverly Hills, CA: Sage.

BRANTINGHAM, P. and BRANTINGHAM, P. (1981). 'Introduction: The Dimensions of Crime'. In Brantingham, P. and Brantingham, P. (Eds.), *Environmental Criminology*. Beverly Hills, CA: Sage.

BRIGHT, J. and PETTERSON, G. (undated). *The Safe Neighbourhoods Unit*. London.

BURBIDGE, M. (1982). 'Vandalism on Public Housing Estates'. In Hough, M. and Mayhew, P. (Eds.), *Crime and Public Housing*. London: Home Office.

BURBIDGE, M. (1984). 'British Public Housing and Crime—A Review'. In Clarke, R. and Hope, T. (Eds.), *Coping with Burglary*. Boston: Kluwer-Nijhoff.

CLARKE, M. (1975). 'Survival in the field'. *Theory and Society*, 2, pp. 95–123.

CLARKE, R. (1982). 'Chairman's Introduction'. In Hough, M. and Mayhew, P. (Eds.), *Crime and Public Housing*. Research and Planning Unit Paper No. 6, London: Home Office.

COLEMAN, A. (1985). *Utopia on Trial*. London: Hilary Shipman.

COLEMAN, A. (1986). Interview 21.2.1986.

COLEMAN, A. (1986b). Talk delivered at the London School of Economics, 25.2.1986.

CURTIS, L. and KOHN, I. (1982). 'Citizen Self-Help and Environmental Design: The Theory and Practice of Crime Prevention in American Subsidised Housing'. In Hough, M. and Mayhew, P. (Eds.), *Crime and Public Housing*. Research and Planning Unit Paper No. 6, London: Home Office.

DAMER, S. (1974). 'Wine Alley: The Sociology of a Dreadful Enclosure'. *Sociological Review*, pp. 221–248.

DAVIES, C. (1978). 'Crime, police and courts'. *New Society*, 23 February, pp. 424–5.

DEPARTMENT OF THE ENVIRONMENT. (1981). *Reducing Vandalism on Public Housing Estates*. London: HMSO.

DEPARTMENT OF THE ENVIRONMENT. (1984). *Local Housing Management: A Priority Estates Project Survey*. London: Department of the Environment.

DOUGLAS, J. (1977). *The Nude Beach*. Beverly Hills, CA: Sage.

GILL, O. (1977). *Luke Street: Housing Policy, Conflict and the Creation of the Delinquent Area*. London: Macmillan.

HEDGES, A., BLABER, A. and MOSTYN, B. (1980). *Community Planning Project: Cunningham Road Improvement Scheme Final Report*. London: Social and Community Planning Research.

HERBERT, D. (1979). 'Urban Crime: A Geographical Perspective'. In Herbert, D. and Smith, D. (Eds.), *Social Problems and the City*. Oxford: Oxford University Press.

HOPE, T. (1986). 'Crime, Community and Environment'. *Journal of Environmental Psychology*, 6, pp. 65–78.

JACOBS, J. (1961). *Death and Life of Great American Cities*. New York: Random House.

LAND USE RESEARCH UNIT, (undated). 'Mozart Estate Disadvantagement Report'. London: Land Use Research Unit.

LIEBOW, E. (1967). *Tally's Corner: A study of Negro Street Corner Men*. Boston: Little Brown.

MAYHEW, P. and CLARKE, R. (1982). 'Crime Prevention and Public Housing in England'. In Hough, M. and Mayhew, P. (Eds.), *Crime and Public Housing*. Research and Planning Unit Paper No. 6, London: Home Office.

NACRO. (1982). *Neighbourhood Consultations, A Practical Guide*. London: NACRO.

NACRO. (1983). *Thirlmere Estate Report*. London: NACRO.

NACRO. (1983b). *Annual Report 1982–83*. London: NACRO.

NACRO. (1985). *The Titford Link Project Action Plan Review*. London: NACRO.

NEWMAN, O. (1972). *Defensible Space: Crime Prevention Through Urban Design*. New York: Macmillan.

NEWMAN, O. (1981). *Community of Interest*. Garden City: Anchor.

113

OSBORN, S. (1982). 'Crime and Public Housing: Community Planning Approach to Tackling Crime'. In Hough, M. and Mayhew, P. (Eds.), *Crime and Prevention Housing*. Research and Planning Unit Paper No. 6, London: Home Office.

OSBORN, S. (1986). Interview 19.2.1986.

PARKER, T. (1983). *The People of Providence*. London: Hutchinson.

PEPTALK. (1985). *Peptalk*, 3. London: Department of the Environment.

POWER, A. (1981). 'How to rescue council housing'. *New Society*, 4 June.

POWER, A. (1985). *The Development of Unpopular Housing Estates and Attempted Remedies (1895–1984*. Ph.D. London School of Economics.

POWER, A. (1986). 'Crisis on Run-Down Housing Estates'. Paper delivered at London School of Economics Sociology Department Weekend School. 1.2.1986.

POWER, A. (1986b). Interview 14.2.1986.

POWER, A. (1986c). Interview 4.3.1986.

POYNER, B. (1983). *Design against Crime*. London: Butterworths.

PRIORITY ESTATES PROJECT (undated). *Priority Estates Project 1984–87—Tackling hard-to-manage housing estates*. London: Department of the Environment.

PRIORITY ESTATES PROJECT. (1985). *Peptalk*, 2. London: Department of the Environment.

REYNOLDS, F. (1986). *The Problem Housing Estate*. Hants: Gower.

SAFE NEIGHBOURHOODS UNIT. (1985). *After Entryphones: Improving Management and Security in Multi-Storey Blocks*. London: Safe Neighbourhoods Unit.

SAFE NEIGHBOURHOODS UNIT. (1985b). *Annual Report 1985–86*. London: Safe Neighbourhoods Unit.

SIMMEL, G. (1908). *Sociology*.

WILSON, R. (1963). *Difficult Housing Estates*. London: Tavistock Publications.

WILSON, S. (1978). 'Updating Defensible Space'. *The Architects' Journal*, 11th October.

WILSON, S. (1980). 'Vandalism and "defensible space" on London Housing Estates'. In Clarke, R. and Mayhew, P. (Eds.), *Designing Out Crime*. London: HMSO.

WILSON, S. (1982). 'Crime and Public Housing: Evidence from an Investigation of Unpopular Housing Estates'. In Hough, M. and Mayhew, P. (Eds.), *Crime and Public Housing*. Research and Planning Unit Paper No. 6. London: Home Office.

ZIPFEL, T. (1985). 'Hard work transforms a "nightmare estate" '. *Peptalk*, 2. London: Department of the Environment.

ZIPFEL, T. (1986). 'Broadwater Farm Estate, Haringey: Background and Information Relating to the Riot on Sunday 6th October 1985'. Unpublished.

Community Involvement and Policing

Using the term community in its more generalized sense to refer to citizen-based crime prevention strategies, these three chapters provide insights into both the potential for and the limitations of policies which make use of 'watching and action against crime' or informal social control. Chapter 7 discusses the stereotypes which tend to be invoked when informal control is considered, and the assumption that either such control is no longer possible in an urban setting, or that its encouragement will necessarily result in a vigilante presence. Based on a recent study of informal social control in a number of small rural and urban communities, the chapter argues that informal action against crime is indeed prevalent in both rural and urban settings, although rarer in urban areas where the opportunity for communal action seems small. Informal control is limited, however, by the extent to which people are prepared to take action against crime or nuisance behaviour. People's expectations of the police would appear to compliment informal action in dealing with problems in consultation with local residents, and only in cases of serious crime do they expect prosecution, and there appears to be a clear case for public and the police to work together at the local level.

Chapters 8 and 9 provide complimentary material on the scope for neighbourhood watch in Britain, and the experience of the development of schemes in the USA, over a number of years. Thus Chapter 8 examines the 'theoretical underpinnings of this popular strategy' on the basis that our knowledge of how it actually works and what its real effects on community residents are is extremely limited. While such schemes seem to be attractive to homogeneous, often middle-class, areas where informal social controls are strong, the fundamental question of whether it is possible to *implant* informal social control through neighbourhood watch programmes remains unanswered. The majority of evaluations are, it is argued, flawed. The results of the first quasi-experimental test of the assumptions underlying watch programmes are examined, finding not only no improvements between treated and untreated areas, but some increase in fear and perceptions of crime. Chapter 9, with the benefit of North American experience, explores the extent of support of watch schemes in England and Wales based upon responses to the British Crime Survey. Such information has value for those setting up schemes in identifying the kinds of communities where additional resources may be needed to stimulate participation. The results suggest a complex model linking perceptions to behaviour. Personal proximity to crime, the level of disorder in their neighbourhood, the extent to which they worry about such things, satisfaction with their neighbourhood and other assessments all affect people's willingness to take part. It is also evident that care is needed in presenting the concept to reassure people that their privacy is protected.

7. Policing with the public?

Joanna Shapland[1]

Discussion about informal social control—policing carried out by ordinary people within their own neighbourhoods—has been marked by the use of a number of extreme and mutually contradictory stereotypes. Some hark back to an idea of a mythical golden age, when communities were close-knit, wrongdoing was quickly stamped upon and the police were personified by the friendly, local bobby. Others have pointed out that the closeness was itself restricting and intolerant of deviation, and that policing tended to reflect the interests of certain groups and classes. Many people, whichever view they hold of the past, pour scorn on the idea that any informal control is possible today—citing the anonymity and lack of cohesion of modern neighbourhoods. Most of these, however, take as their reference point run-down inner-city council housing estates. Finally, people cite the shadowy presence of vigilantes as indicating the likely result if informal control were to be encouraged.

Unfortunately, discussion about communities, crime and policing has largely jumped from the stereotypes above to action—policy and executive initiatives—leaving out any study of whether those stereotypes represent reality or whether the initiatives and projects have any chance of being accepted by the public or are compatible with action the public is already taking. Unfortunately, this scenario of leaping from thought to action, because problems are pressing, is typical of both police initiatives (Weatheritt, 1986) and those in the crime prevention field, though the latter tend to be better evaluated (see, for example, Bright *et al.*, 1985; Hope, 1982).

This paper attempts to explore the themes which run through the stereotypes about informal control and its relation to the police—its potential scope; its limitations, current and intrinsic; its tendency to reflect only a small part of the views in any area; its likely use of coercion; and the problems in matching up policing by the public and policing by the police. It draws heavily upon a recent research study done by Jon Vagg and the present writer, designed to elicit the current pattern of ideas about crime and problems and the resulting action taken in several small rural and urban areas.

The study

The areas in which the study was done comprised two groups of villages and four small parts of the inner residential area of the county town of a shire county in the Midlands. These types of area, which contain a mix of houses, shops and industry, obviously do not include run-down inner-city areas or

1. The research on which this paper is based was carried out with Jon Vagg and many of the ideas expressed here were developed jointly with him. The project was funded by the Home Office. Any mistakes or errors are, however, the author's responsibility.

116

substantial council housing estates (though one of our urban areas did have a crime rate three times the national average). They are, however, typical for the majority of the population of England and Wales. In considering measures for crime prevention and policing, it is important to weigh up whether it is more beneficial to concentrate on the small number of areas with the highest crime rates, or, rather, the more numerous ones with slightly lesser crime rates (but in which most crime overall is committed). It may be more beneficial to develop a crime policy for the 'average' area and then see what changes need to be made in a 'high crime' area, rather than vice versa.

The study was designed to be detailed and explanatory. It used, therefore, as many methods as possible in order to build up a picture of reactions to crime and problems in the areas. A total of 322 residents and business people were formally interviewed; a total of 27 months spent informally being present in the areas, talking to people and watching what went on; 90 formal periods of observation were conducted; a total of 53 police officers involved in those areas were interviewed; and a whole year of crime reports and 72 days of calls on police services analysed. The result was a mass of information on people's experiences of crime and problems and their attitudes as to what should happen, including a log of all the incidents that had occurred over a period of about 18 months.

The extent of informal social control

A plethora of different kinds of informal action were being taken in both urban and rural environments. People, particularly the elderly and business people, were actively engaged in watching out for anything suspicious and this watching and noticing was, in general, considered a positive thing to do—it was caring, rather than nosiness. Residents might even 'adopt' some public spaces, like the pavement outside their house or a small grassy patch, and watch over them, as well as taking care of factories situated near their houses. This watching was, however, quite localised. It extended only to a handful of houses adjacent to the watcher's house or business (a much smaller area than the typical neighbourhood watch scheme). Large public spaces, such as parks, were too much for any individual to adopt.

Watching and noticing what was seen was focused on centres of activity in the areas—typically business and services serving that area. These might be the corner shops and newsagents cited by Jacobs (1965), but they might equally be post offices, garages, spare parts dealers, secondhand shops, pubs and community centres—some of whose proprietors had very equivocal relationships with the police. These commercial centres of life in villages and urban areas appeared to be essential to the communication of information about what was going on. Current planning fashions for zoning of residential and commercial districts may inadvertently be destroying the infrastructure for community crime prevention and social control.

It was also found that a wide range of types of informal action was being adopted to deal with anything thought to be suspicious. This might involve direct action by the watcher (perhaps watching ostentatiously, perhaps going out and challenging the suspicious person); or it might involve further action initiated by the watcher (telling the victim; initiating discussion and action through groups such as councils, schools and 'responsible people').

One of the limitations on the effectiveness of informal action is obviously the willingness of watchers or victims to do anything about the problem or to take action themselves. Here considerable differences between areas were found. In one village, which was policed by several officers coming from outside the village, people seemed to be more prepared to rely on their own resources (as opposed to ignoring the problem or bringing in the police). In another village, where there was a resident, local police officer, calling in the assistance of the police was a more frequently used option (though keeping the matter to oneself was also common). In the urban areas, informal action was rarer—people did call in the police more often, but they also ignored more problems as well. In particular, there appeared to be few options for communal informal action—using organisations or groups to deter further offending.

Another feature of the informal action taken was its purpose. Action was primarily aimed at coping with problems individually—stopping that offence or catching that offender—rather than deterring or preventing future offending. It aimed to comfort and to make aware and was, perhaps, designed to a greater degree to preserve the order and peace of that community than to promulgate the traditional aims of the criminal justice system. There was some deterrence—for example, warning people thought about to commit an offence either directly or by showing them that someone was about; or 'punishing' by spreading knowledge about the misdeeds of individuals or by telling off children directly or informing their parents. There was also some preventative activity—'target hardening' by local bodies and individuals, repairing damage quickly, looking after empty houses and businesses.

There was little hint of direct punishment for misdeeds and no formal patrolling of areas. There was no vigilante activity (by which is meant organised informal activity which goes further than just patrolling the streets to involve contact with suspected offenders). Such activity requires the assumption of certainty as to who has done a certain deviant act—it requires the punisher to be confident that the person being punished is the offender. In contrast, people in both the rural and urban areas in the study were very wary of pointing a finger at an offender unless they had direct, eye-witness proof (they were equally dubious about naming possible suspects to the police). Coercion, including direct punishment and dealing with offenders who do not admit wrongdoing (or just continue to do it), was felt to be a matter for the police or for other, formal bodies. Equally, informal action could not deal with offenders who were not local. People could not follow offenders to where they lived or collate information about offences committed in different districts.

We may conclude that informal action does exist, even in relatively anonymous urban areas (few of our urban residents felt they belonged in any way to that part of the city). People watch, notice and sometimes take action. And that action, being designed to cope, not to punish, is unlikely to lead to vigilante activity. It is interesting that the only publicised examples of organised vigilante activity in England recently have involved very specific issues and have arisen following the perceived failure of the relevant authorities to take action.

People's views about crime

A straight description of informal action, such as has been given above, does not indicate the limitations of informal activity, the problems in the interaction between informal action and police activity, or the reasons why people will do something about some problems and not about others. For this, it is necessary to explore people's ideas about the areas in which they live and the problems and crimes with which they are afflicted.

The perception of crime as a major problem only occurred in urban areas, but vandalism was as much a problem in rural areas as urban (and it appeared as though as many incidents of vandalism were occurring). Most people thought there was at least one major problem of disorder in their area. People from different parts cited similar kinds of problems—parked cars, noise, damage, groups of teenagers—and the problem cited correlated with the objective measurements we were able to make of that problem. The particular problem that seemed to affect any one household, however, depended on the precise location of that household—problems were extremely localised in space and usually spasmodic in their occurrence over time. So, at one point in time, one street or part of a street would be afflicted by noise from a club, the next by vandalism to cars, the next by youths hanging around a bus stop and so on. It was the occurrence of one of these events, rather than the personality or attitudes of the residents, that affected whether it would be cited as a problem. But there would be considerable disagreement about how severe that problem was, and what should be done about it.

To criminologists, those involved with criminal justice policy and the police, crime is very important. To residents and business people, crime and crime prevention may become important at particular times, or because of specific episodes (such as being victimised), but generally it is a background factor. Other things, such as personal life or work, are far more immediate and pressing. So, though people in the study had thought about crime prevention, their willingness to take action was confined to particular times when it seemed to be most appropriate. For the rest of the time, they reverted to habitual behaviour which was the most convenient for them given their daily lifestyle.

This can be illustrated with respect to burglary. People often had quite definite views about their likelihood of being burgled and the factors that would contribute to or diminish the risk. People's estimations of their likelihood of being burgled followed very closely their perceptions of the amount of crime in general, with urban residents and business people quoting much higher probabilities than rural residents and business people. The factors they cited were weighted towards the action they had taken to combat burglary and the factors they had considered, rather than helpless worry. People might even be said to display a crime prevention set. They cited factors such as difficult rear access, possession of a dog, lack of valuables, special locks or hardware, and watchful neighbours. Rural residents and business people cited primarily surveillance factors and urban residents and business people, design and hardware factors. It is difficult to assess the accuracy of these beliefs, as work on the effectiveness of design, hardware and surveillance factors in combating burglary is only in its infancy (though see Bennett and Wright, 1984; Winchester and Jackson, 1982). However, though all these factors seem relevant, it is possible to suggest, tentatively, that urban residents may have a less useful set of beliefs than rural residents. Urban residents both minimised the effectiveness of surveillance and did not seem to realise the extent of informal social control operating in urban areas. It is possible that crime prevention has been a victim of its own publicity about the anonymity of urban areas!

Set beside the considerable unease about burglary in urban areas, people's crime prevention behaviour seems illogical. As has been found in other surveys, there was a considerable minority of people who did not lock both front and back door when going out. Windows were even more likely to be left unlocked. Why are people so lax? It is not due to a lack of care about their possessions—or even a lack of awareness of the need to take precautions against crime. This is shown clearly in the study by the large numbers who bothered specifically to inform someone when they went away (not the police—it was felt they should not be bothered by such a mundane task). The reasons for not locking up seemed to be a combination of judgements about the relatively low risk of an individual being burgled, incorrect stereotypes about the abilities and *modus operandi* of burglars, perceptions of the inconvenience of current crime prevention hardware and perceptual blind spots about the rear of premises. These views were rarely challenged and so did not change. There was no feedback from the police about local crime (stories about local burglaries stopped at '. . . and then the police arrived' and usually did not contain details of who the burglars were or how they got in). Media information and national campaigns were, by their nature, not targeted to the most appropriate times, when crime prevention was in people's minds, and produced only such responses as 'I must get round to that' (see Riley and Mayhew, 1980; Winkel, 1987). Police contact with individual households or businesses for crime prevention was very rare (as it must be, if it is left to specialised crime prevention officers). And the stereotypes of burglars given in both official publicity and media reports were very inaccurate (burglars are not usually large men, total strangers to the neighbourhood, aged about 40 and dressed in stripes with a bag over their shoulder).

The two occasions on which crime prevention did become important were when going away and when moving into a new property. It would be possible to target accurate publicity and suggestions on these times. This is likely to be far more effective than trying to raise people's level of awareness in general—for this, the likelihood of burglary would have to be stressed to an extent beyond the current levels of crime in most areas, so that it would be perceived as a major problem and a constant threat. That would increase the number of people who really fear burglary and whose lives are being severely curtailed because of that.

The problem is that, although awareness of crime prevention is perhaps not as high as policy makers might like, fear of crime has reached the level of a major social problem in many urban areas. This is currently mostly fear of assault, physical or sexual, rather than fear of burglary, although there were signs in this study of some fear of burglary. Here, fear of crime is separated from concern about crime. Concern about crime is related to knowledge about actual occurrence in that area and to recorded crime levels. It feeds to some degree into crime prevention practices and informs people's beliefs about their areas. However, for some people, concern seems to have become transmuted into fear. Fear is fear of the unknown, of strangers, of something undefined 'out there waiting to come in and get me'. It is not necessarily related to the crime rate in the area, and is fed by media reports of violent crime from completely different areas. In this study, fear of assault was most prevalent among women, particularly middle-aged women, and resulted in a drastic curtailment of their activities outside the home. Fear of burglary occurred in men as well and also restricted people to their homes (this time to protect the home). In the urban areas, there were almost no women walking on their own or in a group of women on the street after dusk.

If informal social action, in the sense of watching and taking action, is to be encouraged in the context of community crime prevention, then attention will need to be paid to the intrinsic contradiction between the need to raise people's awareness of crime and the potential this has for increasing fear of crime. Crime prevention publicity, particularly national campaigns, are an obvious potential source of concern. The images they convey may produce unintended reactions, such as increased defensiveness, fear or aggression (see, particularly, Winkel, 1987). Such publicity needs rigorous monitoring in pilot studies. Perhaps there is also now a need to produce publicity designed specifically to reduce fear of crime, to promote informal action positively and to stress the low absolute level of both assaults and burglaries.

Informal action and the police

People's responses to incidents they see as suspicious depend very much on their beliefs about the seriousness of that kind of incident and the kind of offender they suspect has done it. Most people in this study divided incidents up into 'real crime' and 'the things that kids do' or 'nuisances'. The dividing line between real crime and other crime varied greatly between individuals, but real crime generally comprised only sexual assaults, serious physical assaults (using weapons), robberies, and burglaries of dwellings in which something was taken. For these, no matter who the offender was, almost everyone would call in the police and wish the matter to be dealt with through the traditional channels of the criminal justice system.

People's responses to other crimes were much more varied. The offence, the offender and the victim would be seen as a unit and perceived seriousness judged on the whole. The legal insistance on treating offences as divorced from their setting (sometimes reflected in police thought as well) is alien to victims' and witnesses' ways of thinking. In respect of other crime, victims and watchers expected to be able to take decisions about reporting themselves, without proactive action by the police. If the watcher knew the offender, he or she would be more likely to intervene personally and deal with the situation (unless, of course, the offender was feared—as a member of the local gang of youths, for example). If the offender was a child or a youth, the watcher was much more likely to take direct action. Owning any property involved, or feeling responsible for it (because the owners were known to be absent, or because the watcher was in charge or on a committee running it) also strongly promoted intervention. This latter factor is being utilised in the Dutch proposals to increase guardianship over public places (Ministerie van Justitie, 1985). The potential consequences of the action or inaction being contemplated were also important—not just in terms of retaliation, but also potenti-

social embarrassment if the person being challenged turned out to be there legitimately. The greater willingness to intervene actively against a childish or youthful offender was due not only to their lesser powers of retaliation, but also to the feeling that it was more permissable socially to tell a child off mistakenly.

Calling in the police to an instance of other crime was often a result of the perceived inappropriateness of other options, rather than a positive decision that this was definitely a matter for the police and that any offenders caught should be processed through the criminal justice system. The main desire was often that the problem should stop, rather than a specification of any particular method for this. This is probably the most difficult area for the police, as there will be not only definite local views, but also disparate local views. Without sensitive policing by local officers in tune with public ideas, mistrust and resentment can easily arise. Disagreement between victim, watcher or neighbours and the police can arise in both directions—either if the police take action perceived to be too serious (for example, if they prosecute a local youth for a 'minor' offence such as burglary of outbuildings) or if they fail to take action (for example, against people parking cars on the pavement or groups of youths playing football in the street). Equally, on occasions people would report other crime to the police in order for action to be taken, but on other occasions had no expectation that anything was possible and were merely letting the police know what was happening. The problem is that the police are not currently equipped to perform all these roles, even should they think them desirable. The processing of reported crime tends to follow a well-worn path, with, perhaps, little thought as to alternative solutions, such as informal reparation or apologies. The facility for treating reports as information is often totally lacking, with officers neither being trained in the arts of mapping problems and thinking out their solutions, nor encouraged by supervisors to ascertain local views and local difficulties.

Action against crime in the community

It has been seen that people are actively taking action against instances of crime and problems occurring in their own local area and that they are interested in crime and in crime prevention. This is not a surprising finding. Crime reported by the public to the police can be seen as merely the tip of the iceberg of ignored crime and informally dealt-with crime. If informal action had disappeared in the last century or so, the likelihood is that the reporting of crime would also have reduced significantly. Instead, it appears that public interest in crime and in the workings of the police is, if anything, increasing. The 'rediscovery' of informal action that is not vigilante action may be similar to the apparent discovery over the last ten years of the importance of victims to the running of the criminal justice system.

But, unlike the role of victims, the role that is played by informal social _____ _____ _____re limitations. Some of the constraints could be removed or _____ ____ ley stem from the inadequate informational base given to the _____ ___ .ncompatabilities between current police and public modes of _____ .: are explored in more detail below. Some, however, are _____ ____ natures of informal social control and of formal policing. If informal control is not to become vigilante action, then it cannot use physical coercion. It can only persuade, suggest, reason or negotiate. It will always be vulnerable to those who refuse to accept its mandate. The only way to back up that mandate is to bring in the police.

The police, however, are not currently seen as in the business of supporting individuals' rights or solutions but as 'enforcing the law'. The precise meaning of this imposing platitude is the subject of the current controversies about the accountability of the police. In the current context, it is, however, clear that, given the extent of the discretion not to prosecute, the formal machinery of the courts and statutory interpretations cannot give clear guidance to an individual constable as to what exactly he should do when faced with the local gang of youths. It can only produce constraints as to what will be an illegal use of his powers. Equally, his decision would be relatively simple if everyone in the local community, including the youths and the victim(s), agreed on the seriousness of the problem and what should be done about it. What is quite clear from this study, however, is that below the level of 'real' crime, there is very considerable disagreement within local areas about just those topics. This is exacerbated by the very localised extent of knowledge about problems. The likely result of constables constantly being faced with these difficulties is the development of a local 'police view' (or several police views, varying with rank and with specialism) on appropriate action.

It has been argued elsewhere (Shapland and Vagg, 1987) that these problems, combined with ineffective means of consultation between police and public, have led to a relationship between police and public that can best be termed 'separate policing'—policing by the police and by the public independently from each other. The police are currently remarkably isolated from the public in their day-to-day working practices. It has also been pointed out that the police may be unwilling to see this situation change by sharing more information and responsibility with the public (Fielding, 1987). Even if there was such willingness (and I believe that its encouragement will take a very long time), there will still be barriers to effective partnership between informal and formal social control. One, as cited above, is the disparate views within communities. Another is the discrepancy between the very localised concerns of residents and business people and the area subsumed at the level of operational command in the police force and in local authorities. Division, district council areas, even subdivisions, are far too large to have any meaning in crime terms to residents and businesss people (though they may be the appropriate level for minority groups and trade associations). If consultation and the sharing of responsibility is to be promoted, it will need to take place at sub-beat level as well as at beat level, subdivisional level and above. And that implies not only mechanisms and willingness across the police-public divide, but also greater priority given to beat work within the police force and effective channels of communication upwards through the ranks and between specialisms.

On a less depressing note, it is possible to suggest some ways of improving communication to tackle the inadvertent, as opposed to structurally generated, lack of interaction between police and public. One is to provide the public with accurate information about crime and with feedback on what has been done by the police when problems are referred to them (see Burrows, 1986, for a cogent argument for this in respect of burglary victims and Shapland *et al.*,

1985, in respect of victims of violent crime). Feedback will provide a basis for a reasoned appraisal of public and police action. Equally, crime prevention information could be targeted at the times when it is most needed and marketed to suit the needs of different groups (separate leaflets for the common house and business design styles, for example). Finally, the major target of police deployment—providing 'ground cover'—could move in the direction of providing that cover by local officers dealing with most calls, with leadership, information backup and problem-solving instruction by supervisors (see Shapland and Vagg, 1985). Only local officers talking to local residents will have a chance of moving towards an ideal of policing with the public.

References

BENNETT, T. and WRIGHT, R. (1984). *Burglars on Burglary*. Aldershot, England: Gower.

BRIGHT, J., MALONEY, H., PETTERSON, G. and FARR, J. (1985). *After Entryphones: Improving Management and Security in Multi-storey Blocks*. London: NACRO, The Safe Neighbourhoods Unit.

BURROWS, J. (1986). *Burglary: police actions and victims' views*. Home Office Research and Planning Unit Paper No. 37. London: Home Office.

FIELDING, N. (1987). 'Being used by the police'. *British Journal of Criminology*, 27, pp. 64–69.

HOPE, T. (1982). *Burglary in Schools: the prospects for prevention*. Home Office Research and Planning Unit Paper No. 11. London: Home Office.

JACOBS, J. (1965). *The Death and Life of Great American Cities*. Harmondsworth, England: Penguin Books.

MINISTERIE VAN JUSTITIE, (1985). *Society and Crime: a policy plan for The Netherlands*. The Hague: Ministerie van Justitie.

RILEY, D. and MAYHEW, P. (1980). *Crime Prevention Publicity: An Assessment*. Home Office Research Study No. 63. London: HMSO.

SHAPLAND, J. and VAGG, J. (1985). *Social Control and Policing in Rural and Urban Areas*. Final Report to the Home Office. Oxford, England: Centre for Criminological Research.

SHAPLAND, J. and VAGG, J. (1987). 'Using the Police'. *British Journal of Criminology,* 27, pp. 54–63.

SHAPLAND, J., WILLMORE, J. and DUFF, P.(1985). *Victims in the Criminal Justice System*. Farnborough, England: Gower.

WEATHERITT, M. (1986). *Innovations in Policing*. London: Croom Helm.

WINCHESTER, S. and JACKSON, H. (1982). *Residential Burglary: The Limits of Prevention*. Home Office Research Study No. 74. London: HMSO.

WINKEL, F. W. (1987). Response generalization in crime prevention campaigns: an experiment'. *British Journal of Criminology*, 27, pp. 155-173.

8. A critical eye on neighbourhood watch: does it reduce crime and fear?

Dennis P Rosenbaum[1]

Over the past five years, community crime prevention in North America and Europe has become a visible and accepted part of community life for millions of individuals. To some extent, the appeal of collective citizen action stems from the hope that strategies such as Neighbourhood Watch will serve to correct or replace almost reflex responses to crime, including heightened levels of fear and behavioural withdrawal from social environments that are perceived as dangerous. Research in the United States indicates that restricting one's behaviour and installing security devices are among the most common reactions to crime by community residents (Lavrakas *et al.*, 1980). In discussing this 'retreat behind locks, bars, alarms, and guards', the National Advisory Commission on Criminal Justice Standards and Goals (1973) in the United States noted that 'although these prophylactic measures may be steps in self-protection, they can lead to a lessening of the bonds of mutual assistance and neighbourliness' (p. 46). In the context of discussions about 'neighbourhood decline' (cf. Taub *et al.*, 1982), there is talk about a declining sense of community or a reduction in social cohesion. One of the main explanations for high levels of crime, incivility, and fear of crime in certain neighbourhoods is the erosion of informal social control processes that are believed responsible for maintaining order (Jacobs, 1961; Greenberg *et al.*, 1985; Wilson and Kelling, 1982).

Neighbourhood Watch has been recommended as a feasible and attractive solution to these crime-related neighbourhood conditions. This crime prevention strategy has been conceptualised as a collective, 'public-minded' strategy as opposed to the individual-focused, 'private-minded' responses to crime that are typical of most citizens (cf. Schneider and Schneider, 1978). Essentially, Neighbourhood or Block Watch involves citizens coming together in relatively small groups (usually at the block level) to share information about local crime problems, exchange crime prevention tips, and make plans for engaging in surveillance ('watching') of the neighbourhood and crime-reporting activities. The first block meetings are often arranged by crime prevention officers from the police department or 'community organisers' employed by local community organisations. Block group meetings involve presentations regarding the opportunity to participate in property marking (engraving) and home security survey programmes offered by the police, as well as to set up a 'phone chain' or 'tree' for surveillance and support. The meetings frequently involve informal discussions of feelings and perceptions among participants regarding the local crime problem and what can be done about it.

Although Neighbourhood Watch is often described in the media as a highly effective programme, our knowledge of how this strategy works and what real

---

1. Portions of this article are excerpts from 'The Theory and Research Behind Neighbourhood Watch'. *Crime and Delinquency*, 33, pp. 103–134, 1987.

effects it has on community residents remains extremely limited. This chapter takes a critical look at this scheme from both a theoretical and empirical standpoint. Emphasis is given to articulating the models and assumptions underlying this strategy and examining the quality of evaluation research that addresses the question of programme effectiveness. Particular attention will be given to the fear-reduction hypothesis.

Theoretical foundation

Watch programmes are consistent with the two primary theoretical models used in community crime prevention today, namely, informal social control and opportunity reduction. Jane Jacobs (1961) articulated the basic principal behind the informal social control model as it pertains to crime control:
> 'The first thing to understand is that public peace ... is not kept primarily by the police, necessary as police are. It is kept primarily by an intricate, almost unconscious network of voluntary controls and standards among the people themselves, and enforced by the people themselves.' (p. 31–32).

Recently, researchers have sought greater theoretical precision in making the connection between informal social control and community crime prevention programmes such as Neighbourhood Watch. Specifically, the hope for Watch programmes is that they will produce the social contact and social interaction necessary to strengthen informal social control bonds and thus enhance community social cohesion (see Chapter 14; DuBow and Emmons, 1981; Greenberg et al., 1985; Rosenbaum et al., 1985; Silloway and McPherson, 1985; Yin, 1979). Perhaps the biggest hope for the Watch model, as articulated by these theorists, is that it will reduce fear of crime via this collective process. Residents would be stripped of their reasons for social isolation and distrust after developing friendship patterns with neighbours and working jointly toward reducing the common problem of crime.

The opportunity reduction model as it applies to Neighbourhood Watch is actually a derivative of earlier theorising about how changes in physical design characteristics will reduce criminal opportunities (Jacobs, 1961). At the core of what became known as 'crime prevention through environmental design' (Jeffrey, 1971) and 'defensible space' theory (Newman, 1972) is Jane Jacobs's (1961) argument that there must be natural surveillance ('eyes on the street') to reduce the opportunities for crime. Neighbourhood Watch, one could argue, was historically built upon research showing an inverse relationship between surveillance opportunities and crime rates (e.g. Newman, 1972; Reppetto, 1974). Through social (rather than physical) means Watches seek to encourage *intentional* surveillance rather than merely create *natural* surveillance opportunities. Thus, Neighbourhood Watch holds the promise of increasing collective surveillance of the neighbourhood, where residents become the 'eyes and ears' of the police and report any suspicious or criminal activity in the area. This type of territorial 'neighbouring' is expected to reduce the opportunity for criminal activity by letting would-be criminals know that the risk of detection and apprehension has increased. Also, to the extent that block meetings stimulate residents to take individual measures to protect themselves or their property (although unrelated to the hypothesised surveillance effect), then the opportunities to engage in personal and property offences in that particular neighbourhood should diminish. This opportunity reduction model suggests that fear of crime will decrease as residents perceive a decrease in their risk of victimization.

Empirical support and its limitations

Two primary types of empirical information have been used to support the concept of Neighbourhood Watch—(a) neighbourhood studies on citizen participation and reactions to crime and (b) evaluations of crime prevention programmes. The reactions-to-crime research has provided the basis for most scholarly support for the Watch concept, as it provides considerable support for the informal social control model (see Greenberg *et al.*, 1985, for a review). For example, research has shown that fear of crime is lower in neighbourhoods where residents feel more responsibility and control over what happens in that area (Greenberg *et al.*, 1982; Skogan and Maxfield, 1981), where the number of incivilities or disorders, such as litter and teenagers hanging out, is low (Skogan and Maxfield, 1981; Taub, Taylor and Dunham, 1981), and where neighbours are perceived as available to provide assistance when needed (Sundeen and Mathieu, 1976). Thus, fear of crime appears to be influenced by the perceived level of social order in the neighbourhood, leading Greenberg and her colleagues to recommend that communities 'develop programmes that familiarise local residents with each other and with the neighbourhood to help intervention and to reduce fear' (Greenberg *et al.*, 1985, p. 17). While the enhancement of informal social control in neighbourhoods characterised by disorder is a seemingly desirable objective, our ability to accomplish this through programmatic efforts remains very questionable, as this paper will address in more detail later.

Another aspect of the reactions-to-crime literature that has been interpreted as supportive of watch-type programmes is the research focused on citizen participation in local community organisations—groups that often serve as vehicles for Neighbourhood Watch programmes. For example, studies have shown that 'participators' in local voluntary organisations exhibit higher levels of informal social interaction in the neighbourhood than 'non-participators' (Kasarda & Janowitz, 1974; Hunter, 1974). The assumption that more social interaction will reduce the level of crime or fear of crime in the community will be examined later.

Unfortunately, there are many problems in seeing the research on reactions to crime as supportive of Watch-type programmes. Perhaps the most fundamental problem is the low internal validity of the typical research design used. This body of research is based, almost exclusively, on *cross-sectional* data that do not easily allow causal inferences. Hence, we have little confidence that the behaviours which distinguish participants from non-participants are attributable to the act of participation or the influence of the groups, rather than pre-existing differences between the two groups. Self-selection is one of the biggest threats to the validity of non-experimental evaluation research in many fields, and it is no less of a problem in this case. The research has been quite clear about who participates in community activities and where these individuals live, and thus serves to document this self-selection process. Studies have consistently shown that participation in voluntary organisations is largely a middle-class phenomenon, i.e., participants tend to be in the middle-income range, married with children, home-owners, and well educated (Lavrakas *et al.*, 1980; Skogan and Maxfield, 1981; Wandersman, Jakubs and Giamartino, 1981). Furthermore, these individuals tend to live in neighbourhoods characterised by a shared set of norms regarding public behaviour. In their re-analysis of survey data from three American cities and 60 neighbourhoods, Greenberg *et al.*, (1982) found that collective crime prevention programmes like Neighbourhood Watch were more prevalent in neighbourhoods with racial and economic homogeneity.

A number of studies indicate that these homogeneous, typically middle-class areas are generally characterised by much stronger informal social controls. That is, residents feel more control over their environment (e.g. more willing to intervene), feel more responsible for crime prevention (i.e. less reliant on police), and generally feel more positive about, and similar to, their neighbours than residents of typical lower-class neighbourhoods, (Boggs, 1971; Greenberg *et al.*, 1982; Hackler *et al.*, 1974; Taub *et al.*, 1982; Taylor *et al.*, 1981).

All of these empirical observations leave unanswered the fundamental question of whether the *introduction* of a community crime prevention programme (and Neighbourhood Watch in particular) can make a difference in the perceptions, attitudes, and behaviours of local residents. The important question here is whether informal social control (and other processes supposedly activated by Watch-type programmes) can be *implanted* in neighbourhoods where they have not developed naturally. I have referred to this as the 'Implant Hypothesis' (Rosenbaum, 1987). Let us examine some of the empirical support for this proposition. What evidence can be amassed to show that crime, fear of crime, and related neighbourhood responses have declined as a direct result of Neighbourhood Watch-type intervention?

Evaluation research findings

Titus (1984) has reviewed the findings of nearly three dozen evaluations of burglary prevention programmes (including more than a dozen Watch programmes) and found that participating individuals were less victimized and/or target areas had lower burglary rates than their comparison groups. However, showing participator-nonparticipator differences, again, is not quasi-experimental because participator characteristics may be confounded with intervention effects. In addition, the self-selection process which can explain pre-intervention differences between participators and nonparticipators also applies to blocks and neighbourhoods as well.

At our request, Leonard Sipes (using documents at the National Criminal Justice Reference Service) identified 111 programmes that claim 'success' with Neighbourhood Watch by reporting reductions in crime (Lurigio and Rosenbaum, 1986). While many writers in the mass media and elsewhere have been quick to conclude that these success stories are truly indicative of the power of Watch-type programmes, these conclusions are not based on hard evidence. For example, 92 per cent of the projects collected data using the one-group pre-test—post-test design—a very weak research design that is subject to many threats to validity (see Campbell and Stanley, 1966; Cook and Campbell, 1979). Most of these programmes were implemented in the late 1970s and early 1980s when crime rates were peaking and beginning to decline across the United States, thus introducing the possibility that statistical regression artifacts can explain the observed declines. Often, only police crime statistics were examined in the target area.

The low quality of evaluation research in this field has been recognised by several researchers (Greenberg *et al.*, 1985; Lurigio and Rosenbaum, 1986; Skogan, 1979; Yin, 1979). To summarise these concerns, the programme evaluations are 'characterised by weak designs, an under-use of statistical significance tests, a poor conceptualisation and definition of treatments, the absence of a valid and reliable measurement of programme implementation and outcomes, and a consistent failure to address competing explanations for observed effects.' (Lurigio and Rosenbaum, 1986, p. 2.)

If the large majority of evaluations in the field are seriously flawed, what evidence can be amassed to test the implant hypothesis? While strong community crime prevention evaluations have been conducted in Hartford, Connecticut (Fowler and Mangione, 1982) and Portland, Oregon (Schneider, 1975) neither of these interventions was limited to Neighbourhood Watch. Only two evaluations to date can be viewed as reasonably strong tests of the Neighbourhood Watch model—the well-known Seattle evaluation (Cirel *et al.*, 1977; Lindsay and McGillis, 1986), and the recently completed Chicago Evaluation (Rosenbaum *et al.*, 1985; 1986). Briefly, the Seattle evaluation yielded generally positive results, showing a reduction in residential burglary in the target areas relative to the control areas. In contrast to the Seattle evaluation, the Chicago evaluation found generally negative results, showing increases in a variety of social problem areas, including fear of crime. Because the Chicago evaluation is the first quasi-experimental test of the full range of hypotheses derived from both the informal social control and opportunity reduction models, a brief description of this research is provided.

The Chicago evaluation

The Ford Foundation funded Northwestern University to conduct a rigorous process and impact evaluation of community crime prevention programmes being planned in Chicago Neighbourhoods (see Lewis *et al.*, 1985: Rosenbaum *et al.*, 1985). The intervention was an attempt by experienced volunteers from local community organisations to organise the residents of selected neighbourhoods using door-to-door canvassing, block meetings, and neighbourhood meetings, with emphasis on the Block Watch model. A quasi-experimental research design was employed for the impact evaluation, namely, an Untreated Control Group Design with Pre-test and Post-test (cf. Cook and Campbell, 1979). A one-year lag was scheduled between the pre-test (n = 3357) and post-test samples (n = 2824), from February 1983 to February 1984, and extensive telephone surveys were conducted with residents using both panel and independent random samples. Control groups included three carefully selected neighbourhoods in Chicago for *each* of the four target neighbourhoods, and a city-wide random sample.

Seven primary hypotheses were tested which capture the current theorising about the impact of such programmes (Rosenbaum *et al.*, 1985). Specifically, Neighbourhood Watch was expected to: (a) stimulate residents' awareness of, and participation in crime prevention meetings, (b) enhance feelings of efficacy and personal responsibility for preventive action, (c) produce a number of behavioural changes related to preventing victimization and informally regulating social behaviour, (d) enhance social cohesion in the neighbourhood, (e) reduce crime and various types of disorders, (f) reduce fear of crime and related perceptions of crime, and (g) improve citizens' general perceptions of the neighbourhood and attachment to the community as a place to live.

The results of the Chicago evaluation indicate that although residents' awareness of the programme and levels of participation increased significantly (indicating *some* success with programme implementation), there was a consistent lack of support for the main hypotheses stated above. That is, the large majority of comparisons revealed no significant differential change over time between the treated and untreated areas. Target area residents did not allow the Watch meetings to influence their crime prevention behaviours, nor did the programme have any consistent effects on levels of crime or incivility. Furthermore, the majority of the significant findings ran *counter to* the main hypotheses. Specifically, the three neighbourhoods with the strongest evidence of programme implementation showed significant *increases* in a number of areas, including increases in fear of crime, perceptions of the crime problem, personal knowledge of recent crime victims, concern about the future of the neighbourhood, and the likelihood of moving out. Additional analyses were conducted to rule out rival hypotheses.

Given a very serious effort by experienced organizers to implement the Neighbourhood Watch programme in one neighbourhood, there is some justification for pointing the finger at the theoretical model guiding these actions. While the Chicago evaluation should not be viewed as the 'final word' on the effectiveness of Neighbourhood Watch, these data should encourage us to take a closer look at the theoretical underpinnings of this popular strategy.

Challenging theoretical assumptions

The attraction of Neighbourhood Watch rests on a number of key assumptions about neighbourhood processes and social behaviour. While several of these assumptions are theory-based, others are simply popular beliefs accepted by the general public as statements of fact. In any event, these assumptions (which are rarely challenged) need to be stated explicitly and examined critically. Five of the more problematic assertions are discussed below, but the reader should note that the list of assumptions is much longer.

Assumption 1: Neighbourhood Watch can be easily implemented on a large scale to provide citizens with an opportunity for participation in crime prevention activities.

The feasibility of implementing Neighbourhood Watch on a large scale will depend, to some extent, on public receptivity to the concept. If citizens are unaware of the programme's existence or hold negative attitudes about the benefits to be derived from their participation, then high levels of involvement are unlikely. However, survey data from the United States and Britain suggest that the Watch concept is attractive to most citizens in these two countries. A 1982 Gallup Poll revealed that 72 per cent of the American public has 'heard or read about' the programme (Gallup, 1982). Furthermore, the concept has spread quickly to Britain, as indicated by the results of the 1984 British Crime Survey (BCS) (see Chapter 9).

In addition to these fairly high levels of awareness, citizen attitudes about Neighbourhood Watch are quite positive. The 1982 Gallup poll revealed that 81 per cent of Americans were interested in joining a Watch programme, and the 1984 BCS found that 62 per cent of respondents were prepared to join the Watch scheme (Chapter 9).

Citizen participation

A problem emerges when we look at the opportunities to participate in the programme and actual levels of participation at the national level. In the United States, the 1984 Victimization Risk Survey, used as a one-time supplement to the National Crime Survey (NCS), offers the best data on these variables (N = 21,106 persons aged 16 or older from 11,198 households). In terms of the *opportunity* to participate, respondents in approximately one-fifth of the households (19%) reported that a Neighbourhood Watch programme exists in their area (Whitaker, 1986). (This shows a slight increase over the 17 per cent figure produced from the 1982 Gallup poll survey. Comparable data from Britain are not yet available.) In terms of *actual participation*, the levels are quite low when compared to the level of interest described earlier. The 1984 NCS found that only 7 per cent of the American public has participated in a local Neighbourhood Watch.

Apparently, Neighbourhood Watch is an attractive idea to many people, but the gap between favourable attitudes and actual participation is rather sizeable. Some insight into this discrepancy can be obtained by examining the responses of persons who are openly reluctant to join a Watch programme (see Chapter 9). Clearly, the concept is much newer in Britain than in the United States, and thus, the opportunities to participate have been limited until quite recently. However, the 1984 level of 7 per cent attained in the United States is indicative of what can be expected (up from 5% in 1981). Much depends on the attractiveness of self-help anti-crime measures in Britain, although in the United States this movement is rather strong.

Police participation

Another part of the low participation problem is the lack of opportunity to get involved. In the United States, although only 7 per cent of the public participated in Neighbourhood Watch, almost 38 per cent of the households participated in areas where the programme already existed. A big determinant of opportunity is local law enforcement and their level of commitment to the programme. Anecdotal evidence and local surveys indicate that the level of investment in crime prevention activities among law enforcement agencies remains very minimal despite all the talk about this being their top priority. For example, a rare survey of 'municipal crime prevention practitioners' in the state of Pennsylvania revealed that the average low enforcement agency devotes only 2 per cent of its total person-time to crime prevention activities. (Pennsylvania Commission on Crime and Delinquency, 1984). The Commission report concludes that 'although there is an abundance of crime prevention activities in many local municipalties, those with planned, targeted programmes involving Neighbourhood Watch on an organised basis are not common' (p. 11). These observations are consistent with the preliminary findings of the National Assessment of Neighbourhood Watch which indicate that Watch programmes are not as 'systematic' or 'co-ordinated' as the popular definition suggests (Garofalo and McCleod, 1985).

Assumption 2: If given the opportunity to participate in Neighbourhood Watch, most citizens would find the programme appealing and would become involved regardless of social, demographic, or neighbourhood characteristics.

There is a widespread belief that Neighbourhood Watch can be successfully implemented anywhere and anytime if only the effort is made. This important belief is the cornerstone of the 'shotgun' crime prevention policies adopted by many local governments, but it conflicts strongly with research findings regarding the natural distribution of citizen participation and informal social control.

As noted earlier, research suggests that collective participation is largely a middle-class phenomenon that emerges in more stable neighbourhoods, and Watch-type programmes are no exception. A recent national survey of 530 Neighbourhood Watch programmes in the United States revealed that residents living in the areas served by these programmes are predominantly white, have middle or upper incomes, are single-family home owners, and have lived in their current location for at least five years (Garofalo and McCleod, 1985). A similar pattern of participation was apparent in the British Crime Survey, where residents in areas of 'modern family housing' (i.e. non-manual, higher-earning, home-owners with children) expressed the greatest desire to join Neighbourhood Watch (Chapter 9). In addition, there is a long line of scholarly work on urban neighbourhoods which suggests that informal social control is less likely to develop in low income, and culturally heterogeneous neighbourhoods (see Greenberg *et al.*, 1985, for a review).

Thus, the notion that programmes like Neighbourhood Watch will be adopted in *any* neighbourhood is based on a number of assumptions that are inconsistent with prior research. Greenberg *et al.*, (1985) have articulated some of the relevant assumptions:

'A basic assumption of crime prevention programmes with a neighbourhood orientation is that their success depends on collective citizen involvement. It is assumed that neighbourhood residents already know one another or would like to get to know one another; are willing to co-operate with each other in such activities as watching each others' houses and intervening in crimes; and, most importantly, have shared norms for appropriate public behaviour. Many of the activities of community crime prevention programmes depend upon mutual trust and a willingness to take responsibility for each others' safety.' (p. 19).

The problem, as research suggests, is that neighbourhoods which need the most help (i.e. have the most serious crime problems) will be the least receptive to such programmes because these residential areas are characterised by suspicion, distrust, hostility, and a lack of shared norms regarding appropriate public behaviour.

While these studies of urban neighbourhoods and citizen participation suggest some limitations on programme applicability, they do not directly test the Implant Hypothesis because we do not know whether non-participating neighbourhoods or blocks can be motivated to get involved in Watch-type programmes regardless of their characteristics. Only the Minneapolis project offers a careful examination of this issue in the context of a quasi-experimental evaluation.

The Minneapolis test

Perhaps the strongest test of the hypothesis that citizens *will* participate in Block Watch *if* given the opportunity is currently underway in Minneapolis. What is noteworthy about the Minneapolis project is the wide variety of neighbourhoods that were exposed to this intervention, and the intensity of this systematic effort to organise Block Watch in each area. The preliminary results are now available and strongly challenge the Implant Hypothesis (DuBow, McPherson, and Silloway, 1985; Silloway and McPherson, 1985). The findings show that even after a substantial organising effort (averaging 25 hours per block), the level of citizen participation was quite low. While residents on 85 per cent of the target blocks were invited to attend at least one block meeting, only one-fifth of the households responded affirmatively. On the average, fewer than nine people per block attended the meetings.

Perhaps the most important finding in Minneapolis is that different levels of success were experienced when seeking to organise different types of neighbourhoods. Organisers tried significantly *harder* (i.e. arranged more meetings, made more contacts) in neighbourhoods with lower socio-economic status and less homogeneity, but experienced *less* success in terms of citizen attendance. Thus, organisers did not give up on blocks that were initially difficult to organise, but the extra effort did not pay off.

In sum, there is now some evidence to suggest that Neighbourhood Watch is not a suitably strategy for certain neighbourhoods or blocks. If this strategy does not stimulate substantial levels of participation, even after serious attempts by trained community organisers, then the theoretical underpinnings of the approach should be scrutinised. Silloway and McPherson (1985), in discussing the Minneapolis findings, concluded that the assumption of '*voluntary* participation' which underlies the Block Watch model is 'highly problematical'.

Assumption 3: If and when citizens get together at Block Watch meetings, the assumption is made that this interaction and discussion will produce a

134

number of immediate effects, including a reduction in fear of crime and an increase in both individual and collective crime prevention behaviours.

The social interaction that takes place at Block Watch meetings is poorly documented, yet we entertain wonderful ideas about these meetings—how they alleviate the fears of local residents and set in motion an organised plan for fighting neighbourhood crime. Field-work in this area suggests that citizens use these meetings to discuss informally the local crime problem, learn about individual and home protection measures and set up a 'phone tree' of block residents to share information about suspicious activities observed in the area (Lewis, *et al.*, 1985; McPherson and Silloway, 1980). With the exception of meetings that are well organised by crime prevention officers or community organisers, there is usually an open agenda for residents to exchange thoughts and concerns and take the meeting in whatever direction is suitable to their immediate needs.

Fear reduction

One of the most critical (and troublesome) assumptions of the Neighbourhood Watch model is that this strategy is a promising mechanism for reducing fear of crime in urban communities. The opportunity reduction model suggests that fear is the result of exposure to crime and, therefore, fear can be directly reduced by lowering residents' actual risk of victimization. The social control model suggests that fear is the result of a perceived decline in informal social control and, therefore, fear can be indirectly reduced by somehow restoring a sense of social organisation and cohesion in the community.

Neither of these models provides a clear basis for predicting that the Watch meeting *itself* will directly reduce fear of crime. However, consistent with the social control model, a reduction in fear has been assumed (cf. Feins, 1983; DuBow and Emmons, 1981; Rosenbaum *et al.*, 1985). The idea behind this hypothesis is that social interaction at these meetings provides concerned citizens with social support and reassurance that something can be done, both collectively and individually, to affect the local crime problem. Indeed a basic derivation of social comparison theory (Festinger, 1954) is that people affiliate with similar others to reduce anxiety (cf. Schacter, 1959). Moreover, in many cases, the meetings provide participants with a plan of action (i.e. watching out for suspicious activity and improving personal and household security) that seems efficacious, and thus might be expected to alleviate fear of crime.

This line of thinking sounds plausible, but to date the author is not aware of evaluation research (with a reasonably strong design) that shows a significant reduction in fear of crime. To the contrary, there is evidence that could be interpreted as supportive of the alternative hypothesis that Watch meetings serve as a mechanism for *heightening* fear of crime.

The Chicago evaluation found, contrary to expectation, that fear of personal crime *increased* significantly in three of the four target neighbourhoods (relative to control groups). In other quasi-experimental work, the exemplary Seattle programme, although showing a reduction in burglary, was also associated with a marginally significant increase in fear of crime (see Cirel *et al.*, 1977, p. 68). Research on the personal correlates of participation in community crime prevention is not inconsistent with this less favourable hypothesis. In their review of literature, DuBow *et al.*, (1979) conclude that 'participants of all types generally have higher fear levels' (p. 31), and that collective participation is associated with both fear and perceived risk of victimization (see also Chapter 9). A look at more recent literature on crime prevention suggests that the results are mixed. Participation in collective crime prevention activities has been found to be associated with a higher perceived risk of victimization in one study (Yaden *et al.*, 1973), but a lower fear of crime in another (Skogan and Maxfield, 1981). Several studies suggest that fear and participation are unrelated (Lavrakas *et al.*, 1980; Podolefsky and DuBow, 1981; Rohe and Greenberg, 1982). Again, these correlational studies do not solve the 'direction-of-causality' problem, but they at least suggest that participation is not a clear path to fear reduction.

The fear-exacerbation hypothesis

Why might we expect that fear of victimization would increase as a result of participation in Watch-type meetings? One possible explanation is that fear is exacerbated when participants exchange information about local crime (Greenberg *et al.*, 1985; Rosenbaum *et al.*, 1985; Skogan & Maxfield, 1981). Our field work suggests that participants often use this opportunity to describe their direct and indirect victimization experiences and express the i.e. personal concern about the neighbourhood crime problem (Lewis *et al.*, 1985). In fact, Block Watch organisers in Seattle and Chicago are trained to encourage a discussion of personal victimization experiences. (*Citizen's Guide to Organizing a Block Watch*; Seattle Police Department, n.d.; Citizen Information Service of Illinois, 1982, p. 12.)

With this type of discussion, more criminal activity is brought to the group's attention, as well as the fears of individual group members. Consistent with this explanation for possible increases in fear, Greenberg *et al.*, (1982), in a study of six Atlanta neighbourhoods, discovered that worry about crime increased as more information was exchanged with neighbours. Similarly, Pennell's (1978) analysis of data in three American cities revealed that participation in neighbourhood groups was associated with a greater knowledge of and concern about crime.

Informal discussions of victimization experiences can be as important as actual crime rates in shaping residents' fears and perceptions. The Reactions to Crime Project (Skogan *et al.*, 1982) in three American cities found that 'vicarious' victimization (i.e. knowing someone who has been a victim of crime recently) was an important predictor of fear of crime.

Small group discussion may even serve as a 'consciousness raising' experience whereby participants leave feeling *more* (rather than less) helpless in the face of uncontrollable political and social forces. For example, citizens may discover that residential transition is beyond their control, or that the police have not been responsive to their pressures, or that criminal victimization is not always prevented by precautionary measures and may strike anyone at anytime. This perceived lack of efficacy could, in turn, exacerbate fear of crime and fear of neighbourhood decline.

In addition to one's knowledge of local crime and exposure to expressions of

136

fear, another factor that may contribute to feelings of vulnerability are the discussions of home security measures that are a commonplace at Watch-type meetings. Whether it happens via informal discussions or a formal security check, residents can be made to feel that their home is quite vulnerable to burglary or home invasion. Using a randomised experimental design in Evanston, Illlinois, Rosenbaum (1983) found that burglary victims who were given a home security survey by an experienced crime prevention officer were significantly more fearful of revictimization, felt less control over their chances of revictimization, were more upset and angry about the incident, and reported less emotional and psychological recovery than victims who did not receive a home security survey. Hence, we cannot assume that well-intended efforts to share information about crime prevention will have unconditional positive effects. Although programmatic attempts to increase public *concern* and knowledge about crime without simultaneously increasing public *fear* have previously been advocated (Lavrakas, Rosenbaum & Kaminski, 1983), this separation of effects may not be easy to accomplish.

Insights from psychological research

A long history of social psychological research on group dynamics gives us some insight into the functions and decision-making processes of small groups. Festinger's (1954) classic social comparison theory suggests that people participate in group activities not merely to accomplish group tasks, but to evaluate (and validate) their own feelings, opinions, and abilities against those of other group members. This process opens the door for interpersonal influence.

There is a significant body of research which indicates that small group discussions—when not constrained by structure or authority—will produce a more extreme group consensus than would be expected by averaging the initial positions of the individual group members (Kogan and Wallach, 1964). In fact, the direction of change is predictable from the group's *initial* inclinations, leading researchers to label this process 'collective polarisation' (Doise, 1969, Moscovici and Doise, 1974; Moscovici and Zavalloni, 1969). Myers and Bishop (1970), for example, have demonstrated that groups comprised of racist individuals have become even more racist after having the opportunity for discussion. Research on small group discussion also suggests that informational influence is operating—that is, groups will shift their judgements in response to more frequent and persuasive arguments, and that the outcome could go either way.

Social psychological theory and research do not directly answer the question of whether group discussion in Watch-type settings will increase, decrease, homogenise, or have no effect on the fear level of group participants. However, the implication of this work is that the outcome will depend on the precise interactional circumstances and content of the discussion. One task for future research will be to specify the conditions under which different fear outcomes are observed. At a minimum, social psychological theory can take us beyond the more general criminal justice models to identify some of the social processes that are worth attending to in this type of small group setting, including modelling, labelling, and informational persuasion. Through careful observation or manipulation, researchers could explore the importance of types of models (e.g. calm vs. anxious), level of group structure, initial group inclination, and other factors that may predict fear responses.

Post-meeting behavioural effects

Finally we must confront the important empirical question of whether Watch-type programmes actually produce the types of residential behaviour which the social control and opportunity reduction models posit as the causal preconditions for reducing fear, incivility, and crime. Specifically, will citizens begin to interact more frequently, engage in territorial surveillance, and practice a variety of victimization prevention behaviours? Several studies have found that citizens who elect to participate in crime prevention programmes are more likely than non-participants to engage in various crime prevention behaviours which, in turn, *may* reduce their chances of victimization (Lavrakas *et al.*, 1980; Pennell, 1978; Schneider and Schneider, 1978). However, in the Chicago evaluation—which avoided much of the self-selection bias inherent in these participation studies—we found that neighbourhoods (and blocks) exposed to the Watch programme generally did not differ from unexposed neighbourhoods (and blocks) in terms of residents' levels of social interaction on the street, neighbourhood surveillance (i.e. watching each other's home while away), home protection behaviours, self-protection behaviours, or intervention behaviours. Thus, while target-area residents participated in crime prevention meetings at significantly higher levels than members of the control group, they did not allow these meetings to influence their behaviour in any measurable way. Clearly, these data suggest theory failure, but more research is needed to further substantiate this conclusion.

Assumption 4: Neighbourhood Watch organisers (both police and community volunteers) invest in this strategy with the belief that such activities, once initiated, will be sustained.

Even if Watch programmes could be successfully implemented, they would still face a serious problem, namely how to maintain themselves. Researchers have documented the decline in participation and discontinuation of watches that frequently occurs with the passage of time (Garofalo and McCleod, 1985; Lindsay and McGillis, 1986; McPherson and Silloway, 1980). Block group members become inactive for a variety of reasons, and the importance of maintenance activities has been emphasised repeatedly by experts in the field. One of the main problems is the single-issue focus of many watches. Once the crime problems appear to have dissipated, the reason for the group's existence has also been removed.

This observation has led researchers to conclude that *multi-issue* community organisations are the best vehicle for sustaining citizen involvement in crime prevention activities (Lavrakas *et al.*, 1980; Podolefsky and DuBow, 1981). However, there is also the problem of expecting too much of voluntary community groups (see Chapter 13). There should be little doubt that local government (and its many resources) plays a critical role in starting and sustaining community-based programmes, as well as maintaining public order. As Yin (1986) notes in his synthesis of 11 major community crime prevention evaluations, the programmes which had the strongest positive effects on crime and fear were those where 'citizens and police either collaborated directly or were both involved in the intervention'.

Assumption 5: The collective citizen actions implied by the Neighbourhood Watch scheme, if set in motion, would reduce the level of criminal activity and disorder in the neighbourhood, thereby setting the stage for a reduction in fear of crime and other neighbourhood improvements.

Assuming for the moment that this strategy could be successfully implemented as specified by theory, the question then becomes—would Block Watch be an effective means of controlling crime and incivility? Even under optimal conditions, there are still several reasons to question the efficaciousness of this approach.

One problem is that the Neighbourhood Watch concept, as explained by the informal social control or opportunity reduction models, does not give sufficient attention to the factors that limit our ability as residents to regulate the behaviour of either 'good' or 'bad' members of the community. First, the social control model suggests that Watch programmes will restore a sense of community (through increased social interaction), and this will, in turn, pressure criminally-inclined individuals and families to abide by the norms of the community. However, 40 years of social psychological research remind us that social control is a *group* process, and the many principles of group behaviour that have been uncovered through controlled research still apply. Theories of small group processes do not posit mechanisms by which a group can exercise effective control over 'non-members'. Individuals are controllable to the extent that they are committed to the group and the group is a cohesive unit (Festinger, Schacter and Back, 1950). Social control processes should have little influence over strangers or criminals who do not perceive themselves as group members and feel no pressure to conform. In fact, the very same problem applies to 'good' citizens as well, who are not members of the 'group'. If they do not view themselves as belonging to the Block Watch group, neighbourhood organisation, or even the larger 'community', then group members have little leverage to regulate or change the social perceptions and behaviours of these individuals.

A crucial question that emerges from this discussion is—who belongs to the target 'group'? Is it everyone on the block, everyone living in certain apartment buildings, the entire neighbourhood, or some other social unit? Perhaps the hypothesised effects of Watch-type programmes are limited to those individuals who actively participate in the group meetings, contrary to the widely-held assumption that such programmes can alter the pattern of informal social control at the neighbourhood level.

Implicit in this discussion is another critical question, namely, what 'dosage' of the 'treatment' would be sufficient to modify the community's social control mechanisms, and thus reduce crime and incivility? What scope, duration, and intensity of effort is needed to alter these social patterns? As noted earlier, the typical levels of participation in Watch programmes are hardly sufficient to produce occasional surveillance, let alone permanently change residents' day-to-day interactions. Social norms and control processes do not develop as a result of a few people attending one or two Block Watch meetings over the course of a year. Again, we are looking at the credibility of the Implant Hypothesis, and find it wanting. DuBow and Emmons (1981) summarise the point nicely: 'The descriptions of informal social control that are found in the literature ... illuminate processes that are the outgrowth of unplanned social forces at work over a long period of time' (p. 177).

Behavioural mechanisms

Certainly we can envision potentially efficacious ways of enhancing informal social control, such as parental efforts to monitor and collectively regulate the behaviour of children and young adolescents in the neighbourhood. However, Neighbourhood Watch is not a complex strategy for shaping social behaviour, but rather a simple programme designed to encourage people to watch for suspicious behaviour (especially residential burglary) and call the police if necessary.

Nevertheless, the main hypothesised consequences of Neighbourhood Watch that are relevant to informal social control are (a) more social interaction, (b) more surveillance, and (c) more bystander intervention. The role of each of these citizen behaviours in controlling neighbourhood crime remains very uncertain. If Watch programmes could stimulate more social interaction among neighbours, and if this effect is documented, there is still a need to show that this change in behaviour will, either directly or indirectly, reduce crime and/or acts of incivility. While the bystander intervention literature provides some empirical basis for thinking that people who interact or know one another are more likely to help one another in time of need (Bickman and Rosenbaum, 1977; Latane and Darley, 1970), the relationship to crime reduction or fear reduction has not been established (Greenberg *et al.*, 1985).

Surveillance and bystander intervention are also problematical behaviours. The field studies involving staged crimes suggest that bystanders have difficulty (a) noticing the incident, (b) interpreting the suspicious behaviour as a crime, and (c) actually intervening to provide help (Latane and Darley, 1970). Will collective Watch programmes contribute to or help alleviate such problems? Furthermore, what percentage of the local crime can be witnessed by local residents? Clearly, most residents are not home during the day when most residential crime occurs, and if they did attempt to 'watch' out of their windows, many buildings are not designed to allow adequate surveillance of the area. After reviewing research on 'the surveillance effect', Mayhew *et al.*, (1979) conclude that '... the chances of witnesses behaving in ways which will have consequences for [the offender] are often small' (p. 2). Even so, one might ask what 'dosage' of surveillance is needed to deter or apprehend criminals, assuming that we could motivate citizens to be vigilant? This is another empirical question that cannot be answered at the present time.

The opportunity reduction model, besides placing a high premium on surveillance, also suggests that 'target hardening' measures (i.e. efforts to make access to dwelling units more difficult), such as those commonly discussed at Watch meetings, will reduce the opportunity of criminal activity in the neighbourhood. The limitations of target hardening for controlling crime have been discussed elsewhere (e.g. Clarke and Hope, 1984) and will not be reviewed here. However, emphasis should be given to the fact that this strategy is limited almost exclusively to property crimes and does not address the violent street crime that is primarily responsible for residents' level of fear (cf. Baumer, 1978). Moreover, when a strategy is employed that seeks to protect individual households from victimization (and thus change the behaviour of potential victims rather than offenders), there is always the possibility for displacement to occur, i.e., a change in criminal activity (*not* the prevention of criminal activity) as a result of prevention efforts (see Gabor, 1981). We know very little about the nature and extent of displacement effects, but this problem could be very critical to a strategy such as Neighbourhood Watch that is forced to settle for low levels of participation scattered across individual households, blocks, and neighbourhoods (cf. Repetto, 1974). If one block, for example, is well organised and simply displaces criminal activity to the adjacent block, then the 'collective benefit' for the community is questionable.

Conclusions

While Neighbourhood Watch is an attractive concept, this paper has raised a number of questions about the theoretical and empirical foundation of this approach to community crime prevention and fear reduction.Going beyond the correlational neighbourhood research, there is a paucity of good quasi-experimental evaluations which directly test the Implant Hypothesis, i.e., that citizen participation, and, eventually, informal social control mechanisms, can be 'implanted' in the neighbourhoods where they do not presently exist. Theory failure is suggested by the current absence of support for some basic assumptions regarding this strategy of crime control. Specifically, there is some North American evidence to suggest that: (a) if given the opportunity to participate, residents in the majority of high-crime neighbourhoods would not participate; and (b) when citizens do participate, the social interaction that occurs at meetings may lead to increases (rather than decreases) in fear of crime and other crime-related perceptions or feelings. More importantly, there is little evidence that these block/neighbourhood meetings *cause* local residents to engage in neighbourhood surveillance, social interaction, bystander intervention, and specific crime prevention activities— behaviours that are posited as the central mechanisms for strengthening informal social controls and reducing the opportunities for crime. Finally, there is little evidence that Block Watches (as typically implemented) are self-sustaining.

In a nutshell, this field needs more precise theories of both implementation and impact to better estimate programme effects. More precise and controlled research is needed to test the Implant Hypothesis under a variety of conditions, including differences in neighbourhood and individual character-istics, as well as difference in the content of the intervention. Substantially more work is needed on the effects of crime prevention meetings on participants and, eventually, on the perceptions and behaviour of potential offenders.

In terms of current policy and practice, this analysis suggests that Watch-type programmes have been oversold. There is a need to recognise that Neighbourhood Watch cannot be easily implemented and sustained in all types of neighbourhoods. One policy question is whether to *try harder* to implement Neighbourhood Watch in high-crime areas where obtaining citizen participation is the most difficult (cf. Greenberg *et al.*, 1985) *or* take a more sceptical view that this type of programme may be *inappropriate* for such neighbourhoods (cf. Silloway and McPherson, 1985; DuBow *et al.*, 1985). In any event, organisers should recognise that a single strategy such as 'watching' is unlikely, by itself, to curtail a deeply rooted crime problem and that multiple approaches will be necessary.

This analysis also suggests that planners should not assume that Watch programmes are 'wired' to produce only pro-social effects and that untoward effects are impossible. Contrary to prior theoretical statements about *fear reduction*, there are both theoretical and empirical reasons to be concerned that residential meetings, left to themselves, may heighten residents' fears. Thus, if the strategy is pursued, the responsibility of organisers reaches beyond simply organising an initial meeting, to encouraging discussion of the 'right' subject matter in the 'right' way.

The goal of *fear reduction* that has moved to the forefront of United States national policy on community crime prevention may need to be re-examined. Fear reduction may not be possible or even desirable given the objective of increasing citizen crime prevention behaviours. While people would agree that large increases in fear of crime would be dysfunctional, models used to predict preventive health behaviours suggest that moderate increases in perceived vulnerability may be necessary to induce behaviour change directed at minimising the risk of victimization (cf. Rosenstock, 1966). Fear arousal is unlikely to be destructive if it can be channelled into action that is perceived to be efficacious.

References

BAUMER, T. L. (1978). 'Research on fear of crime in the United States.' *Victimology*, 3, pp. 254–264.

BICKMAN, L. and ROSENBAUM, D. P. (1977). 'Crime reporting as a function of bystander encouragement, surveillance, and credibility.' *Journal of Personality and Social Psychology*, 35, pp. 577–586.

BOGGS, S. (1971). 'Formal and informal crime control: An exploratory study of urban, suburban and rural orientation.' *Sociological Quarterly* 12, pp. 319–327.

CAMPBELL, D. T. and STANLEY, J. L. (1966). *Experimental and Quasi-experimental Designs for Research*. Chicago: Rand McNally.

CIREL, P., EVANS, P., McGILLIS, D., and WHITCOMB, D., (1977). *Community Crime Prevention Programme in Seattle: An Exemplary Project*. Washington DC: US Government Printing Office.

CITIZEN INFORMATION SERVICE OF ILLINOIS. (1982). *Community-Directed Crime Prevention: An Alternative That Works*. Final Report to the National Institute of Justice. Chicago: Citizen Information Service of Illinois.

CLARKE, R. and HOPE, T. (Eds.) (1984). *Coping With Burglary*. Boston: Kluwer-Nijhoff.

COOK, T. D. and CAMPBELL, D. T. (1979). *Quasi-experimentation: Design and Analysis Issues for Field Settings*. Chicago: Rand McNally.

DUBOW, F. and EMMONS, D. (1981). 'The Community Hypothesis'. In Lewis, D. A. (Ed.), *Reactions to Crime*. Beverly Hills, California: Sage.

DUBOW, F., McPHERSON, M., and SILLOWAY, G. (1985). 'Organizing for the State: Neighbourhood Watch as a strategy of community crime prevention.' Paper presented at the annual meeting of the American Society of Criminology, San Diego.

DUBOW, F., McCABE, E., and KAPLAN, G. (1979). *Reactions to Crime: A Critical Review of the Literature*. Washington DC: US Department of Justice, National Institute of Justice.

DOISE, W. (1969). 'Intergroup relations and polarization of individual and collective judgments'. *Journal of Personality and Social Psychology*, 12, pp. 136–143.

FEINS, J. D. (1983). *Partnerships for Neighbourhood Crime Prevention*. Washington, DC: US Department of Justice, National Institute of Justice.

FESTINGER, L. (1954). 'Motivations leading to social behaviour,' in Jones, M. R. (Ed.), *Nebraska Symposium on Motivation*. Lincoln: University of Nebraska Press, 2, pp. 191–219.

FESTINGER, L., SCHACTER, S., and BACK, K. (1950). *Social pressures in formal groups*. Stanford, Ca.: Stanford University Press.

FOWLER, F. J., JR., and MANGIONE, T. W. (1982). *Neighbourhood Crime, Fear and Social Control: A Second Look at the Hartford programme*. Washington, DC: US Department of Justice, National Institute of Justice.

GABOR, T. (1981). 'The crime displacement hypothesis: an empirical examination.' *Crime and Delinquency*, 27, pp. 391–404.

GALLUP, G. H. (1981). *The Gallup report 187*. Princeton, N.J.: The Gallup Poll, p. 12, 13.

GALLUP, G. H. (1982). *The Gallup report 200*. Princeton, N.J.: The Gallup Poll, p. 22, 23.

GAROFALO, J. and McCLEOD, M. (1985). 'A national overview of the Neighbourhood Watch Programme.' A paper preprared for the annual meeting of the American Society of Criminology, San Diego.

GREENBERG, S. W., ROHE, W. M., and WILLIAMS, J. R. (1982). *Safe and Secure Neighbourhoods: Physical Characteristics and Informal Territorial Control in High and Low Crime Neighbourhoods*. Washington, DC: US Department of Justice, National Institute of Justice.

GREENBERG, S. W., ROHE, W. M., and WILLIAMS, J. R. (1985). *Informal Citizen Action and Crime Prevention at the Neighbourhood Level*. Washington, DC: US Government Printing Office.

HACKLER, J. C., HO, K. Y. and URQUHART-ROSS, C. (1974). 'The willingness to intervene: differing community characteristics.' *Social Problems*, 21, pp. 328–344.

HUNTER, A. (1974). *Symbolic Communities*. Chicago: University of Chicago Press.

JACOBS, J. (1961). *The Death and Life of Great American Cities*. New York: Vintage Books.

JEFFREY, C. R. (1971). *Crime Prevention Through Environmental Design*. Beverly Hills, Ca.: Sage.

KASARDA, J. D. and JANOWITZ, M. (1974). 'Community attachment in mass society.' *American Sociological Review*, 39, pp. 328–339.

KOGAN, N. and WALLACH, M. A. (1964). *Risk Taking: A study of Cognition and Personality*. New York: Holt, Rinehart.

LATANE, B. and DARLEY, J. (1970). *The Unresponsive Bystander: Why doesn't He Help?* New York: Appleton-Century-Crofts.

LAVRAKAS, P. J., and LEWIS, D. A. (1980). 'The conceptualization and measurement of citizens crime prevention behaviours.' *Journal of Research in Crime and Delinquency*, July, pp. 254–272.

LAVRAKAS, P. J., NORMOYLE, J., SKOGAN, W. G., HERZ, E. J., SALEM, C., and LEWIS, D. A. (1980). *Factors Related to Citizen Involvement in Personal, Household, and Neighbourhood Anti-Crime Measures. Final Report* (National Institute of Justice) Evanston, Illinois: Northwestern University, Center for Urban Affairs and Policy Research.

LAVRAKAS, P. J., ROSENBAUM, D. P., and KAMINSKI, F. (1983). 'Transmitting information about crime and crime prevention: the Evanston Newsletter Quasi-Experiment,' *Journal of Police Science and Administration*, 2, pp. 463–473.

LEWIS, D. A., GRANT, J. A., and ROSENBAUM, D. P. (1985)1. *The Social Construction of Reform: Crime Prevention and Community Organizations*. Final Report Vol. 2 to the Ford Foundation, Evanston, Ill.: Northwestern University, Center for Urban Affairs and Policy Research.

LINDSAY, B. and McGILLIS, D. (1986). 'Citywide community prevention: An assessment of the Seattle programme.' In Rosenbaum, D. P., (Ed.), *Community Crime Prevention: Does it Work?* Beverly Hills, California: Sage.

LURIGIO, A. J., and ROSENBAUM, D. P. (1986). 'Community crime prevention: A critical look at programme evaluation in the field.' In Rosenbaum, D. P., (Ed.), *Community Crime Prevention: Does it Work?* Beverly Hills, California: Sage.

MAYHEW, P., CLARKE, R. V. G., BURROWS, J., HOUGH, J. M. and WINCHESTER, S. W. C. (1979). *Crime in Public View*. Home Office Research Study No. 49. London: HMSO.

McPHERSON, M., and SILLOWAY, G. (1980). *Programme Models: Planning Community Crime Prevention Programmes*. Minneapolis, Mn: Minnesota Crime Prevention Center.

MOSCOVICI, S., and DOISE, W. (1974). 'Decision Makings in Groups.' In Nemeth, C., (Ed.), *Social Psychology: Classic and Contemporary Integrations*. Chicago: Rand McNally.

MOSCOVICI, S., and ZAVALLONI, M. (1969). 'The group as a polarizer of attitudes.' *Journal of Personality and Social Psychology*, 12, pp. 125–135.

MYERS, D. G. and BISHOP, G. D. (1970). 'Discussion effects on racial attitudes.' *Science*, 169, pp. 778–779.

NATIONAL ADVISORY COMMISSION OF CRIMINAL JUSTICE STANDARDS AND GOALS. (1973). *A National Strategy to Reduce Crime*. Washington, DC: US Government Printing Office.

NEWMAN, O. (1972). *Defensible Space: Crime Prevention Through Urban Design*. New York: Macmillan.

PENNELL, F. E. (1978). 'Collective vs. private strategies for coping with crime.' *Journal of Voluntary Action Research*, 7, pp. 59–74.

PENNSYLVANIA COMMISSION ON CRIME AND DELINQUENCY (1984). *Crime Prevention Activities in Pennsylvania: A survey of Municipal Crime Prevention Practitioners*. (Prepared by Bureau of Crime Prevention, Training and Technical Assistance.)

PODELEFSKY, A. and DUBOW, F. (1981). *Strategies for Community Crime Prevention: Collective Responses to Crime in Urban America*. Springfield, Ill.: Charles C. Thomas.

REPETTO, T. A. (1974). *Residential Crime*. Cambridge, Ma.: Ballinger.

ROHE, W. M. and GREENBERG, S. (1982). *Participation in Community Crime Prevention Programmes*. Chapel Hill, NC: University of North Carolina, Department of City and Regional Planning.

ROSENBAUM, D. P. (1983). 'Scaring people into crime prevention: The results of a randomized experiment.' A paper presented at the 91st annual convention of the American Psychological Association, Anaheim, California, August.

ROSENBAUM, D. P. (Ed.) (1986). *Community Crime Prevention: Does it Work?* Beverly Hills, Ca.: Sage.

ROSENBAUM, D. P., LEWIS, D. A. and GRANT, J. A. (1985). *The Impact of Community Crime Prevention Programmes in Chicago: Can Neighbourhood Organization make a Difference?* (Final Report, Vol. 1). Evanston, Ill.: Northwestern University, Center for Urban Affairs and Policy Research.

144

ROSENBAUM, D. P., LEWIS, D. A. and GRANT, J. A. (1986). 'Neighbourhood-based crime prevention in Chicago: A look at the impact of community organizing.' In Rosenbaum, D. P., (Ed.), *Community Crime Prevention: Does it Work?* Beverly Hills, California: Sage.

ROSENSTOCK, I. (1966). 'Why people use health services' *Milbank Memorial Ford Quarterly*. 44, pp. 94–127.

SCHACTER, S. (1959). *The Psychology of Affiliation.* Palo Alto, Ca.: Stanford University Press.

SCHNEIDER, A. L. (1975). *Evaluation of the Portland Neighbourhood-Based anti-Burglary Programme.* Eugene, Or.: Institute of Policy Analysis.

SCHNEIDER, A. L. and SCHNEIDER, P. R. (1978). *Private and Public-Minded Citizen Responses to a Neighbourhood-based Crime Prevention Strategy.* Eugene, Or.: Institute for Policy Analysis.

SEATTLE POLICE DEPARTMENT (n.d.) *Citizens Guide to Organizing a Block Watch.* Seattle, Wa.: City of Seattle.

SILLOWAY, G. and McPHERSON, M. (1985). 'The limi:·s to citizen participation in a government-sponsored community crime prevention programme.' Presented at Annual meeting of the American Society of Criminology, San Diego.

SKOGAN, W. G., LEWIS, D. A., PODOLEFSKY. A., DUBOW, F., GORDON, M. T., HUNTER, A., MAXFIELD, M. G., and SALEM, G. (1982). *Reactions to Crime Project: Executive Summary.* Washington, DC: US Department of Justice, National Institute of Justice.

SKOGAN, W. G., and MAXFIELD, M. G. (1981). Community crime prevention programmes: Measurement issues in evaluation.' In *How well Does it Work?* (Compiled by the National Criminal Justice Reference Service.) Washington, DC: US Government Printing Office.

SUNDEEN R. A. and MATHIEU, J. T. (1976). 'The fear of crime and its consequences among elderly in three urban areas.' *Gerontologist*, 16, pp. 211–219.

TAUB, R. P., TAYLOR, D. G., and DUNHAM, J. D. (1981). *Crime, Fear of Crime, and the Deterioration of Urban Neighbourhoods.* Chicago: National Opinion Research Center.

TAUB, R. P., TAYLOR, D. G., and DUNHAM, J. D. (1982). *Safe and Secure Neighbourhoods: Territoriality, Solidarity, and the Reduction of Crime. Final Report.* (National Institute of Justice) Chicago: National Opinion Research Centre.

TAYLOR, R. B., GOTTFREDSON, S., and BROWER, S. (1981). *Informal Control in the Urban Residential Environment. Final Report.* (National Institute of Justice). Baltimore: John Hopkins University.

TITUS, R. M. (1984). 'Residential burglary and the Community Response.' In Clarke, R., and Hope, T., (Ed.), *Coping with Burglary.* Boston: Kluwer-Nijhoff Publishing.

WANDERSMAN, A., JAKUBS, J. F. and GIAMARTINO, G. D. (1981). 'Participation in block organizations.' *Journal of Community Action*, 1, pp. 40–47.

WHITAKER, C. J. (1986). 'Crime prevention measures: Bureau of Justice Statistics special report.' US Department of Justice: Bureau of Justice Statistics.

WILSON, J. Q. and KELLING, G. L. (1982). 'The police and neighbourhood safety: Broken windows.' *Atlantic Monthly*, 127, pp. 29–38.

YADEN, D., FOLKSTAND, S., and GLAZER, P. (1973). *The Impact of Crime in Selected Neighbourhoods: A Study of Public Attitudes in Four Portland Census Tracts.* Portland, Oregon: Campaign Information Counsellors.

YIN, R. K. (1986). 'Residential and commercial crime prevention: A synthesis of eleven evaluations.' In Rosenbaum, D., (Ed.), *Community Crime Prevention: Does it Work?* Beverly Hills, California: Sage.

YIN, R. K. (1979). 'What is citizen crime prevention?' In *How Well Does it Work?* (Compiled by the National Criminal Justice Reference Service) Washington, DC: US Government Printing Office.

9. Support for neighbourhood watch: a British Crime Survey analysis.

Tim Hope

The development of Neighbourhood Watch in England and Wales has been dramatic. In 1983 there were a handful of experimental schemes. In April 1987, police returns to the Home Office registered 29,000 schemes in operation in England and Wales—just over twice as many as were registered in June 1986, and three and a half times as many as were registered at the end of 1985. Without doubt, Neighbourhood Watch is one of the most significant attempts to involve the British public in crime control for many years. It is as yet too early to tell whether it will make an appreciable impact on crime rates in Britain. There is also still a way to go in making it widely available. At this stage of growth, though, it would seem useful to ask whether there might be any limits to the public demand for Neighbourhood Watch. Knowledge of the extent of support for the idea is likely to be helpful in forecasting necessary resources for growth and for highlighting people and places where special effort would be needed to stimulate participation.

Differential participation

A recent supplement to the US National Crime Survey found only about 7 per cent of households to be participating in a Neighbourhood Watch programme (Whitaker, 1986; and Chapter 8). Figures such as these, however, are a misleading indicator of public support because they include people who live in areas where no Neighbourhood Watch scheme operates and who therefore do not have the opportunity to take part, even if they wanted to. When only those households living in areas which had schemes were considered, a greater proportion of households said they participated, but these were still in a minority (38%). In addition, there were significant differences between participants and others: participants were wealthier, more likely to live with others than alone (including living as families), and twice as likely to own their home as to rent it.

These differences in individual disposition to participate are reflected in a number of smaller American surveys of participants in neighbourhood organisations and community crime prevention programmes (see, for reviews, Titus, 1984; Greenberg, Rohe and Williams, 1985; and also Shernock, 1986). In summary:

> '... fear of one's own victimisation seems less important [as a predictor of participation] than do concern over crime as a neighbourhood problem, interest in other neighbourhood quality-of-life issues, a tendency to join and participate in other sorts of local voluntary organisations, and being acquainted with neighbourhood adults and children. Participation in collective activities also increases with income, having children at home, length of residency, homeownership, sense of attach-

ment to the neighbourhood and being black.' (Titus, 1984, p. 103.)

It seems pertinent then to ask whether similar factors might be related to participation in Neighbourhood Watch schemes in England and Wales and, more importantly, to see what they might tell us about people's motives for joining or avoiding Neighbourhood Watch.

The British Crime Survey

One approach to studying participation in Neighbourhood Watch would be to look at current group members. But, as noted in Chapter 8, there is the general problem of the representativeness of current group members of the wider population who might be inclined to join if they had the opportunity. Current membership may be a product of two factors: differences between police forces in the rate of success with which they are implementing Neighbourhood Watch; and the self-selection of new members to a novel and expanding idea. A wealth of studies of the diffusion of innovations of many kinds suggest that new ideas or organisations may initially attract a different kind of person (e.g. more confident, open-minded, etc.) than those who join later. There thus needs to be another way of assessing demand.

The second sweep of the British Crime Survey in February and March 1984 provided an opportunity to ask some questions of a representative sample in England and Wales of heads of household, or their spouses (n = 5600), about the potential scope for Neighbourhood Watch (details of the survey can be found in Chapter 2, and in Hough and Mayhew, 1984, where some preliminary findings from this particular analysis are reported). At the time, Neighbourhood Watch was beginning to receive media attention but only a few schemes were in operation. Though around 57 per cent of respondents had heard of the idea, less than 1 per cent of households were actually involved in a group. The purpose was to elicit a measure of 'support' or general disposition towards the idea as expressed by respondents' views of the feasibility of Neighbourhood Watch and their willingness to join a scheme. Of course, this can only ever be a very crude predictor of actual participation in a Neighbourhood Watch group—which may be shaped by a host of more immediate considerations (see Chapter 8)—but it may nevertheless afford some yardstick against which to judge the progress of implementing Neighbourhood Watch.

The extent of support

Bearing in mind the low level of actual participation at the time, respondents were shown (or had read to them) a description of a typical Neighbourhood Watch scheme. This read as follows:

Neighbourhood Watch Schemes are being introduced by the police to help prevent burglary and other crimes. They are based on the idea of 'good neighbours'.

Police ask residents to get to know others who live nearby.

People in the schemes keep an eye on each others' homes and tell each other about when they will be away from home, holidays, deliveries and so on.

Then if they notice anyone acting suspiciously, they call the police.

The police may ask one or two local people to play an active part in the scheme by, for example, keeping a list of members' telephone numbers.

People may be asked to put stickers in their windows saying they belong to Neighbourhood Watch. Street signs may also be put up.

Neighbourhood Watch does not mean people 'having a go' nor does it involve patrolling the streets. People are simply asked to keep watch and inform the police.

They were then asked about their 'support' for the idea, which was assessed by i. whether they thought Neighbourhood Watch would work in their area *and* ii. whether they were personally prepared to join. Though most people thought that Neighbourhood Watch might be effective in preventing burglary and other crimes (89%), the number who could be defined as potential supporters, though still a majority, was rather less (62%). There seems then to be some shortfall between support for the idea in principle and a stated willingness to participate in practice.

Those who were reluctant to join gave a variety of reasons. Ten per cent of the sample (27% of non-supporters) said they would not join even though they thought that a scheme would work in their area; the reasons most often advanced were that they were away too much, too busy, too ill, or too old. Seventeen per cent (or just under half the non-supporters) thought that Neighbourhood Watch might generally prove effective but would not work in their own area; they cited the lack of motivation and untrustworthiness of local people, physical difficulties in keeping an eye on each other's homes and problems in distinguishing between intruders and legitimate callers. Finally, 11 per cent were sceptical about the effectiveness of *any* Neighbourhood Watch scheme.

But how important are these reasons, and do those who support Neighbourhood Watch have contrary attitudes? Supporters were not asked explicitly why they were favourably disposed to Neighbourhood Watch (a question which is not easy to answer), rather, their responses to a battery of questions in the British Crime Survey were compared to those given by non-supporters. In this way, it would be possible to identify those personal characteristics, attitudes and experiences which might distinguish between the two groups and which might provide insight into the motives behind participation in Neighbourhood Watch.

Modelling support for Neighbourhood Watch

The task for analysis was to identify those factors which distinguished supporters from others and to measure the strength and form of their independent influence. This would allow inferences to be drawn about the potential scope for participation in Neighbourhood Watch and might suggest some of the things which influence people's disposition towards the idea.

The analysis ('stepwise' logit modelling) produced two kinds of result. First, it provided an estimate of the relative importance of each variable in accounting for differences between supporters and others, taking into account the other variables in the model. These are reported in Table 1. Second, estimates were derived of the relative, independent probability of supporters of Neighbourhood Watch being in the individual categories of each of the variables, denoted in the text by the symbol 'e'.

Table 1 *Potential influences on support for Neighbourhood Watch*

Variables in the model	relative importance (S)	degress of freedom (d.f.)	significance (p.<)
Null model (S(0))	12,310	5,593	–
HOUSEHOLD CHARACTERISTICS			
1. Household tenure	52	7	.001
2. Marital status	25	5	.001
3. Household income	22	6	.005
Combined influence (S,1–3)	144	18	.001
EFFICACY, FEASIBILITY AND ACCEPTABILITY			
4. Belief in efficacy of Neigh-bourhood Watch	700	3	.001
5. Willingness to tell neighbours when home left empty	272	3	.001
6. 'Neighbourhood Watch needs to be organised''	197	3	.001
7. Ease with which neighbours can watch home	165	5	.001
Combined influence (S,4–7)	1,749	14	.001
TYPE OF AREA			
8. ACORN Type (S,8)	33	12	.001
COMMUNITY AND NEIGHBOURS			
9. 'People in neighbourhood help each other'	60	4	.001
10. Neighbours regarded as friends or acquaintances	31	3	.001
11. Type of 'Home-minding' arrangements made	32	5	.001
Combined influence (S,9–11)	133	12	.001
CRIME			
12. Worry about burglary and contact with a recent victim (S,12)	94	19	.001
Full fitted model (S(f))	2,690	74	.001

Note

S(f) is the value of the likelihood function (the 'scaled deviance') of the fitted model, and S(0) the maximum value of the likelihood function of the null model. The importance of individual variables, and sub-groups of variables, is assessed by the quantities $S(v,1-12) = S(x) - S(f)$, where S(x) is a model fitted with all the variables as the full model S(f) but without the respective variable or group of variables (v,1–12). The significance of the difference between models is assessed by comparing $S(v,1-12)$ with the chi-squared statistic with $df(x) - df(f)$.

149

Table 1 lists the twelve most important variables which differentiate supporters from non-supporters, along with their relative independent contribution to the model. These are grouped into different related sets:

i. *efficacy, feasibility and acceptability*—respondents were asked some questions about their attitude to various aspects of the Neighbourhood Watch idea;

ii. *household characteristics:*—i.e. the social and demographic characteristics of respondents;

iii. *type of area*—the ACORN classification of the census enumeration district in which the respondent lives (see Chapter 2);

iv. *community and neighbours*—respondents were asked questions about their relations with their neighbours, their feelings about their neighbourhood, and the arrangements they make for having their homes looked after when they are away;

v. *crime*—respondents were also asked about their experiences of crime, and their feelings and perceptions about it.

The remainder of this chapter provides an interpretation of the findings of this model.

Efficacy, feasibility and acceptability

A perception of the efficacy of Neighbourhood Watch in preventing burglary was the strongest predictor of support. This suggests there might be a powerful instrumental motive underlying participation, for nobody was prepared to join who did not believe in the efficacy of Neighbourhood Watch as a crime prevention measure. Nevertheless, as will be seen below, a belief in the efficacy of Neighbourhood Watch is not by itself sufficient to encourage some people to participate.

Most people regard their neighbours as friends or acquaintances (89%) and those who do are more likely to be supporters of Neighbourhood Watch (66%e) than those who do not (28%e). Unwillingness to inform neighbours when one's home is left empty (expressing the lack of trust one has in them) seems part of the reason for the lack of support for Neighbourhood Watch—whereas 75 per cent (e) of those who were willing to tell their neighbours were also supporters of Neighbourhood Watch, only about 25 per cent (e) of those who would not be willing were supporters. The feasibility of neighbourly surveillance might also be a factor—wheras 70 per cent (e) of those who thought it would be easy for neighbours to keep a watch on their homes were supporters, only 19 per cent (e) of those who thought it would be very difficult were supporters.

Though most people are at least acquainted with some of their neighbours, neighbours are not always called upon to look after their homes. Of those who asked someone to mind or watch their homes the last time they were away, just over half (56%) asked their immediate neighbours, 20 per cent asked other people who lived nearby and the remaining 24 per cent asked other people, including the police (4%). Those who never leave their homes unoccupied for lengthy periods seem to have less of a need to join (59%e) than those who do go away and usually ask their neighbours to look after their homes (68%e).

Yet the greatest support seems to come from those who ask local people, but not their immediate neighbours, to mind their homes (88%e). In particular, the small number of people who ask the police to keep an eye on their homes all (e) seem likely to be supporters. Perhaps these two groups may be looking to Neighbourhood Watch to provide an opportunity to come to a home-watching arrangement with their neighbours.

The principal feature which distinguishes Neighbourhood Watch from everyday practices of home-watching is that the former entails some degree of formal organisation. Respondents were asked 'do you think the idea of neighbours looking after each others' homes needs to be organised or should people be left to make their own arrangements?' Surprisingly, a majority of the sample (69%) thought people should be left to make their own arrangements. It follows that a significantly greater proportion of those who thought schemes needed to be organised were likely to be supporters (78%e) than of those who thought people should make their own arrangements (35%e). Interpretation of this finding is not without difficulty. With hindsight, the question contained a number of meanings and might have been better put. 'Organisation' implies a need for co-ordination but also has overtones of coercion. It is difficult to know whether people are reacting to being organised by their neighbours or by the police. Nevertheless, such a widespread reaction, and one which differentiates between supporters and non-supporters, suggests that associating Neighbourhood Watch with conno-tations of formal organisation produces an adverse response, even though belief in its efficacy, and declared support, are common.

The importance of perceptions of the efficacy, feasibility and acceptability of Neighbourhood Watch in differentiating potential supporters from others, though obvious, should not be over looked. Researchers have had some success in using a 'rational-cognitive' approach to account for people's willingness to take preventive action both in the public health sphere and in crime prevention specifically (see Chapter 13). The approach suggests that once people have formed a 'readiness to take action' based on assessments of risk and seriousness (see below), then, not surprisingly, they will adopt those measures which seem to them effective, feasible and acceptable (Skogan, 1981). Additionally, Lavrakas and Bennett (Chapter 13) see an instrumental motive distinguishing between secondary prevention schemes like Neighbour-hood Watch and offender-oriented community schemes.

Nevertheless, belief in the efficacy of Neighbourhood Watch is not all there is to the decision to participate. Scepticism about effectiveness may be one of the reasons for not wanting to join, and perceived efficacy seems an essential ingredient of joining, but in neither case is it the only reason. The model suggests that these other reasons are over and above whether people think that participation in Neighbourhood Watch will reduce their chances of being burgled.

Personal and household characteristics

Three personal characteristics in particular seem to mark out supports from others: household tenure; household income; and martial status. Owner-occupiers seem more likely to support Neighbourhood Watch (68%e) than council tenants (46%e) or private tenants (52%e). The poorest households are less likely to be supporters (39%e) than other income bands; and those currently married are most likely to be supporters (66%e) compared with the divorced, widowed, separated or single (48%e) (though household composition—i.e. whether living alone or with others, especially children—seems virtually interchangeable with marital status in its relationship to support for Neighbourhood Watch). Age also seems related to participation (though just failing to reach the criterion of model selection), with the middle-aged somewhat more likely to be supporters than younger or older age groups.

As noted above, American research suggests a somewhat similar pattern to this with household tenure, in particular, being important in relation to a readiness to take crime prevention measures. Lavrakas (1981), for instance, found home-ownership to characterise households who were likely to take *any* kind of crime prevention measure. Owner-occupiers may perhaps feel a greater sense of personal responsibility to take steps to protect their homes from crime. Renters may initially seek protection from their landlords. This is understandable as far as household security measures are concerned, but there may also be a generalisation to communal protective measures (Greenberg, *et al.,* 1985). Council tenants, for example, may be inclined to see the protection of their estates as the formal responsibility of the council and police rather than as amenable to their informal collective control.

Participation in Neighbourhood Watch may also be similar to participation in other forms of voluntary work and activity. Some common explanations of participation in local activities are: greater identification with local neighbourhood concerns (i.e. amongst owner-occupiers or those with families); social confidence and competence (excluding the young, the old, and the poor) and the availability of free time (i.e. including the middle-aged, and excluding families where both parents work, and single parents amongst the divorced, widowed or separated). The British Crime Survey contains no information on involvement in voluntary activities but the General Household Survey in 1981 (OPCS, 1983), and another survey conducted by Social and Community Planning Research (Field, 1982) both found that those who do some kind of voluntary work differ from the rest of the population in ways very similar to those which distinguish supporters of Neighbourhood Watch from others. Some people therefore may be generally disposed to joining community groups, including Neighbourhood Watch.

Neighbourhood characteristics

So far, support for Neighbourhood Watch has been related to a possible disposition towards joining community-based groups, and to a cognitive process of choosing an effective, feasible and acceptable way to protect oneself against becoming a victim. Neighbourhood Watch, though, is a collective, community-based measure and there are differences between supporters and others which reflect this. Support for Neighbourhood Watch varied according to the areas where respondents lived (as measured by the census-based ACORN classification of census enumeration districts—see Chapter 2) over and above the characteristics of individual households, suggesting that the fact of living in particular areas is related to an individual's willingness to join a scheme.

The American literature suggests (Chapters 3, 8 and 13) that communities which are socially homogeneous and where there are dense social networks may be better hosts to community crime prevention groups than other kinds of areas. Thus respondents were asked a question which has been used in a number of American surveys:

'In some neighbourhoods people do things together and try to help each other while in other areas people mostly go their own way. In general, what kind of neighbourhood would you say you live in?'

Those who thought people mostly went their own way were less likely to support Neighbourhood Watch (47%e) than those who thought people helped each other (68%e).

Nevertheless, a comparison of the characteristics of those ACORN areas with a high versus a low likelihood of participation (Table 2) does not reveal any simple relationship between likely participation, community cohesion and the socio-demographic characteristics of the local neighbourhood. The two lowest participating areas are at either extreme of perceived community cohesiveness, the highest groups are in between. A large private rental sector supposedly denotes an unstable population but this is not the case in agricultural areas. An elderly population might be less active but the poorer neighbourhoods of terraced housing have an elderly population and high support for Neighbourhood Watch. Finally, two out of the three areas of highest support have higher proportions of semi- and unskilled manual workers than those areas exhibiting lowest support. In sum, though support for Neighbourhood Watch varies between neighbourhoods this does not seem to be a direct consequence of their social composition or cohesiveness. The effect of crime on these neighbourhoods would appear more crucial.

Table 2 *Support for Neighbourhood Watch and characteristics of area (percentages)*

ACORN group classification	estimated support for NW	'most people help each other'	households in private rental	persons over 65	semi- and unskilled manual workers
HIGHEST PARTICIPATION					
B. modern family housing, higher incomes	86e	40	7	7	16
D. poor quality older terraced housing	78e	45	20	17	35
E. better off council estates	75e	37	3	11	32
LOWEST PARTICIPATION					
A. agricultural	54e	62	28	16	30
I. high status non-family areas	52e	28	38	16	17
GREAT BRITAIN	–	–	10	15	26

Neighbourhood Watch is distinguished from other neighbourhood activities by affording protection from crime. What role, then, does the experience of crime play in encouraging support from Neighbourhood Watch? In the first place, there seems no direct relationship—supporters were no more nor less likely to have been the victims of any kind of crime than others. Yet the indirect experience of crime—in particular its potential threat—does seem to be related to support, though mediated in important ways by people's feelings about their neighbourhood.

Support for Neighbourhood Watch is related to being worried about becoming the victim of burglary. Yet it is the 'fairly worried' who seem more likely to be supporters (69%e) than either the 'very worried' (62%e) or the 'not at all worried' (46%e). Thus although support increases with worry about burglary, suggesting that Neighbourhood Watch might be seen as a means of alleviating the fear of being burgled, there may also be a 'threshold' effect where too much worry begins to inhibit participation. As Chapter 8 suggests, a certain level of 'fear arousal' may be necessary to stimulate a decision to join Neighbourhood Watch, but too high a level of fear may paralyse participation, promoting a withdrawal behind closed doors.

The source of people's worries about crimes comes less from personal experience (which may be infrequent) than from knowledge of other people who have been victims—i.e. 'vicarious' victimisation (Skogan and Maxfield, 1981). We know from the first British Crime Survey that fear of crime generally increases with the closeness with which one has experience of crime—victims are more fearful than non-victims, and non-victims who know victims are more fearful than those who do not know victims (Maxfield, 1984). Again, proximity to crime seems to have a threshold effect on suport for Neighbourhood Watch. On the one hand, people who did not personally know any recent burglary victims were least likely to support Neighbourhood Watch (55%e). On the other hand, of those who knew a recent victim, it was the ones who knew a victim who lived *outside* the local area who seemed more disposed to participate (88%e) than those whose victimised acquaintances were local people (66%e) or who had been victims themselves (60%e). Our model, then, suggests that both the source and intensity of fear may prompt participation but in a kind of 'threshold' manner. Support may be aroused by contact with victims who live some way away (personifying a growing but as yet not immediate threat) but becomes inhibited (because worry about crime begins to inhibit positive activity) when victims begin to appear too close to home.

A number of chapters in this book have drawn attention to the role played by neighbourhood disorder (or incivilities) in reducing people's satisfaction with their neighbourhood and their sense of community. Crime and incivility are seen as a threat to community life. Table 3 suggests that Neighbourhood Watch might be seen as a means of fighting back, though this depends on how the neighbourhood is valued.

Neighbourhood Watch may be seen as a community resource to combat incipient neighbourhood problems and support for the idea may increase with rising neighbourhood disorder, at least initially. But again there seems to be a threshold in the use of Neighbourhood Watch as a community resource, related in this case to the general level of satisfaction with the neighbourhood.

Table 3 *Neighbourhood satisfaction, incivility and support for Neighbourhood Watch (e = model estimates)*

Neighbourhood satisfaction	Incivility Scale		
	low 0	1	high 2 +
positive ('very satisfied')	65%e	73%e	79%e
neutral or negative	62%e	71%e	54%e

Source: British Crime Survey. Weighted data; unweighted N = 5600

These estimates are derived from a model excluding variables 4–7 (in Table 1) plus this interaction term; S = 710, d.f. 53, p.< .001. The incivility scale was computed by summing the scores over five items of incivility (see Chapter 2) where those who thought any of them were 'common' or 'very common' were scored 1, while the others were scored 0.

Support for Neighbourhood Watch as a community defence may become even stronger for those who remain satisfied with their neighbourhood despite increasingly high levels of disorder. Eventually, however, demoralisation and withdrawal might set in amongst those who are less than satisfied with their neighbourhood, and with increasing disorder, these people are likely to exhibit much lower support for Neighbourhood Watch.

Table 4 *Support for Neighbourhood Watch: neighbourhood satisfaction and changes in burglary in the neighbourhood (e = model estimates)*

Neighbourhood satisfaction	Burglary in neighbourhood		
	has decreased/ none here	is the same	has increased
positive ('very satisfied')	58%	68%e	77%e
neutral/negative	64%e	60%e	59%e

Source: British Crime Survey. Weighted data; unweighted N = 5600

These estimates are derived from a model excluding variables 4–7 (in Table 1) plus this interaction term; S = 710, d.f. 54, p.< .001

Table 4 shows a similar reaction to perceived changes in burglary in the neighbourhood. Where people are satisfied with their neighbourhood, support for Neighbourhood Watch increases with a perceived increase in burglary but somewhat declines for those who are less than satisfied.

The above results suggest that support for Neighbourhood Watch may grow with increasing worry about burglary, and a perceived increase in the proximity and extent of crime and disorder, but only up to a certain point from where it diminishes. Two characteristics of this threshold of support seem relevant: first, the psychological proximity of crime (e.g. when it begins to affect people directly as victims, or people just like them in their own communities); and second, personal satisfaction with the neighbourhood. The British Crime Survey shows that personal satisfaction with the neighbourhood tends to diminish with increased worry about crime and support for Neighbourhood Watch similarly declines. Commitment to the neighbourhood may therefore be a crucial precondition for participation. Yet, as Tables 3 and 4 suggest, for those who remain highly committed to their area, despite rising incivility and crime, Neighbourhood Watch may be seen as an important resource against further community decline.

Crime risk versus community cohesion

The primary purpose of Neighbourhood Watch is to help protect participants from residential crime. For it to work, it needs neighbours prepared to help each other. Therefore, for people to give their support to Neighbourhood Watch, it may be necessary for them to feel enough at risk to make the effort of participation worthwhile and *at the same time* for them to have sufficient confidence in their community to warrant participation in self-help activities. Table 5 confirms this hypothesis. The greatest support for Neighbourhood Watch comes from those who thought it likely they would become the victim of burglary in the next year *and* who think their neighbourhood is socially cohesive. Both conditions are necessary: where a sense of community is lacking, perceived risk does not by itself seem to affect participation.

Table 5 *Support for Neighbourhood Watch: % prepared to participate in Neighbourhood Watch by perceived risk of burglary and neighbourhood cohesion (e = model estimates)*

	Neighbourhood cohesion	
Risk of burglary	'most people help each other'	'most people go own way'
'likely'	74%	38%e
'unlikely'	59%e	38%e

Weighted data. Source: British Crime Survey 1984

These estimates are derived from a mode excluding variables 4−7 (in Table 1) plus this interaction term $S = 690$, d.f. 54, ($p < .001$).

If these two conditions are necessary for supporting Neighbourhood Watch, the highest rates of participation might then be found in areas where: i. there was perceived to be a risk of crime; and ii. where there was confidence that people would help each other. Unfortunately, it is also to be expected that, in general, areas of high crime risk would also be those where trust and co-operation in the community was diminished (cf. Chapter 3). Support for Neighbourhood Watch might be greatest, therefore, in areas where the risk of crime is perceived to be likely but where there is still a sufficient sense of community. Support would be low: i. where there was little risk of crime (though a great sense of community); and ii. where there was little sense of community (though a great risk of crime).

This hypothesis finds reasonable confirmation in Table 6, at least for areas with the highest and lowest levels of support for Neighbourhood Watch. Lowest levels of support can be found in agricultural areas (type A) where there is little crime and in urban non-family areas where there is little sense of community (type I, i.e. gentrifying areas with few children and areas of furnished flats and private rented houses in multi-occupation). In contrast, highest levels of support can be found in higher income areas of modern family housing (type B), areas of poor quality older terraced housing (type D), and on the economically better-off council estates (type E). In all these areas, crime may be felt to be an increasing threat though community ties may still be strong.

Table 6 *ACORN areas: participation, risk and community*

ACORN group classification	Estimated participation in Neighbourhood Watch (percent)	percent seeing burglary as likely	percent thinking 'most people help each other'
		(Standardised scores)	
HIGHEST PARTICIPATION			
B. modern family housing, higher incomes	86e (+1.9)	36 (−0.4)	40 (−0.2)
D. poor quality older terraced housing	78e (+1.1)	42 (+0.2)	45 (+0.4)
E. better-off council estates	75e (+0.9)	36 (−0.4)	37 (−0.5)
LOWEST PARTICIPATION			
A. agricultural areas	54e (−1.2)	19 (−2.1)	62 (+2.3)
I. high status non-family areas	52e (−1.4)	46 (+0.6)	28 (−1.5)

Weighted data. Source: 1984 British Crime Survey.

Without detailed attitudinal data it is unwise to speculate too much about the place of Neighbourhood Watch in these communities' collective sentiments. It is, however, tempting to see ACORN type B as representing newly developing communities who seek to buttress themselves against crime while simultaneously reinforcing their recently acquired community identity. These could be contrasted with type J—the older established suburbs—which seem to exhibit less support than might have been expected (58%e). Perhaps community identity has been forged long ago and residents need to look less to organised collective means to defend themselves from crime; perhaps also they may prefer, or have the resources, to invest privately in security hardware for the home. In contrast, ACORN type D may represent the older declining working-class communities of the industrial regions of Britain where there may still be a residue of community spirit.

Areas within the public housing sector display a marked contrast in support for Neighbourhood Watch. High levels of support come from the better-off council estates (type E). As Bottoms and Wiles point out (Chapter 5), various developments in housing markets and policies may be helping to bring about a convergence between these areas and their private sector counterparts (type B). In contrast, average council estates (type F) have a lower likelihood of participation (61%e), though being older and more established, they have higher proportions of older residents, which probably militates against active community participation (according to the 1981 Census, 20% of residents are over 65 years in type F areas compared to 11% in type E).

The three high risk areas—where over one in ten households are likely to suffer at least one attempted or successful burglary each year (see also Chapter 2)—exhibit different levels of support. The poorest council estates, in particular, seem to have a greater potential for support than might have been expected (69%e). Despite very high burglary rates, people on these estates seem to retain some faith in their community and perhaps some willingness to act in a communal way—37 per cent of residents thought people mostly helped each other, the same proportion as on the better-off estates and only 3 per cent less than the residents of modern, private family housing (type B). Multi-ethnic areas (type H) also have about an average level of potential support (65%e) while non-family areas (type I) exhibit the lowest support (52%e). Again, community cohesiveness seems higher in the former (38%e) than in the latter (28%e) type of inner-city area.

Implications

The foregoing analysis has sought to identify the independent correlates of support for Neighbourhood Watch contained in the British Crime Survey. These have been used to make inferences about the scope and possible influences affecting people's decisions to take part in Neighbourhood Watch schemes. It would be unwise to see these findings as predictive of actual participation. Rather, they provide an indication of the nature and extent of a favourable disposition towards Neighbourhood Watch which may exist before schemes are introduced into neighbourhoods—information which may help police and community planners to implement schemes efficiently.

The pattern of the results may also tell us something about perceptions of the role of Neighbourhood Watch in the context of public reaction to crime. Criminological theory contains a paradox about the impact of crime on communities—on the one hand, crime is held to integrate community members by drawing them together against a common enemy; on the other, crime is seen as undermining community ties by breeding fear and sowing mistrust (Chapter 3, Lewis and Salem, 1981). Neighbourhood Watch embodies this paradox for it appears to rely upon community cohesion and at the same time is a possible means for achieving it. The evidence presented here suggests that both processes may be at work. For some, Neighbourhood Watch may be seen as a way of defending the community against the encroaching threat of crime, though this may only occur if the threat has not yet fully materialised into an immediate and pressing problem. In the latter circumstance, the basic ingredients of community have disappeared, leaving little foundation upon which to build Neighbourhood Watch defences.

As many researches have found, individual 'reactions to crime' are not straightforward (Skogan, 1981). As in this study, participation in crime prevention does not automatically increase with risk nor, indeed, with fear of crime. The results do, however, conform to some more complex models linking perception to behaviour. In the first place, support for Neighbourhood Watch may involve people in making a conscious decision based on an assessment, as they see it, of the costs and benefits of participation. The results suggest a number of thresholds in people's (and communities') support for Neighbourhood Watch, having to do with their personal proximity to crime, the level of disorder in their neighbourhood, the extent to which they are worried about these things, satisfaction with their neighbourhoods, perception of the degree of risk facing them and assessment of the 'community spirit' of their neighbours.

Amongst the 'costs' of Neighbourhood Watch may be the risk one takes in altering the relations one already has with neighbours and other local people. Neighbourhood Watch may require a certain degree of trust, reciprocity and loss of privacy between people and their immediate neighbours. Relations with one's neighbours rest upon a fairly complex set of implicit, informal rules, governing the acceptable limits of neighbourly behaviour (Bulmer, 1986). Moreover, these shared understandings between neighbours may represent a kind of negotiated outcome from a set of contradictory expectations—arguably, a good neighbour is someone who is at once friendly, helpful and distant (cf. Abrams, 1977). Where there is little risk of crime, there may be little point in disturbing amicable and informal neighbourly relations.

Conversely, where the risk of crime is high, people may be inhibited from engaging with their neighbours because trust has broken down. The British Crime Survey shows that people who think they are likely to be a victim of burglary are also more likely to believe that burglars are local people. It may be difficult to tell your neighbours when you are going out if you also suspect that they, or their children, might be inclined to burgle your home. Where the strongest spontaneous support for Neighbourhood Watch seems to reside is in those communities where people are sufficiently worried about crime, where they feel the need to do something about it, and where they feel positively towards their neighbours and to the community in general. Here, rather than a threat, Neighbourhood Watch may be seen as a positive means of affording protection from crime and of establishing communal and neighbourly relations.

A second conclusion to be drawn from the findings is the suggestion that the social characteristics of those favourable to Neighbourhood Watch may be similar to those of the wider group in the population who particpate more generally in voluntary activities (they may indeed be virtually the same people). Though some have pointed to a middle-class, home-owning and middle-aged bias (cf. Donnison, Scola and Thomas, 1986), this may be less to do with any deliberate conspiracy in the implementation of Neighbourhood Watch (cf. Bridges and Bunyan, 1983) than with the fact that some people may have greater personal resources to organise themselves collectively (e.g. more time, education, social confidence and experience). The difficulties which Neighbourhood Watch may face in involving the poor, or renters, or the elderly, are those which it shares with a broad range of other participatory activities.

Finally, the credibility of Neighbourhood Watch as a feasible, and, above all, effective means of crime prevention may also be very important in encouraging those favourably disposed to opt for this particular solution. At the time of the British Crime Survey, 89 per cent believed in the efficacy of Neighbourhood Watch and the rapid growth of schemes, presumably in the kinds of fertile soil identified here, is a witness to this belief. As long as community conditions are favourable, Neighbourhood Watch has lower costs than the only other alternative open to the householder—investment in security hardware. At present, 64 per cent of British Crime Survey respondents think that more or better locks on doors and windows are the best thing people can do for themselves to prevent burglary. The decision to opt for one or the other solution—communal or private—presumably depends upon the relative costs and benefits with which they are perceived.

With little else than a brief description to go on, it may be that people exaggerate the 'costs' of Neighbourhood Watch. Perhaps a careful present-ation and explanation of the concept, and the provision of safeguards in schemes to reassure people that their privacy is protected, will overcome their fears and encourage those in high crime neighbourhoods to take part. However, successful implementation of Neighbourhood Watch in high crime areas may need to overcome a paradox which Neighbourhood Watch embodies: the presentation of a solution to a problem (crime in the community) by means (community co-operation and trust) which are themselves part of the problem and are affected by it.

References

ABRAMS, P. (1977). 'Community care: some research problems and priorities'. *Policy and Politics,* 6, pp. 125–151.

BRIDGES, L. and BUNYAN, T. (1983). 'Britain's new urban policing strategy—the Police and Criminal Evidence Bill in context'. *Journal of Law and Society,* 10, pp. 85–107.

BULMER, M. (1986). *Neighbours: the work of Philip Abrams.* Cambridge: Cambridge University Press.

DONNISON, H., SCOLA, J. and THOMAS, P. (1986). *Neighbourhood Watch: policing the people.* London: Libertarian Research and Education Trust.

FIELD, J. (1982). *National Survey of Volunteering* (interim summary report). London: Social and Community Planning Research.

GREENBERG, S. W., ROHE, W. M., and WILLIAMS, J. R. (1985). *Informal Citizen Action and Crime Prevention at the Neighbourhood.* Washington, DC: National Institute of Justice.

HOUGH, M. and MAYHEW, P. (1985) *The 1984 British Crime Survey: first report.* Home Office Research Study No. 76. London: HMSO.

LAVRAKAS, P. J. (1981). 'On Households'. In Lewis, D. A. (Ed.), *Reactions to Crime.* Beverly Hills, CA: Sage Publications.

LEWIS, D. A. and SALEM, G. (1981). 'Community crime prevention: an analysis of a developing strategy'. *Crime and Delinquency,* 27, pp. 405–421.

MAXFIELD, M. G. (1984) *Fear of Crime in England and Wales.* Home Office Research Study No. 78, London: HMSO.

OPCS (OFFICE OF POPULATION CENSUSES AND SURVEYS) (1983). *The General Household Survey 1981.* London: HMSO.

SKOGAN, W. G. (1981). 'On attitudes and behaviours'. In Lewis, D. A. (Ed.) *Reactions to Crime.* Beverly Hills, CA: Sage Publications.

SKOGAN, W. G. and MAXFIELD, M. G. (1981). *Coping with Crime.* Beverly Hills, CA: Sage Publications.

SHERNOCK, S. K. (1986). 'A profile of the citizen crime prevention activist'. *Journal of Criminal Justice.,* 14, pp. 211–228.

TITUS, R. M. (1984). 'Residential burglary and the community response'. In Clarke, R. and Hope, T. (Eds.) *Coping with Burglary.* Boston, MA: Kluwer-Nijhoff.

WHITAKER, C. J. (1986). *Crime Prevention Measures.* Bureau of Justice Statistics Special Report. Washington, DC: US Department of Justice.

Community Interventions

The two chapters in this section provide accounts of programmes which are concerned with tackling the causes of crime based on a broader analysis of the contribution of the community in the genesis and prevention of crime. Thus the concept of community for these studies goes much wider than the creation of links between the police and residents anxious to protect their property. It involves the role of employment and relevant job training and experience, the role of families, wives, parents and siblings, as well as friends and community leaders, in helping to generate a supportive and involving environment for young people. Chapter 10, based on a series of projects carried out over the past decade, is concerned with the development of approaches to the problem of football hooliganism in Britain, and the need to locate resources and action in the communities from which the hooligans come, building on the football club as a local resource, rather than relying on defensive and opportunity-based approaches around the sites of hooliganism.

Chapter 11 is based on a range of experience in the development of community crime prevention in America. It attacks with vigour a number of the current assumptions about crime prevention: that it is a waste of time and money to try to tackle the causes of crime because they are too costly, or do not work, or that opportunity-based approaches provide the most efficient and effective means of reducing crime. It deals too with the barriers to implementation, including assumptions that the voluntary sector should be able to establish and maintain viable programmes within the community with little if any government support, and that charisma is a rare commodity; and that funding tends to be tied to research and 'knowledge' rather than to administrative needs. It sets out a powerful case for locating a policy to prevent crime in the places where crime and its causes are most prominent, and particularly in the inner-city ghettos.

10. Professional football and crowd violence in England: the case for a community approach

John Williams, E G Dunning and P Murphy[1]

Introduction

This paper attempts to evaluate the appropriateness and potential effectiveness of a 'community' approach to the problem of football hooliganism. It does so against the backcloth of a sport which is in considerable turmoil. Even its most committed supporters would probably admit that professional football in England—the game seems to be undergoing something of a minor resurgence in Scotland—is in the depths of the latest and, arguably, the most serious of a long series of recent crises. Crowds are leaking away fast from the game's delapidated and caged terraces and ill-equipped stands. Television audiences are down, too. As financial decline continues, and as top players are attracted abroad by the seemingly limitless salaries on offer there, the major English clubs have recently been seeking and securing an ever greater share of the sport's dwindling domestic financial cake. They have also succeeded in achieving more power over their smaller neighbours in the lower divisions, many of whom are now seriously threatened with 'official' part-time status or even liquidation. English league football's major sponsor, Canon, the photographic group, recently withdrew its financial support from the sport and, at a time when sports sponsorship is something of a thriving industry, replacement sponsors of a suitable kind—tobacco companies, for example, are deemed unsuitable for health reasons, though brewers seem to be looked upon more kindly—have been noticeably slow in coming forward. English club sides, regularly European champions in recent years, are currently banned, indefinitely, from European competition and, consequently, they are divorced from the benefits in terms of finance and the international exposure accrued from that source. A Football Association campaign launched in the 1985–86 season in a blaze of publicity is trawling around attempting to recruit 'Friends of Football' in an attempt to rescue the English game from its present malaise. A final measure of the depths to which the game has recently sunk can perhaps be gauged by the fact that a recent proposal from the authors and others, to an independent television company, for a series of programmes on the history of the game and an analysis of its current crisis, was rejected on the basis that such a project would be linking 'the wrong channel with the wrong sport at the wrong time'.

No single factor can explain football's present troubles, of course. But there is one which seems to provide a dissoluble link between almost all the major recent damaging developments in the game; it is, needless to say, that of football hooliganism. There is a widespread but mistaken tendency within the

1. This paper emerged out of a series of research projects on football hooliganism undertaken by the Football Crowd Research group in the Sociology Department of Leicester University. The group's work is currently funded by the Department of the Environment and the Football Trust.

English game to blame *all* football's present ills on the dreaded hooligan. There is, however, little doubt that hooliganism and its coverage by the mass media has played a substantial part in producing the recent shortfalls in football match attendances in England and in the development of the game's generally poor public image. Surveys of lapsed supporters and of those 'interested' in the game regularly highlight crowd violence as being among the major reasons for the withdrawal of live support (Williams *et al.*, 1984a; Canter *et al.*, 1987).

Trends of this kind were undoubtedly exacerbated in the 1985–6 league season by the appalling tragedies in the spring of 1985 at Bradford City and at the Heysel Stadium in Brussels in which 95 football fans lost their lives. Despite persistent attempts by the British press to link the Bradford fire to crowd misbehaviour the disaster highlighted, instead, the moribund state of the game's finances and more general attitudes towards spectator provision in what is still, despite its recent relative decline, the country's most popular working-class spectator sport (Taylor, 1985). The Heysel affair spoke loudly, too, of poor spectator facilities as well as of the dangerously incompetent administration of the sport by its European governing body, UEFA. However, the tragedy in Brussels can only be fully understood within the framing context of the violence perpetrated over the past 20 years or so by young English football followers at home and, since 1974, increasingly abroad (Williams *et al.*, 1984b).

Despite its frequent manifestation elsewhere, football hooliganism is known, almost universally it seems these days, as the ' English disease', following a long series of violent and often destructive visits by English fans to continental Europe. Football hooliganism in various forms seems to be a growing problem in countries like West Germany and Holland (Dunning *et al.*, 1986; Pilz, 1984; De Vriesbosch, 1983). It was even reputed to have been 'imported' into England from Italy sometime during the early 1960s. Today, of course, it is the English who seem to 'export' their football violence more readily and to more dramatic and damaging effect than any other footballing nation (Williams, 1986). This is the prime basis for our current standing as the *bêtes noires* of the international game and for the concern expressed at governmental levels about the nature of the 'national image' abroad.

Managing hooliganism: the policy response

Over the past 20 years there have been a total of seven official or quasi-official reports on football hooliganism in Britain: J.A. Harringtons's *Soccer Hooliganism,* (1968); J. Lang's *Crowd Behaviour at Football Matches* (1968); F. McElhone's *Report of the Working Group on Football Crowd Behaviour* (Scotland) 1 (1977); the Sports Council-SSRC Joint Report *Public Disorder and Sporting Events* (1978); the Department of the Environment's *Football Spectator Violence: Report of an Official Working Group* (1984) and the Interim and Final reports of Mr Justice Popplewell's *Committee of Inquiry into Crowd Safety and Control at Sports Grounds* (1985 and 1986 respectively).

Despite the variations between them, reports produced and commissioned by government during this period have been characterised by a general lack of concern with investigating and explaining hooligan behaviour, or with the development of longer-term policies designed to involve clubs in initiatives aimed at addressing some of the issues and circumstances which seem to be important in generating hooligan activities. A partial exception to this general rule is provided by the rather eclectic approach to explanation given in the Sports Council-SSRC Joint Report and also Mr Justice Popplewell's more recent attempt to sift the evidence about 'causes', which produced a similarly fragmented and an ultimately frustrating conclusion. Football hooligan violence, according to the Judge, has no indentifiable or remedial roots of almost any kind. Throughout history, he argues, and regardless of their structural circumstances, 'there has always been a group, albeit a small group, who find violence attractive' (1986, p.60). No one, of course, would deny this nation's violent heritage. But without further elaboration, assertions of this kind, which seem to reduce violent behaviour simply to the product of free-floating moral choices, are of little help in interpreting the peaks and troughs in the history of violent disorders at football and elsewhere. Moreover, and crucially, it contributes little to our understanding of why football hooliganism appears to be very largely the preserve of lower working-class youths and young men (Dunning *et al.*, 1987).

Issues of this kind rarely seem to be raised in official circles. Nor does the political hue of the administration-in-charge seem to be especially crucial in this respect. Indeed, many of the most recent pronouncements and recommendations of the present Conservative Government are merely stronger echoes of those rehearsed or tried by Labour administrations of the 1970s. If, however, as Mr Justice Popplewell and most of his predecessors seem to allege, football-related violence has no clear structural basis or remedial root, the way is clear for a simple concentration on more 'adequate' *situational* responses to the phenomenon. In short, the recent history of football hooliganism as a social problem in England has been largely one of increasing the burden of responsibility and control of the police in and around football grounds, in conjunction with attempts to deter hooligan offenders *via* the introduction of a wider range of more severe punishments for offenders and the escalating use of more comprehensive crowd control and crowd surveillance techniques and technologies.

Among the many measures recommended in these reports and tried in Britain, and particularly in England, since the mid-1960s are a number which are also widely used abroad. Indeed, the steel perimeter fencing which is now a common feature of most major grounds in England—making them resemble 'medieval fortresses' according to Popplewell—was regularly seen abroad prior to its use becoming widespread in the English context.

The segregation of rival fans practised in England since the late 1960s is now common in many continental countries as is the use of large squads of police officers to ensure good order on match days. More usually associated with Britain, however, and particularly with modern-day football in England, are provisions for: police escorts for 'away' fans to and from matches; the use of special railway disembarkation points to keep visiting fans out of town centres; police 'roadblocks' to aid in segregation *outside* grounds; legislative restrictions on road and rail transport and inside grounds on the carriage and sale of alcohol; the introduction of more seated accommodation inside grounds specifically as an anti-hooligan device; ground closures and the temporary closure of troublesome stands and terraces; heavy fines on clubs found guilty of taking 'inadequate precautions' to combat hooliganism; higher fines and lengthier custodial sentences for convicted hooligans (there have also been repeated calls for greater use to be made of Saturday afternoon attendances centres); the use of plain clothes police officers and security guards inside and outside grounds (culminating recently in the arrest of 7 Chelsea supporters as part of the so-called 'Own goal' operation); bans on young hooligan fans; 'blacklists' of 'known troublemakers' so that their activities can be closely monitored or to enable the authorities to exclude them from grounds altogether; the introduction of closed-circuit television (CCTV) to monitor the behaviour of fans inside and outside grounds and to produce evidence for use in the prosecution of offenders; the introduction of the police 'Hoolivan', a mobile CCTV unit; and, finally, an overall increase in the amount of police resources devoted to football match policing including the regular use of mounted divisions and dogs and, on occasions, helicopters (Dunning et al., 1986a).

Not all these developments are on view in all football grounds in Britain. Football watching lower down the English League divisions, for example, remains relatively free of the sorts of policing levels and most of the newer technological developments mentioned here. Most of them are free, too, of decent size crowds but not always from hooliganism. Despite public concern about football hooliganism in Scotland in the 1960s and earlier—particularly, but not solely, as it occurred in relation to the major Glasgow clubs—the temptation to implement rigid penning arrangements and to provide the enormous matchday police escorts now common in England was, at least partially, resisted. This is probably one of the reasons why the hooligan phenomenon in Scotland does not appear to have developed along the same sort of quasi-dialectical lines of its English counterpart. That is, the English experience over the last two decades seems to have been one in which the actions of fans have led to new control initiatives which, in turn, have led to the employment of new and more 'sophisticated' strategies by hooligan fans and the rise of a new breed of matchday organiser, and so on, in an escalating spiral. According to this view, the rise of organised 'super-hooligan' groups in England like West Ham's 'Inter City Firm' (ICF), Leeds United's 'Service Crew', the '657 Squad' from Portsmouth and comparable groups elsewhere, owe at least something to the mounting attempts by clubs and the authorities to limit and control hooliganism from the middle of the 1960s onwards (Dunning et al., 1986a).

The central aim of core members of groups like these is to engage rival hooligan 'firms' in confrontations and fights and, in doing so, to evade the attentions of the hundreds of police officers who are now turned out at major matches in England and whose presence and operations make the experience of attending matches, particularly as a visiting fan, rather like being part of an elaborate, sometimes intimidating, military exercise. Today, many of these provisions are, of course, desirable, indeed, unavoidable on match days. According to official figures at least, hooliganism in the first season post-Heysel declined considerably. But the conditions under which many major matches are now played in this country hardly seems to provide a long-term recipe for a pacified and popular professional sport in the 1980s. The realisation that this is in fact the case, however, seems to be dawning only slowly on League clubs, most of whom seem content to describe hooliganism and its consequences as, simply, a problem of law and order about which they themselves can do little or nothing.

Research and social policy

Faced with the relative poverty of 'official' responses to hooliganism, academic researchers working in the field have rarely made their mark with policy-makers. Following Heysel, the Government rejected calls for more research into the causes of football hooliganism. (Interestingly, and perhaps revealingly, the reaction to Heysel of the uninvolved West German authorities was to fund *more* research and programmes of preventive intervention.) It did so, on the basis that previous investigations had palpably failed to provide adequate 'solutions' for the hooligan problem. (Though little was said on the extent to which research-based recommendations which *had* been put forward had been implemented or even considered by government in their attempts to counter hooliganism at home and abroad.) None of this is especially puzzling, of course. Politicians for ideological, but also for more immediately pragmatic, reasons tend to veiw what are often deep-seated and complex social problems as being amenable to 'feasible' (cheap), 'popular' (often demonstrably tough), and 'practical' (immediately enforceable, concrete and short term, preferably with 'results' which can be documented) policy initiatives. Sociologists, on the other hand, in their general concern to examine the effects of longer-term social *processes* and to seek to *understand* (politically, 'go soft on') the much unloved hooligan, have seldom been popular with those charged with making difficult policy decisions. The, mostly political, complexities involved in work in this area have played no small part in producing academic responses to the hooligan problem which have done little to impress or even assist policy-makers. Instead they have tended to give prominence to uncomplicated 'offender as victim' theses; calls for what amount to policies of radical non-intervention at football matches; theories which seem to concentrate almost solely and uncritically on the rational 'resistance' expressed in working class youth violence, almost regardless of its targets and the expressed motivations and experiences of those involved in it; obscuring conspiracy theories which, in attempting to explain what is actually *involved* in hooligan outbreaks, point only to the damaging and distorting exaggeration of the phenomenon by the media. When faced with the vexing 'policy question', potentially constructive approaches—for example those which involve a legitimate 'community' emphasis, or the improvement of facilities—have been too readily dismissed (though not always without reason) as simple attempts by clubs to move up market. Indeed, for some theorists, the only *possible* option in dealing with problems like football hooliganism, seems to be either to await the 'inevitable' outcome of class or other forms of 'popular' struggle, or else to simply insist that the state and its agents, kindly, look elsewhere for sites at which to flex their repressive muscle (Young, 1986). Such positions often seem to ignore the need to confront the immediate and damaging *realities* of football hooliganism, e.g. its effects on the often multiple-disadvantaged residents who live around football grounds; its frequent promotion of racist and violently sexist ideologies; and its effects on a popular and predominantly working-class spectator sport. In short, they give too little emphasis to the linking of constructive short-term policy proposals inside and outside the game to the development of longer-term, more ambitious, initiatives aimed at addressing some of the structural 'causes' of hooliganism.

Some brief suggestions on policy were made in *Hooligans Abroad* (Williams *et al.,*1984b). They were meant to be the first, small steps towards establishing more constructive links between short-term strategies and longer-term policy goals, i.e. an attempt to bridge the *impasse* between the utopianism of some researchers and the narrow expediency of policy-makers. In the concluding sections of the book a short-term strategy was suggested which aimed at regulating and Controlling the passage to, and behaviour of, English fans on the continent which did as little as possible to contradict or obstruct longer-term objectives of reducing hooligan behaviour. Its aim was to involve football *supporters* in a project designed to establish greater self-discipline and control among travelling fans, without avoiding the necessary option of excluding serious offenders from football match travel on the Continent. Almost 18 months prior to Heysel the package of measures was recommended by the Department of the Environment working group which produced the report on *Football Spectator Violence* of 1984 'as a model to provide a basis for discussion' and, more particularly, as a scheme which 'could deter hooligans and potentially have a significant effect in reducing violence' (p.31). However, the plan was never implemented or used even on an experimental basis.

Football and football violence

As English fans continued to carve their reputations abroad throughout the 1970s, in England a largely spurious and ultimately fruitless debate was prominent in discussion on the prospects of curbing the hooligan phenomenon. Football clubs and the football authorities, on the one hand, were, unsurprisingly, keen to deny any sort of responsibility—beyond the requirements for fencing and penning—for the football hooligan problem. The game, caught in a pincer movement between rising costs and falling attendance and attempting to woo sponsors and patrons from the higher classes was ill-disposed to the matchday rituals of the increasingly disruptive terrace gangs who were accused of 'attaching' themselves, uninvited and unwanted, to major clubs. On the other, the game was adjudged by radical and some liberal commentators to have 'caused' hooliganism. It had done so, according to this view, by relinquishing its cultural purchase within working-class communities precisely because of its 'new' emphasis on bourgeois forms of commercialism and competition. In short, the game and its players had largely servered their cultural connections to disastrous effect (Taylor, 1971, Clarke, 1978).

Since the 1970s, the football v. society debate about 'causes' has moved on but not very far. However, if research at Leicester University on the roots of football hooligan violence has been more warmly received in football circles than previous academic accounts, it is almost certainly because the findings may have been interpreted by the game's officials as being broadly supportive of the 'helpless victim' position which seems to have been so readily adopted by the clubs and the football authorities. It is certainly the case, for example, that the Leicester research suggests that the heavily masculine values and standards expressed in serious football hooligan confrontation are largely the product of slowly changing but deep-rooted and long-established structural features of lower working-class life. It suggests that within the context of the shifting structural constraints which shape the future of each new generation of lower working-class people, hooligan behaviour routinely contains elements of the largely masculine *celebration* of community, and of cultural traditions as well as elements of resistance.

This being the case, the research raises a number of seemingly paradoxical questions about a 'community' approach to the football hooligan problem. For example, much of the behaviour involved in football hooliganism seems to reflect less the simple *lack* of local community attachments than it does the *strength* of *particular kinds* of local identifications and experiences. Indeed, when young males travel to football they often, in effect, take their (male) communities with them. In this sense, many of the youth and young men involved in hooliganism are less in need of *stronger* local attachments—which are generally expressed at football and elsewhere in the guise of an aggressive parochialism—than they are of forms of local identification, attachment and integration which are of a qualitatively different kind from those generated in the male-dominated public domain of the street, i.e. forms which are more equally expressive of the experiences and values of *all* community members and not just males. In addition to this, it is clear that a constructive 'community' approach to a problem like football hooliganism must have as a central goal not only an emphasis on local attachments of this kind but also a stress upon knowledge of, and respect for, *other* cultures and *other* communities.

More generally, it has been argued that hooligan behaviour is expressive of the sorts of differential social standards which are liable to arise in modern industrial societies which exhibit *inter alia*:

i.   deep-seated forms of social division and inequality, perhaps particularly as they are articulated and experienced along the lines of gender as well as class;

ii.   the production and reproduction of cultural and ideological representations which seem to support and which act to reinforce such social divisions (see Dunning *et al.*, 1987).

Thus it is clear that, in our view, football hooliganism is not 'caused' in any simple sense by the shifting pattern of relations between football clubs and their audience. Football can neither be held responsible for, nor be expected to deal in an effective way with, hooliganism. Our research expressly does *not* rule out the probability, however, that hooliganism in its present-day form and distribution owes at least something to the differential nature and experience of club/fan relations. Football, after all, despite the protestations of those largely within the game who prefer to conceptualise the problem in terms of a specious football/society dichotomy, cannot be *abstracted* from the complex network of interdependencies which serve to structure the life experiences and limited life chances of many working-class men and women. Indeed, for a substantial, if declining, number of them—and especially for males—it remains not simply a 'product' or an 'entertainment' which is purchased, but, rather, a major focus of their leisure lives. (This is a form of relation, of course, which clubs celebrate when it suits them to do so and which they prefer to play down when it does not.) Moreover, to the extent that this is the case, football provides a prime site—if a relatively insubstantial one when compared with the potential provided by the prospects of broader social and economic reforms—for the performance of broadly *equalising,* integrative functions.

These, of course, are among the major the reasons why a more pronounced 'community' emphasise in football, i.e. a greater emphasis on the role of the football club and its staff as a local *resource* in partnership with other local agencies, and as an authentic symbolic representative of members drawn from different local communities and including females and members of ethnic minorities, is likely to be both desirable and beneficial from a local community and a societal point of view. Football clubs, however, at a time when finance is tight for many (though one *Second* Division manager/director is reported to have earned in excess of £160,000 in a season) and when they seem increasingly concerned to maintain their traditional conservative stance towards 'outside interference' in the game, are unlikely to succumb to arguments of this kind. More forceful and effective are likely to be the pressures generated by a stress on the cost *to local communities* of harbouring an insular, often poorly supported club—in terms, for example, of policing and public transport costs and loss of local retail business on match days—and, more particularly, those which emphasise the importance of 'football and the community' initiatives to the future marketing and financial well-being of the game. The latter argument, when allied to their dire financial position has, unsurprisingly, been in the forefront of a recent upsurge of interest among clubs in the use of 'community' initiatives as a means of reducing hooliganism and of regenerating support for an ailing sport. The remainder of this paper looks, briefly, at some initiatives which are now in operation and others which are proposed or planned for implementation in the near future.

Football and the community initiatives: some examples

In answer to a Parliamentary Question on the 'community approach' in football Mr Richard Tracey, the Minister for Sport, said on 19 March 1986:

> 'In our continuing discussions with the football authorities we are giving very active encouragement to strengthening family and community involvement with football clubs. This will help to encourage participation in sport, it represents effective marketing for football and in the longer term it will help to remove the threat of violence. Many clubs now have family enclosures and links with the community. Grants are available for community schemes from local authorities, the Sports Council and the Football Trust.'

The general optimistic air of the Minister's answer masks a considerable degree of *ad hoc* and uneven development and a lack of commitment among some clubs for a community input. It also obscures the complex and often contradictory connections between 'effective marketing' and the removal of 'the threat of violence' from in and around football grounds as well as the increasingly limited capacities of local authorities, under pressure from central government, to provide finance for schemes. Finally, his assertions also mask the real *lack of knowledge* we have about how and why community initiatives are supposed to work. Watford Football Club are generally lauded, for example, for what is certainly a 'progressive' approach to club/fan relations and for the good behaviour of the club's supporters. But are the two connected? If so, how and why? Are the lessons from Watford (if, indeed, there are any) likely to be easily and effectively transferable to, say, Leeds? These are not easy questions to answer, even with the aid of research. At the moment, little comparative data of a suitable kind exists to allow us to make informed assessments about the success or otherwise of local schemes in relation to the goal of reducing or discouraging hooliganism or to their potential transferability.

Roger Ingham's research for the Sports Council on the 39, mostly football, clubs involved in the first phase of the Council's 'Football and the Community' initiative launched in 1978 provides one of the few useful sources of comparative data on the community approach (Ingham, 1981). In the first phase of the initiative, Sports Council funds of £1.7 million, along with one-quarter that amount contributed by the clubs, were used to establish sports schemes aimed at developing better links between young people and football clubs, and at increasing the activities of professional clubs in the area of sports provision for the local community. It was also hoped that the schemes 'may help reduce soccer hooliganism by giving supporters a link with clubs outside match days' (p.3). Developments as part of the initiative included the updating of club facilities and the provision of all-weather playing surfaces. In some cases local authority employees were used to staff projects, with clubs committed to involving playing staff on a regular basis in coaching sessions and other activities.

A number of projects which grew out of the 1978 initiative, such as the Manchester City Platt Lane scheme in Moss Side, for example, have continued and grown with considerable local success. The Manchester scheme enjoys today a great deal of local support from community groups and organisations drawn from a variety of ethnic backgrounds and increasingly caters in a more equal way for the leisure needs of females as well as those of males. The scheme encourages a wide range of sporting and cultural activities and maintains a high level of commitment and involvement from the local football club. Levels of vandalism on the project are low and the club regards the initiative as an important facet of its local community links and as part of its general anti-hooligan drive.

Despite the relative success of schemes like those in Manchester, Ingham's conclusions on the overall experience of the first phase of the Football and the Community initiative are undisguisedly gloomy. He points to only *nominal* involvement on the part of many clubs and a lack of emphasis on the needs of youngsters. Ingham also warns of the dangers of public money perhaps being used by clubs to fund 'strictly commercial enterprises ... to enable football clubs to improve their own viability' (p.118). On a slightly more positive note, Ingham points to what are, on balance, the advantages of local authority involvement in the Football and the Community initiative and recommends the joint representation of football clubs and local authorities on scheme management committees as a means of maximising potential advantages in this respect. It seems likely, from recent developments, that local authority involvement in initiatives designed to give clubs a greater community emphasis will increase in the next few years and this issue will be returned to, briefly, later.

Currently research at Leicester is focusing on a variety of initiatives and proposals involving football clubs and, in some cases, local authorities. They vary considerably in their scope and aims but are all designed to improve relations between clubs and local people and to reduce the incidence or effects of hooliganism. The first group includes those which fall broadly within the confines of a *community defence* approach, emphasising such issues as membership enclosures and club membership schemes. The Leicester City experience and some new proposals from Luton Town illustrate these kinds of initiatives.

Membership schemes

Most major clubs have family enclosures, family membership schemes or clubs or other forms of 'family' commitment. The precise emphases in these schemes vary, but most seem to be premised on the historically dubious notion that clubs must aim to 'attract back' into the game the family audience (including females) and that to do so family groups—who also seem to be identifiable by their capacity to pay—must be protected, at least inside the ground, from involvement in hooligan incidents. A mini industry has grown up around this idea including the S.A.F.E. (Soccer as Family Entertainment) project and a series of meetings and conferences on improving (or developing) football's 'family' image.

A number of commentators have noted the generally *macho* and male-dominated atmosphere of the English game when compared with that of its continental counterparts (Vulliamy, 1985; Williams, 1986). Such experiences cannot be easily divorced from the general nature of, and the unequal power balance involved in, gender relations as they are more widely experienced in British society (Taylor, 1985). Football's aim to attract more women into the sport is important and potentially significant as part of an anti-hooligan drive, but the game's approach to female fans is riddled with contradictions and inconsistencies. There is only space to mention two here. Firstly, football's widely publicised 'family commitment' has yet to open up many club boardrooms to females, even, simply, as guests of the club. Secondly, the FA's recent 'Friends of Football' campaign adopted a breathtakingly insensitive, not to say outmoded, view of the female role commending the woman's 'involvement' in the sport in the sole guise of kit washer!

The proposal that football clubs should use identity/membership cards more generally as a means of regulating access to stadia, thereby exercising a greater degree of control over hooligan fans has cropped up repeatedly since the early 1960s. In 1985, however, following the serious crowd disturbances at Chelsea, Luton, Birmingham and later in Brussels, the Prime Minister's 'War Cabinet' on football hooliganism increased the political pressure for the introduction of a *national* identity card plan. The football authorities and representatives of the police force strongly opposed these proposals, largely on the basis of their impracticality. (One club, Manchester United, envisaged issuing up to 100,000 membership cards.) Football clubs were also opposed to a comprehensive national scheme because of its likely detrimental effect on

173

already falling attendances (the exclusion of the so-called 'casual' supporter). In response to government proposals, the Football League Management Committee recommended, instead, that 50 per cent of ground capacities be covered by membership criteria. Under the new arrangements, many clubs seemed to interpret season ticket holders as constituting club members, raising important and hitherto unresolved questions about the role and status of members. In any case, season ticket holders or no, few clubs (if any) approached the 50 per cent guidelines last season, though a small number of lower division clubs proceeded on the basis of their own local membership plans.

The members' scheme at a First Division club, Leicester City, illustrates this type of approach (for a fuller account see Murphy *et al.,* 1986). Leicester City's members' plan was launched following serious crowd disturbances in the club's Main Stand during a match with Arsenal in October 1984. Disturbed by the scenes and complaints from season ticket holders and others who were caught up in fights and missile assaults between rival fans, the club decided to convert the Main Stand area of the ground, including the standing enclosure in front of it, to a members-only section. Season ticket holders were awarded membership free of charge. Other Leicester fans who wished to become members, thereby making themselves eligible for access to these parts of the ground on match days, were required to pay £3 for a plastic member's card which was posted to their home address on application. As an incentive for local fans to join the computerised scheme, ticket prices were raised in non-members' sections of the stadium while they were held constant in members' areas. Members were also allowed to purchase up to three guest tickets per match at slightly increased prices. At the end of the 1984–85 season the members areas (stand and enclosure), with a total capacity of 8,500 places had 2,400 registered members plus 2,280 members/season ticket holders. The club had made a profit from the new arrangements of something approaching £35,000.

With respect to hooliganism, the main aim of the Leicester scheme is to improve the conditions under which members watch matches while reducing the likelihood of them being involved in hooligan incidents at least *inside* the ground. Groundside fences have been removed from in front of the members' enclosures, for example. Police have been replaced in the members' areas by low profile security guards who have stewarding rather than policing functions. Local police are pleased with the new arrangements primarily because they mean that during matches police resources can be concentrated in limited, non-members' sections of the Filbert Street stadium.

As numbers of members rise, Leicester hope their plan will 'creep' around the stadium thus enveloping an increasing proportion of it. The scheme promises to concentrate those hooligan outbreaks which occur inside the ground—thus far there have been *no* incidents in members' areas—and to aid with the identification and exclusion of offenders as the scheme spreads. Among the possible disadvantages of schemes of this kind are their potential for increasing the social distances between members and non-members with the latter perhaps increasingly forced into sections of the ground in which hooliganism is likely or expected to occur. Moreover, the Members Plan at Leicester seem to have had little effect on *levels* of hooliganism occurring in association with matches at Filbert Street. Indeed, while hooligan arrests declined substantially almost everywhere in the 1985–86 season, figures for Leicester City showed an upward trend from previous years, with a number of major hooligan incidents taking place in and around the city centre and outside the Filbert Street ground.

During the present season (1986–87) Luton Town have introduced a comprehensive computerised membership card system, the first English football club to do so. As with Leicester City, Luton was sparked into action by serious crowd problems during home matches, notably those involving the visit of Millwall in 1985. Under the new arrangements no supporters outside the club's immediate catchment area are eligible for club membership. No visiting fans are allowed into Kenilworth Road (Luton's home ground) on match days.

This appeal *solely* to local people, coupled with a programme of stadium redevelopment, is an attempt by the club to regenerate local support and to change the general context and atmosphere of football match attendance by eliminating the element of conflict which is frequently present between members of rival fan groups. In this sense it is, in some ways, similar to the ill-fated all-seated/flexible pricing policy scheme adopted by Coventry City in the early 1980s and dismantled soon afterwards. A major reason for the failure of the Coventry scheme seems to have been a lack of consultation with fans and an explicit attempt to move 'up-market' (Williams *et al.*, 1984a). Stadium redevelopments in Scotland aimed at *maintaining* the 'traditional' football audience seem to have achieved a much greater degree of success (Centre for Leisure Research, 1984; Moorhouse, 1984).

The recent rise and spread of 'alternative' national football supporters' organisations like the Reading-based Supporters United and, especially, the Football Supporters Associations (FSA) based in Liverpool, suggest that growing numbers of fans are less willing these days to accede to calls for them to act 'with responsibility' at matches (for example, as 'ambassadors' for the game) while they have little effective power or even rights of representation within the sport. The FSA has radical aims for supporters' representation throughout all levels of the game and is stressing the part football supporters can play in discouraging and limiting hooliganism (Centre for Contemporary Studies, 1986).

Football clubs, the game's governing bodies, and official enquiries seldom solicit views from regular supporters on issues like football match policing, football hooliganism and anti-hooligan initiatives. Luton Town did at least hold public meetings to explain the club's new approach. Major concerns which remain about their new proposals, however, include the reactions of other clubs and supporters to the exclusion of visiting fans from Luton—at a time when organisations like the FSA are attempting to bring fans *together* in closer relations—and the capacity of local police to cope effectively with visitors who continue to arrive for matches in Luton without members' cards. Such situations provide the potential for the *raising* of levels of hooliganism in and around 'closed' grounds which have, in the past, produced policies of admitting 'ineligible' fans. The Bedfordshire police and Luton Town FC with the support of local councillors and community organisations have committed themselves firmly to the effective exclusion of non-Luton Town supporters from Kenilworth Road ground. Other clubs and police forces will look on the Luton experiment in the 1986–87 season with more than a passing curiosity.

Early indications are that the scheme has been successful in limiting hooliganism, but it may not be appropriate for other clubs (Williams *et al.*, 1986).

The two proposed anti-hooligan community initiaties with which this paper ends have a more pronounced *community reform* emphasis. The first scheme, which has recently begun under the control of the Professional Footballers Association, focuses on the role of local clubs in developing their community appeal and the use of club staff and resources in improving community links. The second, which has been developed by the Liverpool City Council over the past year favours a multi-agency approach and emphasises the role local authorities could play in addressing the hooligan problem.

Working together: the PFA Scheme

In January, 1986, approval was given through the Manpower Services Commission (MSC) for a pilot 'Football and the Community' scheme to be launched under the Community Programme (CP) and supervised from the Manchester offices of the Professional Footballers Association as part of the PFA's commitment to further education and vocational training for its members.

Six north-west clubs are involved in the pilot study which it is hoped will lead to a national programme. The scheme's central administration unit—a general administrator, three permanent supervisors and office staff—will be based in Manchester. Each of the six clubs involved will also have a club-based unit of nine employees: one full-time permanent worker, six part-time workers with 'outreach' capabilities and responsibilities and two part-time office staff.

The PFA scheme has five main objectives:

a. The provision of temporary employment within the local community and the enhancement of long-term employment prospects. (Under CP conditions non-permanent staff must be appointed on yearly contracts only, an obvious disadvantage for a project aiming to build up community links.)

b. The promotion of closer links between professional clubs and the community, centring on the role of players, club staff and scheme workers in providing easier community access for both males and females to their collective skills and to other club resources. (Three of the clubs involved in the pilot schemes will have artificial playing surfaces next season, enhancing their potential for community use.)

c. The greater involvement of members of ethnic minorities in club activities and the general community use of club resources and facilities.

d. The reduction of hooliganism and vandalism through 'good practice' and by 'a programme of talks/visits involving professional players aimed at educating and influencing young people'.

e. The maximisation of the use of club facilities and outside specialists and resources to provide services for the community with the professional football club as a focal point.

These are generally noble aims and if carried through would undoubtedly constitute a constructive element of a policy aimed at developing a community-based anti-hooligan initiative. The plan to *target* hooligan groups and the sorts of communities which typically produce hooligan fans also distinguishes these proposals from previous initiatives which have acted as more or less *marketing* strategies for clubs. The PFA also has a greater leverage with one of the most important (and most reluctant) resources available to projects of this kind, namely *the players*. (A small number of clubs including Watford, insist on a 'community' clause in players' contracts.) The PFA scheme would also seem to fit easily with a broader set of proposals currently being developed by the Liverpool City Council.

Local authority involvement

The model for the Liverpool approach can be found in the Association of Metropolitan Authorities (AMA) report on Football Violence (1984). The report calls on a multi-agency approach to prevention and control involving a wide range of agencies as well as a local authority input. Taking this model as a marker, the council in Liverpool established a number of working parties in the autumn of 1985 involving representatives from a range of voluntary and statutory organisations and from the two football clubs in the city and football supporters' groups. These working parties have general responsibilities for the development of initiatives in the areas of:

    a. the role of social factors and education;

    b. the football clubs and the community;

    c. planning, transport and the ecology of the football grounds;

    d. publicity and the media;

    e. legal considerations including the disposal and treatment of offenders.

    The authorities in Liverpool are well aware, of course, that the role they can play in alleviating some of the material inequalities which play an important part in generating hooligan behaviour is, especially in the present circumstances, slight. But they are concerned with developing a coherent educational response to the problem of the heavily aggressive forms of masculine parochialism of the kind which are expressed at football and elsewhere. The Liverpool project is also concerned to address the part played by sport on the social construction of gender. As part of a more general aim to reshape the relationship between young people of both sexes and football, in a city in which the sport provides a considerable psychological buffer against the effects of material and other forms of disadvantage, information is currently being collected from local school children of all ages on their images and/or experiences of the sport. It is hoped that the material will be used to construct an educational package on gender and sport which makes particular reference to male aggression at football and elsewhere.

    Plans for better links between the major Merseyside clubs and local people include the aim to establish, along PFA lines, community liaison officers at each of the clubs; a development in the role of spectators in establishing greater self-discipline among fans; and the use of supporters' groups in attempts to 'rehabilitate' young hooligan offenders. The West German authorities have already appointed 'streetworkers' to work with young fans at a number of projects throughout that country. These schemes claim some degree of success, though no such development seems to be in the offing in this country (Knaust and Linnemann, 1984; Pilz, 1984).

In recent months local councils in Leeds, Birmingham and Derby have all announced 'community partnerships' with local football clubs. A growing number of local authorities now own League grounds and, almost for the first time, they are in a favourable position to open up club resources and skills for their greater and more efficient local use. These new developments, even if they are supported by the football clubs concerned, will not, of course, rid British society of the major, structural 'causes' of hooliganism. But they may be constructive first steps in the establishment of more effective preventative programmes which make these longer-term and ambitious goals just a little less distant.

References

ASSOCIATION OF METROPOLITAN AUTHORITIES, (1984). *Football Violence: the Metropolitan Viewpoint*. Report of the AMA joint working group on football violence. London.

CANTER, D. and COMBER, M. (1987). *Football in its Place*. London: Methuen.

CENTRE FOR CONTEMPORARY STUDIES, (1986). *Contemporary Affairs Briefing*, 2, No. 17.

CENTRE FOR LEISURE RESEARCH, (1984). *Crowd Behaviour at Football Matches*, Dunfermline: Football Trust.

CLARKE, J. (1978). 'Football and working class fans: tradition and change'. In Ingham, R. *et al.*, (Eds.), *Football Hooliganism: the Wider Context*. London: Inter Action.

DEPARTMENT OF THE ENVIRONMENT WORKING GROUP, (1984). *Football Spectator Violence*. London: HMSO.

DUNNING, E. G., MURPHY, P. J. and WILLIAMS, J. (1986). *Spectator Violence Associated with Football Matches: A State of the Art Review*, paper prepared for the Sports Council on behalf of the Council of Europe.

DUNNING, E. G., MURPHY, P. J. and WILLIAMS, J. (1987). *The Roots of Football Hooliganism: an Historical and Sociological Study*. London: Routledge and Kegan Paul.

HARRINGTON, J. A. (1968). *Soccer Hooliganism*. Bristol: John Wright.

INGHAM, R. (1981). *Football and the Community: Monitoring Report*. London: Sports Council.

KNAUST, M. and LINNEMANN, L. (1984). 'Das Bremer Fan Projekt: Sozialpadagogik um Unfeld des Profi-Fussballs'. In Kaeber, H. and Tripp, B. (Ed.), *Gesellschaftliche Funktionen des Sports*. Bonn: Schrift-enreihe der Bundeszentrale fur politische Bildung.

LANG, J. (1969). *Crowd Behaviour at Football Matches*. London: HMSO.

McELHONE, F. (1977). *Report of the Working Group on Football Crowd Behaviour*. London: HMSO.

MOORHOUSE, H. F. (1984). 'Professional football and working class culture: English theories and Scottish evidence'. *Sociological Review*, 32, pp. 285–315.

MURPHY, P. J., DUNNING, E. G. and WILLIAMS, J. (1986). *House of Cards: the Development of the Leicester City Members Plan*. London: The Football Trust.

PILZ, G. (1984). 'Fussball ist fur uns krieg'. *Psychologie Heute*, August, pp. 53–59.

POPPLEWELL, O. (1985). *Committee of Inquiry into Crowd Safety and Control at Sports Grounds: Interim Report*. London: HMSO.

POPPLEWELL, O. (1986). *Committee of Inquiry into Crowd Safety and Control at Sports Grounds: Final Report*. London: HMSO.

SPORTS COUNCIL/SSRC. (1978). *Public Disorder and Sporting Events*. London: Gavin Martin.

TAYLOR, I. (1971). 'Soccer consciousness and soccer hooliganism'. In Cohen, S. (Ed.), *Images of Deviance*. Harmondsworth: Penguin.

TAYLOR, I. (1985). 'Putting the boot into a working class sport: British soccer after Bradford and Brussels'. Paper delivered to the annual conference of NASS, Boston, Mass.

DE VRIESBOSCH, H. (1983). *Achtergronden van Vandalism bij Voetbalwed-Strijden*. Haarlem: Publisher unknown.

VULLIAMY, E. (1985). 'Live by aggro, die by aggro'. *New Statesman*, 7 June, pp. 8–10.

WILLIAMS, J. (1986). 'White riots'. In Tomlinson, A. and Whannel, G. (Eds.), *Off the Ball*. London: Pluto Press.

WILLIAMS, J., DUNNING, E. G. and MURPHY, P. J. (1984a). *All-Seated Grounds and Hooliganism: the Coventry City Experience, 1981–84*. A report for the Football Trust.

WILLIAMS, J., DUNNING, E. G. and MURPHY, P. J. (1984b). *Hooligans Abroad*. London: Routledge and Kegan Paul.

WILLIAMS, J., DUNNING, E. G. and MURPHY, P. J. (1986). *A Preliminary Report on the Luton Home Only Members Plan*. London: The Football Trust.

YOUNG, J. (1986). 'The failure of criminology', in Young, J. and Matthews, R. (Eds.), *Confronting Crime*. London: Sage.

11. The march of folly—crime and the underclass

Lynn A. Curtis

'[Folly] is the pursuit by governments of policies contrary to their own interests ... In its first stage, mental standstill fixes the principles and boundaries governing a political problem. In the second stage, when dissonances and failing function begin to appear, the initial principles rigidify ... Rigidifying leads to increase of investment and the need to protect egos; policy founded upon error multiplies, never retreats ... In the third stage, pursuit of failure enlarges the damages until it causes the fall of Troy, the defection from the Papacy [during the Protestant Reformation], the loss of a trans-Atlantic empire [in the case of George III, and] the classic humiliation in Vietnam.'

Barbara W. Tuchman
The March of Folly

Since the late nineteen sixties, serious crime in the United States has doubled and levels of fear have increased. American crime and fear are by far the highest in the industrialized world. Given disproportionate minority investment, crime and fear have helped perpetuate segregation in schools and racism in our national consciousness (Curtis, 1985).

In terms of policy, these numbers over two decades suggest the march of folly. During this time, the federal government made 'hardware' fashionable. Its grants included money for several tanks to one police department and for a submarine to another. Crime didn't go down—all that went down was the federal agency making the grants (Curtis, 1985).

'Deterrence' was fashionable for a while, but it has been demonstrated that, for the most part, more and more police or longer and longer sentences do not result in less and less crime (Currie, 1985).

If one believes that society should be protected from serious offenders and that punishment is a valid reason for incarceration, the notion of incapacitation—taking criminals off the street to prevent them from committing more serious crimes—seems to be common sense. Yet careful research on incapacitation, another trendy policy of recent years, shows that 'the potential reduction in serious crime is disturbingly small, especially one balanced against the social and economic costs of pursuing this strategy strenuously enough to make much difference to public safety' (Currie, 1985). It should be borne in mind that the US already has the highest rates of imprisonment in the industrialised world—with the possible exceptions of South Africa and the Soviet Union. At current rates, every fifth black man in America will spend some time in a state or federal prison (with the proportion much higher for specific inner-city communities) (Currie, 1985). It has been estimated that, in order to have any significant effect on the rate of serious crime—say, to try to reduce it by 20 per cent—we would have to triple this prison population. The cost is about $70 billion in new construction (American prisons being filled to capacity) and, conservatively at present prices, $14 billion in new annual operating costs. The $70 billon is well over *double* the amount needed to lift *every* poor family above the poverty line. The $14 billion could provide one million unemployed inner-city youths solid jobs at an entry level wage of $7.00 an hour (Currie, 1985). In addition, prison is the best school for crime. 'Not only do a greater number of those who receive punitive treatment ... continue to break the law, but they also commit more serious crimes with greater rapidity than those who experience a less constraining contact with the judicial and correctional system' (Wolfgang *et al.*, 1972).

Even though crime and fear have risen dramatically while so much money has been poured into police and other criminal justice social engineering over the last twenty years, one still observes state legislatures churning out laws to 'lock them up and throw away the key' and similar advocates arguing that, if we just got still tougher, we would see some light at the end of the tunnel. United States policy against crime, then, appears well into Tuchman's second stage of folly, where failures appear, principles rigidify, investment increases to protect egos, and policy founded upon error multiplies.

Community Based Prevention

Over the same twenty years, however, there has been at least one line of action that has reflected the courage to cut our losses and try something both more effective and less costly. Citizen-based crime prevention in the community involves descriptions like 'indigenous self help', 'grass-roots mobilisation' and 'bubble up' rather than 'trickle down'. It is not intended to define the concept of community crime prevention here because it has become a projective test. People read into it what they want. The point of this paper is to identify alternative visions of the concept, as theorised, implemented and measured for success in the US—and to warn that, while promising, it can also become a footsoldier in the march of folly.

In certain ways, the coming years may mark a crossroads in the notion of community-based crime prevention. Will it reflect a truly grass-roots process of citizen empowerment that addresses the underlying issues, as one might argue was the recent experience of the relatively bloodless revolution in the Philippines? Or will official agencies co-opt citizens, and use public relations gimmickry to camouflage underlying and continuing problems, as one can interpret some of the actions of the South African Government?

Granted, these are extreme foreign examples that translate imperfectly to the American scene. But they help to clarify an alternative future for the nine million or so people estimated to be in the American underclass,[1] especially in

---

1 Auletta (1983) provides a working definition of the American underclass.

For most of 25 to 29 million Americans officially classified as poor, poverty is not a permanent condition. Like earlier immigrant groups, most of these people overcome poverty after a generation or two. There are not precise numbers on this, but an estimated 9 million Americans do not assimilate. They are the underclass. Generally speaking, they can be grouped into four distinct categories: (a) the passive poor, usually long-term welfare recipients; (b) the hostile street criminals who terrorise most cities, and who are often school dropouts and drug addicts; (c) the hustlers, who, like street criminals, may not be poor and who earn their livelihood in an underground economy, but rarely commit violent crimes; and (d) the traumatised drunks, drifters, homeless shopping-bag ladies and released mental patients who frequently roam or collapse on city streets.

inner-city ghettos—where the residents are disproportionally non-white and disproportionally involved as perpetrators and victims in crime. This is not to deny that crime is complex and associated with many other aspects of levels of American life. The premise is simply that a policy to prevent crime using a citizen-based approach ought to initially focus on where crime, and its causes, are most prominent.

A detailed interpretation of the causes of American crime would be out of the question here, but I do not disagree with Currie's conclusion (1985):

> 'If I wanted to sketch a hypothetical portrait of an especially violent society, it would surely contain these elements: it would separate large numbers of people, especially the young, from the kind of work that could include them securely in community life. It would encourage policies of economic development and income distribution that sharply increased inequalities between sectors of the population. It would rapidly shift vast amounts of capital from place to place without regard for the impact on local communities, causing massive movements of population away from family and neighbourhood supports in search of livelihood. It would avoid providing new mechanisms of care and support for those uprooted, perhaps in the name of preserving incentives to work and paring government spending. It would promote a culture of intense interpersonal competition and spur its citizens to a level of material consumption many could not lawfully sustain.'

Based on this view, to what extent do various versions of American community-based crime prevention address the causes of crime? How successful are they, and how valid and reliable are the indices of success? What are the ideas underlying them? Politically and technically, how difficult is it to implement them?

Addressing causes

Illustrative programmes and their measures

Three neighbourhood based self-help organizations are among the most widely used illustrations of how to directly address the causes of crime: the Argus Community, the Center for Orientation and Services and the House of Umoja.

Argus. The Argus Learning for Living Center is physically located in a former school in the South Bronx. Begun in the late nineteen sixties, it has an eight-hour non-resident programme as well as a resident programme. Argus works with young people aged 12–21, mostly black and Hispanic, both young men and young women, chronic underachievers, runaways, addicts and criminals. Many are directed from the juvenile justice and school systems, while others walk in from the neighbourhood.

Argus provides an extended family of staff and peers, a safe and therapeutic environment, a moral climate with strict rules and daily routines, and a concrete programme—which includes counselling, high school and vocational education, recreation, practical job training and job placement. A great deal of the work is remedial—emotionally, socially, academically and vocationally.

Led by its founder, Elizabeth Lyttleton Sturz, and a staff who often themselves were runaways, addicts and criminals, Argus seeks to provide for these young people what their natural families and the other schools in New York City often do not provide—an opportunity for bonding (forming two-way trust relationships), a safe and orderly place (sanctuary), encouragement in the airing of emotions and a strong emphasis on the accumulation of knowledge (Sturz, 1983).

At any one time, Argus has between 100 and 200 youth, working through one of two phases. Phase one involves becoming part of the Argus extended family, working in the classroom, accepting the rules, learning to trust the staff and controlled peer feedback, gaining a sense of responsibility and developing self-esteem. Phase two—training, work and, eventually, a non-subsidised job—is not pegged to academic progress but to behavioural, attitudinal and emotional growth. For those who are not academically talented, there are alternative avenues to knowledge and self-esteem (such as being an artist or peer group trainer) (Sturz, 1983).

Argus measures outcomes in terms of improved ability to function self-sufficiently—at a personal level and in real world legal labour markets. By these standards, it has been successful. For example, in a recent cohort of 149 high-risk girls who passed through Argus, only 5 were on welfare after the experience. Most of the rest were in college, advanced training or non-subsidised jobs; returned to their parents; or returned to regular high school. In terms of non-subsidised job placement, 67 per cent of Argus enrollees reached this goal in 1980. This is a much higher job placement rate than for similar 'high risk' youth who are not involved with Argus (Sturz, 1983). Studies by the Vera Institute and the Criminal Justice Coordinating Council have shown lower recidivism rates for Argus graduates than almost all other programmes in New York City which work with such high-risk offenders (Sturz, 1983 and 'phone conversation with Elizabeth Sturz, 10 July 1986).

Argus defines success through what happens to *individuals* who pass through its programmes. Argus does not (now at least) define success via changes in the surrounding South Bronx *community* (like a drop in crime or fear in the neighbourhood).

El Centro. The Centre for Orientation and Services (El Centro) was begun in 1970 in Ponce, Puerto Rico's second largest city, by a Catholic nun with training at Fordham University, Sister Isolina Ferre.

The La Playa community where Sister Isolina began was at that time almost written off by the public and private sectors. It had high poverty, high unemployment, high crime and physically deteriorated housing.

El Centro started with ten full-time 'advocates'—local residents trained to work with and represent young people in trouble with the law. Eventually, the number of advocates increased and their role embraced the larger community. They began to organise, lead recreational and cultural programmes, encourage residents of La Playa to become involved in community issues (transportation and street paving), and serve as brokers between the people in need and the services provided by El Centro.

Today, the goal of El Centro is to enhance self-respect and reduce dependency among young people in trouble with the law. El Centro is primarily a day-time programme, though there is temporary housing for young people. Both young Puerto Rican men and women are involved—many diverted from the juvenile court, but also some high-risk non-adjudicated teenagers from La Playa.

183

Community, as well as individual, competence is developed, so that all in La Playa can gain more control over their lives. The view is that, in the last analysis, it is the disorganisation of the community at large—the evidence on all sides that their parents are unable to control their own lives, unable to impose sanctions on people who threaten their own or their community's well-being—which persuades the young that the cards are hopelessly stacked against them, that fate (or the omnipotent and omnipresent 'they') will not permit them to 'make it' in any legitimate form, thereby allowing crime to seem a rewarding alternative (Silberman, 1978).

Beyond the extended family of the advocates and other immediate staff, which operate out of a physical facility built through the US Department of Housing and Urban Development, El Centro has over thirty programmes, which include:

Education—An alternative school has been established for young people who are dropouts or need more individualised instruction.

Family Counselling and Support—Counsellors work with young people and families in crisis.

Vocational Training—Training is provided to youth in cosmetics, horticulture, sewing, electrical engineering, computer technology and nursing assistance.

Enterprise Development—Some of the activities that were started in the early years of El Centro have become employment opportunities for youth and adults in La Playa (where, as in the South Bronx, the unemployment rate is over 50 per cent). These small industries include bookbinding, silk-screened Christmas cards, calendars, agricultural products, ceramics, landscaping and laminating.

Runaway Counselling—The Department of Health and Human Services has funded a programme that provides counselling, referral services and shelter for runaway youth.

Independent Living—The Department of Health and Human Services has funded a programme that provides housing for delinquent and non-delinquent young men and women who are on their own.

Typical statements about the great success of El Centro are in terms of community-wide measures in La Playa, rather than in terms of what happens to young people who pass through El Centro (as is the case with Argus). Thus, in his Ford Foundation study, Charles Silberman called El Centro 'the best example of community regeneration I found anywhere in the United States.' He reported that, since 1970, the number of adjudicated delinquents has been reduced 85 per cent and the delinquency rate cut in half, despite an exploding delinquency population (Silberman, 1978). Because El Centro is the prime moving force for delinquency prevention in La Playa, the community-wide measures also imply a low rate of repeat crime for the individual young people who pass through the organisation. Reduced fear in the neighbourhood does not appear to be a measure that has been used, or deemed necessary in demonstrating success.

Umoja. The House of Umoja was begun in the late nineteen sixties in the West Philadelphia home of David and Falaka Fattah. Today, the Fattahs have developed the 'first inner city Boystown in the US'. Up to forty young men—mostly Black—are in residence at any one time along a city block of rehabilitated row houses in West Philadelphia. A non-resident programme has operated, but presently Umoja is residential. Most residents are adjudicated offenders (for any offences except sex crimes), though some are high-risk youth from the community.

Umoja, a Swahili word which means 'unity', defends its notion of extended family in terms of African culture. The extended family means that the African mother and father are mother and father to all children. Applying this belief to the urban situation, Umoja considers the teenagers living with them to all be sons of Sister Falaka and David Fattah, and therefore brothers. Within this context, Umoja creates a sanctuary—a sheltered environment which (Curtis, 1985):

Requires adherence to a strict sense of house rules and order, underscored through a signed contract between each resident and Umoja.

Assures individual counselling to each youth to help determine his immediate and life goals, define his educational needs and resolve his internal conflicts and problems.

Involves the youth in the operation of the house—including household chores and food preparation.

Ensures that the youth attends school.

Assists youth in securing employment or enrolling in a training programme.

Fosters a sense of togetherness and group unity by imparting the values inherent in African culture.

Addresses the youth's well-being—including repair health check-ups, clothing, food and recreation.

A recent television documentary captured much of the process whereby the house parents (the Fattahs), 'Old Heads' (Umoja graduates), peer pressure by other young men in residence, and African ethnic identity all operate to build self-respect, a sense of control and a willingness to channel one's energy into a future based on education, employment and family. For example, the documentary shows Sister Fattah sitting at a table with several young men. She is leading the Adella—a Swahili word for 'just' and 'fair'. It is a vehicle for character building, mediation, and self-government. Problems are raised and resolved. Sister Falaka shows her concern that James got fired from a construction job for talking back to the foreman. 'If you were hanging on a rope by your mouth, and you just had to get in that last word, you'd be gone. Isn't that right?' (Curtis, 1985).

There is classroom training in Umoja youth enterprise ventures and job placement. The youth enterprises within the Boystown include the Umoja restaurant, the Umoja moving company, the Umoja printing company, the Umoja Security Institute (which is accredited to train for the private security industry), and driving (for later work as taxi, bus and truck drivers).

Most of the new youth enterprises are just getting started. They provide sheltered training opportunities but, for the most part, cannot (yet) provide full time employment for all Umoja youth—who therefore often eventually seek work, with the aid of counsellors, outside of the Umoja community in the course of becoming self-sufficient. The Black youth unemployment rate in

185

West Philadelphia is above 50 per cent, job placements require extensive work by the counsellors.

Umoja is geared to independent living after six months to one year of residence, if family re-union is not a realisable goal.

Success at Umoja is defined mainly in terms of frequency of recidivism for adjudicated offenders who pass through. The most cited study is by the Philadelphia Psychiatric Center, which reported a 3 per cent re-arrest rate for the first 600 Umojans who lived at the Boystown—compared to a rate of 70 to 90 per cent for young people released from conventional juvenile correction facilities (Curtis, 1985). Umoja does not measure success through changes in crime and fear in the surrounding West Philadelphia community.

A Note on Measurement. These examples of successful programmes still require more careful measurement. We need to follow age cohorts of individuals in the community programmes over longer time to see how they fare *vis-à-vis* control groups in quasi-experimental designs. Measures need to include reduced recidivism, increased employment, increased self-sufficiency and (for young women) reduced teenage pregnancies. Some of this kind of work is now being initiated by the Eisenhower Foundation with Argus.

In spite of the measurement gaps, there appears to be a consensus along a broad political spectrum of observers that these groups are on the right track and are cost-effective, compared to the alternatives.

In this verson of community crime prevention, neighbourhood-wide measures of crime and fear reduction are not central. The only success story of the three that includes neighbourhood-wide measures is El Centro. Much of the reason has to do with El Centro serving just the La Playa community, so enough reduced crime by individuals eventually results in fewer victims in the neighbourhoods where they live (Argus and Umoja draw youth in city-wide.) Fear reduction rarely appears to be involved as a measure—simply because it is not direct enough. Why do we need to look at perceptions of crime (that is, fear) if we are going to the heart of the matter by reducing actual crime and its causes?

Conceptual framework

Other successful community programmes which operate on many of the same underlying principles as Argus, El Centro and Umoja include the Dorchester Youth Collaborative in Boston, the Inner City Roundtable on Youth in New York, Delancy Street in San Francisco and Project New Pride in several locations around the nation.

Most fundamentally, those principles are to create an extended family setting with strict rules and nurturing—through which self-respect is instilled, education is pursued, training is undertaken and employment is found. The ultimate measures of success are reduced crime, reduced welfare dependency and increased personal and economic self-sufficiency.

Although this paper has focused on private sector community successes, it is interesting to note that one of the most successful public sector programmes to reduce crime, the residential Job Corps, uses the same basic principles. According to Labour Department statistics, during the first year after the experience, Job Corps members were a third less likely to be arrested than non-participants. Every \$1.00 spent on Job Corps results in \$1.45 in benefits to society, including reduced crime and substance abuse (which account for \$.42 alone in benefits), reduced welfare dependency, and increased job production, income and taxes (Taggert, 1981).

The conceptual framework of Argus, El Centro and Umoja is opposed by those who, for example, ask, 'What agency do we create, what budget do we allocate, that will supply missing parental affection and restore to the child consistent discipline by a stable and loving family?' The same critics argue that they have 'never seen the causes of crime' and that there is no relation between unemployment and crime. (For a critique of such issues, see Curtis, 1985 and Currie, 1985.)

The inextricable involvement of extended family and employment in Argus, El Centro, Umoja and similar successful programmes underscores the nonsense in such academic posturing. The real theoretical and evaluative work is how better to define and understand the relation among the terms in the equation that extended family + employment = less crime and dependency. For example, to what extent, if any, are residential programmes more cost-effective than non-residential programmes, and for what kinds of youth? What is the significance of El Centro's drawing the entire community into its extended family, compared to Argus and Umoja, where the surrounding community appears less involved (though each has fledgling businesses serving the community)?

That the principles underlying these successful organisations are on the right theoretical path can be further verified by the results of the most exhaustive review of the employment-crime relationship, by the Vera Institute for the US Justice Department (Thompson, *et al.*, 1981).

For high-risk dropouts aged 14–18, Vera concludes that we cannot assume a direct, one-to-one, short-term relationship between employment alone and reduction in crime by those employed. Rather, Vera suggests that a number of components are necessary to successfully reduce (at least theft and related) crime by those employed:

Employment training and the actual jobs for high risk youth ideally should provide a 'bridge' from less secure and promising 'secondary' labour market employment to more secure 'primary' labour market employment, where the work is steady and holds promise of upward mobility.

Employment opportunity must exist. Training and bridge employment mean nothing if the private and public sectors cannot supply the jobs. Importantly for the focus here on the inner city underclass, Vera found that the private supply was much more limited for poor black than poor white youth. Therefore, although more private sector employment needs to be identified for minority youth, we cannot rule out the public sector sources which in recent years have often been more accessible to poor minorities than private sector opportunities. Examples are local government, civil service and postal service jobs.

Employment networks are crucial for linking the demand for bridge employment by high-risk youth to the supply of jobs. The Vera findings were that black high-risk youth had far fewer contacts than white high-risk youth with family, friends and others who provided access to opportunities. In the absence of such contracts, alternative sources, such as community organisations where high-risk youth feel comfortable, were seen as needed to make the linkages between the youth and employees.

Family help and alternative extended families are required. Vera found that white high-risk youth were able to utilise family resources for employment more than black high-risk youth. Because so many minority high-risk youth are from single-parent families and because it often is harder for a single parent to maintain control over potential delinquent youth, Vera found that there need to be ways of either strengthening the control of natural families or of providing both discipline and psychological support through alternative, extended families. Vera also found that high-risk youth need more accessible role models who have made it in legal labour markets to work with them. As youth grow older, the formation of their own families can be a stabilising influence which both makes employment more important to them and also encourages a non-criminal lifestyle.

Peer networks need to be tapped. Among high-risk youth, Vera suggests that many decisions are not made based on 'rational' cost-benefit calculations between legal and illegal market behaviour—at least not 'rational' as defined by, say, many academics and policy-makers. Rather, the decisions are often determined by peer influence—for example, pressure to conform to what friends say, behaviour required to join and stay in a gang, and advice by friends regardless of its wiseness. The Vera findings suggest that it is naive to deny, try to break up or try to compete with such peer influence. Rather, a crucial lesson from the Vera work appears to be that the influence of peers needs to be incorporated into an employment programme as another essential support to the job itself.

High school education is another support which the Vera study suggests is important, influencing reduced crime by those employed. Although considerable variations existed among ethnic groups, there were clear payoffs associated with high school degrees or more advanced education. However, while school was seen as valuable, the schools for minorities in the Vera study often were disorganised, full of conflicts and unhelpful in providing personal contacts and job opportunities. This raised the possibility of alternative settings, like community organisations, which can provide more order and a refuge for study—or at least counsellors and role models who can assist and motivate high-risk youth who remain in high school.

In sum, the Vera findings read like a theoretical advertisement for the components that Falaka and David Fattah, Isoline Ferre and Elizabeth Sturz long have identified as the commonsense core of their work. All probably would add that, in their neighbourhoods of over 50 per cent joblessness, the component most outside of their control is employment opportunity.

Barriers to implementation

Even these community successes in reducing crime and the underclass face, as they key implementation issue, the need for adequate funding to finance basic operating programmes and avoid cash flow difficulties. Police do little to prevent crime (see below), but their funding has quadrupled over the past 40 years. The 88 cities of at least 100,000 or more people in the US now spend a total of about $3 billion per year on policing (*Criminal Justice Newsletter*,

1986). That is an average of over $34 million per city per year, compared to core budgets at Argus, El Centro and Umoja that range from $200,000 to $2,000,000.

One reason why these community programmes are underfunded has to do with inadequate knowledge among the citizenry and federal, state and local government about their successes—combined with American values that still inaccurately relate prevention to the criminal justice system. Another reason has to do with the fact that rarely do programme-specific grants to such organisations provide anywhere near sufficient support for general administrative and management operations. And desperately needed 'unrestricted' grants for general operations are hard to come by. Since the Tax Reform Act of 1969, both the public and private sectors tend to require programme-specific applications and one- to three- year 'research' and 'knowledge development' projects. Hence, often a game must be played, with community organisations 'attempting to manipulate and squeeze their needs out of the "research" while their "adversaries", the funding agencies, tighten controls' (Sturz, 1983).

Argus, El Centro and Umoja are aware of the rhetoric of the times—that commmunity organisations need to become more 'financially self-sufficient', particularly by learning to become more sophisticated fund raisers in a traditional sense, as well as by striving to transform some activities from social programmes to profit-making businesses. But this is not easy to do, especially in the markets available in low income communities and given the scarcity of start-up capital for what private public sources alike view as high risk ventures. Even a passing understanding of these realities leads to the conclusion that the new rhetoric can rarely lead to anything close to complete financial self-sufficiency. Similarly, some would lead us to believe that, if we only had enough volunteers, we could solve all of our domestic problems. While successful inner-city organisations make ample use of unpaid individuals, ideological posturing about volunteerism is treated with the same scepticism as bombast on self-sufficiency by the street wise community programme director. Only the assurance of steady, paid employment draws a sufficient core staff to run a community programme like the successes documented here.

To compound the strain on resources, funding agencies, especially in the public sector, often require far too much in administrative paperwork. "How can we create, sustain and continuously modify . . . an entire environment, act as an extended family, incorporate kids into a structure and a value system and in addition find the time to record our every interaction?" (Sturz, 1983).

Improved management is an implementation issue as well, mostly related to inadequate funding of community programmes rather than to some innate inability to administer efficiently. All other things being equal (especially resources), there has been no demonstration that community organisations are managed less well than corporations, the police, small business, government, academic departments, foundations or think tanks.

Community-based organisations which house at-risk youth can sometimes face problems from neighbours who are frightened by the residents. This issue can and has been addressed by careful location in areas with appropriate zoning and well-planned community organising which demonstrates to neighbours how they will benefit. This is perhaps best demonstrated by El Centro, which has motivated the entire surrounding community to serve as, in

189

effect, support staff for the common good. It helps if the at-risk youth come from the immediate community, so the programme can be said to support 'our own'. On balance, hostility by the surrounding neighbourhood against a community organisation probably is a lesser implementation obstacle than hostility by minorities against police in police-led prevention. (This is especially so if the police are white, as is usually the case.)

But the *community* always takes the lead *vis-à-vis* the police among the successes. Umoja began *in spite* of opposition by then Police Chief Frank Rizzo. Argus has always used police support, which varies over time, based on the attitudes of precinct captains. At one point in the nineteen seventies, when Anthony Bouza was in charge of the Bronx, an officer was given two years leave to teach building trades at Argus. The Puerto Rican police initially were hostile to and suspicious of El Centro. Today, the police rely more and more on El Centro's advocates. Unless a crime is very serious, the police will avoid arrest, instead bringing a juvenile to an advocate for counselling. When police are asked to settle a domestic dispute, they often will ask an advocate to meet them in the barrio to help mediate. Several advocates have police 'hot lines' in their homes, so they can be contacted immediately after hours when there is trouble (Silberman, 1978; phone conversations with Elizabeth Sturz on July 10 1986).

The failure by the private sector, in particular, to provide employment opportunity to high-risk youth, however well designed a community organisation's training programme may be, is a serious implementation impediment. Currently, public sector programmes do not compensate for the private sector deficiencies—because the public job training 'creams' the most qualified young people and does not automatically provide the extra resources needed for the kind of high-risk youth at Argus, El Centro and Umoja.

Beyond reducing these impediments in the implementation of the relatively few American community crime prevention programme that currently address causes, the priority is to replicate the principles underlying these successes and facilitate new Arguses, El Centros and Umojas that vary according to local circumstances. It has become a cliché for observers to say that one can't replicate a Fattah, Ferre or Sturz. But all of these pioneers say that natural leaders are present in every minority community and that we only need the financial and political mechanisms to nurture their development. With support from the Departments of Health and Human Services and Labour, leveraged against funds from other sectors, the Eisenhower Foundation is beginning what presently is anticipated to be a slow process of replication in several locations around the nation.

In the nineteen eighties, is there the political will to address causes, change values, publicise the success documented here and begin replication on a large enough scale to make a national impact? Ronald Reagan has praised Umoja before the National Alliance of Business, saying that Umoja has done 'what all the police and social welfare agencies have failed to do'. Argus has been praised in the *Wall Street Journal* as 'an inner city school that works' (Curtis 1985). The advocate who sought 'community action' and sponsored 'mobilisation for youth' in the nineteen sixties came from a different philosophic position than the observer who today wants people to 'pull themselves up by their bootstraps'. Yet there is some political common ground here, a certain shared support of 'self-help' by American liberals and conservatives.

George Orwell observed that the left asks, 'How can you improve human nature until you have changed the system?' The right asks, 'What is the use of changing the system before you have changed human nature?' (Auletta, 1983). The genius of Argus, El Centro and Umoja is that they work on human nature, motivating and disciplining youth, yet they also create a system—the extended family—in which the individual can function and find models to emulate on the way to employment. That still leaves the inequities and racism in the broader American system—as best illustrated here by inadequate funding and lack of job opportunities. But limited success through the extended family can be a leveraging tool for more basic reform. If this sounds too naive and idealistic, we can return to cost-effectiveness and the economics of self-interest in support of the political feasibility suggested by the Reagan and *Wall Street Journal* endorsements. Measured in terms of recidivism, Argus, El Centro, Job Corps and Umoja are much more effective than prison. And money wise, the cost per year, per person is $24,186 for Minnesota prisons, $22,433 for a federal maximum security prison, $19,339 for California prisons, $18,472 for New York prisons, $16,000 for Argus residents, $16,000 for Umoja residents $13,000 for Job Corps residents, $2,000 for Argus non-residents and $200 for El Centro non-residents (*New York Times,* 1985: 22E; Auletta, 1983; 'phone conversations with Falaka Fattah, Isolina Ferre and Elizabeth Sturz on July 10, 1986).

Federal resources and leadership will be needed—for the level of replication necessary, the employment opportunity, and substantive and management technical assistance. With some of the red tape created by federal bureaucracies, the vehicles for targeting increased federal resources directly to community organisations, providing technical assistance, leveraging additional corporate and foundation money, and guiding evaluations may be the kind of national private sector 'mediating institutions' which evolved in the nineteen seventies and eighties—like the Institute for Local Self Reliance, the Enterprise Foundation, the Local Initiatives Support Corporation, the Management Training Institute, the Manpower Demonstration Research Corporation, Public/Private Ventures and the Eisenhower Foundation.

Addressing causes and reducing opportunities simultaneously

A somewhat different variety of citizen-based community crime prevention also addresses causes—on a more modest scale than Argus, El Centro and Umoja—but also includes opportunity reduction. Opportunity reduction strategies are those which make the victim a 'harder target', lowering the probability of victimization. Traditional opportunity reduction includes block watches, patrols, escort services, property identification, improved locks or physical security of a household to make it more difficult to enter, and 'defensible space'-type physical configurations.

The Eisenhower Foundation programme

Today, a number of crime prevention programmes in the US seek to both address causes and reduce opportunities. The largest scale national attempt

191

currently underway that is carefully being evaluated is run by the Eisenhower Foundation, initially at ten locations across the country: Baltimore, Boston, the Bronx, Brooklyn, Cleveland, Miami (Liberty City), Minneapolis, Newark, Philadelphia and Washington, DC.

Most of the following observations are based on this programme, a national effort running from 1983 to 1987 which builds on some of the lessons learned from the Urban Initiatives Anti-Crime Programme run by the US Department of Housing and Urban Development, (see Police Foundation, 1984; Hayes, 1982; Catalyst, 1986) and especially draws on the principles of Argus, El Centro and Umoja. When completed, the demonstration will cost about $2 million—which covers grants to inner-city community organisations, technical assistance (by the Foundation), and a process/impact evaluation (by North-western University). The majority of funds have come from the Ford Foundation, but other national funders include IBM, Exxon, the Burden Foundation and the federal government. There are also over fifty local fund-matching partners.

The programme and its measures

The Eisenhower Foundation has selected cities where there are qualified inner-city community organisations and local funding institutions (public and private) which understand community development. If local funders can sufficiently match the Foundation, a programme is begun. All funders sit as a selection committee. Usually, there is an open competition among qualified inner-city community organisations. (Sometimes the locals only will match if a certain organisation is chosen. The Foundation may or may not agree, depending on whether the organization is highly qualified.) The Foundation does not ask for traditional detailed proposals—and selection is made on the basis of a much briefer 'capacity statement' in which each applicant seeks to demonstrate that it has, for example, a good management track record, a competent staff and board and experience in organising. Site visits also are made. In its initial selections, the Foundation has mostly chosen community groups with organising experience in economic development and sought to integrate in crime prevention programmes (though some youth service agencies also have been chosen).

After selection, each organisation undertakes a planning period of roughly six months. A survey of community residents is undertaken by 'phone to collect information on victimization, fear, quality of life and perceptions on the neighbourhood's problems. In-person interviews are undertaken with community leaders and businessmen. The professional evaluators guide the assessment, but the interviews are done as often as possible by community residents, to give them a stake in the programme. The assessment is quickly written up and presented to the community organisation. The document becomes an objective basis for planning the programme. Is unemployment a major problem? Are older women being mugged on the way back from shopping? Will some business people move out unless the commercial strip is made more secure? Through a series of mini town meetings in which all persons in the neighbourhood are invited, the community organisation 'bubbles up' a programme tailored to the community's specific needs.

The Foundation does not 'trickle down' programme dictates—except to require a general framework in which each locality addresses the causes of crime (for example, through employment training and support to extended families), reduces opportunities for crime, and creates a financially self-sufficient mechanism for carrying on the programme after initial Eisenhower Foundation-facilitated support ends. The Foundation provides a guidebook which summarises all past significant work by others in each of these areas. The local organisation often draws on these ideas, but also innovates its own solutions.

After a workplan is bubbled up over the planning period, the programme runs for about twenty-four months. The community survey then is repeated (in the neighbourhood where the programme operates as well as in a control neighbourhood). Along with other before and after measures of changes in high-risk individuals involved in the programme, the pre-post surveys allow us to measure for success. If the programme is making good progress, the Foundation continues to assist the community organisation in reaching the goal of financial self-sufficiency. In some cities, 'self-help funds' are being set up—financial pools based on yearly corporate and foundation contributions, as long as the programme continues to do well. The Foundation seeks *quid pro quo* from local business—by communicating successes (e.g. in reducing crime and fear), pointing out that this helps business, and asking for financial support to help continue the programme. The Foundation also assists local organisations in better using the media to generate free publicity (which can lead to financial support) and in beginning for-profit enterprises that provide funds for the programme. In selecting community organisations to participate, the Foundation usually looks for multi-faceted operations which draw income from many sources, some of which (like housing syndication) may be used to help finance the ongoing programme.

Even before month twenty-four, the Foundation works with localities to finance expansion of programmes that are doing well. For example, Foundation executives will write proposals to federal agencies for funds which pass through the Foundation to local programmes, which otherwise probably would not have access to such monies.

Most programmes involve the police in important supportive roles, but the decision is made by community organisation.

Of the ten initial programmes, the effort in Washington, DC has become one of the most ambitious. The Foundation began by helping to organise the Adams-Morgan neighbourhood against crime—to create through opportunity reduction a more secure setting for the low income housing rehabilitation work of Jubilee Housing, Inc, which is the national 'model' for developer James Rouse's Enterprise Foundation. This led to a home rehabilitation and weatherisation business which employs minority youth who are at risk of crime. The federal Department of Health and Human Services granted $250,000 to better capitalise the business, which will become profit making in two years. Some of the new jobs created will be for single mothers affiliated with a teen parent self-sufficiency centre in the same neighbourhood. Single teen fathers also will be eligible for employment in the business if they use some of their earnings to support their infants. The physical facility for the centre is being financed by two real estate companies, which are purchasing the property (with the aid of a below market loan from a local bank) and

193

rehabilitating it at no cost to the programme. The property is being rented to the centre at $100 per month for five to ten years. The Foundation and the real estate companies hope that the rehabilitation will help to revitalise the neighbourhood and increase the value of the property—which eventually will be sold by the real estate companies, hopefully at a price that will cover their social investment in the centre. (If there is an actual profit, it would be shared with the centre.) The Foundation has a grant from the federal government to replicate such financing in other locations; this will be part of the effort to more completely replicate Argus, El Centro and Umoja.

The process and impact evaluation of the first ten sites will not be completed by Northwestern University until 1988. While this proscribes cost-benefit comparisons now, the important point is the sophistication and ambitiousness of the evaluation design. Argus, El Centro and Umoja operated for considerable time before evaluations began, whereas Northwestern University undertakes pre-tests before a local programme starts up. In addition, the twenty-four months of operation before the post-test in the Foundation programme defines the minimum period which experience has suggested is needed over which to expect a difference.

The evaluation encompasses pre-post tests for both community and individual measures. For opportunity reduction strategies, like block watches, which are thought to operate through co-operation among neighbours, a community-wide 'phone survey is appropriate (except when too few people have 'phones—in which case personal interviews are undertaken). For strategies that address the causes of crime, the measures more often focus on changes in individual high-risk youth—for example, reduced recidivism over time by those employed. The exact composition of community versus individual pre-post measures in any one site is a function of the opportunity reduction versus causes of crime strategies that are bubbled up in planning the programme. There are comparison groups for both community and individual measures, as well as an assessment, for opportunity reduction, on whether crime actually declines in a neighbourhood or is merely displaced into adjoining neighbourhoods.

Success is being measured in terms of intervening (or proximate) measures as well as ultimate outcome measures. For opportunity reduction, intervening measures include greater social cohesion and less fear, while outcome measures include greater willingness to report crime and reduced victimisation. For causes of crime strategies, intervening measures include higher self-esteem and more goal setting by individual youth, while outcome measures include less recidivism, higher employability, and more personal and economic self-sufficiency.

The Foundation will consider programmes modestly successful if there is progress in achieving at least some of the intervening goals over twenty-four months. But—unlike programmes that concentrate only on opportunity reduction (see below)—the Foundation will not take a safer route by defining success mainly in terms of intervening measures. Rather, the local sites will be considered totally successful only when they show progress in meeting ultimate goals—like actual crime reduction and increased legal market economic self-sufficiency among at-risk youth.

It is here that the requirement that a programme creates its own financial self-sufficiency after twenty-four months of operations comes into play. What if changes in intervening and outcome variables are only modestly positive after twenty-four months, but the community organization has done extremely well in creating financial self-sufficiency and hence in continuing the programme? Here financial self-sufficiency can have a 'multiplier effect'—limited success in, say, recidivism reduction becomes more pronounced if we have money to continue and have learned what to do better in the future.

Use of the community survey pre-test to plan the programmes means that the evaluation has a direct role in the programme's action—yet without any violation of research objectivity. Similarly, after the post-test is undertaken and if there is good evidence of success, the pre-post test comparison is used as a marketing tool to raise funds for the continuation of the programme. (The evaluators are writing individual site assessments which will be used in this way, but also are concluding with a 'summative' evaluation which combines all the data.)

Conceptual framework

Why create a framework in which a community organisation must both address causes and reduce opportunties? While Argus, El Centro and Umoja were outstanding models, it seemed unwise, from a developmental and financial viewpoint, to seek to directly replicate them, especially the residential parts, in the early nineteen eighties when the Foundation began crime prevention. Simply put, money was scarce. There are pronounced limitations to opportunity reduction, but it can be done at low cost. Even if opportunity reduction does not in and of itself address the causes of crime, it is increasingly associated in the American public's eye as something worth undertaking. It therefore was decided to begin the present ten sites with very modest budgets (in the range of $50,000 to $80,000 for all six months of planning and twenty-four months of implementation). Hopefully, opportunity reduction would be implemented rapidly and lead to positive impressions among the public. This would allow more time for other strategies to develop that addressed causes of crime and for us to build up local constituencies which would assist in the financial continuation for the programmes. The Washington, DC programme turned out to be a good illustration of how this strategy could work—and work well—beginning with community organising and leading to the weatherisation business and the teen parent centre.

In addition, the Foundation framework required opportunity reduction to be carried out not as an end in itself—as is so often the case—but as a means to the end of addressing the causes of crime. Thus, for example, the programme in East Brooklyn makes extensive use of block clubs, but the overall plan is to reduce fear and secure the neighbourhood for the economic development of a business strip, which will help provide jobs for neighbourhood youths.

Through the bubble up planning process, the Foundation also is attempting to empower community organisations to gain expertise in crime prevention and take the lead in many forms of community action. The Foundation tries to provide technical assistance without being overbearing. Part of the demonstration is to test how a mediating, national level institution can leverage funds from many sources and facilitate technical assistance for localities—producing the kind of supply to community organisations that Argus, El Centro and

Umoja often did not have during their formative periods. As part of the empowerment, the community organisation always takes the lead *vis-à-vis* police, which play a supportive role, building on the experiences of Argus and El Centro.

Barriers to implementation

To date, implementation in the private sector has proceeded more smoothly than public sector programmes though some problems needed to be solved. For example, when the Foundation was searching for cities in which to match funds and start programmes, some more traditional local funders could not understand how we could ask them to commit funds and select on the basis of capability, rather than on the basis of a detailed 'proposal'. But there were far more local funding leaders who understood how the bubble up planning process could lead to better workplans and more genuine community empowerment than up-front proposals. When, at the insistence of local matchers, community organisations were funded without open competitions, the organisations sometimes tended not to plan and implement as completely as organisations which won competitively. The relatively low level of funding to the sites—an exercise in 'lean and mean' programme management for the eighties—placed too great a burden on local programme directors and denied a sufficient level of staff support. (Volunteers were very helpful, especially senior citizens, but the experience points to the limits of volunteerism). A budget with more Eisenhower Foundation technical assistance would have been desirable, in retrospect. In one community, much of what was originally promised as local match failed to materialise, but alternative sources were found. In a few cases, police have not co-operated in providing statistics for the evaluation or in supporting programme operations, but more often police have been quite helpful.

The Violent Juvenile Offender Programme

These Eisenhower Foundation implementation experiences will be much more thoroughly written up in 1987, at which time the results from six other sites in a comparable national venture will become available. As part of the US Justice Department's Violent Juvenile Offenders Programme, in the early nineteen eighties the Center for Community Change provided technical assistance to community organisations in the Bronx, Chicago, Dallas, Los Angeles, New Orleans and San Diego. The effort was to both reduce opportunities and address causes. It followed a bubble up community planning and implementation process very similar to that of the Eisenhower Foundation. The Urban Rural System Associates (URSA) Institute is now completing a process and impact evaluation which uses comparable individual and community measures.

196

Opportunity reduction alone

Opportunity reduction as a more singular strategy, especially when it concentrates on block watches and citizen patrols, originally assumed that residents can be mobilised by community organisations or the police; that such participation strengthens community cohesion, interaction and control; and that this reduces crime and fear.

Some examples and their measurement

Community organisation-led opportunity reduction is popular today through-out the country. Federal government supported opportunity reduction programmes begun in the nineteen seventies and nineteen eighties, often were undertaken without adequate evaluations. When impact evaluations were undertaken, the conclusions often were that the opportunity reduction did not reduce crime—as is the case, for example, with evaluations in Washington, DC (Henig, 1984) and Chicago (Rosenbaum, 1985). Such studies are not without methodological criticism. For example, the Chicago study undertook pre-post comparisons only twelve months apart, compared to the twenty-four month period used by the Eisenhower Foundation, based on past experience in the field. Twelve months simply does not allow enough time for a programme to develop. Nor was it likely that the (relatively low) degree of block organising activity and resident involvement in Chicago was sufficient over that time period to expect much success.

Over the last fifteen years there has been an important methodological development in community-led opportunity reduction. The uncertainties about whether crime was reduced in those impact evaluations that were undertaken, the many problems associated with the use of police statistics to measure for changes in crime, the relatively high costs of using 'phone and personal victimization surveys to collect victim-based data to measure crime, and the political pressure on sponsoring agencies to show results—all of this combined to produce a new measurement mentality. Impact evaluations were still seen as necessary (at least by some), but reduced crime as a measure of success began to be de-emphasised, in favour of reduced fear of crime, a perception measure with a better track record for showing positive results.

This same evolution has occurred in police-led opportunity reduction. Experiments in the nineteen seventies with police footpatrols showed little, if any, reduction in crime (see a review in Silberman, 1978), but citizens appeared less fearful in some experiments.

The die was cast. By the mid-nineteen eighties, the cover of a summary report to the Justice Department on police-led opportunity reduction was titled 'Reducing Fear of Crime in Houston and Newark' (Police Foundation, 1986). The title almost seems constructed in a way to avoid any expectations of crime being reduced. This was wise, for there was only slight evidence of crime reduction, but fear was reduced by some police actions—like establishing small storefront police stations in neighbourhoods; sending officers to make door-to-door contact with residents to identify problems and solutions; and encouraging officers to establish community organisations, like block watches.

197

Police strategies in Newark and Houston which did not work to reduce fear included clean-up campaigns to reduce signs of physical deterioration and social disorder. This was a significant finding, given a great deal of recent rhetoric that neater neighbourhoods and less garbage would increase community cohesion and so reduce crime and fear. (For a critique, see Curtis, 1985). The lack of empirical verification of this position is not surprising. One underlying assumption is that cleaning up garbage and pushing out street people will better protect the neighbourhood from invasions by outsiders. This is oblivious to the simple truth that, in high crime inner-city neighbourhoods, perpetrators are just as likely to live next door or be in one's own family than attack from outside perimeters. (As far back as 1969, The National Violence Commission warned that 'challenges from within' presented a greater danger than outside threats.) In addition, the get-folks-to-clean-up-garbage-and-then-crime mentality ultimately rests on the hope that citizens will not so much address the causes of crime as become surrogate police—in spite of the contrary evidence that police do not reduce crime.

Perhaps most important for the focus here on the underclass, police efforts in Newark and Houston to reduce fear had some success with white middle class home-owners but no success with less affluent black renters. This reinforces the findings of Podelefsky and DuBow (1981), that citizen-led opportunity reduction without accompanying strategies to address causes is unsuccessful—and often resisted in lower income minority neighbourhoods.

The interventions in Newark and Houston appear to see fear reduction as an end itself. It *is* a worthy goal to protect people from victimization, especially where it disproportionately occurs, in inner cities. But few, if any, of the Newark-Houston strategies appear to consciously orchestrate a total package in which fear reduction is immediately used as the means to achieve ends like economic development, business reduction, and job creation. This is not surprising, given that the police are the first to admit that such programmes are out of their control and expertise.

In sum, while Argus, El Centro and Umoja continue to be measured as successful in terms of crime reduction and also demonstrate success in increasing employment and reducing self-sufficiency among at-risk youth, opportunity reduction, whether by community organisations or by police, has gravitated to the less direct measures of fear—and fear primarily is reduced for the middle class, rather than the underclass. Through interventions with specific youth, 'causes of crime strategies' have been measured as successful by following cohorts of such youth over time and demonstrating reduced recidivism in comparison to control groups. This method of measurement has rarely been attempted for opportunity reduction strategies, presumably because they only impact on high-risk youth indirectly, through social control by the entire community.

Conceptual framework

Conceptually, the minimal success of opportunity reduction in underclass locales, even when measured by the more workable measure of fear reduction, reflects barriers to trust and social cohesion among poor families living in harsh and hostile social environments. The minority poor recognise, in ways that some academics do not, that crime prevention is a farce in their communities if it does not include strategies to address causes:

'Many of these opportunity reduction programmes are bad because they get people together to defend themselves against "criminals". Those people who are criminals are part of the community too. Programmes like this have to protect the whole community. People get into crime because of socioeconomic reasons.' (Podolefsky and DuBow, 1981)

Nor does it go unnoticed among the poor that block clubs can be the organising means through which whites gentrify their neighbourhoods (Henig, 1984). For example, concern over gentrification is a major issue in the Eisenhower Foundation's Washington, DC programme, discussed above.

To explain the mixed success of community-led opportunity reduction alone, in the form of block clubs, in reducing crime and fear, Rosenbaum (1985) has added that meetings of volunteers, through the exchange of victimization stories, might lead to *increases* in fear in some circumstances and to feelings of helplessness in light of uncontrollable political and social forces.

As Henig (1984) has concluded:

'The best that can be hoped for may be the recognition that the neighbourhood watch programme is not the simple cure-all that overly enthusiastic exponents have suggested. It is a worthwhile programme that can be helpful in some neighbourhoods. If a real dent is to be made in crime, and if the needs of all neighbourhoods are to be met, other substantial initiatives must be designed and put into effect.'

But at least *community*-led opportunity reduction offers the possibility of empowerment by citizens at the grassroots level, so that, through success, community members hopefully gain control of their turf and their lives. This is less likely when opportunity reduction is led by *police*. In American cities, most police do not live in the neighbourhoods that they patrol, and therefore do not necessarily have a deep personal stake in the community. They are outsiders—professionals like social workers, who come in to do a job and, however dedicated, leave for home at the end of their working day. In less friendly circumstances, inner-city residents can perceive police as representing a colonial mentality, being sent in to insure control.

By comparison, in Japan, police are assigned to small geographic areas where they often live with their families, try to become integrated into neighbourhood life, make door-to-door visits with their wives, are known as neighbours of most people there and consequently receive much more co-operation from citizens—for example, in reporting crime—than do American police. Reforms in this direction would be welcome in the United States, but they probably will be slow in coming (Curtis, 1985).

Compared, then, to the conceptual frameworks of strategies that address causes or that combine causes and opportunity reduction, police-led opportunity reduction alone makes community empowerment difficult. (In some cities, this may be precisely why police want to lead opportunity reduction.) The Newark-Houston experiment was trickle down, in that predetermined strategies were imposed on citizens by police. It did not allow for a bubble up community planning process. (As an illustration, while police in Newark were orchestrating citizens in one part of Newark, the bubble up programme in another part of Newark, facilitated by the Eisenhower Foundation, had its directors complaining that the police were not adequately supporting their initiatives.) There was little attention paid to teaching community groups how to become financially self-sufficient, to continue on their own, in the Newark-Houston demonstration. Nor were individual at-risk youths motivated into psychological and economic self-sufficiency.

Barriers to implementation

There has been certain resistance to opportunity reduction—by the underclass when strategies to address causes are not part of the package and also by some traditional police chiefs, who, at most, are prepared to send an 'officer friendly' to teach 'civilians' what to do.

But the salient reality is the *lack* of resistance—the widespread acceptance of opportunity reduction in spite of its relative ineffectiveness compared to an Argus, El Centro or Umoja.

The trick has been the institutionalisation of fear as an accepted measure of success. With the failure of individual and community measures of crime in opportunity reduction, fear as the impact measure gives a new lease on life for researchers seeking grants and for the budgets of federal and local government agencies running opportunity reduction programmes. This is especially so for the police. With police making arrests for less than ten per cent of all serious crimes (when one takes into account unreported crimes), having little success in reducing crime through opportunity reduction, and spending $3 billion per year in the 88 cities in the US with populations of 100,000, there is a pressing need to rationalise police cost-effectiveness.

Fear reduction, then, has in part become a public relations vehicle par excellence. Some cities report success in reducing fear—yet they also have reported increases in actual crime. What might it mean if people feel less fearful even though crime is very high or even increasing? Are we merely altering their perceptions through public-relations gimmickry—while making them more vulnerable?

We need to remember Paul Lavrakas (1985):

> 'Too many of our supposed crime prevention experts and policymakers may well be expert about the workings of criminal justice system agencies, but they do not appear to recognise the implications of acknowledging the limitations of these agencies in our democratic society. Until we change the emphasis of our public policies away from considering the police, courts, and prisons to be the primary mechanisms for reducing crime, I believe that we will continue to experience the tragic levels of victimisation with which our citizens now live. These criminal justice agencies are our means of reacting to crime—they should not be expected to prevent it by themselves.'

Conclusion

In the next two years, it will be important to undertake careful cost-benefit and cost-effectiveness analyses of the Eisenhower Foundation programme. This has addressed both causes and reduced opportunities, at a cost of $2M in operations, technical assistance and evaluation over ten sites, compared to the

Newark-Houston programme which only reduced opportunities, at a cost of $2M in operations, technical assistance and evaluation at two sites. Similarly, we need more careful comparisons of real crime reduction and costs for groups like Argus, El Centro and Umoja *vis-à-vis* prisons.

Even if the Eisenhower Foundation experiences only modest success, of the order of the Newark-Houston experiment, it will be done at a much lower cost and with the additional benefit of empowering the minority poor—so the cost-benefit ratio will be more favourable. Whatever the level of success, the first ten Eisenhower sites will provide guidelines for how the next round of sites can best approximate the level of success already apparent at Argus, El Centro and Umoja (even when we discount for the need for better measures of such model programmes). For example, will our relatively low cost partial replications, combined with opportunity reduction, prove to be effective, or will we conclude that only more complete replications make sense?

There also is room for confidence that perceptive police leaders will recognise the strong supportive role that the police need to play with established community organisations, as has been the case with Argus and El Centro. (When there are no such organisations in an inner-city neighbour-hood, we can hope that the police will help to establish them.) More demonstrations on exactly how the community and the police can best work together, at different class levels and in different racial settings, surely are in order.

Still, the march of folly has strong institutional momentum. In the late nineteen sixties, many were sceptical when the 'National Commission on the Causes and Prevention of Violence saw a future with armed guide guards in schools and on buses, television surveillance, window bars on city apartments with the look of 'fortified cells', and 'santizied' expressway corridors leading to (some) suburban safety and often running through inner-city areas 'out of police control' after dark (National Violence Commision, 1969).

All of that has come to pass. Today, an update of the Violence Commission's final report predicts possible domestic urban terrorism (Curtis, 1985). If that is our future, along with $70 billion more in prison building and imaginative new measures of 'success' that George Orwell would appreciate, then we will all have to answer to the fourteen-year-old Argus enrollee who wrote (Sturz, 1983):

> One day I said grandma
> What do you think America
> Will be when I get 53?
> Will it be like a big ugly
> Tree or a pretty little butterfly
> Sitting on my knee?
> She said 'Baby I cannot say,
> But if I had my way
> I would surely try and make it
> A better day.'

References

AULETTA, K. (1983). *The Underclass*. New York: Vintage Books.

CATALYST (February 1986). 'Resident Involvement Key to Crime Prevention in Charlotte's Public Housing Projects'. Washington, DC: National Crime Prevention Coalition.

CURRIE, E. (1985). *Confronting Crime*. New York: Pantheon Books.

CURTIS, L. A. (Ed.), (1985). *American Violence and Public Policy*. New Haven: Yale University Press.

CURTIS, L. A. (1986). 'New Ways to Cut Crime'. *Baltimore Sun*. May 6.

HAYES, J. G. (1982). *The Impact of Citizen Involvement in Preventing Crime in Public Housing*. Charlotte, NC: Public Housing Authority.

HENIG, J. R. (1984). *Citizens Against Crime*. Washington, DC: George Washington University.

LAVRAKAS, P. J. (1985). 'Citizens Self-Help and Neighbourhood Crime Prevention Police.' In Curtis, L. A. (Ed.), *American Violence and Public Policy*. New Haven: Yale University Press.

NATIONAL VIOLENCE COMMISSION. (1969). *Final Report*. Washington, DC: Government Printing Office.

NEW YORK TIMES, (1985). 'Breaking Up Government's Monopoly on Prison Cells'. March 3

PODOLEFSKY A. and DuBOW, F. (1981). *Strategies for Community Crime Prevention*. Springfield: Charles C. Thomas.

POLICE FOUNDATION, (1984). *Evaluation of the Urban Initiatives Anti-Crime Programme*. Washington, DC: US Department of Housing and Urban Development.

POLICE FOUNDATION, (1986). *Reducing Fear of Crime in Houston and Newark: A Summary Report*. Washington, DC: US Department of Justice.

ROSENBAUM, D. P., LEWIS, D. A. and GRANT, J. (1985). *The Impact of Community Crime Prevention Programmes in Chicago*. Evanston, IL: Northwestern University.

SILBERMAN, C. E. (1978). *Criminal Violence, Criminal Justice*. New York: Random House.

STURZ, E. L. (1983). *Widening Circles*. New York: Harper and Row.

TAGGERT, R. (1981). *A Fisherman's Guide*. Kalamazoo: The Upjohn Institute.

THOMPSON, J. W. (1981). *Employment and Crime*. Washington DC: US Department of Justice.

TUCHMAN, B. W. (1985). *The March of Folly*. New York: Ballantine Books.

WOLFGANG, M. E., FIGLIO, R. M. and SELLIN, T. (1972). *Delinquency in a Birth Cohort*. Chicago: University of Chicago Press.

Implementation

This section details experience, from both sides of the Atlantic, of some of the issues which have to be confronted in trying to implement programmes of crime prevention in the community. Chapter 12 questions what communication and co-ordination really amount to in the development of inter-agency projects at the local level. The policy drift towards a 'community orientation' is welcomed, 'but what does it add up to on the ground?' The policy contribution of agencies other than the police seems to be rarely spelt out in detail, and some may fear too close a liaison with the police, or be ambivalent about the objectives and purposes of local crime prevention initiatives. The authors build on their current research on inter-agency projects in three inner-city neighbourhoods, and their findings, although at an early stage, represent an essential step in the clarification of the kinds of problems which are likely to arise in setting up such programmes. They provide a necessary reminder that the development of community crime reduction will not be a simple task, and warn against the replacement of the myth of rehabilitation with that of crime prevention.

Chapter 13 starts from the premise that the accumulated evidence of a number of years of community and citizen crime prevention projects in the USA suggests that such projects have failed on the whole to stimulate citizen involvement, or to show reductions in crime and fear, and that they may even have increased fear of crime. It questions whether this is because the theories underlying such projects are wrong, and/or because they have not been implemented successfully, and sets out to examine the latter issue. Three levels of crime prevention are considered and the psychological dynamics appropriate to each. The authors argue that any programme which sets out to involve citizens and the community must consider the public or private-minded motivations which volunteers have in taking part, and the incentives appropriate to each, which are essential for the establishment and maintenance of programmes. The chapter builds on the authors' current experience in evaluating a five-year 'Neighbourhood Anti-Crime Self-Help' programme.

12. Inter-agency co-operation; rhetoric and reality

Harry Blagg, Geoffrey Pearson, Alice Sampson, David Smith, Paul Stubbs

Recent official discourses and policy debates on crime and criminal justice have generated and mobilised a number of key terms: 'community', 'participation', 'inter-agency co-operation' and 'crime prevention' are among those which frequently cluster together in these discussions. Implying a co-ordinated effort by both state agencies and voluntary bodies, a closer involvement between services and the public, an avoidance of wasteful duplication and policy confusion, these discourses convey the sense of an unproblematically 'good thing'. When, as they frequently are, they are yoked together in such formulae as 'inter-agency co-operation in community crime prevention' their positive connotations tend to be reinforced. Who could possibly argue that agencies should not co-operate to such worthy ends?

And yet, there are counter-arguments to be put and some of these are explored in this paper. The precise meaning and practical application of these terms is also problematic, as when it is sometimes suggested that inter-agency forums might be merely 'talking shops', or that the terms themselves are little more than rhetorical devices which have become dominant in recent official discourse on crime and criminal justice. In reviewing this field, this paper draws both upon aspects of general policy debates and the small amount of available British research, as well as current research by the authors into inter-agency working practices in three localities in a Lancashire town (Milltown) and inner London [1]. Finally, the paper makes some critical comments on the scope and nature of 'crime prevention' as it is usually defined.

The state of the art

The focus of the research (which is still in its early stages) was in part defined by awareness of the growing official consensus that effective crime prevention required both co-ordination between official agencies and a sensitivity to local crime problems. The Home Office Circular 8/84, which is perhaps the clearest example of this position can offer a starting point. Here it was claimed that 'crime prevention schemes are more successful where the police and local agencies work together in a co-ordinated way towards particular aims', and that, since patterns of crime vary, 'preventive measures are therefore more likely to be successful when designed to reflect local characteristics and focused on particular types of crime' (Home Office 1984a, p.2). This means, according to the circular, that it is not possible to specify how its 'broad approach' should be implemented in practice, since this will depend on local circumstances. As we shall see, the problem of specifying (and agreeing) a course of practical action recurs at local level, partly because of difficulties in reaching agreement on what the significant local crime problems are.

Another example of the apparent consensus is the collection of papers from the Home Office Research and Planning Unit published as *Managing Criminal Justice* (Moxon, 1985) which lays a great deal of emphasis on the need to view the criminal justice system *as a system*. That is, each agency should be aware of the inter-connectedness of its activities with those of other agencies; and planning and innovation should take account of possible effects beyond the agency's own boundaries, on the work of other agencies and on the system as a whole. Thus, fairly obviously, sentencing practices have an impact on the prison system, the probation service and social services departments (cf. Parker *et al.,* 1981). Or an increase in prosecutions will affect the courts, and ultimately the agencies charged with implementing court sentences. Even so, this invocation of the importance of systemic thinking and therefore of inter-agency co-operation is more evident in the general arguments than in the substantive papers in the collection. Moreover, it is less obvious that this inter-connectedness applies equally across the agencies. For example, a charge in probation service practice is likely to have only marginal implications for other agencies. It might mean that magistrates spent less time reading social enquiry reports, or that some police officers spent more time attending liaison meetings; but it is unlikely to have much impact on the prison population (e.g. Smith *et al.*, 1984) or indeed on the volume of crime (e.g. Folkard *et al.*, 1976).

In any liaison or collaborative efforts the different agencies do not start on equal terms. Some, so to speak, are more inter-connected than others. Autonomous, pro-active policies by the police or courts can have considerable impact on other agencies, but this effect cannot be reciprocated. This inequality of power is an important factor in shaping the forms actually assumed in practice by inter-agency co-operation, liaison, collaboration, co-ordination, or whatever term is preferred. Indeed, the tendency to neglect power differentials between various agencies which might come together in an inter-agency initiative is a serious weakness in current policy thinking, which constrains the practical feasibility of multi-agency work as it is presently conceived. In the current fieldwork it is already clear that both voluntary bodies and other state agencies are particularly worried that the 'police view' of local problems and crime prevention will come to dominate inter-agency forums and practical initiatives, to the exclusion of all other interested parties. These worries also reflect the fact that the consensus on the desirability of such co-operation is not entirely universal, in that it is sometimes feared that it might have 'net-widening' effects or lead to infringements of civil liberties through unaccountable systems of information exchange (cf. Birley and Bright, 1986; Cohen, 1985).

Having acknowledged the existence of such worries, we now turn to some more specific matters of practical application in the field of situational crime prevention where one might expect that fewer problems would arise when local objectives are (or can be) relatively clearly defined. It is necessary first to recognise, however, that too much commonality of experience should not be expected. A widely divergent set of practices is already subsumed under the rubric of 'local crime prevention'—from major co-ordinated efforts directed towards a range of local problems such as of NACRO's Safe Neighbourhoods Unit (Bright and Petterson, 1984), through more specifically focused 'target hardening' schemes, to rather diffuse inter-agency forums at a local level. Where these experiments have been evaluated, the results are not always encouraging. The project first described by Gladstone (1980) and evaluated by

Hope and Murphy (1983), for example, had a clear focus aimed at reducing vandalism in schools. Nevertheless, 'unanticipated technical difficulties', together with failures of co-ordination and the high cost of increased surveillance, conspired to produce a disappointing outcome to what must have looked (on paper) like a modest and realisable project. (The 'technical difficulties' were not entirely separate from lack of co-ordination, in that City Architect had prohibited the use of one type of damage-resistant glass on safety grounds, something that could presumably have been known at the outset, although it was not.) Reviewing this project, Hope (1985, p.7) commented that 'even when parties appear to agree at the decision-making stage, co-ordination can break down in practice', and this seems likely to be a message with some general validity. Allatt (1984a and 1984b) has reported some similar problems with an otherwise successful project designed to improve the security of dwellings on a 'difficult to let' housing estate in Newcastle. While helping to stabilise the burglary rate and reducing the fear of crime in the short run, both technical and organisational problems arose. The security devices that were fitted were not adequately maintained, for example, and did not appear to have worked in half the reported cases of successful burglaries—and this in spite of a prior local authority commitment to their proper maintenance. In eight out of ten of the security device failures, Allatt (1984a, p.108) concluded that the victims could not be blamed for these failures, despite the fact that on this estate 'the public image of the typical resident is one of heedlessness'. The success of such a project, as she saw it, depended not only on the efficient installation of the security devices but also on 'overcoming problems of long-term maintenance that will be encouraged by local authority housing and maintenance departments' (Allatt 1984a, p.109).

It has been fairly clear for some time that increased surveillance can be effective in reducing particular types of crime in particular settings (cf. Mayhew *et al.*, 1976; Clarke and Mayhew, 1980). It is even clearer (Hope and Murphy, 1983) that this is going to cost money which may not be available to local authorities which have to take account of other, competing, priorities. Considerations of cost are likely to limit the expansion of both surveillance schemes and 'hard target' security projects (cf. Bright *et al.*, 1985). Indeed, it is not outside the bounds of possibility that questions of cost have helped to promote interest in 'softer', more 'social' crime prevention measures. It is to this sphere of activity that the paper now turns.

Areas of inter-agency tension

It was suggested above that the problems of liaison and coordination found in situational crime prevention were likely to be intensified where the goals are less clearly defined and apparently achievable; and there is often a lack of clarity about what kind of a contribution to crime prevention agencies other than the police are supposed to make. At a general level, there remain hopes (which re-appear in Circular 8/84) that programmes of social reform and improvement may have the effect of reducing crime. Indeed, as part of a process which might be termed the criminalisation of the discourses of social policy, crime reduction is sometimes presented as the main justification for such programmes (cf. Pearson, 1983, pp 238−9). These cover a very wide range, from economic policy proposals aimed at reducing unemployment, through programmes of housing and environmental improvement, the provision of recreational facilities, to schemes of social education (e.g. on drugs and alcohol) and social work services (cf. Parliamentary All-Party Penal Affairs Group, 1983; Birley and Bright, 1985), despite a lack of convincing evidence that they are likely to have an impact on crime rates (cf. Baldwin and Bottoms, 1976).

The recent emphasis on more focused and specific crime prevention, whether situational or social, might well reflect some disillusionment with grand-scale reforms and correctional optimism; although the recent grounds-well of 'community-oriented' ideology has also helped to shape this local emphasis, offering points of connection between otherwise quite disparate social movements and policy innovations such as 'community work', 'community arts', 'community education', 'community policing' and 'community social work' (cf. Willmott, 1984).

This policy drift towards a 'community orientation' is impressive in the range of different activities that it encompasses, but what does it add up to on the ground? A report of NACRO's Juvenile Crime Unit (1985) on an attempt to develop inter-agency consultative processes in relation to juvenile crime in ten different areas gives some indication of the difficulties. Crime prevention was part of the Unit's brief, although it seems clear from the text that much less progress was made on this front than, for instance, in increasing the use of cautions and reducing the use of custodial measures for young offenders. Although suggesting that there were 'considerable improvements in the arrangements for communication, consultation, co-operation and co-ordination', the Juvenile Crime Unit concluded that:

'Joint planning and action on crime prevention is still at a fairly early, unsophisticated stage. Some local authorities and other agencies have been slow to realise that crime prevention cannot simply be left to the police. Schools for example could do far more to prevent juvenile crime through the development of appropriate ethos, pastoral care and a consistent approach to discipline. School buildings which could be opened in the evenings and at weekends are often kept closed outside school hours'(p. 28).

It may be significant that no other examples are given, and that even those possible initiatives which are mentioned remain highly problematic to crime prevention. It is unlikely that an 'ethos' can be changed quickly, for example, or even at all as a matter of conscious policy; and the relationship between school discipline and levels of crime and vandalism is not at all straightforward (cf. Reynolds, 1976). Moreover, while it should be noted that the proposal to keep schools open longer has major cost implications, it is not at all clear that this would necessarily reduce crime.

In the case of the probation service, there have also been some encouragements to ease the focus of work only with offender-clients, reflected in the fact that the 1984 Probation Rules incorporated a duty 'to take part in crime prevention schemes, victim support and other work in the wider community'— a broad remit which is echoed in the Statement of National Objectives and Priorities issued by the Home Office (1984b). (cf. Henderson, 1986). Along similar lines a major staff development initiative over seven years in the North of England had aimed at establishing closer neighbourhood and community involvement (cf. Pearson, 1986) and some of the experience of this initiative has been recently brought together by Scott *et al.*, (1985) under the theme of *Going Local in Probation*. One difficulty commonly encountered by probation officers in this context is how to reconcile the traditional focus of their work with client-offenders (which has been relaxed only to a small extent either by the Statement of National Objectives and Priorities or the new Probation Rules) and the different demands of neighbourhood involvement schemes. Stone (in Scott *et al.*, 1985) states the problem in the following terms:

'Then how do we appropriately expand our horizons to tackling "crime"? If we operate from a neighbourhood base, then because much *client* crime will not have a local effect, being committed elsewhere, a client focus is likely to be on indirect issues of quality of life. If on the other hand, locality crime is addressed, this is likely to be of a particular kind, e.g. vandalism, rowdiness and petty theft, important in themselves but not necessarily involving significant numbers of clients' (pp. 15–16).

This is an interesting observation on a number of counts. Because while it certainly echoes the difficulties which probation officers commonly face in attempting to develop a focus and rationale for neighbourhood work, it probably does not reflect the actualities of criminal victimisation in that victims and offenders will often live in close geographical proximity to each other. What this lack of 'fit' between probation workloads and local problems might reflect, on the other hand, is that the probation service is routinely involved with particular kinds of crime and particular kinds of offender which do not correspond to the locally perceived crime problem.

Given the traditional focus to the work of the probation service, however, there are also more direct and formal objections sometimes voiced to the extension of the probation officer's role implied by neighbourhood work. 'The service should be cautious about its involvement in 'preventive work' and "crime prevention" schemes', writes Falkingham (Scott *et al.*, 1985, p.129), drawing on his experience of neighbourhood work in West Yorkshire, and his 'scare quotes' reflect a widespread ambivalence within the probation service towards loosening the offender-focus of its work which might dilute attempts to provide alternatives to custody. For example, Shaw (1983, p.128) has suggested that the effect of 'community involvement' on actual crime rates is by no means certain, carrying with it 'a danger in some quarters of replacing the rehabilitation myth with the myth of crime prevention'.

A more positive view, on the other hand, is that put forward by Laycock and Pease (1985) which is also unusual in attempting to go beyond rhetorical flourishes and to specify more clearly what the nature of probation involvement in crime prevention might be. They suggest, for example, that probation officers' knowledge of offenders and their habits might enable them to design individual crime prevention 'packages', taking into account environmental factors. Probation officers, they argue, also have access to knowledge which could be useful to other agencies attempting to develop crime prevention strategies such as local authorities, the police and community groups; and developing a more political theme they suggest that probation involvement could promote a greater awareness of social approaches, thus reducing the risk of the 'fortress mentality' which might easily develop if crime prevention were defined in purely situational 'target hardening' terms. Probation officers, Laycock and Pease suggest, may also be able to introduce into local debates issues which might not be defined as important by the police, or of which they may be unaware, citing the example of 'racially motivated attacks centring on particular public houses'. And it is certainly true that with their dual welfare/justice role, probation officers can often draw upon local information networks which are not always accessible to the police, within which such information might come to light. One final point suggested by Laycock and Pease is, however, more arguable. In their view, public support for liberal penal measures (such as those traditionally upheld by the probation service) is unlikely in so far as people fear crime and feel helpless to do anything about it, and they argue that situational crime prevention approaches offer the best hope of reducing such feelings. But this is unfortunately not always the case, in that our fieldwork suggests that an emphasis on locks and bolts can sometimes help to fuel the 'fear of crime' on an estate, by giving such a high prominence to crime prevention. Nevertheless, Laycock and Pease have laid out a basis for the rationale of probation involvement in crime prevention schemes which goes beyond the confines of customary debates and preoccupations: one, moreover, that is unusually direct in attempting to reconcile the traditional concerns of probation work with those of crime prevention schemes.

Some space has been devoted to the policy and practice issues around the involvement of the probation service in crime prevention because there is probably a commonsense assumption that probation is particularly fitted among the relevant agencies for such involvement. Its organisational focus on offenders and its close integration within the criminal justice system both contribute to this view. It might as a consequence be thought of as an obvious candidate for a leading role in local liaison efforts, in that probation officers might be less likely to experience tension and conflict in their relations to the police than social workers often do (cf. Holdaway, 1986). This is not supported by Garton's (1980) research, however, which found vast areas of disagreement in the mutual perceptions of police and probation officers. Indeed, the preliminary indications of the current research both in Milltown and inner London are that, in spite of the active policy debate on the wide community role of the probation service, it is generally perceived to be the agency least involved in liaison on crime prevention, whether in formal multi-agency initiatives or in routine contacts. So that whereas recent research on drug liaison initiatives in the North of England (cf. Pearson et al., 1986) found that it was the probation service which of all non-specialist agencies had the best working knowledge of local drug problems, more generally the probation service might prove to be marginal to multi-agency crime prevention initiatives.

A partial explanation for this marginality is the lack of 'fit' between probation caseloads and local concerns about crime which we have already noted. However, this is certainly not only a question which affects the probation service. A major obstacle to multi-agency initiatives in a number of spheres of action (e.g. alcohol-related problems, heroin misuse, burglary) is to be found in the ways in which any identified problem will tend to make widely varying impacts on the routine workloads of different agencies (cf. Friend et al., 1981; Pearson, 1985; Pearson et al., 1986).

These difficulties alert us to the fact that the formal differentiation of roles and objectives between different agencies means that areas of great

209

uncertainty are touched upon in multi-agency liaison. Mutual respect for necessary confidentiality and different working practices might seem to be indicated when one Milltown police officer expressed the view that:

> 'We shouldn't have liaison with probation: it would make their job impossible ... Clients wouldn't be able to trust a probation officer who had dealings with the police.'

A similar view came through repeatedly in the Northern England heroin project whereby drug liaison committees would deliberately distance themselves from the police because they feared that close police liaison would endanger the trust of their target audience of drug-users and their families (Pearson *et al.*, 1986). Even so, this same police officer in Milltown could complain to the researchers about the unhelpful response he had received from the probation office when he made what was to him a routine enquiry about a probation client's whereabouts. An even balder criticism of the probation service, which related to another aspect of the structural differentiation of roles, came from an inner London police officer who voiced his routine impressions of probation officers in the court setting:

> 'I go to court, and I know that 'chummy' has done some horrible deed or another ... a real villain. And this probation officer gets up and says how 'chummy' is really quite a nice bloke, doing his best by his family and that kind of thing. That's how I see it, and it starts to get to you. It really does.'

It is reasonable to assume that these kinds of tensions, which are also found in case committees called on suspected cases of child abuse and which are an unavoidable aspect of the 'checks and balances' of the criminal justice system, must play themselves out in the broader context of crime prevention. Indeed, the early indications of the research in Milltown and inner London suggest that they do, and in what follows it is hoped to shed some light on these and other issues where agencies are brought together on locally devised crime reduction schemes.

Inter-agency relations in three localities

The research has so far been concentrated in three localities (one in Milltown, two in inner London) each of which is defined in some way as a 'problem estate'. In many other respects, however, these localities are quite different. The Milltown estate, Saxon Lane, lies on the outskirts of town, a low-rise development, conventionally built and a showpiece estate of the 1970s. It is the site of a multi-agency initiative, and was chosen as a location for the research because of widely held official beliefs that extreme social difficulties have developed there, although 'official' imagery of the estate as being a particular problem is not necessarily borne out by social indicators.

Saxon Lane was already being identified by some local professionals as a 'problem estate' in the late 1970s, with a gathering of local opinion that it contained a disproportionate number of single-parent families and other potentially 'troublesome' sections of the population. However, these judgements are difficult to reconcile with the demographic indications of the Small Area Statistics of the 1981 Census, when the estate was already becoming locally notorious.

For example, the proportion of single-parent households in the five Enumeration Districts which define the core 'problem area' of the estate was no more than 15 per cent, which is quite a low figure in comparison with other identified 'hard-to-let' districts within 'problem estates' in the North of England (cf. Pearson *et al.*, 1986). Moreover, although Saxon Lane generates a high childcare workload for the social services area team, this was by no means out of line with the age composition of the estate where more than one-third of the population were under 15 years of age. There is no reason to dispute that this was a poor estate, with 25 per cent of the male labour force unemployed, nor that its difficulties would have been aggravated since the 1981 Census reflecting the deep recession in the North West region. But Saxon Lane was already coming to earn its local reputation as a 'problem estate' in the early 1980s, and the broad areas of disagreement between official perceptions of the estate and its actual demography begin to make one wonder what subtle processes of stereotyping were beginning to encircle this deprived neighbourhood, both in terms of state agency responses and those of the local press. In the wake of the eruptions in Brixton and Liverpool 8 in the summer of 1981, for example, an outburst of youthful unrest outside the local chip shop was labelled Saxon Lane's 'riot', and the press subsequently headlined the area as an 'Estate of Fear'. This was one of the triggers to the formation of Saxon Lane's 'multi-agency' initiative. One further complexity of the estate's image is that public agencies do not agree either on its precise geographical boundaries or its name. So that although it is generally known as 'Saxon Lane', the police employ a different definition of its geography and refer to the area as 'Cowmarsh'.

By comparison, Empire Gardens in inner London represents an unmistakable territory, consisting of a somewhat forbidding grid-development of three-storey tenement-style blocks built in the inter-war years, although once again as an architectural triumph of its time. Its name is known London-wide, and it is associated with a history of crime and trouble of different descriptions. But here the easy definitions stop, just as they did with Saxon Lane. According to the local police, for example, the estate has deteriorated sharply in the past 10 to 15 years, whereas a local councillor tells us that it was a much worse place in the past and has improved itself since the early 1970s. The police do not define it as a 'high crime' area in terms of official statistics on burglary and other targeted crimes, although it is significant that they fear it as a potential location for violent 'disorder'. The police do, however, see Empire Gardens as the home for 'problem tenants' and 'problem families', and therefore as a problem for the social services. The social services team, on the other hand, do not see Empire Gardens as any different in terms of their workload from the surrounding locality—even though on the basis of the 1981 Census more than one-fifth of households with children were 'lone parent' households, with 45 per cent of such households containing one or more single-parent families. But whereas this contrasts very sharply with the demography of Saxon Lane in Milltown, it is nevertheless true that Empire Gardens is no different in these respects from the immediately surrounding area which is characterised by a high proportion of single-parent households. Indeed, one social work team leader directly challenged the decision to site research on Empire Gardens as possibly resulting from 'prejudice' which might simply reinforce the estate's awful reputation.

211

The police perception of crime within the immediate area of its divisional responsibilities is that burglary and other targeted crime is concentrated in a middle-class area one mile away which begins to merge with suburban London. And whereas a great deal of emphasis has been given to the development of 'neighbourhood watch' schemes in this police division, with different levels of success and application, an attempt to establish a neighbourhood watch scheme in Empire Gardens was a complete failure. A very recent initiative to establish an inter-agency forum on the estate has not yet got beyond the point of devising an appropriate mechanism, with no stated objectives. Even so, in a forum meeting to which police were invited, tensions have already emerged between the police view of Empire Gardens and that of other relevant agencies who will insist on seeing crime as a more important local issue than the police do.

Finally, Queen's Reach is a high-rise development of the 1970s with a number of spectacularly innovative architectural features. A disturbing maze of walkways and balconies connects the dramatic tower blocks which comprise the estate. It quickly became known as a 'problem estate'. With a large proportion of single-parent households very similar to that of Empire Gardens and well over one-third of the population aged under 15 years, there are common allegations of a housing policy which uses it as a 'dumping ground', together with some local rumour associating the estate with a major drugs problem, although this is not the view of the police drugs unit. More generally it is felt to be characterised by a high degree of social isolation (a view held by health visitors, social workers and the community worker because of its structural design, a significant proportion of tenants with substantial rent arrears (housing officer and social workers) as a possible consequence of very high rents, and a fear of crime among the elderly population identified by the representative of a sheltered housing scheme. The probation service, on the other hand, do not see Queen's Reach as a particular problem.

An inter-agency forum has been in existence for 5 years on Queen's Reach, and its preoccupations reflect the problems mentioned above. The police are represented on this forum by the home beat officer, although crime is not regarded as an exceptional problem either by the police or by the other local agency representatives, and nor by the local residents' group which tends towards a 'normalised' picture of the estate. But crime prevention technology recently installed—in the form of card-operated lock devices—is now a major focus for concern for everyone, including both the agency representatives and local residents. Indeed, it is the view of some agency personnel that these crime prevention measures (which were introduced as part of a major initiative by the police and housing authority) may be helping to fuel the 'fear of crime' phenomenon, by giving crime prevention such a high physical profile, while also leading to difficulties of access. There are complaints that old people are quite inaccessible to their neighbours who try to keep an eye on them.

Empire Gardens and Queen's Reach in inner London, and Saxon Lane (or Cowmarsh) in Milltown do not share anything remotely resembling a common history or tradition. In spite of their obvious differences, however, each of these localities points to the problematic nature of the definition of a 'problem estate', with attendant difficulties in reaching agreement between agencies on a common focus for inter-agency work—in spite of agreement in each area that close inter-agency co-operation could provide a possible answer to local problems.

Conflict and consensus in inter-agency work

Only in Saxon Lane might one say that there is a consensus about what the 'problem' is, although as we have seen this definition seems to be sharply at variance with much of the available evidence. The Saxon Lane multi-agency initiative has already thrown up a number of interesting inter-agency tensions, however, which seem a far cry from the confident tone of the Chief Executive's original policy document:

'Integration is ... important to ensure a common purpose to the delivery of services and, perhaps of greater importance, to enable residents (whose needs are not fragmented into 'departmental boundaries') to relate more clearly to our initiatives. A co-ordinator for the area should now be appointed.'

As a consequence a 'Housing and Joint Agency Base' has recently opened on Saxon Lane, in a pair of houses near its centre. It is staffed by the co-ordinator and three 'community wardens', with rooms for the police and the social services department. The police who use it are the 'permanent beat officers' for (in police terms) Cowmarsh. It is in this case, however, the co-ordinator from the Chief Executive's department who is the central figure in this 'inter-agency' initiative, partly because of the enthusiasm of the individual concerned, but more significantly because of the pattern of available finance for specific projects. In order to obtain central government funds for crime prevention, it might be that it has been necessary to 'talk up' the estate's problem status and serving this end some unsubstantiated (but widely accepted) figures are in circulation: for example that Saxon Lane's unemployment rate is 79 per cent, with 83 per cent on some kind of state benefit, although it is not clear what these figures mean other than as a dramatised version of the estate's difficulties.

Low level tensions have already appeared between workers actually on the estate. The community wardens, for example, who are supposed to respond helpfully to tenants' problems, have expressed anxiety that sharing information with the police may threaten what they see as their present good standing with the local community, and lead to them to being 'alienated from the estate'. They see their liaison with the police as a 'one-way flow of information from us to them, with nothing in return'. The information concerns vandalism to specific properties, suspected child abuse, burglaries and thefts from meters. The wardens fear that this focus on crime may undermine their ability to do their 'real job' of protecting housing stock. They also feel that the police may use the liaison machinery to off-load tedious enquiries into incidents of vandalism. For example:

'Policemen have told locals who ring up about vandalism, "See the wardens, we can't do anything about that". They are shifting the time and cost on to us.'

An anecdote from one of the wardens reveals how far official pronouncements about liaison can differ from actual practices:

'I saw a window that seemed to be left wide open by someone. I rang the police and suggested that they come and take a look at it. The policeman said that this was not worth coming out for, and why didn't I just close the window? I said I didn't want to get my finger-prints on it in case there were a burglar's on it already. He was right offensive, he said, "Why, are you known to us? Have you got something to hide?" That's what they're like. I'll not bother reporting anything again.'

As a backcloth to these emerging tensions, there is a complex interplay of different inter-agency and intra-agency emphases on what might consitute an appropriate strategy for Saxon Lane. The local police view of crime prevention tends to be purely situational. They want any available funding from central government directed towards providing stronger doors, with stronger locks, together with window locks for all ground-floor windows. The Chief Executive's department, on the other hand, leans towards a more 'social' approach which would entail the establishment of 'residents' committees' to seek local views on police priorities, on the grounds that crime prevention must begin with 'restoring public confidence in the police'. As one further indication of these local shifts of emphasis, crime prevention within the Milltown police is no longer a separate function, having been merged within the newly created 'Community Affairs' department which also covers juvenile liaison and accident prevention—a reorganisation which has not met with universal approval. Some police officers express disquiet about what they see as an increasing trend towards 'social' crime prevention at the expense of the 'real' variety. Social approaches are dismissed as 'Playschool' policing, just as police officers in inner London will sometimes deride inter-agency efforts on juvenile crime as the work of the 'Toy Squad', 'Care Bear', and the 'Teeny Sweeny'. These attitudes, moreover, are not merely matters of individual whim. Rather, they reflect (as the emergence of a derisory argot might suggest) significant aspects of the police culture at the level of the rank-and-file which cuts across otherwise obvious differences between Milltown and inner London (cf. Reiner, 1985).

Meanwhile at a local level, as already suggested, the police on Saxon Lane remain the primary definers of the problem of crime prevention and the leaders in seeking solutions, with little mutuality existing in their relations with other agencies. Community-oriented approaches such as neighbourhood watch are not thought to be feasible for the 'abnormal' population of Saxon Lane. In its pattern of crime the estate is thought to commit too many 'own goals'—such as crime committed locally by local residents, including thefts from their own gas and electricity meters. The non-offending population—the still, just about 'decent' people—are seen as apathetic and fatalistic.

So that whereas one aspect of this declared inter-agency strategy leans towards 'bottom-up' definitions, involving local residents' committees, the police tend towards what we have come to think of as a 'Rambo' model of 'real' crime prevention. And such liaison as is necessary for this model is directed towards security firms, the media and possibly charitable funding organisations. Central to this model is an 'ideal citizen' who is committed enough to call in the crime prevention experts and for whom it is worth organising roadshows and mounting displays of security equipment. But this virtuous, well-motivated public is supposedly not well represented on Saxon Lane. The police do nevertheless distinguish within this overwhelmingly 'feckless' population special groups, such as the vulnerable elderly and juveniles whose activities, at least at the younger end, are seen as a troublesome, time-consuming nuisance rather than as real crime. And it is at real crime that real crime prevention should be directed. Hence, as things stand, an extensive area of policy confusion underlies the surface agreement on the 'problem' of Saxon Lane. For the police, this confusion is evidenced in the fact that although the estate is regarded as a problem, it is an area which generates a workload characterised as one of largely a nuisance-value, that is time-consuming, messy and unrewarding.

An inter-agency forum on Queen's Reach in inner London has indicated a quite different set of problems for multi-agency work, and we can briefly describe some of these. The forum has already been in existence for five years, and members of a variety of agencies meet once a month in order to discuss common problems. Representatives of different agencies hold widely conflicting views of what problems exist on Queen's Reach, with a major preoccupation at the moment centring on recently introduced crime prevention technology. However, the forum members rerely confront the conflicts which exist between themselves, or when they do these conflicts come to be seen as a threat to the forum's very existence. For example, some time ago a major issue was the housing department's renting policy which was resulting in very high rent charges and the forum made some effort to get the housing department representative to challenge this policy. But this met with no success, and although high rents are an ongoing problem the matter is now rarely, if ever, discussed. Similarly, there was a recent change in the territorial boundaries of home beat officers which proved to be unpopular with forum members. However, when the home beat officer (who is a member of the forum) was confronted with this, he simply said that it was 'typical of the management, who are always chopping and changing without consulting us'. In other words, the home beat officer neither attempted to justify his agency's policy nor to argue the forum's case with his superior officers.

What seems to be at issue in this and other instances of evading conflict is the question of 'representation'. Forum members are not representatives of their agencies, in the sense of being delegated either to represent their agency's policies within the forum, or to represent the forum's views to their agency. The forum has come to be an end in itself, with members apparently taking the view that by simply sitting down together and reaching surface agreement on a number of issues this is doing something which will contribute to an improvement of the quality of life on Queen's Reach. Unlike Saxon Lane where agency conflicts are still in an emergent phase, the Queen's Reach forum has reached a 'cosy' stage of development where maintaining the coherence of the group itself, in terms of conflict-free face-to-face relationships between members, has come to be more important than identifying areas of conflict and attempting to remedy them. When asked what the forum does for their working relationships with other agencies, forum members will typically say that it has improved them. They are now on 'first name terms' with their opposite numbers who have become 'real people' to them, and 'not just the voice on the other end of the telephone'. A more critical way of describing these relationships, however, would be to say that the forum is drifting, with no adequate sense of the representative status of its members, and without a clear direction in terms of identifying and confronting actual areas of policy

215

tension and conflict. The meetings have no pre-arranged agenda, for example, they are sometimes cancelled at short notice, and at the beginning of meetings it is uncertain who will chair them. There is certainly now a more flexible approach to information exchange between forum members, but even this is sometimes highly questionable in that it takes place on a case-by-case basis, with no over-riding policy to guide it, and in a manner that is sometimes highly unaccountable. The issue of the troublesome crime prevention technology on Queen's Reach meanwhile remains unresolved, with most time and energy devoted to the question of who will be allowed a card which gives them access to the estates—so that at the moment, for example, the milkman and the CID do have cards, but the social services department and the home beat officer do not. Crime prevention techology has thus come to be a definer of status within the forum, with possibly unintended consequences for future inter-agency relationships.

Neglected issues

The manifest recent official enthusiasm for inter-agency co-operation (or some synonym) in crime prevention has been noted in this paper. It has been suggested that this enthusiasm often remains at the level of rhetoric or sloganising, so that its importance may be symbolic or ideological, rather than indicating much about what is feasible. There is also a significant tendency within the police (or certain subdivisions of the complex machinery of the police service) to define 'social' approaches to crime prevention as something other than real police work, and a similar scepticism may be important in (at least) the probation service. Further, some of the dilemmas which a commitment to liaison may produce for agencies other than the police have been noted, although there are dilemmas for the police too. In conclusion, it is argued that both the reality and the rhetoric of crime prevention remain highly selective with regard to the types of crime whose prevention is considered important, and inter-agency co-operation is correspondingly more developed in relation to some types of crime than others. It is not surprising that work in crime prevention should reflect dominant conceptions of what kinds of crime constitute a problem. Indeed, the present form of the official discourse on crime and its prevention significantly privileges some activities over others, and although it has not been possible to develop this point here, it is nevertheless important to register what seem to be particularly neglected themes.

The two most obvious silences in the field of crime prevention and inter-agency working are those of violence against women in the home and racial attacks. [2] As far as racism and racial attacks are concerned, although this problem has a high public profile and has generated a large amount of political controversy, as things stand it is so neglected in existing ' crime prevention' practices that one can perhaps do no more than register the fact of its neglect, together with the likely effect which this has upon the confidence and trust which ethnic minorities place in the police (cf. Home Office, 1981; Home Affairs Committee, 1982; Field, 1984; Benyon, 1986). In relation to domestic violence, on the other hand, it is possible to be a little more specific.

The positioning of the concept of a 'domestic' in operational policing is a matter that has received a fair degree of attention in recent years. While acknowledging that many 'domestics' are comparatively trivial, for example, a small-scale observational study by Faragher (1985) noted the reluctance of the police to execute an arrest in such cases. Studies of the police occupational culture have also identified the ways in which 'domestics' are defined as 'rubbish' cases that are unworthy of police attention (cf. PSI, 1983; Reiner, 1978 and 1985). This 'structured indifference' towards violence against women in the home is no less notable in research on the work of social workers (cf. Maynard, 1985; Borkowski et al., 1983). There is no shortage of evidence of the extent of violence against women in the home, nor of the reluctance of official agencies to intervene (Hanmer and Saunders, 1984; Pahl, 1985; Dobash and Dobash, 1980). But what is most striking is the contrast between the neglect of domestic violence as a site upon which to enact measures of crime prevention (in other words, to regard such violence as 'crime') or to invoke the concept of inter-agency co-operation, when set against the elaborate liaison apparatus which is arranged around child protection.

The question of gender is something which might also be expected to influence the form which inter-agency relationships take, especially when these are between the police service which is such a dominantly male (not to say macho) organisation, in contrast with the predominantly female domain of the social services at fieldworker level. Indeed, the neglected issues which we have identified might well have much wider ramifications within the entire field of local crime prevention, reaching far beyond the specific issues of racial attacks and violence against women in the home. Little attention has been given in this field, for example, to the nature of informal neighbourhood care networks, which might be thought of as a natural constituency upon which to build effective local crime prevention initiatives. It has been noted how, in localities with a substantially mixed racial composition, a neglect of racial issues is unlikely to encourage public participation in police-led crime prevention schemes. More generally, informal neighbourhood networks tend to be predominantly concerned with women's concerns, and to be supported largely by the time and energy of women (cf. Bulmer, 1986; Finch and Groves, 1980), so that again the likelihood that local crime prevention initiatives will be successful in recruiting local interest and support might well depend upon their ability to address women's concerns more directly than they do at present.

But these are large questions, which cannot be settled here. The extent to which crime prevention and inter-agency initiatives previlige certain kinds of crime as against others can hardly be disputed. The circumstances which shape and determine these areas of relative priority and neglect are matters which it is intended to pursue in the subsequent development of this research.

Notes

1. This paper is based on a research project, 'Crime, Community and the Inter-Agency Dimension', funded by the Government and Law Committee of the Economic and Social Research Council (Grant No.ED 6250035) for two years from 1 November 1985. This is a collaborative project between staff of Middlesex Polytechnic and the University of Lancaster: Geoffrey Pearson, Professor of Social Work at Middlesex Polytechnic; Mr Harry Blagg, Lecturer

in Social Policy and Mr David Smith, Lecturer in Social Work at Lancaster University. Ms Alice Sampson and Mr Paul Stubbs are Research Fellows on the project, and Mr John Friend of the Tavistock Institute of Human Relations acts as a management science consultant to the research team.

2. This is an area of fluid policy change and innovation, and since this paper was written significant new policy initiatives have emerged from the Metropolitan Police in order to give a higher priority to both domestic violence and racial attacks. In the case of racial attacks, 'Best Practice Guidelines' include not only the requirement to establish improved reporting and monitoring procedures, but also where local circumstances permit the encouragement of multi-agency structures such as Local Authority Sub-Committees, Racial Incident Panels and sub-committees of Police Consultative Groups as established under Section 106 of the Police and Criminal Evidence Act of 1984 (cf. Metropolitan Police, 1986). However, it is too early to assess the impact of these policies at operational level.

References

ALLATT, P. (1984a). 'Residential security: containment and displacement of burglary'. *Howard Journal of Criminal Justice,* 23, pp. 99–116.

ALLATT, P. (1984b). 'Fear of crime: the effect of improved residential security on a difficult to let estate'. *Howard Journal of Criminal Justice,* 23, pp.170–82.

BALDWIN, J. and BOTTOMS, A.E. (1976). *The Urban Criminal: A Study in Sheffield.* London: Tavistock.

BENYON, J. (1986). *A Tale of Failure: Race and Policing.* Policy Papers in Ethnic Relations No.3 Centre for Research in Ethnic Relations, University of Warwick.

BIRLEY, D. and BRIGHT, J. (1985). *Crime in the Community.* Labour Campaign for Criminal Justice.

BORKOWSKI, M. *et al.* (1983). *Marital Violence: The Community Response.* London: Tavistock.

BRIGHT, J. and PETTERSON, G. (1984). *The Safe Neighbourhoods Unit Report.* London: NACRO.

BRIGHT, J., MALONEY, H. PETTERSON, G., and FARR, J. (1985). *After Entryphones: Improving Management and Security in Multi-Storey Blocks.* London: Safe Neighbourhoods Unit, NACRO.

BULMER, M. (1986).*Neighbours: The Work of Philip Abrams.* Cambridge: Cambridge University Press.

CLARKE, R. V. and MAYHEW, P. (Eds.), (1980). *Designing out Crime.* London: HMSO.

COHEN, S. (1985). *Visions of Social Control.* Cambridge: Polity Press.

DOBASH, R. E. and DOBASH, R. P. (1980). *Violence Against Wives.* London: Open Books.

FARAGHER, T. (1985). 'The police response to violence against women in the home'. In PAHL, J. (Ed.), *Private Violence and Public Policy,* London: Routledge and Kegan Paul.

FIELD, S. (1984). *The Attitudes of Ethnic Minorities.* Home Office Research Study No. 80. London: HMSO.

FINCH, J. and GROVES, D. (1980). 'Community care and the family: a case for equal opportunities?' *Journal of Social Policy*, 9, pp. 486–511.

FOLKARD, M. S., SMITH, D. E. and SMITH, D. D. (1976). *IMPACT. Intensive Matched Probation and After-Care Treatment. Vol II. The Results of the Experiment.* Home Office Research Study No. 36. London: HMSO.

FRIEND, J. K. *et al.,* (1981). *Alcohol Related Problems: A Study of Inter-Organisational Relations. A Report to the SSRC.* London: Tavistock Institute for Human Relations.

GARTON, A. (1980). 'Mutual perceptions between police and probation officers: a research note'. *British Journal of Social Work*, 10, pp. 87–9.

GLADSTONE, F. J. (1980). *Co-ordinating Crime Prevention Efforts.* Home Office Research Study No. 62. London: HMSO.

HANMER, J. and SAUNDERS, A. (1984). *Well-Founded Fear: A Community Study of Violence to Women.* London: Hutchinson.

HENDERSON, P. (1986). 'Community Work and the Probation Service'. *Research Bulletin*, No. 20, Home Office Research and Planning Unit.

HOLDAWAY, S. (1980). 'Police and social work relations: problems and possibilities'. *British Journal of Social Work*, 16, pp. 137–60.

HOME AFFAIRS COMMITTEE, (1982). *Racial Attacks.* Second Report from the Home Affairs Committee, Session 1981–82, HC. 106. London: HMSO.

HOME OFFICE, (1981). *Racial Attacks.* London: HMSO

HOME OFFICE, (1984a). Crime Prevention, Circular HO 8/84. Home Office, DES, DoE, DHSS, Welsh Office.

HOME OFFICE, (1984b). *Statement of National Objectives and Priorities.* London: Home Office.

HOPE, T. (1985) *Implementing Crime Prevention Measures.* Home Office Research Study No. 86. London: HMSO.

HOPE, T. and MURPHY, D. J. I., (1983). 'Problems of implementing crime prevention: the experience of a demonstration project'. *Howard Journal*, 22, pp. 38–50.

JUVENILE CRIME UNIT, (1985). *Juvenile Crime: Co-ordination and the Community.* London: NACRO.

LAYCOCK, G. and PEASE, K., (1985). 'Crime prevention within the probation service'. *Probation Journal*, 32, pp. 43–47.

MAYHEW, P., CLARKE, R. V. G., STURMAN. A, and HOUGH, J. M., (1976). *Crime as Opportunity*. Home Office Research Study No. 34. London: HMSO.

MAYNARD, M. (1985). 'The response of social workers to domestic violence'. In Pahl, J. (Ed.), *Private Violence and Public Policy*. London: Routledge and Kegan Paul.

METROPOLITAN POLICE, (1985). *Estates Policing: A Method of Approach to Multi-Agency Co-operation*, London A2 (3) Branch, Metropolitan Police.

METROPOLITAN POLICE, (1986). *Recording and Monitoring Racial Incidents: Best Practice Guidelines*. London: Territorial Operations Department, Metroplitan Police.

MOXON, D. (Ed.), (1985). *Managing Criminal Justice*. London: HMSO.

PAHL, J. (1985). 'Violent husbands and abused wives: a longitudinal study'. In Pahl, J. (Ed.), *Private Violence and Public Policy*, London: Routledge and Kegan Paul.

PARKER, H. J., CASBURN, M. and TURNBULL, D. (1981). *Receiving Juvenile Justice*. Oxford: Blackwell.

PARLIAMENTARY ALL-PARTY PENAL AFFAIRS GROUP, (1983). *The Prevention of Crime Amongst Young People*. Chichester: Barry Rose.

PEARSON, G. (1983). *Hooligan: A History of Respectable Fears*. London: Macmillan.

PEARSON, G. (1986). 'Developing a local research strategy'. In Wedge, P. (Ed.), *Social Work: Research into Practice*. Birmingham: British Association of Social Work.

PEARSON, G., GILMAN, M. and McIVER, S. (1986). *Young People and Heroin: An Examination of Heroin Use in the North of England. A Report to the Health Education Council*. London: Health Education Council and Aldershot: Gower.

POLICY STUDIES INSTITUTE, (1983). *The Police and the People in London*. 4 vols. London.

REINER, R. (1978). *The Blue-Coated Worker*. Cambridge: Cambridge University Press.

REINER, R. (1985). *The Politics of the Police*. Brighton: Harvester.

REYNOLDS, D. (1976). 'When pupils and teachers refuse a truce: the secondary school and the creation of delinquency'. In Mungham, G. and Pearson, G. (Eds.) *Working Class Youth Culture*. London: Routledge and Kegan Paul.

SCOTT, D. *et al.,* (Eds.), (1985) *Going Local in Probation*, Norwich: University of East Anglia.

SHAW, S. (1983). 'Crime prevention and the future of the probation service'. *Probation Journal*, 30, pp. 127–30.

SMITH, D., SHEPPARD, B., MAIR, G. and WILLIAMS, K., (1984). *Reducing the Prison Population: An Exploratory Study in Hampshire*. Home Office Research and Planning Unit Paper No. 23. London: Home Office Research and Planning Unit.

WILLMOTT, P. (1984). *Community in Social Policy*. London: Policy Studies Institute.

13. Thinking about the implementation of citizen and community anti-crime measures

Paul J Lavrakas and Susan F Bennett[1]

In the last twenty years, public policy towards the prevention of crime in the United States, Great Britain and other Western nations has taken a significant shift in emphasis from what had been the way of thinking earlier in the twentieth century. Consistent with the call for public responsibility and service made by the American president, John F. Kennedy, in his 1961 inaugural address, citizens are being asked to play a major role in the effort to maintain or, if necessary, increase the levels of security and safety in their own communities.

Historically, humans accepted that *they* were primarily responsible for their own safety and that of their families and communities. As population density grew and governments became more powerful and more bureaucratic, many citizens became dependent on 'the state' for security. And, in those cases where security was threatened by some clearly identifiable collective (e.g., a foreign army) the state could try to marshall collective might of its own to protect its citizens. While this was a successful approach to 'national security', it was basically ineffective in providing security to the public from individual criminals (or terrorists, for that matter) within their own cities, towns and neighbourhoods.

One of the most important outcomes of the US Presidential Commissions on crime in the late 1960s was the call for an involved citizenry in the fight against crime (cf. Curtis, 1985). The reports of those commissions urged the public to engage in many forms of personal, household and neighbourhood anti-crime measures. These included strategies aimed at the presumed 'root causes' of crime and those aimed at reducing criminal opportunities (Lavrakas, 1985). In the past five years, this call for an involved citizenry has become routinised in the United States in the form of the highly visible 'McGruff—"Take a Bite Out of Crime"' public service advertising campaign (National Crime Prevention Council, 1986; O'Keefe, 1985).

As this change in crime prevention policy was occurring, crime prevention research was sponsored by various governments' agencies, most notably the Home Office in Britain and the US National Institute of Justice. This research has uniformly shown that efforts to increase the citizenry's involvement in anti-crime activities are very hard to implement, and not unimportantly, it has been learned that it is very difficult to validly assess the impacts of these efforts.

Despite the logical appeal of citizen (i.e., those anti-crime measures engaged in by individual citizens) and community (i.e., those anti-crime measures engaged in by citizen collectives) crime prevention, many recent American

1. This paper was prepared under the partial support of Northwestern University's Center for Urban Affairs and Policy Research, the Eisenhower Foundation, the Ford Foundation, and the National Institute of Justice. The opinions expressed in this paper are those of the authors and are not meant to reflect the official positions of those funding bodies.

evaluation studies have not found strong evidence that community anti-crime efforts achieve their intended goals (Bennett and Lavrakas, 1986; DuBow, McPherson and Silloway, 1985; Garofalo and McCleod, 1985; Henig, 1985; and Rosenbaum, Lewis and Grant, 1985). In fact, some of these studies have raised the possibility that unintended negative consequences may result (e.g., increased fear of crime).

While knowledge of this approach to crime prevention has accumulated in the past two decades there remain many unknowns about the viability and thus the ultimate attractiveness of the 'citizen/community crime prevention hypothesis' (cf. Rosenbaum, 1986). In fact, much of the evidence that supports the wisdom of this approach falls into the realm of the informed professional judgement of expert practitioners and crime prevention scholars.

While intentions have often been good, too often community anti-crime efforts have not succeeded to the extent expected of them. Does this suggest that the underlying theory is wrong (cf. Rosenbaum, 1986)? Or that these anti-crime efforts have not been implemented in a successful manner? Or some combination of both?

For example, DuBow *et al.*, (1985) have noted that despite concentrated efforts in the Minneapolis anti-crime programme they evaluated, the implementation of the programme failed to stimulate citizen involvement in some neighbourhoods, including those that were most in need of anti-crime efforts. This conclusion reinforces earlier findings (Lavrakas, Skogan, Herz, Normoyle, Salem and Lewis, 1980) that it is typically the 'resource poor' that suffer the most from crime and at the same time often do the least or are apparently least able, either individually or collectively, to 'resist' victimization.

This paper addresses the issue of implementing citizen and community anti-crime programmes, since logic dictates that unless one successfully implements (or in social science terms 'operationalises') an anti-crime measure it is not possible to perform a valid test of the theory (cf. Weiss, 1972).

Levels of prevention and the citizen/community crime prevention process

It has been argued that anything that improves the quality of life in a given locale may have a positive effect on the level of crime and felt safety in that area (Lavrakas, 1985). While some criminal justice practitioners view 'crime prevention' in very mechanistic terms (e.g., locks, bars, timers, lights, etc.) the former reasoning suggests that 'crime prevention' should be viewed in much broader terms.

For the purposes of understanding the issues to be considered in implementing an anti-crime programme, it is suggested that one should first understand the *level of prevention* one is aiming to achieve. It is important to recognise the level of prevention to which an anti-crime measure strives since different psychological dynamics appear to motivate adoption or rejection of measures at each level. Here it is believed a public health model of 'prevention' serves a useful analogy.

Prevention can be viewed as occurring at three levels. First, *primary prevention* is proactive and preventive in the truest sense. It occurs prior to the onset of threat and strives to keep the potential for trouble from even developing. What we call *secondary prevention* refers to proactive measures that prevent specific instances of, or opportunities for, potential threat from developing into instances of actual victimization. At this level of prevention the problem already exists and measures are taken to strengthen the 'resistance' of certain individuals or targets from falling victim. Finally, *tertiary prevention* is what the insurance industry regards as 'loss-reduction'. It is 'preventive' only from the standpoint that it reduces the extent of the damage done in actual instances of harm or attempted harm. In other words, the threat has manifested itself in some manner and the preventive reaction is meant to minimise the harm caused by the threat.

In terms of public health, examples of primary prevention typically occur outside the medical profession and include persons who eat a proper diet and exercise regularly so as to keep in top health. Another example against a specific disease, such as malaria, would be spraying mosquito breeding grounds to kill larvae so as to eliminate potential carriers.

Secondary prevention in the realm of public health includes efforts to reduce individual exposure or susceptibility to particular diseases. This includes vaccines and, in the case of malaria, would include the use of mosquito nets to reduce the opportunity for carriers to bite, and thus infect, a victim.

Tertiary prevention in health occurs *after* individual pathology is present and the medical profession is invoked to minimise the likelihood of further harm. Taking antibiotics for various infections, or quinine for malaria, occurs after the onset of the problem and is preventive only in a reactive sense.

As shown in Table 1, the same levels of prevention can be applied to classify anti-crime measures. Primary prevention measures against crime are those that address the causes of crime. While there is much debate regarding the complex forces that 'breed' criminality, most informed opinion agrees that macro forces such as population demographics, the economy, educational opportunities, and the culture's religious and moral climate play important roles in putting bounds on the amount of criminality that might be expected in a society (Silberman, 1978; Currie, 1985). At the same time, micro forces occurring at the level of the family and the individual must also be considered as causes of individual criminality (cf. Wilson and Herrnstein, 1985). Thus, anti-crime measures meant to improve the quality of life within society strive to keep a predisposition for crime from developing. Measures to improve employment, educational and recreational opportunities, especially for lower-income, minority youth, represent primary crime prevention. Included here are support programmes for the hungry and homeless, and support networks for single parents, in particular unwed teenage mothers. Other measures aimed not directly at crime but meant to rid the general living environment of 'unseemly' behaviours and physical attributes which may create an atmosphere which condones criminal events (cf. Wilson, 1975) would also be included.

For many US criminal justice policy-makers and practitioners, 'crime prevention' does not include what has been identified here as primary prevention. Rather, these persons think of 'crime prevention' as starting with measures aimed at minimising the likelihood (or reducing the opportunity) that some specific target will be victimized. In this classification, however, 'opportunity reduction' is secondary prevention against crime. These measures are not preventive in the sense that they address the primary or underlying

Table 1 *Varieties of citizen/community crime prevention strategies*

Level of prevention	type	purpose	examples
Primary	Causes of Crime	Strengthening non-criminal values and motivations of individuals in the community	Employment programmes Educational programmes Recreational programmes Individual counselling and therapy
Secondary	Opportunity-Reduction	Minimise the likelihood that specific criminal acts will be initiated	Outdoor lighting Timbers on lights Deadbolt locks Blockwatch Citizen patrols
Tertiary	Loss-Reduction	Minimise the severity of loss when specific criminal act is threatened or initiated	Whistle STOP Self-Defence training Weapons (e.g., guns) Insurance (personal and property)

causes of crime, but are nevertheless proactive in that they strive to eliminate the opportunity for a would-be offender to decide (not necessarily in a rational sense) to initiate a criminal event. The use of physical barriers such as double-cylinder deadbolt locks and psychological barriers such as outdoor lights and indoor timers are secondary prevention measures against unlawful entry. Citizens patrolling their neighbourhoods on foot or in cars as well as formal and informal 'neighbourhood watch' programmes operate at this secondary level of prevention.

Finally, at the level of reducing the harm from a specific instance of victimization or attempted victimization, tertiary prevention measures can be invoked. These *reactive* measures have the same intent as chemotherapy and surgery for cancer victims. These measures occur *after* the threat is manifest: the threat is a reality confronting the individual and the individual must react or remain the unresisting victim. Individual use of weapons (guns, canes, mace, etc.) as 'protective measures' is preventive only at a tertiary level (unless the weapon is visible and the would-be offender views the circumstances as an undesirable criminal opportunity). Self-defence training is also tertiary prevention. So too is a programme which originated in Chicago called 'Whistle STOP', whereby individuals carry loud whistles to blow if confronted with a threatening situation.

Research has suggested that citizen involvement in different levels of crime prevention is tied to very different psychological dynamics (Lavrakas *et al.*, 1980; Podolefsky and DuBow, 1981). Unless policy-makers and practitioners recognise these differences they will be less than adequately advised when thinking about implementing various anti-crime strategies.

Based on this interpretation of previous research, it is hypothesised that citizens typically engage in primary crime prevention for *public-minded* or altruistic motives, in secondary crime prevention for both public-minded and *private-minded* (i.e., primarily self-interest) motives, and in tertiary crime prevention for mostly private-minded motives. The planning of an anti-crime programme requiring the participation of citizens *qua* residents should logically develop implementation strategies that address or at least build upon these 'natural' motivations.

The remainder of this paper builds particularly on the experiences of the authors with an on-going five-year evaluation of the Eisenhower Foundation's Neighbourhood Programme. Here, interest is primarily in citizens *qua* residents who help to plan and implement crime prevention programmes as *volunteers*, in contrast to paid staff members or residents who are primarily recipients of programme services. These roles are not always mutually exclusive; volunteers sometimes receive token stipends for their work and may also receive services from the programme (e.g., a home security check or job referrals). None the less, most citizen/community crime prevention programmes are dependent on the assumption that residents will volunteer their time and skills (cf. Lavrakas *et al.*, 1980). Thus, it is suggested that differences in volunteers' motivations for participation affect the resources needed, the means for initiating the programme, and the feasibility of maintaining the programme. These issues are discussed separately for the three levels of crime prevention.

Primary crime prevention

Efforts that strive to involve citizens in primary crime prevention should begin by recognising that only a very small proportion of the public is likely to participate. These are not individuals who are motivated to 'get involved' because they are fearful of crime. Rather, a person's assessment of her/his own vulnerability to crime is likely to be *independent* of the decision to engage in some primary crime prevention effort. Here, participators often are caring individuals who want to help others, especially young people, better their lives.

In the authors' view, involvement in these types of social programmes as a means of crime prevention is also likely to be based on certain assumptions about the causes of crime and about socially just means of reducing crime. It appears that such participation is frequently linked to two basic assumptions about the local crime problem: that the majority of local offenders are fellow residents and that their involvement in illegal activities is due to limited opportunities for legitimate activities (cf. Podolefsky, 1984).

For primary crime prevention programmes, then, a major resource which is needed is a shared understanding or knowledge of the presumed underlying causes of crime in the community and the means by which they can be impacted. Although any programme needs an explicit rationale, it is particularly important for primary crime prevention activities in comparison to secondary or tertiary crime prevention activities. These programmes are based on assumptions which cannot yet be proven and which cannot necessarily be expected to have observable impacts over short time periods. As mentioned above, building consensus among residents for this type of programme is difficult due to the more complicated reasoning (in comparison, for example, to requests for more foot patrols), the longer time period required for observable results, and what may seem to be tenuous relationships between initial results and the local crime problem.

Of the ten Eisenhower sites being evaluated, one of the clearest examples of primary prevention is the youth programme established in Washington, DC.

Programme staff and volunteers at that site have negotiated frequently over the nature of the crime problem in the community and the best way to confront it. It has been an ongoing dialogue, carried on seriously by the participants, and with definite impacts on the programme.

Given the need for a shared 'philosophy' regarding causes of crime and the means to deal with them, it seems likely that an articulate and persuasive leader is another resource particularly useful to primary crime prevention programmes. In fact, an articulate leader, personally committed to the programme, seems the most likely impetus for a primary crime prevention programme. A series of home burglaries in the neighbourhood or street muggings may be the catalyst for the start of new block watch groups (a secondary prevention response), but these types of events seem less likely to stimulate a primary crime prevention programme unless there is a community leader or organisation to explain the rationale underlying it.

(It is important to recognise that although primary crime prevention programmes are a direct response to crime inasmuch as they are intended to impact on the *causes* of crime, they often may not be considered either direct, adequate, or appropriate responses by those residents who are primarily concerned about the likelihood of their home being burgled within the next week or so.)

As already mentioned, volunteers for a primary prevention programme will become involved due to public-minded values. Public-minded citizens who maintain their involvement in such efforts are likely to be those with a high tolerance for delayed gratification or reinforcement, due to the long-term and often ambiguous nature of 'success'. It has also been observed that such individuals must also have adequate intrinsic resources (e.g., self-confidence and self-respect) and extrinsic resources (e.g., stable employment) to maintain the perseverance required for primary crime prevention efforts.

Finally, because these programmes need longer implementation periods in order to have the hypothesised effect, they are more likely to need paid staff members not only to maintain continuity in programme implementation but also to pursue funding. As the Washington, DC programme has made progress in establishing their youth entrepreneurships, it has become increasingly important to have paid staff members who can take care of the myriad of complex administrative tasks usually associated with juggling several funding sources and who can continue to explore new options for expansion to insure that commitments made to local youth by the programme can be fulfilled.

Previous work on the motivations (incentives) for individual participation in voluntary associations suggests that the maintenance of primary crime prevention programmes is problematic. Much of this work (cf. Lavrakas *et al.*, 1980) which looks at the participation in a much broader spectrum of organisations, uses the typology of incentives developed by Clark and Wilson (1961). They define three types of incentives or motivations as follows: '*material* incentives . . . are those related to tangible goods such as jobs, taxes, and market opportunities; *solidary* incentives . . . are the rewards obtained from the socialising and friendships involved in group interaction; and *purposive* incentives . . . are benefits derived from the pursuit of nondivisible goods, [that is, an] ideological satisfaction associated with the organisation's efforts to achieve collective goods "which do *not* benefit the members in any direct or tangible way.''' (Berry, 1978.) Comparing these with public-minded and private-minded motivations, purposive incentives are linked to public-minded motivations, while solidary and material incentives both appear to be forms of private-minded motivations.

Of the three levels of crime prevention, primary prevention relies most heavily on purposive incentives (public-minded motivations). Other researchers have suggested that groups dependent on purposive incentives are particularly unstable, precisely because of the need for maintenance of consensus on the values being expressed through group activities (Salisbury, 1969; Sharp, 1978). Although organisations may be appealing to citizens by offering purposive (public-minded) incentives, there does not seem to be any inherent contradiction in such organisations *also* offering solidary and/or material incentives. The use of some resources to produce solidary incentives for volunteers could be effective in maintaining volunteer commitment (cf. Sharp, 1978). Eisenhower's Washington, DC programme has included a variety of field trips, picnics, a softball league, and other community activities which not only provided recreational opportunities for community members but have also contributed to a sense of 'community unity'. Further, youth members in Washington were explicitly assigned responsibilities for thinking of, and planning, these activities as part of their responsibilities to the community. Such activities provide both solidary and material incentives while also providing leadership training to some local youth, which furthers the goals of primary prevention efforts.

Secondary crime prevention

Participation in some secondary crime prevention measures also arises from public-minded motives, such as engaging in a neighbourhood foot patrol or escorting children or the elderly through areas perceived as dangerous. But here there are important motivational differences from the dynamics of primary crime prevention. The participator at the level of secondary crime prevention is not participating to help potential offenders, but rather to help potential victims. Gratification/reinforcement for these activities is not delayed, but rather occurs each time the activity is performed and no criminal event transpires. Thus, the temperament of participators in this form of crime prevention is often quite different from those engaged in primary prevention efforts, although both may be seen as having public-minded motives.

Other secondary crime prevention measures are most certainly private-minded. Traditional target-hardening measures, and other household-based crime prevention strategies typically recommended by police, are not meant to help others, but rather one's self and one's family. (In fact, in the authors' view, when such measures merely displace crime to more vulnerable—less 'hardened'—targets, society has gained little from this mode of 'prevention'.)

If efforts are made to encourage these private-minded forms of secondary crime prevention, one can appeal to citizens' fear about and concern for crime (cf. Furstenberg, 1971; Lavrakas et al., 1980) to encourage adoption and maintenance of these anti-crime approaches. So as to not overwhelm the audience with a message of hopelessness and despair, however, the levels at which fear and concern messages are targeted to the public must be carefully controlled (cf. Lavrakas, Rosenbaum and Kaminski, 1983; and O'Keefe, 1985). Thus, a rash of burglaries or purse-snatchings near banks may serve as the stimulus to organise residents. A community organiser at Eisenhower's Cleveland site was finally able to form a street club in one of her most difficult areas after a street robbery of an older man which was particularly disturbing to the residents. Similarly, the tenant patrols at Eisenhower's Bronx site formed primarily in response to specific problems (teenagers hanging about, thefts, etc.) which were of immediate concern to the residents (see also Henig, 1985).

As already mentioned, the need to build a consensus of values is less critical for secondary crime prevention efforts. This is related to at least two factors. First, for residents who, for example, are concerned about whether their unoccupied homes will be burgled, programmes which offer a means of apparent protection probably seem a direct and reasonable response. Second, there are general prototypes for a majority of these programmes—e.g., Neighbourhood Watch, Operation ID, civilian patrols, and home security checks—and so there is less need to 'design' a programme. Thus it appears more a matter of choosing the components relevant to one's community. Furthermore, these secondary crime prevention programmes are frequently supported by low enforcement agencies which often enhance their perceived legitimacy and efficacy in the eyes of most citizens (Lavrakas et al., 1980; Lavrakas et al., 1983).

While primary crime prevention programmes focus on the question of the causes of crime, secondary efforts tend to focus on the issue of the most effective means to protect residents from victimization. Residents, especially in high-crime areas, may tend to assume that crime is an unavoidable condition of urban living. Thus, in order to help build a sense of efficacy among residents, secondary prevention programmes need short-term results to demonstrate the effectiveness of their strategies. A community organiser for Eisenhower's Cleveland site explained that one of her street clubs was a success inasmuch as they had come to believe that together they could accomplish things and that they themselves—not an outside agency—were the source of the changes.

Another resource needed by many types of secondary prevention programmes is a minimal level of trust among residents. Volunteer participants at several of the Eisenhower sites have discussed the difficulties of forming block clubs when residents believe or know that drug dealers, burglars, and other offenders are living on their street. An organiser in Brooklyn holds meetings with a new block association but never discusses their drug problem openly: a member's husband is thought to be a drug dealer and so the problem is discussed with the association's officers individually, outside of meetings. Efforts to implement block watches, civilian patrols, and similar secondary crime prevention programmes assume that one can trust neighbours in banding together against offenders. That assumption will not hold initially in all neighbourhoods, which requires that programmes be modified and efforts be made to slowly build trust among residents. This is especially true in racially mixed neighbourhoods (cf. Lavrakas and Maier, 1984). In these instances, solidary incentives serving as 'rewards' for participation in collective efforts seem to become an essential ingredient.

In many ways, secondary crime prevention programmes appear easier to implement and maintain than primary crime prevention programmes. As mentioned, secondary preventive strategies are typically less dependent on a consensus of values and they are more likely to be perceived as a direct response to crime by those residents who are concerned about local crime problems. In addition, they probably offer a more balanced mix of purposive, solidary and material incentives for participants, which may be the best strategy for maintaining participation. In fact, solidary incentives may well be essential to continuation of the programme rather than serving primarily as a beneficial 'side effect' for those participating. Finally, in practical terms, there often are many resources available for the implementation of such programmes through law enforcement agencies and national organisations focused on crime prevention. These agencies provide a variety of resources, including speakers for meetings, brochures, films, identification signs for participants, etc. None the less, secondary crime prevention programmes have their own set of difficulties regarding start-up and maintenance.

First, in many respects the results of secondary programmes are not tangible in a direct sense, i.e., the desired result is the *nonoccurrence* of crime events. Several Eisenhower local programme directors have noted the problems of maintaining a project which has no tangible effects that residents can point to and claim responsibility for—in comparison, for example, to housing rehabilitation efforts which eventually result in renovated structures and new families in the community. Thus, civilian patrols and block clubs at certain Eisenhower sites frequently also engage in clean-up and general neighbourhood maintenance efforts: cleaning up a vacant lot which is then used as a playground provides a tangible outcome to remind participants of their accomplishments.

Second, many of the secondary crime prevention programmes require the presence of numerous potential leaders in the community in order to be successful; that is, people who can run block club meetings, follow-up on requests to city agencies, plan fund-raising, etc. As observed in the current Eisenhower evaluation, in many high-crime communities, residents have little previous experience with organisational activities and will typically need assistance from paid staff members or the police in developing such skills. In fact, in some communities, the identification and development of such leaders should itself be considered a significant outcome of crime prevention efforts. For communities where leadership development is a necessary part of the programme, a much longer period of implementation should be anticipated.

Third, because many secondary programmes may start in response to specific problems or crime incidents, participation in them may well be *cyclical* as people's perceptions of those problems wane. For instance, in Eisenhower's Baltimore site, residents worked hard on forming block watches to report on drug dealing activity in their neighbourhood. After some concerted effort and with the coming of colder weather, they noticed that there were fewer drug dealers in the area and relaxed their efforts. The result, not surprisingly, was an increase in drug dealers in the following spring and summer. To some extent, this ebb and flow in secondary crime prevention programmes is unavoidable and not always a source of serious concern. Some Eisenhower local project directors have commented that although particular block clubs or tenant patrols might be inactive for periods of time, residents of that block or apartment building nevertheless knew how to deal with a variety of problems and would become active on an as-needed basis. Yet in the authors' experience, it is unclear the extent to which that actually happens, at least without direct efforts from a community organisation to re-activate them.

Tertiary crime prevention

With tertiary crime prevention, one is dealing almost exclusively with private-minded motives. This is prevention in a reactive sense, and must be tailored to an individual's physical and mental capacities. In the United States, the self-improvement movement has been popular for the past decade. Self-defence training can be viewed as an extension of the basic desire to equip one's self with self-sufficiency skills. Citizens who are not over-dependent (psychologically and physically) on others for their personal welfare appear prime candidates for adopting tertiary crime prevention measures. In particular, the women's movement in the United States has achieved a considerable amount of 'consciousness raising' among women, who may be more receptive to embracing tertiary crime prevention than previously.

The majority of tertiary prevention efforts seem to offer primarily material incentives. They teach residents various means of self-defence in case of victimization. Sharp's (1978) research indicated that organisations which relied primarily on material incentives to attract and reward participators often experience severe maintenance problems. Participators tend to view those organisations as ones which performed services *for* members, rather than one with which they needed to work to accomplish goals. Certainly several of the Eisenhower project directors expressed consternation over the difficulty of making residents understand the nature of the *collective* efforts undertaken by their programmes. It may be that relying too heavily on material incentives (or private-minded volunteers) only increases that problem.

Motivations for adopting and employing tertiary anti-crime measures appear closely linked to fear of crime. In this context, 'fear' is defined as the extent to which one judges herself/himself to be at risk of becoming a victim of crime. Unfortunately, many of the people who might be most motivated by fear to adopt these tertiary measures are also those least capable of successfully 'resisting' (i.e., minimising the damage done by) instances of victimization, in particular the elderly.

As such, those anti-crime efforts that aim to increase the adoption of tertiary anti-crime measures must consider the credibility of what they are offering in the eyes of those they are attempting to reach. For example, the Eisenhower Cleveland project has considered promoting self-defence training for women residents. Before planning a specific programme, though, they attempted to survey local women to determine the 'market' for such a project. Based on their assessment of needs in the community they now plan to offer community seminars on 'violence against women', in which self-defence training will be only a part of the anti-crime education they will offer to women participants.

In the authors' opinion, then, it is important to recognise tertiary crime prevention measures for what they are: that is, they are reactive and thus cannot serve as the basis of true crime *prevention*. On the other hand, they can be used by an anti-crime programme to attract participants with primarily self-interest motives but who may eventually come to learn that they are also interested in participating in secondary and/or primary crime prevention efforts.

Considerations in implementing citizen/community crime prevention

Based on our evaluation of past work in this area, we recommend the following three-step approach to community anti-crime policy-makers and practitioners who are considering planning and implementing community crime prevention programmes.

First, there is no replacement for a careful assessment (or reassessment) of the areal crime-related problems that need addressing. Too often anti-crime efforts fail because of the failure of planners to match the programme with the specific needs of the local community. Since these programmes, by their very nature, are dependent on community support and participation it is unwise to disregard the concerns of the majority of local residents when starting a new programme. The preferred way to determine local needs is by conducting a valid survey of local residents. Although policy-makers and practitioners may think they 'know' what crime problems need addressing, it is unwise not to consider resident opinions on priorities. Even if the decision is made not to address the top concern(s) of local residents, programme planners who conduct a survey will be better informed about what level of community involvement it is realistic to expect.

Second, once the problems that will be addressed are identified, programme planners should determine what level or levels of crime prevention they will strive to achieve. Too often, anti-crime practitioners appear to use a 'shotgun' approach to anti-crime programming: one that appears to assume that by using different programme strategies which presumably worked elsewhere one has a good chance of success locally. The present chapter has attempted to provide anti-crime programme planners with a structure for reviewing programming decisions. This 'thinking' should be done prior to making the final decision about what programme strategy will be employed. Specifically, we recommend that planners be able to defend the choice of the level of crime prevention their strategy may achieve.

Third, and following directly from the first two steps, a realistic assessment of the likelihood of being able to assemble the voluntary person-time and other resources needed to successfully implement anti-crime measures at the chosen level(s) should be performed. Here we recommend careful consideration of the potential to tap into the existing dispositions of local residents and the specific type(s) of incentives that will be offered to attract participation and then maintain it. Again, a valid survey of the community is invaluable in aiding these decisions. Furthermore, in the United States, it has been recommended that the pre-existing network of local voluntary organisations (e.g., neighbourhood clubs, school groups, and church organisations) be exploited for these ends (cf. Lavrakas, 1985).

Additional research questions

This paper has addressed the issue of volunteer motivations and programme implementation on a general level only. Within the constraints of the paper, it was not possible to consider the impact of the specific characteristics of the local environment, including the local organisational environment.

Additional questions which would have policy implications include the following: (1) how does the socio-economic level and racial composition of the community affect the recruitment and maintenance of volunteers, (2) how does the previous orientation of the community organisation affect the recruitment and maintenance of volunteers, (3) can a community organisation effectively combine primary and secondary crime prevention efforts in its programme, and (4) to what extent can outside agencies (e.g., a city police department) initiate and maintain a community crime prevention programme?

Although advances have been made in the knowledge available regarding the planning and implementation of community anti-crime programmes during the past 20 years, much remains to be learned from carefully planned and executed research and evaluation studies. We do not suggest that policy-makers and practitioners must await the results of future studies before implementing community anti-crime programmes, but it would be prudent for them to remember the rather limited knowledge-base in this topic area. Continued research and evaluations must be supported for the field to advance.

References

BENNETT, S. F. and LAVRAKAS, P. J. (1986). *A Process and Impact Evaluation of the Baltimore Neighbourhood Anti-crime Self-help Programme.* Evanston, Ill.: Center for Urban Affairs and Policy Research.

BERRY, J. M. (1978). 'On the origins of public interest groups: a test of two theories'. *Polity*, 10, pp. 379–397.

CLARK, P. B. and WILSON, J. Q. (1961). 'Incentive systems: a theory of organizations'. *Administrative Science Quarterly*, 6, pp. 129–166.

CURRIE, E. (1985). *Confronting Crime.* New York: Pantheon Books.

CURTIS, L. (Ed.). (1985). *American Violence and Public Policy.* New Haven: Yale University Press.

DUBOW, F., McPHERSON, M. and SILLOWAY, G. (1985). 'Neighbourhood watch as a strategy of community crime prevention'. In symposium: *Public Justice: Crime Prevention, Mediation and the Community.* American Society of Criminology Annual Meeting, San Diego.

FURSTENBERG, F. F. (1971). 'Public reaction to crime in the streets'. *American Scholar*, 11, pp. 601–610.

GAROFALO, J. and McCLEOD, M. (1985). 'A national overview of the neighbourhood watch programme.' In symposium: *Neighbourhood Watch Approaches to Reducing Violent Crime and Fear.* American Society of Criminology Annual Meeting, San Diego.

HENIG, J. (1985). 'Citizens against crime: an assessment of the Washington, DC neighbourhood watch'. In symposium: *Neighbourhood Watch Approaches to Reducing Violent Crime and Fear.* American Society of Criminology Annual Meeting, San Diego.

LAVRAKAS, P. J. (1985). 'Citizen self-help and neighbourhood crime prevention policy'. In Curtis, L. (Ed.), *American Violence and Public Policy.* New Haven: Yale University Press.

LAVRAKAS, P. J., SKOGAN, W., NORMOYLE, J., HERZ, E. J., SALEM, G. and LEWIS, D. A. (1980). *Factors Related to Citizen Involvement in Personal, Household and Neighbourhood Anti-crime Measures.* Evanston, Ill.: Center for Urban Affairs and Policy Research.

LAVRAKAS, P. J., ROSENBAUM, D. P. and KAMINSKI, F. (1983). 'Transmitting information about crime and crime prevention to citizens'. *Journal of Police Sciences and Administration*, 11, pp. 463–473.

LAVRAKAS, P. J. and MAIER, R. A. Jr. (1984). 'Racial differences and a barrier to effective anti-crime programming'. In symposium: *Constructive and Destructive Forces in Community Crime Prevention.* American Psychological Association Annual Convention, Toronto.

NATIONAL CRIME PREVENTION COUNCIL, (1986). *Crime Prevention: Status and Trends 1986.* Washington, DC.

O'KEEFE, G. (1985). 'Taking a bite out of crime: the impact of a public information campaign'. *Communications Research*, 12, pp. 147–178.

PODOLEFSKY, A. (1984). 'Rejecting crime prevention programmes: the dynamics of programme implementation in high need communities'. Paper presented at the meeting of the Academy of Criminal Justice Sciences, Chicago, Ill.

PODELEFSKY, A. and DUBOW, F. (1981). *Strategies for Community Crime Prevention: Collective Responses to Crime in Urban America.* Evanston, Ill.: Center for Urban Affairs and Policy Research.

ROSENBAUM, D. P. (1987). 'The theory and research behind neighbourhood watch: is it a sound fear and crime reduction strategy?' *Crime and Delinquency*, 33, pp. 103–134.

ROSENBAUM, D. P., LEWIS, D. A. and GRANT, J. (1985). *The Impact of Community Crime Prevention Programmes in Chicago: Can Neighbourhood Organizations Make a Difference?* Evanston, Ill.: Center for Urban Affairs and Policy Research.

SALISBURY, R. (1969). 'An exchange theory of interest groups'. *Midwest Journal of Political Science*, 13, pp. 1–32.

SHARP, E. B. (1978). 'Citizen organizations in policing issues and crime prevention: incentives for participation'. *Journal of Voluntary Action Research*, 7, pp. 45–58.

SILBERMAN, C. E. (1978). *Criminal Violence, Criminal Justice.* New York: Random House.

WEISS, C. (1972). *Evaluation Research.* Englewood Cliffs, NJ: Prentice-Hall.

WILSON, J. Q. (1975). *Thinking About Crime.* New York: Basic Books.

International Perspectives on Policy

While making no claim for comprehensiveness, these four chapters provide a working account of how four Western countries are tackling crime prevention. They provide considerable evidence of both recent confidence and energy being put into the problem of how to prevent crime, and of particular programmes adapted to specific conditions, as well as a convergence of views on the need to shift the burden of prevention away from an almost exclusive reliance on the criminal justice system. Chapter 14, based primarily on recent experience in the development of situational prevention, deals with three issues at what it argues are a watershed in the development of a preventive approach to crime in Britain. These are the relationships between social and situational measures of crime prevention, problems of the displacement of crime to other areas—one of the major criticisms of situational crime prevention—and the ways in which this can be circumvented. The final section deals with implementation issues, particularly at the corporate and local authority level.

Chapter 15 traces the changes in attitudes to crime prevention in Canada which have been associated with the evolving role of the police. It describes a range of successful and innovative community crime prevention programmes, and bears witness to a determination to move now towards a broader crime reductive approach with a programme of social crime prevention. Chapter 16 provides an account of the quite dramatic changes which have been taking place in France since 1982 in a determination to confront increased crime, violence and unrest among young people in many French cities. The newly created National Council for the Prevention of Crime has set up a network of local community councils. These have in turn established a wide range of projects ranging from leisure, educational and employment provisions, to victim support and offender rehabilitation. Chapter 17 outlines the factors which led to a reassessment of policies to deal with crime and delinquency in The Netherlands which rose sharply over the period of the 1970s, and describes the programme of projects and research which have been set up since 1985. They constitute the new social crime prevention programme, which includes situational approaches, social crime reduction, and emphasises integrated action by local authorities, the police and public prosecutors. The focus is largely on the prevention of petty crime, and upon the construction of viable alternatives to the former socialising and supervisory structures in Dutch society. Some of the projects are already showing good results.

14. The development of crime prevention: issues and limitations

Kevin Heal and Gloria Laycock

Since the turn of the decade Central Government in England and Wales, together with some police forces, voluntary organisations and local authorities have attempted to change the emphasis of their response to crime. Although each organisation has had its own particular reason, or set of reasons, for contributing to this process those involved have had a common goal in seeking to reinforce the place of prevention in strategies against crime, and a common belief that responsibility for prevention should lie, not solely with the police, but with a range of organisations which collectively shape the community. Within Central Government it is possible to discern a clear trend from initiatives to strategies, and from strategies to policies. Svensson (1986), writing on the basis of Scandinavian experience, comments on the importance of this transition, recalling that the crime rate of a country depends less upon police activity than upon trends in housing design and management, education, modes of production and lifestyles.

The British Government's emphasis on crime prevention is most clearly illustrated by the formation, in 1986, of a Ministerial Group on Crime Prevention. This group, chaired by a Home Office minister, seeks to identify and strengthen the crime prevention activity of the work of twelve separate government departments. The formation of the Group marks not the beginning of a single policy for crime prevention, but the recognition that many policies have a bearing on crime.

Not all national activity has been within Central Government. Within the private sector there have been changes in production and marketing methods moving in favour of prevention. Some companies, for example, are seeking to enter what is seen to be the profitable security hardware market. While this action has been taken for what are judged to be sound business reasons, the commercial advertising campaigns which accompany it have drawn to the attention of the public at large the effectiveness of preventive action against crime. For example, some car manufacturing companies now advertise security as a desirable characteristic of the family car. Of more direct bearing on public behaviour is the decision by several insurance companies to provide premium discounts for those policy holders who choose to improve the security of their homes. Given that the 'add-on' costs of household and vehicle security are minimal at the building and manufacturing stage, there are grounds for believing these developments could mark the start of a trend within which 'good security' becomes a marketable product. If this is so the power of the consumer will promote the development of prevention.

At the local level there has been a noticeable expansion of projects, schemes and initiatives. Some have been seeded by central action: for example the local inter-agency demonstration projects established in 1986 in Bolton, Swansea, Wellingborough, Croydon and North Tyneside with modest Home Office funding. Other local schemes are supported through the Manpower Services

Commission's crime prevention initiative within the Community Programme. In contrast some action is entirely local, with initiative springing up from the community itself. This is the case with 'neighbourhood watch' where the past five years have seen the establishment of some 29,000 schemes.

Despite this activity it would be wrong to assume that all organisations with the capability to prevent crime are actively committed to doing so. Many private sector companies hold the view that the control of crime is a matter for the police not their shareholders; plenty of voluntary agencies have yet to develop a preventive aspect to their work, and comparatively few local authorities have come to accept that the way in which services are provided influences the level of crime within the communities for which they are responsible.

Arguably the preventive response to crime is at a watershed. There has been a significant shift in favour of prevention but much apathy and sceptism remains and recent developments have highlighted a number of key issues. Some of the more important of these are considered in this chapter in an attempt to identify the limitations to preventive action. These are: the relationship between social and situational measures; the displacement of crime, and the implementation of preventive measures.

Social and situational measures

Writing in 1976 Brantingham and Faust divided preventive activity into primary, secondary and tertiary measures:

primary crime prevention identifies conditions in which the physical and social environments facilitate criminal acts, and alters those conditions;

secondary prevention identifies potential offenders (i.e. those at risk) and intervenes in their lives in an attempt to prevent them from committing offences, and lastly

tertiary crime prevention seeks to keep people who have already committed crime from committing further offences by incapacitation.

While there is a degree of overlap between the activities falling into these categories, this chapter focuses on what Brantingham and Faust refer to as primary prevention, within which they place both social and situational measures against crime. During the last three to four years, however, interest has centred largely, although not solely, on situational factors. This emphasis has to some extent been a 'catching up' exercise. As Clarke (1981) argued, the situational prevention of crimes was limited in its scale of effort in the face of a growing crime problem and a great deal of detailed work needed to be done. Although police forces each had a staff of crime prevention officers, and the Home Office supported police training and publicity in this field, as well as a growing number of local crime prevention panels, there was an emphasis on locks and bolts to the detriment of the wider situational possibilities.

Recent activity aimed at the wider situational field has raised yet again the spectre of a 'fortress society': one in which locks, bolts, bars and self-interest dominate. All are unattractive in themselves—but they are also felt to favour those who can afford security, at the expense of those less able to protect themselves and what little property they may have. In the light of this criticism attention is starting to swing back to social measures which have been defined as dealing with the 'fundamental causes of crime' which Clarke (*ibid*) divided into broad social policies intended to promote respect for moral values (i.e. change attitudes) or reduced criminogenic inequalities, and more localised measures meant to increase community solidarity, improve police/public relations and provide diversionary facilities for 'alienated' youth. In contrast, situational measures were seen as operating on the opportunity structure for offending: reducing opportunity and increasing risk in line with an 'economic theory' conceptualisation of offender behaviour (Cook, 1986).

At one level, the social/situational distinction is helpful. It places target hardening and design modification in the situational mould, where some would agree they should best be placed, whilst improvements in housing allocation policy, or increased leisure and work opportunity are seen as social measures. But where should the surveillance element (normally associated with design and closed circuit television) in a neighbourhood watch initiative be placed? Since it relies upon individual action and is clearly distinct from design or target hardening then it should perhaps be seen as a social crime prevention measure. To take further examples, a situational measure such as property marking can affect community relations in some circumstances (Laycock, 1985) and a social measure, such as increased work opportunity, can have situational implications if it involves a lock-fitting scheme for the elderly (Home Office, Crime Prevention Unit, 1986).

Anomalies such as these cast considerable doubt upon the value of attempting to seek out differences between social and situational measures, and weight the advantages of one against the other. The anomalies suggest that in practice social and situational measures are best seen as opposite sides of the same coin—reducing criminal opportunity on the one hand whilst increasing socially acceptable behavioural opportunities on the other, and that the principal issue to be addressed should be not the *separation* of the measures but the development of a framework within which both have a part to play.

While the activity over the past two or three years directed at reducing opportunities for crime has been reasonably successful, and it is important that the work continues, it is also important that steps are taken to increase opportunities for non-criminal activity, that is opportunities for worthwhile employment, leisure and participation in community life. The pre-emptive approach is thus as much concerned with the creation of opportunities for legitimate behaviour as with the blocking of opportunities for illegitimate behaviour in any given locality.

But there is more to this approach than structuring opportunities. There is also a case for ensuring that individuals, particularly those in the age groups frequently engaged in crime, have the necessary economic and social skills to participate in the opportunities for non-criminal behaviour and, as the corollary to this, do not obtain the skills needed to commit crime. The rationale behind this framework is linked to the idea that the individual's behaviour (criminal or non criminal) depends upon the rewards, risks, and effort associated with a particular act. Thus if it is more profitable (in terms of economic or social status) to commit a crime than to engage in some form of legitimate activity, and the risks of apprehension are low, it is likely (indeed some would say sensible) to commit the crime.

In sum if the individual has the skills and opportunities to participate in non-crime behaviour, and if that behaviour brings adequate rewards, then he or she is less likely to turn to crime. This view of behaviour provides a broad objective for pre-emptive action. It also provides a context within which social and situational measures can be seen as complementary.

Crime displacement

The argument most frequently levelled against prevention, particularly 'situational' prevention, is that it will displace crime from one setting to the next, or from one type of crime to another. If this is indeed the case the limits to prevention are considerable.

Displacement is complex and varies in its extent and nature by crime and situation. It is helpful, therefore, in attempting to assess the strength of the argument against prevention, to identify the conditions and situations within which displacement is most likely to occur. To take an obvious example, where crime is primarily an aggressive response to frustrating events or inequalities, there is a greater likelihood that the introduction of preventive measures to block opportunities will lead to displacement. On the other hand, where there is a strong opportunistic element to crime, steps taken to make its commission more risky, difficult or costly will not necessarily result in displacement. The activities of these weakly motivated offenders, who are largely responding to an opportunity, will be more easily diverted to non-criminal behaviour. Bennett (1986) takes discussion a stage further by separating the initial decision to offend, which might be psychologically determined, from the final decision to offend which is more likely to be situationally influenced.

Moving on from the motivation of the offender to the criminal opportunity structure of the environment, the more plentiful the crime targets the more likely the displacement will be. So, for example, if the security of one type of vehicle was to be improved to the extent that it was totally protected, this would not lead to a reduction in auto-crime since the pool of vulnerable cars remains substantial. Even in those situations where it is possible to protect *all* property of a particular type, the criminal may well respond by directing his efforts elsewhere. The point is readily illustrated by reference to attacks on banks, post offices and building societies where the protection of these premises appears to have resulted in an increase in attacks on cash-in-transit, particularly duress attacks where the courier is threatened while outside the protection of his vehicle (Home Office, 1986).

The discussion so far has focused on the traditional view of displacement in which the protection of one target deflects crime to another. There are, however, other ways in which relatively low-risk targets can become vulnerable. For example, work conducted by Hill (1986) has shown that on housing estates containing a high proportion of vulnerable houses (in that they contain pre-payment fuel meters) the burglary risk rate for *all* houses is high. Thus the overall risk rate of burglary on the estate was not dependent upon the risk rates of the houses taken individually, but upon the rates of those houses *most* at risk. It seems, therefore, that while the burglar may be aware that some houses on an estate are worth attacking, he is not sure which houses these are. They act as a 'magnet' to the whole estate, but once there, the burglar attacks at random with the result that houses without meters are attacked as frequently as those with.

There are of course a number of ways in which the probability of displacement can be reduced. Accepting that much crime is associated with the interaction between the criminal and those seeking to prevent crime, it is at least arguable that foresight on the part of the practitioner would do much to reduce displacement. Such is the case in attempts to reduce attacks on commercial premises where the introduction—at the initial stage—of a package of measures (including the provision of secure vehicle loading bays) would have limited the cash-in-transit attacks referred to above.

The risk of displacement may also be reduced by ensuring that measures to reduce opportunities for criminal behaviour are complemented by steps to increase the scope for individuals to meet their needs (economic or social) through acceptable channels. Clearly the behaviour of the offender who is making a good living from crime will not be influenced by the provision of leisure facilities, job training opportunities or welcoming, cohesive communities. However, few are in this position and many show a marked degree of ineptitude in committing crime, characteristics which suggest their decisions for or against criminal activity may well be influenced by the provision of alternative ways of meeting their individual needs, particularly when the risks are less and the rewards equal or greater.

Lastly, displacement can be minimised where a preventive initiative aimed at one type of crime has a *beneficial* effect in terms of reducing other types of crime. Taking the example of a property marking experiment in South Wales, Laycock (1985) showed that, for quite co-incidental reasons, in one area the initiative not only reduced theft of markable goods but also the theft of goods which had not been marked, such as cash.

To sum up, in trying to understand displacement it is necessary to keep several points in mind. These include the characteristics of the individual offender; the vulnerability of targets available to him, and (and this might be different) his perception of those targets; the stages in the offender's decision-making process, with action and counter action between the offender and those seeking to prevent crime; and lastly the possibility that preventive action against crime *can* have a scatter gun approach and protect or endanger, often incidentally, other nearby targets.

Within this framework displacement is more likely to occur following a preventive intervention when:

    a.   the offender's personal motivation or drive is strong;

    b.   when many alternative targets are available or perceived to be available;

    c.   where those designing preventive measures fail to take account of the potential for action and counter action;

    d.   where low vulnerability targets are in close proximity to highly vulnerable targets.

It is understandable why displacement is difficult to predict. Nevertheless there is every reason to believe that well thought out preventive action will result in weakly motivated offenders—or those having alternative behavioural options available to them—refraining from committing crime. It is also true, however, that those remaining may increase the sophistication of their attacks or direct their attention to those who cannot protect themselves. This does not necessarily mean that attempts to prevent crime should stop. While the first round of preventive measures may, in some circumstances, lead to other crimes, many of these can probably be blocked effectively. Moreover the process can continue in such a way as not to constrain the freedom of the public or turn communities into fortresses.

Implementation of crime prevention measures

The prevention of crime, like the prevention of disease, wins popular support from most, if not all sections of society. But the difficulties of translating support in principle to support in practice, have increasingly become the subject of debate (Hope, 1985). In many respects it would be surprising if there were not difficulties. Because of the traditional expectation that the police will take responsibility for crime control, in a variety of areas the development of preventive measures (including situational measures) has fallen behind or simply been disregarded; there is, therefore, much to be done. Comparison can be drawn with the prevention of disease, where we now have a highly sophisticated system ranging from the individual's personal attention to hygiene (on which incidently, action is based on habit rather than fear), to the network of underground sewers and other design features which give further protection. Preventive medicine was built up over many years and called for, *inter alia*, major re-education. The public needed to realise that responsibility for the prevention of disease rested not with the medical profession but with them as individuals and with many other agencies and organisations. In drawing this comparison it becomes clear that crime prevention has some way to go. The vast majority of individuals and organisations persist in the view that responsibility for crime control rests with the police alone.

It is not, however, universally true that preventive possibilities are ignored. The most obvious, and effective, example is in relation to High Street banks. Here, highly vulnerable targets have been well protected for many years, originally through high staffing ratios and rudimentary target hardening; more recently, through advanced technology. In looking at this development it is possible to ask why security provision in this area has progressed whilst, for example, with the development of the supermarket, prevention in relation to the retail trade has declined.

There appear to be a number of factors operating. First the *costs* of crime to the banking industry are potentially high, and in a competitive market losses on such a scale cannot be simply absorbed. Nor can managers ignore the possibility of violence to their staff who would, without protection, be particularly vulnerable to attack. Thus there is a recognised need for prevention over and above that associated with the criminal justice processes of incapacitation and deterrence. Furthermore since the banks have both the resources to take action and the necessary control of the banking environment, they have the *capacity* to act. Banks and other commercial organisations have, therefore, taken their corporate *responsibility* for the prevention of robbery. This leads on to the question of why the development of prevention in other areas is comparatively slow. In the remainder of this section three further offences will be considered—motor vehicle crime, shop crime and domestic burglary—in relation to the costs of crime and the capacity and responsibility for its prevention. This section goes on to consider what needs to be done in relation to these offences if prevention is to move forward.

Taking first the example of the vulnerability of the motor vehicle, manufacturers have the capacity to build security into vehicles at the design stage. Traditionally they have not done so because the cost of vehicle insecurity (i.e. crime) is not borne directly by them, and they have seen crime prevention as a police matter. Moreover, the cost of auto-crime is not a heavy burden for the individual driver, since legislative demands in relation to the protection of potential accident victims mean that insurance for theft of and from vehicles can be provided comparatively cheaply. Crime costs, thus shared, lose their otherwise powerfully motivating potency (*vide* banking) particularly when we disregard the costs to the public purse associated with police investigation of auto-crime, estimated at £10m per annum (Home Office, 1985).

Turning to shop crime, similar factors operate. The move from high staffing level counter service to low staffed supermarket layouts brought with it increased turnover, but also increased crime, since the preventive role of the counter staff was overlooked. The response of the retailer was to introduce closed circuit television and mirrors, but primarily to employ store detectives, thus illustrating the confidence of store managers in the arrest, prosecution and sentencing approach to crime control.

Responsibility for crime control is seen, therefore, as a police matter and, although the stores have the capacity to take effective preventive measures (through for example, changes in layout and selling procedures) these measures tend to be rudimentary since the costs of crime can in most cases be passed on to customers, and the offenders, once caught, can be passed to the police.

Finally, the poor security of many homes is a contributory factor in domestic burglary. There are two issues here in relation to implementation. The *level* of security provision and the *use* of such measures as are provided and installed.

Approaching the problem from the perspective of the local police sub-divisional commander, who is generally held responsible for neighbourhood crime control, it becomes clear that the police need the support of the community which they aim to protect. This could not be more obvious than in relation to the use of security hardware, where it is for the householder to ensure that doors and windows are locked. Thus whilst the local police divisional commander may be regarded as *responsible* for preventing burglary on an estate, as far as security of individual properties is concerned he relies on the residents. In addition, if on a hard-pressed estate few residents could meet the cost of installing window locks and improving the quality of door locks, the divisional commander must look to the local housing department for action. In two respects therefore the capacity to prevent crime does not fall within his control. Where do the costs fall? Primarily with the resident who will suffer the distress of burglary and, if uninsured, will bear its cost directly. In this particular case, therefore, there is a notable mismatch between the costs of the crime, which falls in one direction, the capacity to do something about it, which, in part at least, falls in another, and responsibility for prevention which is assumed to rest with the police.

What can be done to facilitate the implementation of crime prevention measures? There are a number of possibilities which, in their various forms, amount to re-education of the general public, and the relevant agencies and organisations. First, it needs to be accepted that the police do not have sole responsibility for crime control. They can, however, carry out a vital catalytic role in drawing crime problems to the attention of those agencies with the capacity for action. In doing this they may point to the costs of crime to the victim and to the public purse.

Placing the crime facts before an organisation or individual may be a necessary first step toward change but this in itself may not lead to the desired action. The most obvious tactic is to demonstrate that preventive action is in the best interests of the organisation. For example, a local education authority or housing department might do well to consider carefully the advantages of replacing traditional fragile glazing with the more robust material now available on the market so reducing what, in some parts of the country, are bills for broken windows running into hundreds of thousands of pounds. Such action, which could become part and parcel of a refurbishment scheme, removes a major target of crime. Theft of company assets, an expensive item for some employers, can be reduced by changes in management practice (Smith and Burrows, 1986). On a different tack, as consumer interest begins to focus on security and crime prevention, it may well be that a company needs to take preventive action simply to avoid a bad press. The motor manufacturer responsible for the production of a particularly insecure car, or housing contractor noted for skimping material on doorframes, door locks, window jambs etc., may well see advantage in changing current practices simply to maintain the 'image' of the product he is trying to sell.

Self-interest also bears, of course, on the position of the individual who often takes action on the basis of fear. An experiment in Newark, New Jersey (Kelling, 1981) illustrated that where fear was reduced through increased police activity, the public became more lax in their security behaviour. If this is the case, attempts to reduce fear may actually dissuade individuals from taking preventive action.

Clearly a balance must be struck between promoting good security behaviour and not alarming the individual. In practice, how this balance is achieved must be determined by the characteristics of a particular locality. In areas where the risk of crime is high, it is likely that people will have an accurate picture of the extent of offending and any fear is unlikely to be raised by talking about the crime problem. Here people need to be persuaded that crime can be reduced through their own activity. However, in areas where crime is low but fear high, the task is to counter the alarmist impression given, perhaps by the local media, without creating complacency. The message must be that crime is not out of control and that sensible measures will suffice to maintain the existing well-being of the community.

There is, therefore, a need for a degree of care in those situations where fear is a stimulus for action, and it is useful to draw a distinction between fear of crime and concern about crime. Few people are so fearful of becoming a victim of a road traffic accident that they will not venture on to the road. However, most are sufficiently aware of the problem to show a reasonable degree of road sense when out and about, and one might take a similar position in dealing with crime.

Finally, where an organisation is responsible for the provision of a service (e.g. a bus service or medical care) it is possible to argue that responsibility *should* extend to the provision of the service within an environment which is free from crime. Thus it is not sufficient to ensure that passengers are transported from a. to point b; it is also a necessary condition of a good service that they are not assaulted along the way. Taking the point more broadly, and looking to local authorities and those providing services in the community, one might argue that on all occasions the criteria against which a service is judged should include whether or not it contributes to the crime problem or works to minimise it. Within this framework all the planning of communities, design of houses, provision of services (education, housing, health, etc.) can be seen to have crime prevention implications. Those responsible for shaping services and setting the criteria against which they are assessed, need to include the prevention of crime within their considerations.

References

BENNETT, T. (1986). 'Situational crime prevention from the offenders' perspective.' In Heal, K. and Laycock, G. (Eds.), *Situational Crime Prevention: from theory into practice*. London: HMSO.

BRANTINGHAM, P. J. and FAUST, F. L. (1976). 'A Conceptual Model of Crime Prevention.' *Crime and Delinquency*, 22, pp.   .

CLARKE, R. (1981). 'The prospects for controlling crime.' *Research Bulletin* No. 12. London: Home Office Research and Planning Unit.

CLARKE, R. V. G. (1983). 'Situational crime prevention.' In Tonry, M. and Morris, N. (Eds.), *Crime and Justice: an Annual Review of Research vol. 4*. Chicago: University of Chicago Press.

COOK, P. J. (1986). 'The demand and supply of criminal opportunities.' In Tonry, M. and Morris, N. (Eds.), *Crime and Justice: an Annual Review of Research vol. 7*. Chicago: University of Chicago Press.

HILL, N. (1986). *Prepayment Coin Meters: a target for burglary*. Crime Prevention Unit Paper No. 6. London: Home Office.

HOME OFFICE, (1985). *Report of the Working Group on Car Security*. Produced for the Home Office Standing Conference on Crime Prevention, November, 1985. Available from Home Office, 50 Queen Anne's Gate, London SW1.

HOME OFFICE, (1986). *Report of the Standing Conference Working Group on Commercial Robbery*. London: Home Office.

HOME OFFICE CRIME PREVENTION UNIT, (1986). *Crime Prevention and the Community Programme: a practical guide*. Available from the Home Office Crime Prevention Unit, 50 Queen Anne's Gate, London SW1.

HOPE, T. (1985). *Implementing Crime Prevention Measures*. Home Office Research Study No. 86. London: HMSO.

KELLING, G. L. (1981). *'Conclusions' in The Newark Foot Patrol Experiment*. Washington DC: Police Foundation.

LAYCOCK, G. (1985) *Property Marking: a deterrent to domestic burglary?* Home Office Crime Prevention Unit Paper No. 3. London: Home Office.

SMITH, L. J. F. and BURROWS, J. (1986). 'Nobbling the fraudsters: crime prevention through administrative change.' *The Howard Journal of Criminal Justice* 25, pp. 13–24.

SVENSSON, B. (1986). 'Welfare and criminality in Sweden.' In Heal, K. and Laycock, G. (Eds.), *Situational Crime Prevention: from theory into practice*. London: HMSO

15. Crime prevention in Canada

Christopher P Nuttall

The geographic, social, economic, and political characteristics of Canada affect crime prevention as they affect everything else. Some significantly affect crime prevention. The first of these factors is the United States. The United States, with ten times the population, a somewhat richer economy and a world leadership role, affects Canada at all levels. Culturally many outsiders find it difficult to distinguish between McDonald's USA and McDonald's Canada; that is, the two countries are very similar. (At the same time, they are very different.)

Probably the most pervasive American influence is television. Because most Canadians live within a hundred miles of the United States border, many watch United States television news and crime dramas and sometimes confuse themselves as to where they live. Thus Canadian levels of fear of crime are similar to those of the United States, although the actual extent of crime is only one fifth as great *per capita*. Public opinion polls indicate a desire for more and longer prison sentences, due mainly to continuous exposure to American crime problems. Thus US proximity and the myths this produces about crime are major factors in any consideration of Canadian crime and criminal justice. The second major factor is that the USA, with fifty-one criminal codes and a very large number of criminal justice jurisdictions, provides a sort of laboratory where Canadians can observe the successes and failures of new ideas before adopting or adapting them.

Yet Canada is very different from the United States. In the United States the West was opened up more or less at gunpoint, whereas in Canada settlers did not move into the prairies in large numbers until the Northwest Mounted Police had established law and order. Canadians place a great value on social order and indeed Canadian ideals for government have been characterised as Peace, Order and Good Government. Canadians therefore expect, and will pay a considerable price for, a peaceful community. The relatively uneventful passage and general public acceptance of gun control legislation is one example of this attitude.

Demographically the United States and Canada are somewhat different. The US population has significant proportions of black and Hispanic people who have disproportionately high crime rates. Canada's origins lie in two founding groups: one French-speaking and the other English-speaking from the British Isles. This has changed considerably in the latter half of the twentieth century: the population now is approximately one-third French in origin, one-third from the British Isles, and one-third from southern and eastern Europe, and from Asia and the Caribbean. Nevertheless, compared to the United States the society is small and, with respect to the inner city, relatively safe.

Economically, the United States and Canada are not very different in terms of final income per head of population. Canadians have, therefore, compared with many other countries, significant amounts of property to lose and this too may affect their attitudes to crime and crime prevention.

Finally, it is probably true to say that Canadians have a greater feeling of community than many Europeans, and that this has affected the ability of authorities and community groups to persuade citizens of the utility of community action. As such action appears to be essential for crime prevention, Canada would appear to have advantages which many other countries may not possess.

Crime prevention and criminological theory

Canadian academics have not as yet produced any particularly Canadian criminological theory. The theoretical underpinnings of crime and crime prevention in Canada do not differ in any marked degree from those in other Western democracies. Pre-war theories were based upon notions of 'born criminals' and on the works of Freud and Lombroso. Since on this basis people were either criminal or not criminal, depending on upbringing or genetics, crime prevention depended upon incapacitation, segregation and deterrence. In the 1940s and 50s, the emphasis was upon behaviour rather than people. Although their behaviour might be deviant, offenders were fundamentally no different from anyone else. Thus crime prevention could be achieved through rehabilitation of the offender and the abolition of the social conditions which led to crime.

In the 1960s and early 1970s, labelling theory led toward notions of decriminalisation and minimal intrusion into offenders' lives and away from the massive social intervention of the previous two decades. In the 1970s and early 80s, criminologists reacted against all of these theories, and indeed became to some extent anti-theoretical, stimulated by the belief that 'nothing works' and that the search for root causes of crime was pointless. There was a return to positivism and belief in the utility of evaluation. Crime prevention, therefore, became concerned with opportunity reduction, target hardening and swift and sure apprehension.

In the late 1980s there is still a strong anti-theoretical element. Criminal justice has been refocused and academics have become more eclectic. There is no overall belief in any particular school, and pragmatism has almost been raised to an ideology. One area that has received more attention than the past is the notion of community. Both left and right wing ideologies have converged on community. Hence, crime prevention through community development has become a very important theme in Canada, although more recently there has also been a return to modified ideas of crime prevention through social development. Some radical criminologists are asking whether or not belief in communities has not gone too far and have questioned the morality of over-intrusive communities, but further theoretical development is needed in this area.

Criminological theories are, however, compounded by police behaviour, beliefs, and practices. And because the police are and will continue to be central to crime prevention methods and practices, it is police actions and pressures on the police that will largely determine the shape of crime prevention. If crime prevention is to become a fundamental feature of criminal policy then it will achieve this through acceptance by the police. It is not yet a fundamental feature but it may become so over the next few years. Crime prevention in the early 1970s was largely target-hardening. In the later 1970s it was based on what is now known as preventive policing and, so far in the 1980s, on co-operative police-community prevention activities; i.e., the police act in partnership with the community to define problems and solutions.

Policing and crime prevention

No specific emphasis on police or community-based crime prevention as we know it now was evident in Canada before the 1970s, after which it formed part of a broad development in policing methods throughout North America. Prior to this period, so far back as the 1890s, there had been an emphasis on increasing police efficiency and response times through telephones, automobiles, bicycles, and radios. The norm for the police throughout North America was reactive law enforcement.

Up to the 1970s, therefore, the police concentrated mainly on improvements in hardware—fire-power, car performance, technology—and measured their performance in statistics—clear-up rates, arrest rates, response times and Uniform Crime Reports. Such features were measurable and rewardable, unlike some of the more intangible aspects of prevention. The emphasis on these aspects of policing meant that community crime prevention as it is now understood was very largely ignored. Even when lip-service was paid to crime prevention, the agency Crime Prevention Officer was on the whole irrelevant.

An increasing emphasis on crime prevention came from both inside and outside the Canadian police community. With police forces of enormous size and complexity, costs had risen, without clear evidence that the technologically sophisticated force was more effective than its predecessors. Policing was, if not bankrupting Canadian municipalities and provinces, seriously reducing the resources available for other community services. Thus while in countries such as Britain and the USA, social unrest and riots were also a catalyst to change, the primary force for the reappraisal of the role of the Canadian police was financial. During the 1970s, therefore, there was a shift to a form of policing directed to more efficient law enforcement, better police relationships with the community, and improved crime prevention.

For the police, however, the practice of community policing was not easy to accept. It required the police to police their beats alone, rather than in pairs. It required local decision-making and autonomy, and diminished central police control. It required the police to find out what the community needed and wanted rather than making assumptions about those needs. And it provided no easy measures of success or failure. Finally, it did not require extensive hardware or measurement, and it seemed to require a long time to produce tangible results.

Nevertheless, with evidence of some successful community policing programmes such as the Flint, Michigan, Neighbourhood Foot Patrol Programme (Trojanowicz, 1982), there is now wide acceptance of the legitimacy of the concept of community policing, as a 1986 Workshop for senior Canadian police executives demonstrated. (It is perhaps significant that since 1975 there has been very little increase in police numbers in most major Canadian police departments. Indeed, the overall number—about 54,000—seems to have declined slightly over the last two or three years.)

In 1982, the Secretariat of the federal Solicitor General, in collaboration with the Royal Canadian Mounted Police, produced a review of critical community policing issues and a model for development that stimulated a number of initiatives in Canadian police departments and training colleges. Perhaps the most dramatic change, however, has been that along with community policing has come the concept of 'preventive policing'.

Initially, the focus for crime prevention was primarily on 'target hardening': i.e., better locks, lights, alarms and other devices to protect residential and business premises, and on the reduction of opportunities for crime, and only secondarily upon community crime prevention. In Canada this meant that community-based crime prevention programmes normally were implemented or co-ordinated by the police, and oriented towards victims or the environment, rather than towards offenders. Its development in Canada, following upon American initiatives, was marked by the establishment of the highly successful *Block Parents* programme in 1972, by the entry of the Solicitor General into the development of national preventive policing policy in 1976 (including the recruitment of the first senior policeman as National Advisor to the Ministry the following year) and the development of Neighbourhood Watch by 1980. In all of this activity, the Solicitor General played a very influential role in working with the police, publishing and disseminating pamphlets, logos and training manuals, helping to set up courses in crime prevention, and working with police committees on research and policy development.

The Solicitor General's contribution to crime prevention research

In Canada, the federal leadership role has been very effective. Given a country with a population of only 25½ million people, spread across 5,000 miles over a land area of 3½ million square miles, with one federal, ten provincial, two territorial and innumerable municipal governments, and with policing responsibility divided among federal, provincial and municipal agencies, a provincial or municipal leadership capability would be unlikely to develop.

'Working Together to Prevent Crime' is the slogan, combined with a logo of a family group and a police officer, which has been used across Canada to foster the development of the community policing approach to crime prevention. This has been accompanied by the development of police mini-stations, foot patrols, community crime surveys and neighbourhood watch programmes—which now cover a large percentage (about 25%) of the Canadian population, so successful has been the response to this particular idea.

Crime prevention research first received specific attention in the Ministry research programme of 1976–77, together with research on victimization. The programme received considerable funding for external research, and included work on victim surveys originally forming part of a 'Peace and Security Package' passed in 1976 when capital punishment was abolished. Victimization surveys were recommended as one tool for measuring the success of crime prevention programmes.

An extensive series of projects was focused on gun control and robbery prevention, often employing environmental design principles, such as *The Vancouver Convenience Store Robbery Prevention Programme* (Roesch and Winterdyk, 1985). A study of the effects of the gun control legislation introduced in 1975 showed a drop in crimes, accidents and suicides involving firearms.

Apart from its extensive developmental work in community crime prevention, the Ministry initiated a research and demonstration project in 1985 to assist the Crime Prevention Council of Ottawa. While set up in part to improve services to victims, the Council brought together citizens, the police, counsellors and business and legal representatives, in five task forces directed to specific problems, including crimes against the elderly, crime and vandalism in high-rise apartment blocks, drinking and driving, juvenile delinquency and violent crime. Their work is currently being evaluated, and this police/ community crime prevention model is expected to be adopted by other major Canadian cities. Of particular interest is the apartment task force, because it involves rental accommodation where community crime prevention projects have traditionally been difficult to initiate.

Other work within the orbit of community co-ordination in crime prevention, which has served as a model for a number of areas in Canada, is the research on family violence. As a result of a study in London, Ontario, and other work, an approach was established that combined police charging policies for wife assault with legal aid, shelter accommodation for battered women and their children, counselling services for victims, and treatment services for men who batter their wives (Jaffe and Burris, 1984).

Given the problems of enormous distances, large, sparsely populated police areas and limited resources, the development of police/community cooperation in the rural setting was particularly difficult. Rural crime prevention, and indeed all aspects of crime in rural areas, have been neglected by the criminological community. One particularly successful project (in Portage La Prairie, Manitoba) combined thorough crime analysis with research and evaluation. Developed in 1979, it was designed initially to deal with an outbreak of theft of farm chemicals in a rural community, and subsequently extended to deal with break-ins to commercial and residential property. The success of the project, using property marking as the major strategy, stemmed from the combination of careful consultation with the community before implementation, successful use of the news media in publicising the programme, increased police visibility and, in the case of the breaking and entering project, the high priority given by the police to educating the members of the community in crime prevention (Linden and Minch, 1985).

One important project with the Metropolitan Toronto Police Force combines community consultation with police decentralisation policies. This has resulted in the establishment of mini police stations and foot patrols which meet the needs of the local community and help to improve police-community relations (ARA Consultants, 1985). Zone and team policing also has been set up and evaluated in Halifax and Ottawa. The Ministry has produced an important review of the key issues in community policing which has been widely used to stimulate further community projects and enhance police training (Murphy and Muir, 1985).

Since 1975, it has become possible to assess the strengths and limitations of a number of approaches to crime prevention used in Canada. It has become clear that media crime prevention campaigns used in isolation are useless, but become an important tool used in conjunction with personal contact and as one element in a community-based crime prevention programme. Similarly, although people in general are not interested in property marking, and although its value as a deterrent has not been clearly demonstrated, it is useful in specific local campaigns. Finally, neighbourhood watch programmes, which exemplify the central philosophy of community-based crime prevention (in contrast to individual-based prevention strategies) have proved to be very effective where there is a high rate of participation and programme maintenance. Minimum acceptable participation rates vary from city to city, but as a rule in Canada a programme is not considered to be in force unless 50 per cent to 90 per cent of the families in a neighbourhood participate.

Synthesis

The value of community crime prevention is firmly established across Canada, at the federal, provincial and municipal levels. Well-designed crime prevention programmes supported by research reduce both the incidence of crime and the fear of crime. Community crime prevention also embodies the notion of self help. To some extent there is evidence, here, of a rebirth of the ideology of community politics of the 1960s, with an emphasis on partnerships between government, voluntary and private sectors, and upon building networks in society.

The community approach is exemplified by the recent practitioners' handbook (Ministry of the Solicitor General, 1984), and in the annual and remarkably successful 'Crime Prevention Week'. This venture was set up in 1984 and features awards, the distribution of pamphlets and books, and a national effort to stimulate national and local networks of 'Canadians for Crime Prevention'. The partnership is emphasized by the Canadian Crime Prevention Council, which brings together representatives of federal or provincial government, police agencies, and business and voluntary organisations.

Crime prevention through social development

Recently, there has been a further shift in the Canadian approach to crime prevention. Canada took a major part in the 7th United Nations Congress on Crime Prevention and the Treatment of Offenders (August, 1985), emphasising that crime prevention can best be advanced through a multi-faceted approach. Economic policy-makers and urban planners, among others, do not typically make crime prevention a priority, yet true crime prevention can only come through social development. At present, this remains a slogan rather than a programme, and is something to which the Ministry of the Solicitor General is directing its efforts.

The Ministry recently sponsored a conference on social crime prevention and, together with the Canadian Council on Social Development, has begun work towards the development of such a programme. Thus, with financial

251

assistance from the Ministry, the Council, together with the Canadian Criminal Justice Association, has been responsible for the compilation and dissemination of materials designed to stimulate discussion among policy-makers and practitioners and provide guides for pilot projects (Waller and Weiler, undated). Here the emphasis is upon the development of focused programmes designed to support families, schools and those targeted towards adolescents and disadvantaged groups within the community. It is the hope of many Canadian officials that a major national campaign, on the lines developed in Canada in the area of victims (Rock, 1986) and community crime prevention, will now be developed in the area of social development.

References

ARA CONSULTANTS, (1985). *Final Report on the Evaluation of the Toronto Mini Station Pilot Project*. User Report 1985–24. Ottawa: Ministry of the Solicitor General.

JAFFE, P. and BURRIS, C. A. (1984). *An Integrated Response to Wife Assault: A Community Model*. User Report 1984–27. Ottawa: Ministry of the Solicitor General.

LINDEN, R. and MINCH, C. (1985). *Rural Crime Prevention in Canada*. User Report 1985–54. Ottawa: Ministry of the Solicitor General.

MINISTRY OF THE SOLICITOR GENERAL, (1984). *Working Together to Prevent Crime: A Practitioner's Handbook*. Ottawa.

MURPHY, C. and MUIR, G. (1985). *Community Based Policing: A Review of the Critical Issues*. Technical Report No. 6. Ottawa: Ministry of the Solicitor General.

ROCK, P. E. (1986). *A View From the Shadows: The Ministry of the Solicitor General and the Making of the Justice for Victims of Crime Initiative*. Oxford: Clarendon Press.

ROESCH, R. and WINTERDYK, J. (1985). *The Vancouver Convenience Store Robbery Prevention Programme*. User Report 1985–41. Ottawa: Ministry of the Solicitor General.

TROJANOWICZ, R. C. (1982). *An Evaluation of the Neighbourhood Foot Patrol Programme in Flint, Michigan*. East Lansing, MI: University of Michigan Press.

WALLER, I. and WEILER, D. (undated). *Crime Prevention Through Social Development: A Discussion Paper for Social Policy Makers and Practitioners* and *Crime Prevention Through Social Development: An Overview with Sources*. Ottawa: Canadian Council on Social Development and Canadian Criminal Justice Association, 55 Parkdale Avenue, K1Y 1E5.

16. The fight against crime and fear: a new initiative in France

Marie-Pierre de Liège

Like many other countries in the last ten years, France has experienced a significant increase in petty and common crime, particularly in cities. During the same period it has experienced an even larger increase in feelings of fear of crime.

The increase in fear has two basic causes. On the one hand fear of crime became a political issue which was exploited in the battle between the left and the right from 1975–6 onwards. This political use of the phenomenon of crime was regularly covered by the press and thus very quickly penetrated the public consciousness. The development of fear of crime was in addition facilitated by the economic crisis within the country which left large sectors of the population more vulnerable to such anxieties. On the other hand, however, the traditional and established ways of combating crime, through the use of the police and the criminal justice system, did not appear to be well adapted to fighting the type of crime which had increased. Very few of those responsible for such petty crime were caught, perhaps 20 per cent. Secondly the procedures and sanctions available within the criminal justice system were felt to be too heavy and ineffective. Rates of recidivism associated with imprisonment, for example, might be 50 per cent or more.

During this period, two policies for the handling of offenders coexisted in almost total ignorance of each other:

Prevention activities which took place mostly in the social sector, and were mostly focused on juveniles, and

a policy of repression undertaken by the police and the system of criminal justice, which had been reinforced between 1978 and 1981 by a series of legislative reforms.

Only the system for dealing with juveniles, which had been established in 1945, had the capacity to combine both preventive and controlling or repressive approaches. For adults, in contrast, prevention was no longer considered nor was treatment an option. Nevertheless, in 1978 when the government (of the right) was promoting criminal justice policies based on a repressive response to crime, it established a 'National Committee on the Prevention of Violence and Crime', following a report prepared under the chairmanship of Alain Peyrefitte, Minister of Justice from 1978 to 1981. The committee was made up mainly by experts, and its task was to analyse violence and its causes.

In May 1981 there was a change of government which brought the left into power. They had spent their years in opposition denouncing the approach to crime based only on repressive policies, and what they regarded as the political exploitation of fear of crime. However, in the summer of 1981, the phenomenon of collective acts of violence occurred in several cities. This was particularly the case in the area of Lyon. The event included some near riots, indiscriminate drag racing (rodéos) and the setting fire of many cars. This created considerable concern among the public and within the government.

Thus the incoming government was faced with the task of resolving multiple problems, it had:

to be seen to be dealing with the problem of crime and not ignore it;

to attempt to cut short the political exploitation of the events of the summer;

to invent new ways of combating the problem in place of the repressive approach they had rejected in the past, and which would if possible be effective;

to respond in the best way possible without major new expenditure, given the economic situation which required the redeploy of resources rather than the funding of additional ones.

The events of the summer of 1981 had occurred in particular sectors of the cities, especially among young people who had nothing to do. Thus it seemed clear that central government (in the capital) was not the most appropriate to solve the problem, at least not on its own and from on high. To understand what was happening and to work out solutions, the administration needed to involve elected officials and others at the local level, such as local school principals, social service directors, youth and sport administrators, police chiefs and magistrates, as well as the local population.

The Commission of Mayors

In the spring of 1982, the Prime Minister Pierre Mauroy decided to establish a commission composed of mayors from the four main political parties, to formulate concrete proposals to fight against crime and the fear of crime.

This commission gave an opportunity to those with political responsibilities and different outlooks to work together against crime for the first time. Locally elected officials have much to gain from appearing to take seriously the question of crime and fear of crime, and rather than usurp the role of the administration they were prepared to work with it. A socialist mayor M. Bonnemaison was elected chairman of the commission.

At the end of 1982, the commission submitted its report under the title 'Dealing with Delinquency: prevention, repression, solidarity' (Face à la Délinquance: prévention, répréssion, solidarité). The main elements of the report were that to deal with crime, the traditional approach of police and criminal justice was insufficient. To be effective, a policy to fight crime should be flexible and adapted to local circumstances rather than monolithic for the country as a whole. It should bring together all the local partners, including several parts of the local administration such as the police, the judicial system, social service, public health, education, youth and sports, culture and housing. It should include elected officials such as the mayor and assistant mayor, as well as local representatives of the population including trade unions and non-profitmaking organisations. It should co-ordinate and integrate their activities and policies in order to achieve a more consistent and effective approach to crime at the least cost.

255

Fear of crime, the committee reported, should be treated simultaneously and in a co-ordinated manner at all levels. There should be revisions to policies on housing, education and employment to prevent the social isolation or exclusion of young people, but also adults, in difficulties. Punishment should be adapted to the seriousness of the offence and to the circumstances of the case, but consideration should also be given in sentencing to the prevention of recidivism with the development of alternatives to imprisonment such as community service orders (travaux d'intérêt général). There should be an emphasis on the rehabilitation of those imprisoned, with social and educational assistance during sentence and on release from prison. Finally, assistance should be given to the victims of crime.

On all of these points the elected officials on the commission concluded that the only way to achieve any measure of success was through joint effort by local communities and administrators. The report of the commission included 64 practical and precise recommendations covering five themes: the social environment and quality of life, youth protection, reform of administrative procedures, police enquiries and the organisation of permanent structures for crime prevention.

Implementation

The committee's recommendations have inspired subsequent activity and legislation including the establishment of community service orders. They were also the substance of the initiative established by the decree of 8 June 1983. This created the National Council for the Prevention of Crime (Conseil National de la Prévention de la Délinquance) under the chairmanship of the Prime Minister. At a departmental level, Departmental Councils on the Prevention of Crime were created for each Department, chaired by the chief administrator for the region (Commissaire de la République) with the chief judicial officer (Procurer de la République) as vice-chairman. Finally, the decree provided for a Communal Council on the Prevention of Crime for any city which wished to create one.

At each level the councils have three entities represented: the elected officials, representatives from the administration and citizen groups including trade unions and non-profitmaking organisations.

A pragmatic initiative

The approach recommended and adopted by each council is the same everywhere. No attempt is made to study, yet again, the causes of crime and delinquency, but rather to take action to deal with them. The essential point about the work of the councils is that it is carried out by the men and women who are on the ground—at the coal face—and based on their own knowledge of the local problems. Any research or data collection if carried out is 'quick and dirty', supplementary to the action and not systematic.

The method recommended by the Prime Minister's circular of 14 October 1983 was as follows:

   assess prevention action that is already underway,

identify the problems to be resolved locally,

define the objectives and co-ordinated action to which the administration and the local community want to contribute,

monitor the implementation of the agreed measures together.

In 1983 Communal Councils were established in 18 pilot cities selected to represent those with different political parties in power, and by 1984 this number had increased to 42.

The procedure to ensure the collaboration between local administrators and their communities took on a new form in 1985, with the setting up of 'contracts for prevention action'. By 1986, more than 200 cities had proposed such contracts and the National Council had accepted and co-financed 115 of them. By mid 1986 there were more than 400 communal councils and covering half of the towns with more than 9,000 inhabitants.

Once a contract is accepted, the administration is generally responsible for 50 per cent of the operating costs, usually start-up grants which are not renewable in principle. The activities covered by the contracts are very varied and may include the following:

housing and emergency shelter

social and professional preparation

illiteracy programmes

establishment of community service schemes

development of social, cultural and sporting activities in prisons

victims assistance

data processing for police departments

drug addiction projects

recreation programmes for juveniles during the summer.

The National Council made 48 million French francs available in 1985–6, of which about 28 million were used for crime prevention contracts. Decisions on the allocation of funds are taken by an executive committee within general guidelines established by the full assembly of the National Council.

Sensitisation of public opinion

Information campaigns and programmes to educate public opinion about crime set up by the National Councils were also associated with activities at the local level. This might involve short programmes on television or at the cinema which spotlight issues, the use of video tapes on particular themes, circulation of information newsletters, and in some instances the setting up of 'prevention weeks' in such cities as Strasbourg and Toulouse.

Assessment and future

The National Council has been in existence for nearly four years. At the local level, the structure has already demonstrated clearly its benefits in terms of statistical changes in crime levels in certain areas. Thus in the Department of the Val-de-Marne south of Paris, prevention activities undertaken in the summer of 1985 were associated with a 65 per cent drop in the number of juveniles appearing before the courts. Moreover, in the majority of communities where real progress has been made, the local partners report that they are very satisfied with development. New communal councils for the prevention of crime are being created regularly and the new government (of the right) endorses both the concept and the structure of the initiative.

In practice the structure is seen by most to provide several advantages. It encourages collective reflection, discussion and action among the varying local partners. The local communities are in a position to negotiate with central government the extent to which national policies, both preventive and punitive, should be adapted to the local situation, and thus to improve their effectiveness. The structure allows for exchanges of information and views both horizontally and vertically, i.e., both among the local communities and between them and central government.

The effectiveness of this type of action can only be properly assessed in the middle or long term. At present it represents a qualitative transformation of ways of working rather than a quantitative one: the achievement of a smoothly running system and the building up of confidence in understanding and handling crime and its prevention.

The debate on fear of crime has now become the daily responsibility of everyone, including the citizens, rather than taking place in some collective imagination. This is exemplified by the large number of non-profit making organisations which have been established over the last four years to help ex-prisoners, offenders and victims of crime. These organisations are based upon volunteers who, in addition to the traditional kinds of support and help, aim to develop an active 'solidarity' with their fellow citizens. This enables them to regard the offender from a different perspective, and with a different state of mind than hitherto. Thus the initiation, the action and the help replace fear and withdrawal.

Nevertheless, while there are many encouraging elements, it is clear that these are only the first fragile achievements with which we must not be satisfied. The notion that the response to crime lies in the combination of a policy of active prevention and adapted punishment needs to be continually recalled.

The co-ordinated action approach needs to be developed, maintained and assessed. This is necessary in part because relationships between the partners in this type of activity are continally changing or being redefined, but it is also necessary to evaluate and compare results in order to improve the structure. Thus although the initiative is deliberately pragmatic in design, from time to time researchers have become involved in both activities and experiments. The practitioners have begun to realise the complexity of the problems and are learning to make more use of research techniques. Researchers from their point of view are showing greater interest in collaborating with practitioners in committed action projects, serving as methodologists to conceptualise policies for social change and to evaluate their outcome.

It is perhaps important, at a time of decentralisation, for researchers to play an essential role in linking local initiatives with the central administration, by setting out local experience in a form which facilitates the development of broad policy and strategic guidelines.

From the point of view of the judiciary it is necessary to underline the importance in terms of development which this new approach to the treatment of criminality, and the incidence of national and local consultation, have brought about.

In a few years the judiciary has multiplied its contacts with those outside the legal system. Judges and prosecutors have become acquainted with the various local partners, have thought with them about the problems encountered, and worked out possible solutions.

The judiciary have supported, or indeed have initiated the creation of numerous associations capable of taking on and completing their initiatives: rapid investigation services able to make social and professional assessment of the backgrounds of delinquents before the start of proceedings; court-based organisations which provide social and educational help to those charged, before their case is heard, and enable pre-trial prevention to be avoided; associations providing victim assistance, and numerous community service opportunities established mainly at the local level.

Even though these new organisations are at their starting point, it is already possible to say that justice is better articulated with the activities of the outside world because of this development, and that this will continue.

The French 'model' which has been developed over these last few years has awoken the interest of the international community. On 15 and 16 September 1986 a meeting at the Council of Europe was held on 'Urban violence and insecurity: the role of local politicians'. It was organised by the Permanent Conference of Local and Regional Authorities in Europe, the National Council for the Prevention of Crime (C.N.D.P.) and the World Federation of Twinned Towns.

More than 300 European specialists were able to compare the causes of urban disorder and consider the solutions. They were able to establish that one-dimensional policies of 'total repression' or 'total prevention' are always insufficient, and that an effective policy of prevention and treatment of fear and crime must combine technical prevention (protection of property and goods) with a policy of partnership in social development in which the role of local communities and associations is recognised as essential.

Their deliberations resulted in a decision in favour of the creation of 'an association bringing together regional and local groups and associated movements or related organisations working in different countries of Europe, to implement a series of programmes for the prevention and treatment of fear and crime'. France will take the responsibility, in the first instance, for organising the project.

Finally, it was decided to create a European Data Bank which would permit the assembly and collation of information necessary to aid decisions relating to the reduction of violence and insecurity.

This package of initiatives should help in the course of the years to come to reinforce the ties between research and action, nationally as well as internationally, to the profit of a more effective fight against crime.

17. Trends in crime prevention in The Netherlands

Jan J M van Dijk, Josine Junger-Tas[1]

I The New Policy and its Implementation

Introduction

On May 22, 1985 the Dutch Cabinet presented to the lower House of the States General a comprehensive policy plan to improve the maintenance of law and order. This policy plan was called *Society and Crime*.

The government felt that criminal policy in the years to come must be differentiatied in the sense that petty crime requires a different approach to that adopted for the more serious forms of crime. According to the plan, policy with regard to petty crime should primarily consist of social prevention procedures operating at the level of the municipalities. In this the government followed the recommendations of an independent committee of experts set up in 1983 with the task of advising the government on their policies towards petty crime (1). This committee was chaired by Dr H. J. Roethof (MP). The first part of this paper presents statistical information on the extent and development of crime in The Netherlands, and briefly discusses the social background of crime and the basic considerations of the government for future policy. It concludes with an overview of the progress which has been made in implementing the new policy. The last part of the paper written by the second author presents data on some of the local experiments with social crime prevention which were staged as part of the new policy, and which are being evaluated wholly or partly by the Research and Documentation Centre of the Ministry of Justice.

Crime in The Netherlands

Crimes coming to the notice of the police can be expressed in absolute numbers and in numbers per 1000 inhabitants between the ages of 12 and 64. Figure 1 shows a graph of the development of both figures since 1948. This indicates that recorded crimes have increased almost tenfold in absolute figures since 1960. In 1960 130,000 offences were recorded by the police and in 1986 more than one million. The curve also shows that the rate of growth is accelerating. Since the second half of the 1970s annual increases have been particularly high. Since 1985 the increases have been less steep.

Between 1975 and 1983 registered crime (traffic offences not included) per

1. Dr J. J. M. van Dijk served as a member of the Roethof committee and Dr J. Junger-Tas chaired its subcommittee on social control. Both the authors are presently members of the administrative steering committee on the prevention of petty crime.

1000 inhabitants increased from 38 to 76 in The Netherlands (an increase of 100 per cent). During the same period registered crime per 1000 inhabitants in the United Kingdom increased by 44 per cent, from 44 in 1975 to 62 in 1983. In 1975 the crime rate in The Netherlands was still somewhat lower than in the United Kingdom. By 1983 this was no longer the case (source: *Society and Crime*).

FIGURE 1. Crimes, known to police, crimes solved

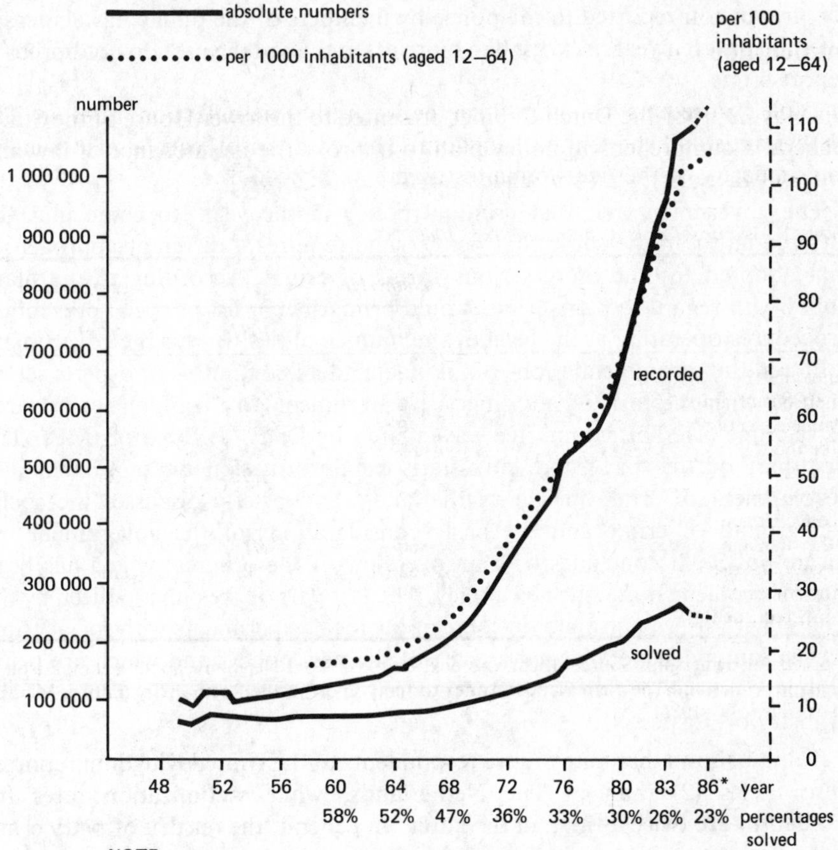

NOTE

*1986 estimated

Source: Netherlands Central Bureau of Statistics

The national crime survey

The victims of a high proportion of incidents of both theft and destruction of property are private citizens. For these types of crime the results of victim surveys which have been carried out in The Netherlands each year since 1975

261

can provide information as to whether the increase in crimes recorded by the police reflects a real increase, or is partly or wholly due to changes in the readiness of citizens to report crimes, or to better recording by the police. A study of the survey results on this point suggests that forms of crime such as breaking and entering private premises and the destruction of private property have almost doubled since 1975. They show that the rise in recorded crime is in the main the consequence of a real increase in the number of crimes committed. The results of the survey also reveal that the real extent of the crime covered by the survey is three to four times greater than that recorded by the police. In the case of some forms of crime it may be noted in addition that the proportion reported to the police by members of the public has decreased over the past ten years. The public more often than in the past do not bother to report crime.

Table 1 presents a comparison between the victimization rates in The Netherlands and the United Kingdom. This comparison can be made due to the similarity of the questionnaires used.

Table 1   *Victim of at least one crime (per 1000)*

	Netherlands		England/Wales
	1984	1981	1981
Auto theft*	5	4	28
Theft out of auto*	126	113	98
Damage to auto*	140	136	62
Bike theft*	69	61	43
Burglary:	24	19	24
some stolen	19		17
none stolen	4		5
Other damage	60	71	24
Assault/threat:	62	50	61
no inj./med.	59		61
inj. req. med.	3		1

*correct for ownership. Source: Richard Block, Crime in Your Neighbourhood: a comparison of England/Wales and The Netherlands. Annex to final report of the Roethof Committee, Ministry of Justice, May 1986.

Table 1 shows that many more respondents in the United Kingdom reported auto thefts (2) than in The Netherlands, while victimization rates for vandalism are twice as high in the latter. In general, the burden of petty crime upon both societies seems to be about the same.

Not only does crime damage its victims and society morally and psychologically, it also has damaging effects which can be valued directly in monetary terms. The total financial loss incurred by individual members of the public, business and industry and the public services each year as a result of theft and vandalism is estimated at four billion guilders (van Dijk, 1984). Private individuals and commercial undertakings each year invest about two million guilders in measures to protect themselves against crime.

The social background

The main thrust of the analysis of the Roethof Committee was as follows. Because of greatly increased prosperity many more goods are in circulation which can be stolen or destroyed, than in the past. The growth in private car ownership in particular has greatly increased the opportunities for crime. On the other hand, there has been a decline since 1960 in the influence of many traditional social institutions within which the behaviour of individuals is effectively normalised, such as the family, clubs and associations, the church and the schools. Society has become more individualistic.

In The Netherlands large parts of the younger generation were traditionally socialised within the framework of the various 'columns' or 'pillars': the social networks established by the various churches and by the Labour movement (Lijphjart, 1975; Bagley, 1973). Since the sixties the 'columns' have lost much of their influence. In the mid-seventies the three main Christian political parties merged into one Christian Democratic party. The Catholic labour union merged with the largest socialist union. The various private probation associations merged into one neutral federation. Many more examples of the 'decolumnisation' or 'depillarisation' of important social institutions could be given (3).

This process was partly the result of the rapid social and political emancipation of the Catholic and Calvinistic population groups during the post war period. The existing columns were also weakened by the growth of the welfare state and the general process of secularization.

Due to these developments, a declining number of the schools, youth clubs, sports clubs, etc. are at present affiliated with one of the columns. Since the columns played a dominant role in the social life of large sections of the Dutch population, the sudden process of decolumnisation has probably undermined some of the traditional socialisation structures in Dutch society (Zijderveld, 1983; Bryant, 1981; Downes, 1986). This may explain why the cultural trend of rebellious individualism in the seventies has been particularly marked among Dutch adolescents, as evidenced by the so-called provo and squatter movements in Amsterdam. In some cases this individualism leads to a tendency to satisfy personal needs at the expense of others or of the community, in short to delinquency or crime. The increased abuse of alcohol and drugs also forms part of this pattern of extreme individualism. Another factor of more recent date, which in the informed opinion of Jongman (1982) has a crime-inducing effect, is long-term unemployment among a section of the younger generation.

In the social and cultural situation which has thus arisen, viable alternatives must be found for some of the socialising functions which were previously performed by the columns. Additional efforts to provide supervision are needed on the part of public and commercial institutions concerned with the maintenance of particular norms of behaviour. The Roethof Committee, however, noted that the level of supervision in many areas of social life is insufficiently attuned to the present more individualistic and non-conformist way of life. Whereas more supervision on the part of officials is now needed than in the past, many forms of surveillance have in fact been relaxed for financial reasons. The numbers of bus conductors, shop assistants and wardens was greatly reduced during the seventies.

Basic considerations for future policy

Introduction

The administration of criminal justice is no longer able to react adequately to serious violations of the law by proper forms of judicial intervention. In this situation it seems obvious to simply bring about a vigorous expansion in the capacity of the various constituent parts of the criminal justice system. There has been pressure from a number of quarters for a drastic increase in the scale of operations of the police and public prosecution service. The government sympathised with the demands imposed on it to combat crime more effectively. However, it rejected the idea that this should be done merely by bringing about quantitative increases in the strength of the police and the public prosecution system. The sharp increase in criminal behaviour over the past few decades is partly the result of structural changes in Dutch society. This fact alone prompts a reappraisal of the place and task of the criminal justice system in the government's general policy with regard to crime. Furthermore, even a doubling of the number of interventions by the criminal justice system would not by any means close the gap between the number of offences committed and the number of responses by the criminal justice authorities. A policy geared exclusively to 'more of the same' would therefore mean that very considerable financial sacrifices would have to be made for action, the ultimate benefit of which is uncertain. Such an approach would also mean that the government would once again arouse expectations with regard to the performance of the criminal justice system which are probably not realistic and cannot, therefore, be fulfilled. This would further compromise the credibility of the administration of justice and of the public authorities in general.

A recent survey showed that Dutch people have no special preference for a mode of tackling crime geared to prevention or one geared to corrective action. A majority of those surveyed were of the opinion that both approaches were of value. Seventy per cent thought that the imposition of harsher penalties was a good way of tackling crime. Even higher percentages, however, favoured measures requiring offenders to pay compensation and the improvement of surveillance in buses and trams, flats, schools and shops (84% and 74% respectively). A majority of those questioned favoured increased surveillance even if it was to mean additional costs to themselves. This pattern of responses indicates that there is widespread support for the recommendations of the Roethof Committee on combating petty crime.

Priorities in social crime prevention

The government shares the view of the Roethof Committee that petty crime is essentially the result of underlying social problems for which the criminal law is not the appropriate mode of approach in the first instance. It is in broad agreement with the recommendations of the Committee on the strengthening of non-police surveillance of possible law-breakers, to be developed in private situations and in the public and semi-public areas of life.

At the same time the government realises that it makes no sense to seek to restore social control in its traditional forms, as a 'nostalgic ideal'. It does consider, however, that even in a heterogeneous society, there is sufficient scope on the one hand for involving the citizen more in the maintenance of law and order, and on the other hand for strengthening the supervisory function of the intermediary structures which together constitute the 'mainstream of society'.

The government discerns three main lines of emphasis in the recommendations of the Roethof Committee:

i. the urban environment should be organised according to town planning and architectural criteria in such a way that, on the one hand, the exercise of surveillance over young people in particular is not made unnecessarily difficult and, on the other hand, the committing of theft and other offences is not made unnecessarily easy;

ii. the bond between the rising generation and society (family, school, work and recreation) must be strengthened as far as possible;

iii. the surveillance of potential law-breakers by persons whose occupational duties cover a wider field, such as drivers, janitors, shop assistants, sports coaches, youth workers, etc., should be extended as far as possible.

The relationship between local authority, Public Prosecutions Department and police (the trilateral consultation)

In formal terms the relationship between the local authority and the Public Prosecutions Department is one of mutual independence. In recent years, however, the realisation has grown that, in material terms, they have a fair number of interests in common. This awareness has taken on concrete form in the trilateral consultation procedure in which the administration, the public prosecution service and the police jointly discuss and decide upon matters relating to the maintenance of law and order. In some municipalities integrated policy plans have been worked out through the trilateral consultation procedure to combat crime. The cabinet sees this as a very positive development. It also feels that the status of the trilateral consultation procedure must be formalised by giving it a basis in the Police Act. A bill has been introduced to the Second Chamber.

At the same time the cabinet thinks that in many areas the scope of that consultation must be widened. The decision in the trilateral procedure should cover all measures—both preventive and corrective—which may contribute to the control of criminal behaviour as well as the question of how optimum co-ordination can be achieved with each party retaining its responsibility.

In the preparation and implementation of integrated plans worked out by the administration and the Public Prosecutions Department together for the control of petty crime, close co-operation must be developed between police officers—including crime prevention officers—who should be given a position and status within the force commensurate with this consultative function, and officials in the various departments of local government and public prosecutors. For the local authority, policy on crime prevention should form part of a much broader local government policy. This means that there must be structured consultation between the organisational units of the local government machine concerned with the control of crime (police, general affairs department and executive) and units whose tasks cover economic policy, physical planning, education, housing etc.

The Burgomaster, in pursuance of his responsibility for public order and safety in the municipality, can play a key role in this consultation. It is incumbent on him, in close co-operation with the municipal council and the municipal executive, to bring home to council departments and services, such as urban development, welfare and housing, the possibilities also open to them of contributing to the fight against crime.

The Public Prosecutor, having regard to his special responsibility for the results of the local crime policy, must have the right to question the Burgomaster in the trilateral consultation procedure on the content and implementation of the local authority's prevention policy. The Public Prosecutor for his part should not only be prepared to consult with his partners in the trilateral consultation procedure on prosecution policy, but also to provide information on the matter, where required, at meetings of the council or the general committee of the council. The Public Prosecutor's Office, since it also exercises formal authority here, may instruct the police to use its specialised resources in providing the best possible preventive support to the administration's activities and should complement the role of the police in following up their action with corrective measures where necessary. The administration and the police may in turn call upon the Public Prosecutor, pursuant to the agreements reached on the matter, to institute those reactions to offences referred to him which are required by the joint decisions taken.

Implementing the new policy

The government has appointed an administrative steering committee which must supervise the implementation of its crime prevention initiatives. The government has also set up a fund of 50 million guilders (around £12 million) to encourage administrative crime prevention from which subsidies can be paid in the period 1986–1990 for promising (local authority) projects. Priority will be given to projects that combine initiatives of the local administration, the police and the local prosecutor. All projects will have to be evaluated by an external agency. The steering committee has a dual task: to monitor the implementation of the new policies on crime prevention by all relevant state ministries; and to act as the advisory committee on the funding of local experiments. In February 1987 the new government published an updated programme of the activities which will be taken to implement the policy plan of 1985 in the coming years.

Progress at the national level

Public transport
In the public transport sector, a decision has been taken on the permanent employment of 1,300 special surveillance officers, called VIC's after the Dutch initial letters for 'Safety, Information and Surveillance', on the city transport

systems in the largest cities. The effects of this measure have been studied by the Research and Documentation Centre. It was found that the percentages of fare-dodging declined substantially on those lines where surveillance officers had been introduced (see below).

Education
The Minister of Education has issued new regulations on the registration of truancy. The minister has also modified the regulations on the replacement of teachers on sick leave with a view to the prevention of delinquency during schoolhours. Schools for secondary education are being given financial incentives to take measures to prevent vandalism.

Youth
Around 25 local projects have been launched aimed at the social integration of high-risk groups (integrated streetcorner work with an emphasis upon work and education facilities). Six additional projects are geared towards youngsters of ethnic minorities. Also £4 million was spent in 1986 on special work projects for permanently unemployed youngsters. Several new employment schemes will be introduced in 1987. The government has set itself the aim to provide training facilities or jobs for all persons in the age range between 16 to 21 in the coming years.

The government will shortly introduce a new licensing Act with more stringent regulations and the sale of liquor will in principle be proscribed on the terraces of professional soccer clubs during matches. The latter proposal has drawn much opposition from the Royal Soccer Association however.

The Roethof Committee also recommended an experiment with the placement of drug addicts in treatment clinics for a fixed period. The placement would be made by a civil judge at the request of the person involved. A bill which will provide the necessary legal instruments for such programmes is pending in the First Chamber (Senate).

Public housing
The Ministry of Public Housing and Planning has published several reports and checklists concerning crime prevention for both planners and architects. The regulations on the technical standards for private or public buildings will be extended with standards of security (target hardening).

Retail stores
The Ministry of Business Affairs has established a national centre for information on the prevention of shoplifting. The Roethof Committee recommended the imposition of civil law sanctions on first offender shoplifters by the retail stores themselves. The government has rejected this proposal. It prefers a system whereby the police may invite first offenders of shoplifting to prevent prosecution by the payment of a small fine. Such a system will be introduced in 1987 on an experimental basis.

Information
The Research and Documentation Centre of the Ministry of Justice issues a regular journal on social crime prevention, aimed at local administrators, youth workers and schoolteachers. The Centre also developed a computerized databank on crime prevention initiatives and their effects.

Progress at the local level

More than a hundred local authorities (city councils) have sent in requests to the national steering committee for the funding of local crime prevention programmes. The committee has selected about 50 different projects for funding in 1986 and 1987.

Fifteen projects are specifically directed towards the prevention of vandalism, a common element being special courses for schoolchildren on the impact of vandalism. For this purpose a standardised teaching package has been provided by the state. In several cities agencies which organise community service orders for young vandals as a diversion option will be established or expanded (see below).

In several cities special programmes will be launched for the prevention of bicycle theft, including the establishment of bicycle-sheds manned by the unemployed. In other cities the prevention of shoplifting will be improved by joint action of retail stores, the police and the prosecutor. The committee has also decided to fund several crime prevention oriented urban renewal programmes. In most cases these initiatives combine technical measures which will improve surveillance and neighbourhood watch projects. Elsewhere neighbourhood watch projects will be sponsored as separate programmes.

In two cities the committee will support comprehensive programmes to prevent truancy in secondary schools (see below). Also sponsored are some new streetcorner-work projects which provide educational and work facilities. Many of these projects will also assist in the organization of community service orders.

Among the various other initiatives, selected by the committee, are two theatre productions about crime (one to be played by high-risk youngsters themselves) a self defence course for girls, an information project on the abuse of alcohol among youth supervisors and in sports clubs, a streetlighting project, and a project aimed at the prevention of the traditional riots during the night of December 31 in The Hague.

II Experiments in Crime Prevention

Introduction

As Part I of this paper indicated, the Dutch Government has decided to subsidise a number of prevention programmes meeting specific criteria and set up by local authorities. Apart from these programmes, the Research and Documentation Centre has initiated and is evaluating a number of such projects. This section of the paper gives a general indication of the types of project concerned and examines an example of each type in more detail.

Experiments in situational prevention

In this approach the objective is essentially to reduce opportunities to commit crime. One such project is addressed to petty crime in shopping centres, such as shoplifting, vandalism, pickpocketing, theft from automobiles and different forms of violence. The experiment will consist of promoting functional forms of surveillance and measures of urban and housing design.

In the city of Amsterdam an experiment with neighbourhood-watch schemes will be introduced, inspired by the experiences in many American, Canadian and English cities. Another experiment aims at reducing burglary and vandalism in large apartment buildings.* A number of measures are designed in collaboration with the occupants of specific 'problem' apartment buildings, such as techno-preventive devices and the introduction of a janitor.

Finally 1,300 SIC-officers (Security, Information, Control) have been introduced in the public transport system of the three largest Dutch cities—Amsterdam, Rotterdam and The Hague—in order to reduce travelling without paying, vandalism and aggressive behaviour.

Social crime prevention

These projects try to meet one of the major objectives of the policy plan 'Society and Crime': 'to strengthen the bond of the coming generation with society'. Apart from a large study of the literature in different disciplines, two school-studies are being conducted. The first one is a comparative study among schools. We know that schools differ considerably in achievement levels, social behaviour, frequency of truancy, and delinquency among their students. We want to find out what factors are most strongly related to social and delinquent behaviour, examining not only teaching styles but also organisational and social aspects within the school. Better knowledge of these factors and processes might improve individual schools' policy as well as the more general policy of the Ministry of Education.

The second study consists of an experiment in a large vocational training school. Its main objective is to reintegrate potential drop-outs in the school system and to reduce truancy and delinquency.

Prevention through integrated action

The municipality of Enschede is one of the first municipalities to have designed an integrated action plan in which the local administration collaborates with the police and the prosecutor to prevent and reduce crime. Four selected 'priority' offences receive special attention by the police and—once detected—are dealt with by the prosecution without delay: offences of violence, vandalism, burglary and bicycle-theft. Local administration supports this policy by specific techno-preventive measures and more functional supervision, in order to reduce opportunities to commit crime. The action plan consists of a great number of sub-projects, most of which are evaluated by our Centre. We also conduct a number of experimental victim

* This evaluation is conducted by a specialised research institute in Amsterdam (Crime Prevention Bureau).

programmes where different approaches to informing and assisting victims are tried out and evaluated.

In the field of diversion two projects should be mentioned. First, we have introduced alternative sanctions for juveniles, modelled on the experiments with Community Service and Intermediate Treatment in the United Kingdom. These sanctions may be imposed on the young person either by the juvenile judge or by the prosecutor. In the latter case the measure should be considered as diversion because if the juvenile completes the community service or training programme satisfactorily, the case will be dismissed and there will be no record. Second, special vandalism projects have been introduced in a number of cities, based on the collaboration between the police, the prosecutor, local administration and social and welfare agencies.

Having presented some of the experiments and studies that have been initiated—mainly in 1986—the remainder of the paper looks more closely at three of them.

The 'SIC' experiment

In order to reduce vandalism, aggressive behaviour and the proportion of travellers who do not pay the fare, the Minister of Traffic and Public Transport has taken two main measures: a modified entry system in buses so that everybody has to pass the bus driver and present his ticket, and the introduction of 1,300 SIC-officers (Security, Information, Control) on tramways and on the underground. The SIC-officers do not operate permanently on predetermined lines, their input is variable according to the 'problematic' character of specific lines and certain peak-hours. These measures have been gradually introduced in the second half of 1985.

For the purposes of evaluating the effects of the experiment at the end of 1985, 3,132 persons in the three cities were approached by telephone. Interviews were held with 1,619 persons using the transport system regularly. It appeared that more women than men use the public transport system and that men of 36–55 years old were under-represented. Both are related to car ownership.

Security

Only 11 per cent of those interviewed thought that security in public transport had improved during the last trimester. The more they used public transport the more they had noticed some change. Generally travellers were fairly satisfied with the security aspects, with persons of 65 years and older among the most satisfied. Knowledge of the presence of SIC's improved the security-scores. A quarter of frequent public transport users occasionally felt unsafe during the last 3 months and half of them sometimes avoided the transport system. This is especially the case with respect to the underground. Feelings of insecurity were strongest when they travelled at night (46%), when there was a bunch of youngsters present (23%), when there were drunks, or drug-users present (18%).

One out of six persons mentioned harassment during transport, but in most

270

cases this happened to someone else; only 5 per cent had been a victim of such incidents. There is a strong relationship between having witnessed harassment, feelings of insecurity and avoidance behaviour. Young women are most often victims of harassment; they more frequently have feelings of insecurity and are more inclined to avoid public transport.

In one third of cases personnel or other passengers intervened during such incidents and this was related to a reduction of feelings of insecurity. However it should be emphasised that there was no relationship between travelling frequency and feelings of insecurity.

Sixteen per cent of all respondents had noticed acts of vandalism during the last three months; 25 per cent five times or more. Specially selected objects are seats, walls and shelters. Witnessing acts of vandalism is related to feelings of insecurity. Among these witnesses, 42 per cent felt insecure and 27 per cent showed avoidance behaviour, whereas among those who had not seen such acts the percentages are 22 per cent and 12 per cent. Those who are frequent public transport users and young persons more often witness acts of vandalism than other passengers, but in general personnel or other passengers did not intervene.

Information

Very few people (8%) had noticed a change in information policy since the introduction of the SIC's. Those who had, mentioned the presence of more personnel and more posters, stickers and brochures.

Although there was some appreciation of the availability of more general information, it was felt that verbal information given on the tram or bus was insufficient, due to lack of personnel. Older people and those who use public transport for recreation, shopping or visiting relatives, are among the most satisfied.

Control

In Amsterdam and The Hague where most of the SIC's have already been introduced, half of the respondents have noticed the changes in control, both the introduction of a modified entering system in buses and the increased number of ticket-controllers.

Overall 13 per cent confessed having travelled without paying during the last three months, most of them on tramways (74%), with about 26 per cent on the underground. Their main justifications for this behaviour were that 'they cannot pay the fare', 'public transport is too expensive', or 'they did not have enough money with them'. Young people more often travel without paying than older persons, and men more than women.

More than half of those interviewed had been subject to the control system during the last three months, most of them several times. Of course this is related to travel frequency. Most people are satisfied and have positive attitudes towards the SIC-officers.

What can now be said about the effects of the introduction of SIC-officers in the public transport system on travelling without paying? Only figures for

Amsterdam and The Hague can so far be compared since the control function was not introduced in Rotterdam at the beginning of the experiment. The modified entering system on buses was introduced in Amsterdam in June 1985, but in The Hague in November 1985, and only on some lines.

Table 2 *Effects of the introduction of SIC's on travelling without paying*

	% of passengers travelling without paying		
	May 1985	November 1985	March 1986
Amsterdam			
tramway	17.7%	8.5%	
underground	23.5%	11.0%	
bus	9.2%	2.0%	
The Hague*			
tramlines without SIC's	13.9%	12.1%	10.4%
tramlines with SIC's	—	4.0%	2.6%
bus	15.1%	4.4%	2.3%

*The Hague has no underground transport system.

As is apparent in the table above SIC-officers have had a great impact on the occurrence of travelling without paying. The impact is especially clear in The Hague where lines with and without SIC's can be compared. Where SIC-officers operate, travelling without paying almost disappeared. The same is true for the modified entering system on buses. However, as far as the effects of SIC's on feelings of insecurity or on information receiving are concerned, results are less convincing. No real effects could as yet be demonstrated.

The school experiment

There is overwhelming evidence showing the role of school failure in the genesis of juvenile delinquency.

Although factors such as the functioning of the family are important, a recent Dutch study found that the strongest predictor of delinquency among adolescents was school failure (Junger-Tas and Junger, 1984).

Other researchers have found the same results (Glueck, 1950; Cohen, 1958; Elliott and Voss, 1974; Polk, 1975; Rutter *et al.*, 1979).

School functioning in terms of achievement, has an impact on the status of a youngster, his or her self-image and self-confidence. Failure has direct effects on social behaviour and may lead to all kinds of disciplinary problems, truancy or dropping out.

A direct relationship between failure at school and delinquent friends had also been found. Marginalised juveniles with status problems join each other and look for other exciting and delinquent activities to increase their status in the eyes of their peers (Junger-Tas and Junger, 1984). Moreover it is a well-known fact that the regular youth agencies and sports clubs have little grip on these youths: they simply cannot reach them.

Considering these facts it seemed to us that in addition to situational or technical prevention, there was a need to conduct some experiments on a more fundamental level. It was also felt that—in our country at least—schools did not really recognise their responsibilities in this field or did not accept them and that some important changes in school policy would be necessary. In some large cities, for example, rates of truancy reach quite unacceptable proportions. Estimates are that there are 10,000 to 15,000 truants on an average schoolday in Amsterdam, and many of these kids will leave school without obtaining a qualification. All this has led us to devise an experiment in a large vocational training school, with a predominantly male adolescent population.

The ultimate objective is to reduce delinquency; sub-objectives are to reduce truancy, to improve performance, and to reintegrate potential drop-outs in the school. First a computerised truancy registration and control system will be set up. This will enable the school to react immediately and warn the parents. In cases of unjustified absences disciplinary action can then be taken. Moreover additional data on all students will be collected such as type of schooling, repeating classes, achievement level, socio-economic status, truancy patterns, discipline measures, etc.

By introducing this control system it is expected that most of the 'ordinary' truancy, by kids that can (too) easily get away with it, will be greatly reduced. There will, however, be a group of more persistent truants, who require more attention. Therefore, in a second phase, a special truant officer will be appointed to use a personal approach with this group. He will examine the background of the truancy problem which can have its origin either in the home situation or in the school system itself. In both cases the truant officer will look for solutions which will reduce the truant-group still more.

However, even then there will be a number of youngsters that present severe school problems and are potential drop-outs. It is the task of the truant officer to select these boys, analyse their problems and refer them to a third experimental set-up, a special class managed by a very experienced and skilful teacher.

It is expected that there will be considerable overlap between those who truant frequently, those who present behaviour problems and those who are school failures: these are essentially the same boys. The teacher's task is in the first place to improve the boy's school performance—eventually in collaboration with others, such as a remedial teacher—promoting in this way his school motivation and social behaviour. If there are related psycho-social problems, the teacher should assist and help the boy, or refer him to outside social agencies. But there is a clear preference for solving problems within the school.

These are the three main experimental conditions that are being introduced. To examine their effects there will be two control schools: one in which the computerised truancy registration and control system will also be introduced and one with no experimental conditions at all. The first control school serves to find out the effects of the introduction of a computerised control scheme: it could be that such a scheme in itself has more effect on school attendance and drop-out than the introduction of special teachers to accompany problem juveniles. We will at least try to distinguish the effects of the different elements.

Another way to do so is to introduce the experimental conditions one after another; thus we will first introduce the computerised control scheme, then after some months the truant officer, and still later the special teacher.

Measures of school performance, truancy, social behaviour and self-report delinquency will be taken before the introduction of each experimental variable.

At the experimental school one of the classes will be more closely followed: in depth-interviews will be held regularly and observations in the classroom will be made. The experiment is planned for a period of two years, although it would be preferable to conduct a cohort study and follow incoming students throughout their school period, which is four years.

Evaluation of vandalism projects

Vandalism projects have been born out of the needs of local administrative authorities, the police and the public prosecutor. The first one originated in Rotterdam, and because almost all programmes that have been set up since took the Rotterdam programme as a model, its major elements will be outlined. The city wanted to undertake action in this field because of the enormous cost to the municipality of acts of vandalism.

While crimes of wilful damage have increased in the whole country, Rotterdam reported that the costs for repairing the municipality's schools increased from about £13,250 in 1975 to about £625,000 in 1980. The programme called HALT—which means 'stop' in Dutch—was initiated in 1980. It was financed by the city, although now the Ministry of Justice is subsidising part of it. The target population included youngsters committing offences against public order and violence against property or persons.

The main objectives of the programme are to reduce vandalism, to take away some of its causes and to prevent vandalism and aggressive behaviour. The programme tries to reach these objectives through three different activities:

i. to provide volunteer work—mostly in the form of repairing or cleaning—for youngsters taken in by the police, as an alternative to prosecution.

ii. to find out the reasons for vandalistic behaviour and assist the youngsters in solving their more obvious and direct problems.

iii. to collect information on situations facilitating vandalism and advise people on how to change these situations.

When a youngster is detained by the police for vandalism the police or prosecutor may refer the boy to HALT. There is no clear practice established, local variations do exist and this is one of the aspects that will be closely examined. In Rotterdam juveniles may be referred to HALT both when there is an official report to the prosecutor and when there is no such report. Participation in HALT is voluntary but in the face of official prosecution the voluntary character of participation may be questioned.

Even in the absence of a report to the prosecutor there may be a claim for damages: HALT then mediates between the two parties and tries to arrange for compensation to the victim by the juvenile.

From October 1981—when HALT officially started—until May 1982 data were collected about its operation (van Hees, 1983). It was found that young persons referred to HALT had an average of 15 years and attended the lower vocational training schools. It is not known how representative this sample is of all those who commit acts of vandalism, since most of these kids are never detected. Thus it is not known whether HALT clients are less smart than the others, or select places where the police patrol more frequently.

More than 60 per cent of juveniles referred to HALT had had repeated police contacts, and had previously committed offences of a rather serious nature such as burglary, theft or violence against persons. Some of them operated in gangs, committing burglaries and thefts. This group more often lived in rather problematic family situations. They were nearly all boys; although girls did encourage the activities, they rarely took part in them. In motivating their behaviour the boys emphasised the excitement and pleasure it produced, and indicated that the acts gave them status and prestige among their peers.

Although HALT officials do not tackle serious family problems they offer direct assistance in problems with education, work, housing, leisure opportunities and the like.

Finally, they have some impact on situations that invite vandalism, in trying to make people change, for example, the organisation of a youth club, to get more control on buses at specific peak hours or on specific itineraries, or to change particular environmental settings. Ten of these programmes are in operation and a lot more are planned. Given the enthusiasm of municipalities setting them up it was decided that evaluation research was necesary to answer three questions:

i. what effect do HALT projects have on the level of vandalism in the municipalities concerned?

ii. what effect do HALT projects have on recidivism of their clients?

iii. under what conditions of administration and organisation do HALT projects offer the best results?

To answer the first question, vandalism will be measured by special indicators—such as telephone boxes—before and after the introduction of HALT in the experimental cities and in some control municipalities. Apart from this the contribution of HALT to situational vandalism prevention will be examined. Any deterrent effects on the general youth population in HALT cities and on peer groups of HALT clients will be examined by interviewing them before, and one year after, the intervention, and by checking police records for information on recidivism and reconviction. Two control groups will be used. The first consists of boys having committed comparable acts but whose case was handled in a traditional way. The other consists of boys who have committed acts of vandalism but were *not* caught by the police: in this case nothing happened to them.

Finally, we will conduct a process-evaluation in which will be examined the general organizational and administrative context, stated objectives and means used, the police and court procedures chosen, the exact target group, the operation of the scheme and all other activities deployed in the field. It is hoped that in this way reasonable insight will be gained about the usefulness of vandalism projects such as HALT.

Summary

This section has covered only three out of a great number of experiments and evaluation studies that the Centre has undertaken. Of the 50 or so local projects that will receive subsidies from the national steering committee, a great number will also get some degree of Research and Documentation Centre supervision. It is clear that—during the coming 5 years—we are engaged in Holland in a gigantic crime prevention operation. It will not be an easy task to keep control of the operation, nor will it be easy to guarantee valid evaluation of all programmes. However, this is the first time that the prevention and reduction of crime has been considered as a matter that concerns society as a whole, public and private instances as well as individual citizens. As such this is an important step forward.

Notes

1. The Roethof Committee defines the term petty crime in its interim report (page 12) as follows: ' ... punishable forms of behaviour occurring on a large scale which can be dealt with by the police on a discretionary basis or, in the case of a first offence, are generally handled by the Public Prosecutor or are dealt with by the courts at the most through the imposition of a fine and/or a conditional custodial sentence and which—mainly because of the scale on which they occur—are a source of nuisance or engender feelings of insecurity among the public'.

2. Previous comparisons of victimization rates have shown that the auto theft rates of Canada and the USA are closer to the Dutch than to the British rates (approx. 10 per 1,000).

3. According to the results of opinion polls, analysed by the Social and Cultural Planning Office, the percentages of the Dutch population who support institutional links between labour unions, schools, youth clubs, sports clubs on the one hand and the churches on the other decreased dramatically since 1966. For example the support for 'columnised' youth clubs went down from 56 per cent in 1966 to 20 per cent in 1986 (Social and Cultural Report, 1986, Social and Cultural Planning Office. The Netherlands, 1986).

References

BAGLEY, C., (1973). *The Dutch Plural Society*. Oxford: University Press.

BRYANT, C. G. A., (1981). 'Depillarisation in The Netherlands'. *British Journal of Sociology*, 32, pp. 56–74.

COHEN, A., (1955). *Delinquent Boys: The Culture of the Gang*. New York: The Free Press.

DIJK, J. J. M. van, (1984). 'Financieel-economische aspecten van misdaad en misdaadbestrijding' (Financial and economic aspects of crime and the control of crime). *Economische Statistische Berichten*, 19/2, December.

DOWNES, D., (1986). *Contrasts in Tolerance*. Department of Social Adminstration, London School of Economics, November.

ELLIOTT, D. S. and VOSS, H. L., (1974). *Delinquency and Dropout*. Toronto and London: Lexington Books.

GLUECK, S. and E. (1950). *Unravelling Juvenile Delinquency*. Cambridge Mass.: Harvard University Press.

HEES, A. van, (1983). *Vandalism en bureau HALT*. Leiden: Stageverslag Rijksuniversiteit, June.

JONGMAN, R. W., (1982). 'Criminaliteit als gevolg van de uitstoting uit het arbeidsproces' (Criminality resulting from the expulsion from the labour market). *Tijdschrift voor Criminologie*, January, pp. 3–20.

JUNGER-TAS, J. and JUNGER, M. (1984). *Juvenile Delinquency—Backgrounds of Delinquent Behaviour*. WODC, Ministry of Justice, The Netherlands.

LIJPHART, A. (1975). *The Politics of Accommodation*. (2nd review ed.), Berkeley and Los Angeles: University of California Press.

POLK, K. FREASE, D., RICHMOND, F. L., (1974). 'Social class, school experience and delinquency'. *Criminology*, 12, pp. 84–97.

RUTTER, M. P., MAUGHN, B., MORTIMORE, P. OUSTON, J., (1979). *Fifteen Thousand Hours—Secondary Schools and their Effects on Children*. Somerset, England: Open Books.

ZIJDERVELD, A. C. (1983). 'Transformatie van deverzorgingsstaat' (Transformation of the Welfare State), in: Idenburg, Ph. A., (ed.), *De nadagen van de verzorgingsstaat* (The autumn of the Welfare State), Amsterdam: Meulenhoff.

Endpiece

The final chapter orginally took the form of a commentary on the papers and discussion which took place at the conference upon which this book is based. It provides an outline of the evolution of thinking and practice in crime prevention in the community in both North America and Europe, and argues strongly for the adoption of an approach to crime prevention which encompasses reform and crime reduction.

18. Two visions of community crime prevention

Elliott Currie

Given the sheer amount of information contained in the chapters of this book, it would not be fruitful—or even possible—to attempt a detailed summary. Rather, this chapter attempts to pull out some key themes which have emerged in the course of the book. I don't pretend that this effort is neutral or unbiased; my aim is to bring out the issues more clearly for the purpose of stimulating discussion and debate.

The chapters brought together in this book reflect two, sometimes conflicting, visions of what community crime prevention is, or should be. This is, of course, an over-simplification, since the visions overlap, and there are many complicated variations and conbinations. But at a more fundamental level, we can discern two ideal types, each with quite different implications for social policy. Moreover, we are witnessing a movement which, I believe, should be encouraged.

Community crime prevention can be seen as having two phases which differ on many crucial dimensions. In the first place they rest on different conceptions of what a 'community' *is*.

Consequently, their views of what it means to *strengthen* a community in order to fight crime differ sharply. Moreover, they differ in their view (and even more in their practice) on what *kinds* of communities should receive the most attention, and, similarly, on what kind of *crime* should be most heavily targeted by community prevention—or indeed whether reducing *crime* is the main priority at all. By the same token, the two 'phases' differ in the degree to which they are concerned with the offender, or potential offender, as a focus of intervention. Finally, they differ on the balance to be struck between public and private responsibility for crime prevention and more generally for the enhancement of community life.

What can be called Phase 1 dominated much of the early discussion of community crime prevention, particularly in the 1970s. It is most typified by Neighbourhood Watch and to some extent the 'defensible space' approaches. The 'broken windows' model associated with James Q. Wilson and George Kelling is a more recent variant that shares many of the same assumptions. What do all these approaches have in common?

Consider first the broad conception of community. The Phase 1 vision leans towards what can be called a *symbolic*, or perhaps a social-psychological, view of community—rather than a more 'structural' or institutional one, which, as will be seen, characterises Phase 2. In Phase 1 thinking 'community' is primarily a matter of collective attitudes and styles of interpersonal behaviour, with the behaviour usually seen as flowing from the attitudes. In this the notion of a 'sense' of community is very important, as is the idea of community 'cohesion'—as though these ideas, on close inspection, are vague and rarely well articulated. Community, in brief, is in people's heads. Consequently, if you wish to improve community conditions you are in essence in the business of changing attitudes, or altering the symbols of community, in the hope that improved interpersonal relations will follow. In the ideal scenario you may thus start a benign cycle: improved attitudes lead to better behaviour, which in turn enhances people's conception of community, which in turn ...

Certainly, this is *part* of what a community is but only one part, and arguably one that, by itself, isn't the most important for crime control. What is missing here is the sense of those more tangible structures and institutions that underlie and shape community attitudes, and also necessarily shape those 'signs' or symbols of crime and disorder so prominent in Phase 1 discussions of crime prevention. In leaving out these things Phase 1 thinking almost seems to suggest—indeed frequently does suggest—that if people just 'get their act together' they will at the very least *feel* better about their community and each other; at best, this feeling will lead to greater participation in a variety of actions that will reverse the cycle of fear and decline—whether it's watching their neighbours' yards or standing up to unruly kids on the corner or (literally) cleaning up their own back yards.

This focus on attitudes is one source of the emphasis in Phase 1 thinking on *fear* reduction—as opposed to crime reduction—an emphasis rooted in the not-well-grounded theory that doing something about fear, an attitude, will result in more tangible crime-preventive behaviour. (There is often another source of that emphasis in Phase 1 thinking, which Chapter 11 touches on, the lurking belief that we *can't* reduce crime but *may* be able to reduce fear, so we should de-emphasise the former effort and settle for the latter.)

This is in many ways an appealing conception, particularly in a culture that has an exaggerated sense of the force of attitudes and of individual participation, and a correspondingly underdeveloped sense of the importance of social structure and of public responsibility for coping with social problems. But the appeal masks some very serious limitations, and these are not just theoretical quibbles. The biggest problem with this approach is that programmes based wholly on it simply do not seem to work well, and sometimes do not work at all, as the serious evaluations of Neighbourhood Watch and the failure to validate the 'broken windows' model show (see Chapters 8 and 3). Moreover, to the extent that they work at all they tend to work (as Chapters 3, 8, 9 and 13 have all argued) for communities with the least serious problems, the lowest risk. They work badly in resource-poor communities where victimization is more severe.

Part of the problem is that Phase 1 thinking typically misunderstands the relationship between the offender and the community. It tends to assume a sort of 'we versus they' attitude. Offenders are outsiders, strangers—as in Neighbourhood Watch, where the job is to monitor your 'turf' to see that 'they' don't get in; or in the environmental design model where you try to design them out in the first place; or in the 'broken windows' model, where they are defined as something like internal outsiders—unruly kids, marginal people—and the task is to get them off the streets and out of the picture.

There is no sense that these offenders against law and civility are *members* of a community—some community—like the rest of us.

There is no sense, for example, that the people you are dealing with might include a neighbour's kid who has a learning problem and hangs about on the corner because he is afraid to go to school, or your sister's abusive husband—hardly a stranger—but an intimate member of a local household. (This is crucially important, because it helps explain why Phase 1 thinking is virtually silent on the issue of community prevention of *domestic* violence. Chapters 10 and 12, for example, comment that gender issues tend to drop out of most discussions of community crime prevention, and this is one of the most unfortunate examples.) They take no account either of the man across the street who lost his job two years ago, and gets a little drunk and crazy on the street on certain nights, or of the young man down the road who has just been released from a secure psychiatric institution, or even *your* own child. But that is the reality of what crime (and disorder) are about in most high-risk communities.

There is little sense, in short, that people who cause trouble or are uncivil or offensive may be part of the community, and correspondingly little sense that they may also be amenable to forms of intervention other than surveillance or aggressive policing; that they might be seen as objects of 'active care', support, and guidance.

Similarly, there is little understanding, in Phase 1 thinking, of where troublesome people come from within the social structure—and what this tells us about strategies of effective crime prevention. Gottfredson and Taylor (Chapter 4) point out that released offenders typically come from 'lousy places' and return to lousy places. The British Crime Survey similarly shows (like the American victimization research) that crime—unsurprisingly—is heaviest in poor areas with high concentrations of poor people (Chapters 2 and 9). All of this suggests the crucial importance of policies directed toward these people and to the damage that a lifetime of residence in 'lousy places' has visited upon them. But this sort of focus is notably lacking in most Phase 1 thinking.

This absence of what we might call 'structural awareness' is especially apparent in the Wilson-Kelling model, which envisions the community exerting its moral authority over bad people who seem to appear from nowhere, and who will surely take over if we don't wave the wand of traditional values at them—through tough policing, among other means. In the 'broken windows' aproach, problematic people become just further 'signs' of local disorder, like litter or graffiti. We do not learn much about how their lives have shaped them, or how we might go about addressing their problems. Given the failure to take these larger realities into account, it is not surprising that this model, in the Police Foundation's Newark experiment, achieved no clear positive impact, and indeed may have made matters worse (Chapters 3 and 11).

Phase 2—the second broad vision of community crime prevention is not yet fully developed, but there are encouraging signs that we are beginning to move beyond some of the limitations of Phase 1. Phase 2, as has been hinted, is more complicated in its understanding of crime and how communities might combat it. But, in my view, it is also far more promising, especially as a strategy for preventing *serious* crime, not merely reducing fear or taming neighbourhood incivilities. It is also, it is suggested, far more attuned to deeper and more fruitful criminological traditions.

Phase 2 begins by looking at 'community' in much more structural, or institutional terms not just as a set of attitudes we can 'implant' or mobilise, but as an interlocked set of longstanding institutions which in turn are deeply affected by larger social and economic forces. Curtis's emphasis on employment opportunities and extended family structures (Chapter 11), Bottoms and Wiles's analysis of how housing estates with different histories generate different patterns of crime (Chapter 5), and van Dijk's notion of the importance of the 'columns' that once served as key socialising institutions for the young in Dutch society (Chapter 17, an idea that parallels the American conception of 'mediating structures'), all illustrate this view of community.

Perhaps the most intriguing possibilities for community crime prevention lie in the recognition—basic to Phase 2 thinking—that real communities thrive or fail to thrive, become healthy or pathological, mainly as a result of the strength or weakness of these basic institutions—work, family and kin, religious and communal associations, a vibrant local economy capable of generating stable livelihoods. When these are weak or shattered, all the Neighbourhood Watches or 'hassling' of street kids on the corner will not put the community back together. Conversely, when these institutions are strong, you need far fewer of the traditional Phase 1-type crime prevention efforts. This does not mean that Phase 1 programmes should be excluded from Phase 2 community crime prevention, only that to the extent that we make use of them at all, it should be as just one part, and not the largest, of a much bigger package.

Several examples of this model of prevention in action are touched on in this book: the Eisenhower programmes, with their stress on employment, family, and local neighbourhood (while often including block watches and security patrols—Chapter 11); the Dutch programmes, which combine some situational measures (like bus surveillance) with efforts to deal with the structural problems of youth in and out of the schools—including proposals for comprehensive job training and development for *all* the young (Chapter 17); the 'on the ground' work of the youth association in Broadwater Farm, combining day care and programmes for single parents with efforts to improve security within the estate (Chapter 6); the development of 'community partnerships' and 'football in the community' schemes to tackle the deep-rooted problem of football hooliganism (Chapter 10), and the nascent social crime prevention programmes of France and Canada (Chapters 15 and 16).

What these examples have in common is the effort to work on the deeper structural problems of tough communities, often by working directly with the members of those communities, with the aim of building or rebuilding the institutions that most directly influence the causes of crime.

On a related point, in some examples of Phase 1 thinking, although Heal and Laycock (Chapter 14) provide evidence to the contrary for Britain, there has been a tendency to dismiss too quickly the role of the formal criminal justice system—especially the police—in favour of 'informal' mechanisms of control. There is some truth in the idea that formal controls are less effective, most of the time, than informal ones; that is a criminological truism. In Phase 1, however, this useful idea is overstated—to the point where it both lets the police 'off the hook' and simultaneously fails to encourage them to innovate and do creative things—some of which may work to strengthen communities and even reduce crime. (See Chapters 7 and 15, and in particular the positive results of some kinds of foot patrol and other community-oriented policing strategies.) It is certainly true, as Lynn Curtis notes (Chapter 11), that the police generally do not and perhaps should not *lead* in community-based crime prevention efforts, but at the same time, we are assuming too much if we expect communities to take care of their immediate crime problems by themselves. In the author's experience, people who live in badly crime-ridden communities desperately want a more effective and visible police presence—especially to cope with some of their toughest and most frightening problems, like street drug dealing or youth gangs.

The neglect of the potential role of the police in Phase 1 thinking is part of a larger rejection of the idea that communities have a fundamental right to good public services, efficiently delivered. At its worst this can slide into a sort of nostalgic voluntarism that exhorts shattered communities to pull themselves up by their own bootstraps, without help—and without money. One of the most important tasks for Phase 2, therefore, is to redress the balance of public and private responsibility for crime prevention.

To be sure, we need to know much more about how Phase 2 programmes work, and how they can be tailored to specific communities. Serious evaluation has not been kind to Phase 1 programmes, as Chapters 3, 8 and 11 suggest. But it is also true that serious evaluation has barely begun for the more complex programmes of Phase 2. Many of them sound marvellous on paper and generate a lot of local support and impressionistic boosting; see for example the discussion by Blagg *et al.*, (Chapter 12) and by Rock (Chapter 6), but with precious little hard analysis to back it up. Here we may need not just more research—but also different *kinds* of research. We could use, in particular, more ethnographic work—as Paul Rock suggests in his comments on how little we know about how various community crime prevention measures influence, and are perceived by, the real people they are designed to affect. (There is a fine model of this kind of ethnographic research in the work of Mercer Sullivan (1984) of the Vera Institute of Justice on crime and opportunity structures in three New York City neighbourhoods.)

Clearly, then, a great deal of research, experiment, and evaluation needs to be done to flesh out and specify the insights of Phase 2 thinking. But these efforts are well worth it. Phase 1 is no longer very impressive as a strategy against serious crime. It may be particularly important to stress this in the United States since, as Dennis Rosenbaum notes, Neighbourhood Watch (and other Phase 1 programmes) have been drastically oversold there. The overselling of Phase 1 ideas has tangible and disturbing consequences: it diverts resources away from other things we might do, while offering facile but easily dashed hopes that quick solutions will stop crime.

Phase 2 thinking, on the other hand, holds a deeper, if more challenging, promise. And it also ties in with earlier, and more ambitious traditions in criminological thinking—traditions that I for one would like to see revitalised. Phase 1 was in part an expression of loss of faith in those earlier and more hopeful traditions. Its retreat to self-defensive models reflects three such losses of faith in particular—none rooted in a careful sifting of the evidence: (1) the loss of faith that troubled and troubling people could (or should) be helped ('nothing works'); (2) the loss of faith that social programmes of any kind could substantially halt the production of such people in the first place; and (3) the loss of faith in the ability of the police or other public agencies to do much about crime either. Despite the up-by-the-bootstraps romanticism of some Phase 1 thinking, much of it actually contains a profound pessimism about the possibilities of conscious social action at its core.

We need to move beyond this. In no sense is such a movement simply a return to the thinking of the 1960s; Phase 2 thinking is much tougher-minded, much more aware of the depth of the personal and structural damage that serious crime reflects, and much more attuned to the need to strengthen the basic institutions of family, neighbourhood, and work—an emphasis which should help the appeal of Phase 2 thinking to cross conventional political boundaries. These are, after all, institutions that most people at all points on the political spectrum, in Britain and America and elsewhere, claim to cherish.

This is not to suggest that we simply discard what is truly useful in Phase 1 thinking, especially the emphasis on local participation, which has been central to the idea of community-based crime prevention at least since Clifford Shaw began organising in the South Side of Chicago. But it is time to transcend its limitations, and to reaffirm the legitimacy of the equally traditional idea of community *reconstruction* as the bedrock of community crime prevention; the idea that we confront crime most effectively by building communities that work, by strengthening local institutions so that they can better do their job of socialisation, nurturance, and support, by building stable community roles in work and family life into which we may guide the coming generations.

This is a lot harder than Phase 1; intellectually harder, programmatically harder, politically harder. But in the long run it will prove both more constructive and more realistic. Considerable momentum in that direction is indicated by the chapters in this book, and it is especially pleasing to have evidence of an international convergence of ideas and sharing of experience.

Reference

SULLIVAN, M. (1984). *Youth Crime and Employment Patterns in Three Brooklyn Neighbour-hoods*. New York: Vera Institute of Justice.

Home Office Research Reports

Reports published in the SCDTO and HORS series are available from HMSO who will advise as to prices (Tel. 01 622 3316). Those marked with an asterisk are out of print, but photostat copies are still available. Reports published in the RUP and RPUP series are available from the Home Office Research and Planning Unit, Information Section, 50 Queen Anne's Gate, London, SW1H 9AT.

Studies in the Causes of Delinquency and the Treatment of Offenders (SCDTO)

1. Prediction methods in relation to borstal training. Hermann Mannheim and Leslie T. Wilkins. 1955. viii + 276pp. (11 340051 9).

2. *Time spent awaiting trial. Evelyn Gibson. 1960. v + 45pp. (34−36 8−2).

3. *Delinquent generations. Leslie T. Wilkins. 1960. iv + 20pp.

4. *Murder. Evelyn Gibson and S. Klein. 1961. iv + 44pp. (11 340054 3).

5. Persistent criminals. A study of all offenders liable to preventive detention in 1956. W. H. Hammond and Edna Chayen. 1963. ix + 237pp. (34−36 8−5).

6. *Some statistical and other numerical techniques for classifying individuals. P. McNaughton-Smith. 1965. v + 33pp. (34−36 8−6).

7. Probation research: a preliminary report. Part I. General outline of research. Part II. Study of Middlesex probation area (SOMPA). Steven Folkard, Kate Lyon, Margaret M. Carver and Erica O'Leary. 1966. vi + 58pp. (11 340374 7).

8. *Probation research: national study of probation. Trends and regional comparisons in probation (England and Wales). Hugh Barr and Erica O'Leary. 1966. vii + 51pp. (34−36 8−8).

9. *Probation research. A survey of group work in the probation service. Hugh Barr. 1966. vii + 94pp. (34−36 8−9).

10. *Types of delinquency and home background. A validation study of Hewitt and Jenkins' hypotheses. Elizabeth Field. 1967. vi + 21pp. (34−36 8−10).

11. *Studies of female offenders. No. 1—Girls of 16−20 years sentenced to borstal or detention centre training in 1963. No. 2—Women offenders in the Metropolitan Police District in March and April 1957. No. 3—A description of women in prison on January 1, 1965. Nancy Goodman and Jean Price. 1967. v + 78pp. (34−36 8−11).

12. *The use of the Jesness Inventory on a sample of British probationers. Martin Davies. 1967. iv + 20pp. (34−36 8−12).

13. *The Jesness Inventory: application to approved school boys. Joy Mott. 1969. iv + 27pp. (11 340063 2).

Home Office Research Studies (HORS)

1. *Workloads in children's departments. Eleanor Grey. 1969. vi + 75pp. (11 340101 9).

2. *Probationers in their social environment. A study of male probationers aged 17−20, together with an analysis of those reconvicted within twelve months. Martin Davies. 1969. vii + 204pp. (11 340102 7).

3. *Murder 1957 to 1968. A Home Office Statistical Division report on murder in England and Wales. Evelyn Gibson and S. Klein (with annex by the Scottish Home and Health Department on murder in Scotland). 1969. vi + 94pp. (11 340103 5).

4. Firearms in crime. A Home Office Statistical Division report on indictable offences involving firearms in England and Wales. A. D. Weatherhead and B. M. Robinson. 1970. viii + 39pp. (11 340104 3).

5. *Financial penalties and probation. Martin Davies. 1970. vii + 39pp (11 340105 1).

6. *Hostels for probationers. A study of the aims, working and variations in effectiveness of male probation hostels with special reference to the influence of the environment on delinquency. Ian Sinclair, 1971. ix + 200pp. (11 340106 X).

7. *Prediction on methods in criminology—including a prediction study of young men on probation. Frances H. Simon. 1971. xi + 234pp. (11 340107 8).

8. *Study of the juvenile liaison scheme in West Ham 1961–65. Marilyn Taylor. 1971. vi + 46pp. (11 340108 6).

9. *Explorations in after-care. I—After-care units in London, Liverpool and Manchester. Martin Silberman (Royal London Prisoners' Aid Society) and Brenda Chapman. II—After-care hostels receiving a Home Office grant. Ian Sinclair and David Snow (HORU). III—St. Martin of Tours House, Aryeh Leissner (National Bureau for Co-operation in Child Care). 1971. xi + 140pp. (11 340109 4).

10. A survey of adoption in Great Britain. Eleanor Grey in collaboration with Ronald M. Blunden. 1971. ix + 168pp. (11 340110 8).

11. *Thirteen-year-old approved school boys in 1962s. Elizabeth Field, W. H. Hammond and J. Tizard. 1971. ix + 46pp. (11 340111 6).

12. Absconding from approved schools. R. V. G. Clarke and D. N. Martin. 1971. vi + 146pp. (11 340112 4).

13. An experiment in personality assessment of young men remanded in custody. H. Sylvia Anthony. 1972. viii + 79pp. (11 340113 2).

14. *Girl offenders aged 17–20 years. I—Statistics relating to girl offenders aged 17–20 years from 1960 to 1970. II—Re-offending by girls released from borstal or detention centre training. III—The problems of girls released from borstal training during their period on after-care. Jean Davies and Nancy Goodman. 1972. v + 77pp. (11 340114 0).

15. *The controlled trial in institutional research—paradigm or pitfall for penal evaluators? R. V. G. Clarke and D. B. Cornish. 1972. v + 33pp. (11 340115 9).

16 *A survey of fine enforcement. Paul Softley. 1973. v + 65pp. (11 340116 7).

17. *An index of social environment—designed for use in social work menum research. Martin Davies. 1973. vi + 63pp. (11 340117 5).

18. *Social enquiry reports and the probation service. Martin Davies and Andrea Knopf. 1973. v + 49pp. (11 340118 3).

19. *Depression, psychopathic personality and attempted suicide in a borstal sample. H. Sylvia Anthony. 1973. viii + 44pp. (0 11 340119 1).

20. *The use of bail and custody by London magistrates' courts before and after the Criminal Justice Act 1987. Frances Simon and Mollie Weatheritt. 1974. vi + 78pp. (0 11 340120 5).

21. *Social work in the environment. A study of one aspect of probation practice. Martin Davies, with Margaret Rayfield, Alaster Calder and Tony Fowles. 1974. ix + 151pp. (0 11 340121 3).

22. Social work in prison. An experiment in the use of extended contact with offenders. Margaret Shaw. 1974. viii + 154pp. (0 11 340122 1).

23. Delinquency amongst opiate users. Joy Mott and Marilyn Taylor. 1974. vi + 31pp. (0 11 340663 0).

24. IMPACT. Intensive matched probation and after-care treatment. Vol. I—The design of the probation experiment and an interim evaluation. M. S. Folkard, A. J. Fowles, B. C. McWilliams, W. McWilliams, D. D. Smith, D. E. Smith and G. R. Walmsley. 1974. v + 54pp. (0 11 340664 9).

25. The approved school experience. An account of boys' experiences of training under differing regimes of approved schools, with an attempt to evaluate the effectiveness of that training. Anne B. Dunlop. 1974. vii + 124pp. (0 11 340665 7).

26. *Absconding from open prisons. Charlotte Banks, Patricia Mayhew and R. J. Sapsford. 1975. viii + 89pp. (0 11 340666 5).

27. Driving while disqualified. Sue Kriefman. 1975. vi + 136pp. (0 11 340667 3).

28. Some male offenders' problems. I—Homeless offenders in Liverpool. W. McWilliams. II—Casework with short-term prisoners. Julie Holborn. 1975. x + 147pp. (0 11 340668 1).

29. *Community service orders. K. Pease, P. Durkin, I. Earnshaw, D. Payne and J. Thorpe. 1975. viii + 80pp. (0 11 340669 X).

30. Field Wing Bail Hostel: the first nine months. Frances Simon and Sheena Wilson. 1975. viii + 55pp. (0 11 340670 3).

31. Homicide in England and Wales 1967–1971. Evelyn Gibson. 1975. iv + 59pp. (0 11 340753 X).

32. Residential treatment and its effects on delinquency. D. B. Cornish and R. V. G. Clarke. 1975. vi + 74pp. (0 11 340672 X).

33. Further studies of female offenders. Part A: Borstal girls eight years after release. Nancy Goodman, Elizabeth Maloney and Jean Davies. Part B: The sentencing of women at the London Higher Courts. Nancy Goodman, Paul Durkin and Janet Halton. Part C: Girls appearing before a juvenile court. Jean Davies. 1976. vi + 114pp. (0 11 340673 8).

34. *Crime as opportunity. P. Mayhew, R. V. G. Clarke, A. Sturman and J. M. Hough. 1976. vii + 36pp. (0 11 340674 6).

35. The effectiveness of sentencing: a review of the literature. S. R. Brody. 1976. v + 89pp. (0 11 340675 4).

36. IMPACT. Intensive matched probation and after-care treatment. Vol. II—The results of the experiment. M. S. Folkard, D. E. Smith and D. D. Smith. 1976. xi + 40pp. (0 11 340676 2).

37. Police cautioning in England and Wales. J. A. Ditchfield. 1976. v + 31pp. (0 11 340677 0).

38. Parole in England and Wales. C. P. Nuttal, with E. E. Barnard, A. J. Fowles, A. Frost, W. H. Hammond, P. Mayhew, K. Pease, R. Tarling and M. J. Weatheritt. 1977. vi + 90pp. (0 11 340678 9).

39. Community service assessed in 1976. K. Pease, S. Billingham and I. Earnshaw. 1977. vi + 29pp. (0 11 340679 7).

40. Screen violence and film censorship: a review of research. Stephen Brody. 1977. vii + 179pp. (0 11 340680 0).

41. *Absconding from borstals. Gloria K. Laycock. 1977. v + 82pp. (0 11 340681 9).

42. Gambling: a review of the literature and its implications for policy and research. D. B. Cornish. 1978. xii + 284pp. (0 11 340682 7).

43. Compensation orders in magistrates' courts. Paul Softley. 1978. v + 41pp. (0 11 340683 5).

44. Research in criminal justice. John Croft. 1978. iv + 16pp. (0 11 340684 3).

45. Prison welfare: an account of an experiment at Liverpool. A. J. Fowles. 1978. v + 34pp. (0 11 340685 1).

46. Fines in magistrates' courts. Paul Softley. 1978. v + 42pp. (0 11 340686 X).

47. Tackling vandalism. R. V. G. Clarke (editor), F. J. Gladstone, A. Sturman and Sheena Wilson (contributors). 1978. vi + 91pp. (0 11 340687 8).

48. Social inquiry reports: a survey. Jennifer Thorpe. 1979. vi + 55pp. (0 11 340688 6).

49. Crime in public view. P. Mayhew, R. V. G. Clarke, J. N. Burrows, J. M. Hough and S. W. C. Winchester. 1979. v + 36pp. (0 11 340689 4).

50. *Crime and the community. John Croft. 1979. v + 16pp. (0 11 340690 8).

51. Life-sentence prisoners. David Smith (editors), Christopher Brown, Joan Worth, Roger Sapsford and Charlotte Banks (contributors). 1979. iv + 51pp. (0 11 340691 6).

52. Hostels for offenders. Jane E. Andrews, with an appendix by Bill Sheppard. 1979. v + 30pp. (0 11 340692 4).

53. Previous convictions, sentence and reconviction: a statistical study of a sample of 5000 offenders convicted in January 1971. G. J. O. Phillpotts and L. B. Lancucki. 1979. v + 55pp. (0 11 340693 2).

54. Sexual offences, consent and sentencing. Roy Walmsley and Karen White. 1979. vi + 77pp. (0 11 340694 0).

55. Crime prevention and the police. John Burrows, Paul Ekblom and Kevin Heal. 1979. v + 37pp. (0 11 340695 9).

56. Sentencing practice in magistrates' courts. Roger Tarling, with the assistance of Mollie Weatheritt. 1979. vii + 54pp. (0 11 340696 7).

57. Crime and comparative research. John Croft. 1979. iv + 16pp. (0 11 340697 5).

58. Race, crime and arrests. Philip Stevens and Carole F. Willis. 1979. v + 69pp. (0 11 340698 3).

59. Research and criminal policy. John Croft. 1980. iv + 14pp. (0 11 340699 1).

60.   Junior attendance centres. Anne B. Dunlop. 1980. v + 47pp.

61.   Police interrogation: an observational study in four police stations. Paul Softley, with the assistance of David Brown, Bob Forde, George Mair and David Moxon. 1980. vii + 67pp. (0 11 340701 7).

62.   Co-ordinating crime prevention efforts. F. J. Gladstone. 1980. v + 74pp. (0 11 340702 5).

63.   Crime prevention publicity: an assessment. D. Riley and P. Mayhew. 1980. v + 47pp. (0 11 340703 3).

64.   Taking offenders out of circulation. Stephen Brody and Roger Tarling. 1980. v + 46pp. (0 11 340704 1).

65.   *Alcoholism and social policy: are we on the right lines? Mary Tuck. 1980. v + 30pp. (0 11 340705 X).

66.   Persistent petty offenders. Suzan Fairhead. 1981. vi + 78pp. (0 11 340706 8).

67.   Crime control and the police. Pauline Morris and Kevin Heal. 1981. v + 71pp. (0 11 340707 6).

68.   Ethnic minorities in Britain: a study of trends in their position since 1961. Simon Field, George Mair, Tom Rees and Philip Stevens. 1981. v + 48pp. (0 11 340708 4).

69.   Managing criminological research. John Croft. 1981. iv + 17pp. (0 11 340709 2).

70.   Ethnic minorities, crime and policing: a survey of the experiences of West Indians and whites. Mary Tuck and Peter Southgate. 1981. iv + 54pp. (0 11 340765 3).

71.   Contested trials in magistrates' courts. Julie Vennard. 1982. v + 32pp. (0 11 340766 1).

72.   Public disorder: a review of research and a study in one inner city area. Simon Field and Peter Southgate. 1982. v + 72pp. (0 11 340767 X).

73.   Clearing up crime. John Burrows and Roger Tarling. 1982. vii + 31pp. (0 11 340768 8).

74.   Residential burglary: the limits of prevention. Stuart Winchester and Hilary Jackson. 1982. v + 47pp. (0 11 340769 6).

75.   Concerning crime. John Croft. 1982. iv + 16pp. (0 11 340770 X)

76.   The British Crime Survey: first report. Mike Hough and Pat Mayhew. 1983. v + 62pp. (0 11 340786 6).

77.   Contacts between police and public: findings from the British Crime Survey. Peter Southgate and Paul Ekblom. 1984. v + 42pp. (0 11 340771 8).

78.   Fear of crime in England and Wales. Michael Maxfield. 1984. v + 57pp. (0 11 340772 6).

79.   Crime and police effectiveness. Ronald V. Clarke and Mike Hough 1984. iv + 33pp. (0 11 340773 3).

80.   The attitudes of ethnic minorities. Simon Field. 1984. v + 49pp. (0 11 340774 2).

81.   Victims of crime: the dimensions of risk. Michael Gottfredson. 1984. v + 54pp. (0 11 340775 0).

82.   The tape recording of police interviews with suspects: an interim report. Carole Willis. 1984. v + 45pp. (0 11 340776 9).

83.   Parental supervision and juvenile delinquency. David Riley and Margaret Shaw. 1985. v + 90pp. (0 11 340799 8).

84.   Adult prisons and prisoners in England and Wales 1970–1982: a review of the findings of social research. Joy Mott. 1985. vi + 73pp. (0 11 340801 3).

85.   Taking account of crime: key findings from the 1984 British Crime Survey. Mike Hough and Pat Mayhew. 1985. vi + 115pp. (0 11 340810 2).

86.   Implementing crime prevention measures. Tim Hope. 1985. vi + 82pp. (0 11 340812 9).

87.   Resettling refugees: the lessons of research. Simon Field. 1985. vi + 66pp. (0 11 340815 3).

88.   Investigating burglary: the measurement of police performance. John Burrows. 1986. vi + 36pp. (0 11 340824 2).

89.   Personal violence. Roy Walmsley. 1986. vi + 87pp. (0 11 340827 7).

90.   Police-public encounters. Peter Southgate. 1986. vi + 150pp. (0 11 340834 X).

91.   Grievance procedures in prisons. John Ditchfield and Claire Austin. 1986. vi + 78pp. (0 11 340839 0).

92.   The effectiveness of the Forensic Science Service. Malcolm Ramsay. 1987. v + 100pp. (0 11 340842 0).

93. The Police Complaints Procedure: a survey of complainants' views. David Brown. 1987. (0 11 340853 6).

94. Validity of the Reconviction Prediction Score. Denis Ward. 1987. (0 11 340   0).

Also

Designing out crime. R. V. G. Clarke and P. Mayhew (editors). 1980. viii + 1986pp. (0 11 340732 7).
(This book collects, with an introduction, studies that were originally published in HORS 34, 47, 49, 55, 62 and 63 and which are illustrative of the 'situation' approach to crime prevention.)

Policing today. Kevin Heal, Roger Tarling and John Burrows (editors). + 181pp. (0 11 340800 5).
(This book brings together twelve separate studies on police matters produced during the last few years by the Unit. The collection records some relatively little known contributions to the debate on policing.)

Managing Criminal Justice: a collection of papers. David Moxon (editor). 1985. vi + 222pp. (0 11 340811 0).
(This book brings together a number of studies bearing on the management of the criminal justice system. It includes papers by social scientists and operational researchers working within the Research and Planning Unit, and academic researchers who have studied particular aspects of the criminal process.)

Situational Crime Prevention: from theory into practice. Kevin Heal and Gloria Laycock (editors). 1986. vii + 166pp. (0 11 340826 9).
(This book is a collection of essays on theoretical, practical and policy issues in crime prevention.)

Research Unit Papers (RUP)

1. Uniformed police work and management technology. J. M. Hough. 1980.

2. Supplementary information on sexual offences and sentencing. Roy Walmsley and Karen White. 1980.

3. Board of visitor adjudications. David Smith, Claire Austin and John Ditchfield. 1981.

4. Day centres and probation. Suzan Fairhead, with the assistance of J. Wilkinson-Grey. 1981.

Research and Planning Unit Papers (RPUP)

5. Ethnic minorities and complaints against the police. Philip Stevens and Carole Willis. 1982.

6. *Crime and public housing. Mike Hough and Pat Mayhew (editors). 1982.

7. *Abstracts of race relations research. George Mair and Philip Stevens (editors). 1982.

8. Police probationer training in race relations. Peter Southgate. 1982.

9. *The police response to calls from the public. Paul Ekblom and Kevin Heal. 1982.

10. City centre crime: a situational approach to prevention. Malcolm Ramsay. 1982.

11. Burglary in schools: the prospects for prevention. Tim Hope. 1982.

12. *Fine enforcement. Paul Softley and David Moxon. 1982.

13. Vietnamese refugees. Peter Jones. 1982.

14. Community resources for victims of crime. Karen Williams. 1983.

15. The use, effectiveness and impact of police stop and search powers. Carole Willis. 1983.

16. Acquittal rates. Sid Butler. 1983.

17. Criminal justice comparisons: the case of Scotland and England and Wales. Lorna J. F. Smith. 1983.

18. Time taken to deal with juveniles under criminal proceedings. Catherine Frankenburg and Roger Tarling. 1983.

19. Civilian review of complaints against the police: a survey of the United States literature. David C. Brown. 1983.

20. Police action on motoring offences. David Riley. 1983.

21. *Diverting drunks from the criminal justice system. Sue Kingsley and George Mair. 1983.

22. The staff resource implications of an independent prosecution system. Peter R. Jones. 1983.

23. Reducing the prison population: an exploratory study in Hampshire. David Smith, Bill Sheppard, George Mair, Karen Williams. 1984.

24. Criminal justice system model: magistrates' courts sub-model. Susan Rice. 1984.

25. Measure of police effectiveness and efficiency. Ian Sinclair and Clive Miller. 1984.

26. Punishment practice by prison Boards of Visitors. Susan Iles, Adrienne Connors, Chris May, Joy Mott. 1984.

27. *Reparation, conciliation and mediation: current projects and plans in England and Wales. Tony Marshall. 1984.

28. Magistrates' domestic courts: new perspectives. Tony Marshall (editor). 1984.

29. Racism awareness training for the police. Peter Southgate. 1984.

30. Community constables: a study of a policing initiative. David Brown and Susan Iles. 1985.

31. Recruiting volunteers. Hilary Jackson. 1985.

32. Juvenile sentencing: is there a tariff? David Moxon, Peter Jones, Roger Tarling. 1985

33. Bringing people together: mediation and reparation projects in Great Britain. Tony Marshall and Martin Walpole. 1985.

34. Remands in the absence of the accused. Chris May. 1985.

35. Modelling the criminal justice system. Patricia M. Morgan. 1985.

36. The criminal justice system model: the flow model. Hugh Pullinger. 1986.

37. Burglary: police actions and victim views. John Burrows. 1986.

38. Unlocking community resources: four experimental government small grants schemes. Hilary Jackson. 1986.

39. The costs of discrimination: a review of the literature. Shirley Dex. 1986.

40. Waiting for crown court trial: the remand population. Rachel Pearce. 1987.

41. Children's evidence: the need for corroboration. Carol Hedderman. 1987.

42. Preliminary study of victim/offender mediation and reparation schemes in England and Wales. Davis, Boucherat and Watson. 1987.

43. Explaining fear of crime: evidence from the 1984 British Crime Survey. Michael Maxfield. 1988.

Name Index

Abrams, P., 26, 27, 159, 161
Adams, R., 60
Allatt, P., 85, 97, 206, 219
Altman, I., 82
Argus, 20, 182–201
Armstrong, G., 100, 113
Auletta, K., 181, 191, 202

Back, K., 139, 143
Bagley, C., 263, 277
Baldwin, J., 39, 42, 44, 84, 88, 89, 91, 97, 104, 113, 207, 219
Barker, R., 64, 81
Baumer, T.L., 141, 143
Bennett, S.F., 143, 151, 221–234
Bennett, T., 85, 119, 125, 239, 245
Benyon, J., 216, 219
Berry, J.M., 227, 233
Bickman, L., 140, 143
Biderman, A.D., 48, 59
Birley, D., 205, 207, 219
Bishop, G.D., 137, 144
Bittner, E., 57, 59
Blaber, A., 97, 101, 104, 106, 109, 113
Blagg, H., 204–220, 284
Block, R., 262
Blumstein, A., 81
Boggs, S., 129, 143
Bonnemaison, M., 255
Borkowski, M., 217, 219
Bottoms, A.E., 7, 17, 27, 39, 42, 43, 44, 84–98, 104, 110, 113, 207, 219, 283
Brantingham, P.J. and Brantingham, P.L., 88, 97, 102, 113, 237, 245
Bridges, L., 159, 161
Bright, J., 101, 102, 103, 106, 113, 116, 125, 205, 206, 207, 219
Brower, S., 60, 64, 66, 82, 145
Brown, J., 13, 28
Bruce, A.A., 81
Bryant, C.G.A., 263, 277
Bulmer, M., 9, 26, 27, 159, 161, 217, 219
Bunyan, T., 159, 161
Burchell, R.W., 52, 60
Burgess, E.W., 63, 64, 81
Burbidge, M., 92, 97, 101, 102, 105, 107, 108, 109, 110, 113

297

Subject Index

ACORN (A Classification of Residential Neighbourhoods), 29, 32–47, 149, 150, 152, 157

A.R.A. Consultants, 250, 254

Architecture and building design, 1, 6, 17, 30, 85, 90, 99–102, 105, 106, 107, 110, 211, 265, 267, 269

Area in crime, 30–47, 62–66, 102, 150, 156–158

   area offence rates, 84–92

   area offender rates, 84–92

   territorial distribution of crime, 3, 6, 7, 13, 15

Association of Metropolitan Authorities (A.M.A.), 175, 179

Autocrime, 40–41, 236, 239, 241–242, 262, 276

Block Parents programme, 249

Block Watch, 126, 130, 134, 136, 141

   see Neighbourhood Watch in U.S.

British Crime Survey (B.C.S.), 15, 18, 29, 30–47, 103, 132, 133, 146–161, 282

Broadwater Farm Estate, 95, 101, 106, 112, 283

'Broken Windows' hypothesis, 16, 29, 280, 281, 282

   testing the theory, 31–39

   see also Informal social control

Burglary, 5, 15, 103, 104, 119, 120, 121, 147, 154, 158, 212, 226, 241, 242, 262

   distribution of, 32–43

   prevention of, 8, 150, 242

   reduction of, 106, 112, 135, 204, 269

   risk of, 239

Canada, 9, 22, 23, 235, 246–252, 276, 283

Canadian Council on Social Development, 251

Canadian Criminal Justice Association, 252

Centre for Contemporary Studies, 175, 179

Centre for Leisure Research, 175, 179

Chicago School, 2, 3, 6

Citizen Information Service of Illinois, 136, 143

'Civility' in criminology, 95

'Columns' in Dutch Society, 9, 263, 276, 283

Community

   community-oriented ideology, 207, 247

   concept of, 1, 26, 64, 66, 204, 207, 280, 282

   development programmes, 10, 11

   disadvantaged, 3

   disorganised, 2, 3, 48–55, 103–104

   groups, organisations, 12, 51, 54, 58, 68, 70, 138, 172

   institutions, 2, 4, 24, 25, 280, 281, 282, 283, 285

socializing role, 2, 9, 10, 50, 130, 163, 263, 265, 285

Fear of crime, 11, 17, 18, 22, 23, 33–39, 48, 49, 52–58, 68, 75, 103, 107, 120, 121, 126, 127, 128, 140, 154, 183, 184, 192, 230, 258, 259, 281

  lack of, 4

  high levels of, 226

  increase in, 180, 181, 254

  reduction of, 106, 134, 135, 137, 139, 140, 141, 183, 186, 193, 196–198, 200, 204, 243, 251, 281

  problems of increasing fear through crime prevention, 131, 135, 136, 141, 199, 209, 222

  over emphasis on, 22, 141, 197, 198, 200, 281

Football Association (F.A.), 164, 173

Football Hooliganism, 19, 20, 22, 163, 164–179, 283

  community approach to, 19, 20, 22, 163, 164–179, 283

  involvement of ethnic minotiries, 176

  involvement of women, 20, 170, 173, 176, 175

  situational response to, 164, 167, 267

Football Supporters Association (F.S.A.), 175

Ford Foundation, 130, 184, 221

France, 9, 22, 235, 254–259, 283

General Household Survey (G.H.S.), 152

Greater London Council (G.L.C.), 101

HALT programme, 274, 275

Holland, *see* the Netherlands

Home Affairs Committee, 216, 219

Home Office, 13, 30, 39, 44, 116, 146, 204, 216, 219, 221, 236, 237, 239, 242, 245

  Circular on crime prevention, 13, 204, 219

  Circular on juveniles, 13

  Crime Prevention Unit, 238, 245

  Ministerial Group on Crime Prevention, 236

  Statement of National Objectives and Priorities (SNOP), 207, 208, 219

  Research and Planning Unit, 1, 101, 205

Housing, 17, 71, 84–96, 99–112, 183, 213, 267

  market, 6, 52, 53, 55–58, 84, 86–96, 99–104, 157

  owner occupied sector, 7, 88, 89, 93–94, 151

  policy, 17, 84–96, 99–102, 157, 212, 215, 238, 256, 283

  private rental sector, 7, 89, 90, 93, 94, 151

  residential community crime career, 84–96

  slums, 4, 7, 10, 14, 100, 101

  tenure, 7, 41–43, 84, 88–94, 151, 152

  see also Local Authority Estates

Housing Action Area, 90

Implementation of preventive programmes, 20, 21, 221–232, 235, 237, 241–42, 256,

  barriers to, 188, 189, 186, 199, 200, 203, 241

  need for careful planning and assessment, 231

Incapacitation, 180

Incivilities, 15, 16, 23, 30–43, 68, 96, 126, 137, 139, 155

Informaal social control, 5, 12, 17, 18, 19, 30, 31, 35, 51, 53, 54, 70, 96, 110,

Printed in the United Kingdom for Her Majesty's Stationery Office.
Dd 289428, 00/87, C30, 000, 5673.